A Register of Old Wycliffians

MR. AND MRS. G. W. SIBLY
who founded Wycliffe College in 1882
(a photograph taken in the Oak Room thirty years later).

A REGISTER

OF

OLD WYCLIFFIANS

1882-1937

Compiled by
R. V. WARD

Privately printed by
JOHN BELLOWS LTD., GLOUCESTER
1937

It's good to see the School we knew,
　　The land of youth and dream,
To greet again the rule we knew
　　Before we took the stream :
Though long we've missed the sight of her,
　　Our hearts may not forget ;
We've lost the old delight of her,
　　We keep her honour yet.

The stars and sounding vanities
　　That half the crowd bewitch,
What are they but inanities
　　To him that treads the pitch ?
And where's the wealth, I'm wondering,
　　Could buy the cheers that roll
When the last charge goes thundering
　　Beneath the twilight goal ?

To speak of Fame a venture is,
　　There's little here can bide,
But we may face the centuries,
　　And dare the deepening tide :
For though the dust that's part of us
　　To dust again be gone,
Yet here shall beat the heart of us—
　　The School we handed on !

Newbolt.

LIST OF CONTENTS

INTRODUCTION

THIS is the fourth time that a Register of Old Wycliffians has been published. A paper-covered Register appeared in 1907, a more comprehensive booklet was printed in 1913, and in 1926 a substantial standard volume of 158 pp., with many illustrations, was issued. But it is in the nature of such books that they must become quickly out of date. The ranks of the Old Boys receive an addition of about fifty new names each year, youthful O.W.s, making their way in the world, change their status and address and often marry and establish homes of their own. Now that more than fifty years have elapsed since the School's first foundation, Death also inevitably begins to take increasing toll of those who were at Wycliffe long ago.

Although much time, trouble and expense have been given to making this Register as accurate as possible, it is almost inevitable that there should be omissions and mistakes, and probably not a few O.W's have changed their address even in the last twelve months, or since this information was collected. For any inaccuracies the Editor expresses his regret, while at the same time making very grateful acknowledgment of the help so freely given by the Honorary Secretaries of the various Branches of the O.W. Society, and continually by the Headmaster, who, with his brother, enjoys what is probably the unique distinction of having been the contemporary, as child, schoolboy, undergraduate and master, of practically all who have ever passed through the School.

It is hoped that the benefits conferred by this Register will be many. It will certainly help to keep some old friends in touch, and—through the common link of the School—may lead to the making of new ones.

By strengthening the ties which unite the School and its Old Boys, such a Register as this may serve other and larger purposes. Like the quality of mercy, it blesses all concerned. The School gains through the widening of the interests of present boys, as they watch ' the giants of old ' winning fame and doing good work upon other and larger fields. Aided also is it in other ways, for it is by the recommendation and support of its loyal sons, and the constant witness of their success and achievement, rather than through any public advertisement, that the School depends for its recruitment, and for public knowledge of its work.

Included in this, as in the last edition, are some brief biographies of the men and women who helped to make the School. We add these without hesitation, for we believe that few O.W.s can read such records without interest, and we are sure that no present masters or boys can study them without receiving some measure of inspiration too, and a clearer conception of the nature of the heritage into which they have entered.

Since the last number of this Register was published Wycliffe has become more intimately associated with its Old Boys than ever before, for it is now their own possession. In 1931 the owners of the School, in the interests of its permanence and stability, disposed of the buildings and estate to a Council which consists almost entirely of Old Wycliffians, and in consequence Wycliffe became a Public School rather than a proprietary one.

There are other gains too, and many an Old Boy is glad to know that, whether he lives in the busy marts of men at home, or in the far-off outposts of the Empire, he is still, in spirit and memory, essentially a member of the old ' commonwealth ' of school. He is not forgotten, and generation after generation of Wycliffe boys can say, in the words of the poet of a larger neighbouring home of learning :

> " Across the world you keep the pride,
> Across the world we mark the score."

THE STORY OF FIFTY-FIVE YEARS

THE story of the School up to the end of the Great War can best be read in the introductory pages of the 1926 edition of this Register, and in the little Memoir of Mr. G. W. Sibly, published by his children soon after his death in 1929. Here we can but summarize the far-off first beginnings.

From 1843 to 1882 Mr. Thomas Sibly was the first headmaster of what is now known as Queen's College, Taunton. Under his enlightened rule the School prospered exceedingly, and in 1878 it contained 280 boys. On a memorial to him in the Temple Church at Taunton it is recorded that " he guided by his instruction and inspired by his example thousands of the youth of this country."

THE ORIGINAL FOUNDATION OF WYCLIFFE

For the last seven years of this headmastership, his second son, Mr. G. W. Sibly, had been his father's chief assistant, and on the retirement of Mr. Thomas Sibly, he applied for the vacant post with a reasonable hope of appointment. The Governors decided otherwise, and the very next day Mr. Sibly journeyed north to Gloucestershire and entered into negotiations for the purchase of the Haywardsfield Hall estate, this being the name of the nearly 200-year-old building which was the original part of the present School House. In September 1882 Wycliffe College was opened with twenty-seven boarders and four dayboys. " Why Wycliffe ? " some may ask. The answer, we believe, is to be found in Mr. Sibly's admiration for this learned and courageous pioneer and forerunner of the English Reformation, and—apart from the problems in spelling which it presents to some—it is a good name anyway. In the same spirit Mr. Sibly chose as motto for his new school the simple English words " Bold and Loyal," instead of a more conventional Latin phrase. ·

With Mr. Sibly there came to Stonehouse a young bride of twenty-one, whom he had married at the beginning of August, and who brought to Wycliffe qualities of gentleness and holiness and high devotion which during the next thirty-three years influenced all who knew her.

He was followed, too, from Taunton by two masters, Mr. John Bramley and Mr. F. H. Sherwell, and a few older boys who formed the nucleus of the new school. There was no secondary school of consequence nearer than Gloucester in those days, and Wycliffe was fortunate in attracting to itself several of the sons of the leading men of the locality, and other boys of marked character and ability from further afield.

EARLY DEVELOPMENT

Thus success came early and quickly. In 1883 Haywardsfield was built as a boarding-house for nearly fifty boys. In 1886 the School House was much enlarged and improved (from a school point of view). Under Mr. Sibly's personal leadership playing fields were levelled, obstructive trees were felled, and many others planted. The first boat-house was excavated or constructed on the banks of the Stroud-water Canal, and the path around the main cricket field was made.

On February 10th, 1886 a Concert and Supper celebrated the fact that the number of boys had reached one hundred.

In 1888 Ivy Grove, an Elizabethan or Jacobean house which is a delightful specimen of Cotswold architecture, was purchased by Mr. Thomas Sibly, who until his death at Taunton in 1892 watched the progress of Wycliffe with pride and satisfaction, and helped its development by his counsels and experience. About the same date a cricket pavilion and cycle house were built.

As far back as 1883 the Debating Society (the " Lit. Soc.") and a Field Club were founded, and in that year appeared the first number of the *Wycliffe Star*, which, as a school magazine of the first magnitude, has continued ever since to shine so brightly.

From all of which it will be clear that these early years contained many " crowded hours of glorious life," and that, in this first decade, the foundations of a prosperous and useful school were firmly laid. During this period, too, Miss Valentine came to be the matron at the School House, and with Mrs. Sibly helped to give to Wycliffe that " homeliness " and unaffected religious outlook upon life which we hope may never be lacking.

THE NEXT DECADE

Between 1890 and 1900 there were no new buildings of much note, but the old football field, now known as the Middle Field, was enlarged by an addition of three acres. For a space of thirty-five years (from 1892–1928) Association took the place of Rugby Football, and in these early years the School produced in both codes some most successful players. One international Welsh three-quarter is commemorated in our midst to-day by the Batchelar-Bowen Memorial Bridge which spans the Stroud road at Ryeford. In 1894–5 the 1st " soccer " XI was unbeaten.

Mr. Bramley accepting a headmastership elsewhere, Dr. Arthur Sibly came to Stonehouse as Housemaster of Haywardsfield, a position which he held for thirty-three years. A tribute to his work will be found in the brief biography at the close of this volume. Although the original suggestion came from Mr. G. W. Sibly, it was Dr. Arthur who was mainly responsible for the formation of the League of Honour, which in one form or another has been for forty years a potent factor in the moral life of the School.

THE NEW CENTURY

Early in the present century there were several building developments, such as the covered playground and a photographic house, but the latter has since disappeared to make place for larger extensions, and the former is likely soon to be displaced by a more modern gymnasium. The first carpenter's shop, and the boat and bathing house which still stands on the Canal, date from the same period. With the return of Mr. Bramley, Springfield was opened in 1904, and the number of boys at Wycliffe was increased to about 160. In these years Mr. J. S. Evans was a leading figure on the staff, adding some striking performances on cricket and football fields to his skill as a teacher. Another Wycliffe master at this period was that strange but public-spirited figure, Melville (or " Max ") Müller.

IN THE YEARS BEFORE THE WAR

During the next ten years there was little structural change, but many new ideas and experiments began to take root in the School. These were stimulated by the return of the present Head-master and his brother from the University and from travel abroad. In 1910 the Seniors and Probationers (as the Prefects and House Monitors then were called) asked by 36 votes to 1 for the complete abolition of tuck-boxes. In the same year Mr. Mervyn Sibly organized the Scout Troop. This had been formed unofficially in 1908 or 1909, and was possibly the first school Troop to be formed in Britain. Summer Camps, chiefly by the Wye, began.

In 1909 and 1912 the first Wycliffe tours on the Continent were arranged, and this period saw the first school excursion to Killarney. Competitions in the study of literature, in rifle-shooting and in cross-country running also date from this period.

THE SPRINGFIELD EXPERIMENT

In 1909 Mr. W. A. Sibly succeeded Mr. Bramley at Springfield, and from 1910 that House, which has been thrice enlarged, has been reserved for boys who are either " life " vegetarians, or who abjure meat by their parents " sanction " or request while at school. Thus for twenty-seven years Springfield has enjoyed the distinction of being the only school boarding-house of this kind in England, and has received many visits from English and foreign doctors, university professors and others, who have been interested in a pioneer experiment.

THE BUILDING OF THE CHAPEL

It was in 1909 that the project of a new Chapel took root, Mr. Bramley—now freed from " House " responsibilities—being the chief mover in this matter. As a result the year 1911 saw successively a sod-cutting ceremony, foundation-stone laying and the opening of the Chapel. Although built upon land given by the School, and with money largely provided by Mr. G. W. Sibly, parents, O.W.s and present boys, it was technically a Methodist Chapel, but a special clause in the trust deed provided for its use by the School without denomination restrictions.

It was the School, or those connected with it, which added the tower, spire and clock as a War Memorial in 1921, and the new Organ at the School Jubilee in 1932, and by the School and its friends (and notably by the gift of an oak reredos and communion table by Mr. J. C. Hayes) this Chapel has been beautified in many ways. Negotiations are now almost complete for the total transference of the Chapel to the School, when its pulpit will be open to preachers of all Protestant denominations.

During a cycle ride in Ireland in 1911 Mr. G. W. Sibly met with the accident which caused the paralysis agitans that troubled the last seventeen years of his life, and led to his elder son succeeding him as Headmaster in 1912.

The Great War

In a beautiful book of over 400 pages, the story of " Wycliffe and the War " has been told in memorable fashion. A large part of that volume is given to memoirs, and to scores of letters descriptive of life on all the battle-fronts, with candid comments on war-time conditions and experiences, but in Chapter XXV " School-Life in War-Time " is described. There one may read how daily life at Wycliffe was affected by the War, and learn of the formation of the School Corps, " chuck-tuck " leagues, and of the Wycliffe Co-operative Potato Estate, or of the help given (a year before any scheme was launched by the Ministry of National Service) to local farmers in hay-harvest and other work, culminating in the harvest camp at Chitterne on Salisbury Plain in August 1918, when Wycliffe boys gave 6,015 hours of labour in the Wiltshire corn-fields.

More than 550 O.W.s served in the fighting forces of the Empire. Nearly 90 received the D.S.O., M.C. or other decoration, or were mentioned in despatches, and about 80 laid down their lives.

Problems and Changes after the War

The rise of prices in war-time, and the high cost of living which prevailed from 1918 to 1921 had been met by no comparable increase of fees, and but for the fact that Mr. G. W. Sibly and Dr. Arthur Sibly possessed private incomes apart from the School, this must almost have gone under. For a time it assumed the nature of a charity, for fees by no means covered costs, but in 1922 the fees were more than doubled, and the position was slowly righted.

On the Staff, too, the old order changed, giving place to new. Mr. G. W. Sibly had retired altogether to Ivy Grove, giving up the control of the School House to Mr. T. M. Sibly. Mr. J. S. Evans had died suddenly at the end of 1919, after twenty-two years as a master at Wycliffe. In the three or four years which followed, Dr. Arthur, Mr. Bramley and Mr. Hugill retired to live at Taunton and Marlborough, and Mr. Sherwell and Miss Jackson gave up class teaching. All these had served the School for an average of more than thirty years apiece. Mr. G. L. Reade became House-master of Haywardsfield, and Mr. E. J. Bevan, Mr. T. S. Dixon, as Master in charge of Music, and several others who have since done fine service, joined the Staff.

BUILDING DEVELOPMENTS

The War had prevented building for a space of six years, and by 1920 the question of whether the School should sink into oblivion, or whether it should live up to its motto and go boldly forward, had squarely to be faced. The bolder course was adopted, and 1921–22 saw the building of a new School Hall, Library and Laboratory and a new Workshop, as well as the erection of the Memorial Spire. At the same time the Berryfield was purchased. These various additions cost more than £10,000.

THE CORPS DISBANDED, BUT THE CAMPS CONTINUE

Some two years after the War, and following a discussion of the problem by the Staff, Old Boys and Prefects, the School declined the offer of the War Office to recognize the Corps as a Junior O.T.C. Instead the Corps was disbanded, but Rover Scouting and the Scout organization were greatly developed. This decision was based partly on the belief that the military training of schoolboys was hardly to be reconciled with the ideals of a new age in which it was hoped that the League of Nations would predominate, and partly by a desire to serve the youth of Britain by providing a steady supply of boys qualified to become Scoutmasters. A doubt was also expressed as to whether any military training possible in schools could have much relation to the actual needs of warfare in a mechanized age, and it was contended that the habits of observa-tion and initiative induced by Scouting would be as valuable even from a military standpoint. Whether that decision was right or wrong only the future can reveal.

As a result Wycliffe Scout Camps on a large scale continued to be held not only by the Wye and the Severn and the Stratford Avon, but also by the Thames at Wittenham, by the English and Bristol Channels and on Cardigan Bay, in the Channel Islands, by the Mediterranean in Sicily and Algeria, and in Bavaria. Many new localities have thus been made familiar to Wycliffe boys in the course of their scout training.

The Opening of the Junior School

For many years it had proved difficult to harmonize the educational and other needs of boys of 18 with those of boys of 10, and in April 1928 Ryeford Hall, known to O.W.s of an older generation as a Girls' School, was purchased, modernized and opened as a Preparatory or Junior School, with an O.W. (Mr. K. C. Bird) as Master in charge.

Rather before this date the School had sought full inspection by the Board of Education, and has since appeared on the Board's list of efficient schools. At the same time the general scheme of work was reorganized, with a two years' course after Matriculation in either the Modern or the Science Sixth. At about the same period the system of "rounds," with "roll-calls" for flagrant offenders, was evolved to take the place of the older punishments of fines and of written tasks.

The Foundation of Wycliffe as a Public School

Mr. G. W. Sibly died peacefully and suddenly at the end of May 1929, leaving the School to his two sons. With the opening of the Junior School and the increasing complexity of school life, these felt that it would be wise to try to establish Wycliffe on a broader and more enduring basis. Just at this time an unsolicited offer of £10,000 for such a purpose, provided that the foundation should be on a basis broad enough to cover the education of boys of all denominations, came from the Farmer Trust. A committee of representative Old Boys was formed, the school buildings and estate were valued independently at £48,000 without Springfield and Ryeford, or at about £58,000 if these were included. (Springfield had been enlarged two years before at a cost of £3,000)

To facilitate the Foundation, the owners agreed to write a large sum off the assessed value, and to ask nothing for goodwill, and to make other financial concessions. The remainder of the purchase money was raised by donations, amounting with the gift of the Farmer Trustees to about £15,000, and by Debentures bearing interest at 5%, and held for the most part by O.W's. At the same time the present Chairman of the Council of Governors, Mr. J. Herbert Edward (O.W.) came forward with an offer of generous assistance, and so, in April 1931, Wycliffe was placed on a permanent foundation as a Public School.

There may be some who regret the change, but there can be no doubt as to its making for stability and endurance as well as for new developments, nor—with the Headmaster and Mr. T. M. Sibly continuing to serve the School, and a Council sympathetic with Wycliffe traditions and ideals—is there likely to be any early change in the general policy and spirit of the School.

DEVELOPMENTS SINCE THIS FOUNDATION

In spite of the economic crisis which swept the world in 1931, the School Council has pursued, under Mr. Edwards' chairmanship, a policy of active improvement. Not only did more money immediately become available, but the expectation has also been realized that gifts could be made far more readily to a public " corporation " than to private individuals. Aided by two further donations from the Farmer Trust, a new Sanatorium was built in 1933, and a new Science Block in 1935. The Sanatorium was skilfully and artistically added to the old Ivy Grove by the late Mr. Thomas Falconer, the School's consulting architect, who has been succeeded by Mr. H. F. Trew of Gloucester. Two noble memorial gifts were also made by O.W.s the Batchelar-Bowen Bridge, which spans the busy motor-road between Ryeford and its playing-fields, given by Mr H. W. Batchelar in memory of his wife and father-in-law, and the reredos and communion table in the Chapel, given by Mr. J. Cecil Hayes in memory of his wife. This was designed by Mr. Lorne Campbell, the consulting architect of the Church of Scotland.

On the occasion of the School Jubilee in 1932 a fine new Organ, one of the most interesting in the West of England, costing nearly £1,800, was dedicated and opened, thanks largely to the labours of Mr. T. S. Dixon in raising the necessary funds.

In 1936 Mr. R. V. Ward, a master at Wycliffe for more than forty years, presented a Swimming Pool to the School, and added a range of dressing-rooms next year. This magnificent and acceptable gift cost about £3,500. Much of the preliminary work of excavation was done by the boys themselves.

In 1937 the Headmaster was presented with a cheque for £1,520 to mark his silver jubilee, this sum being given by Old Boys and other friends. He handed the cheque back to the School, together with the deeds of four adjacent cottages, that the whole might be used for the enlargement and modernization of Springfield.

Meanwhile, under the direction of the Chairman, who has a gift for landscape gardening, the beauty of the already lovely grounds has been steadily enhanced.

Other important changes have also taken place in recent years. In 1931 Mr. T. M. Sibly, on becoming School Bursar, retired from the housemastership of the School House, where he was succeeded by Mr. T. S. Dixon, and purchased the Grove House and part of the Grove Estate. This lies half way between Wycliffe and Ryeford, and gives accommodation for some fifteen boys. In 1933 Miss Enid Sibly built Windrush, to serve as a hostel for some twenty of the youngest Ryeford boys. In the same year Mr. E. J. Bevan succeeded Mr. G. L. Reade as Housemaster of Haywardsfield, Mr. Reade becoming the Master of the Middle School.

New Class-rooms have been built at Ryeford both before and since the Foundation, and a Swimming-pool has been made there.

A new Art Room has been built at Wycliffe, as also an external Common Room for Haywardsfield, and the work of panelling the School Hall in oak makes steady progress.

Serious rowing has begun on the Berkeley Canal, where a boat-house was built by the School, at a cost of £650, during the summer of 1936. In 1937 the Wycliffe 1st IV won the Maiden Fours against strong opposition at Gloucester Regatta.

The only considerable remaining needs of the School on its material side, in the near future anyhow, would seem to be a new Cricket Pavilion (with changing rooms for visiting teams), to take the place of the picturesque but inadequate structure which has served for nearly fifty years, a modern Gymnasium, a small Museum, and further rooms for craft work and other hobbies. If any benevolent O.W. reads these words, here is his chance to help.

Mention should also be made of the Scholarship Fund, by means of which entrance scholarships are now awarded each June, and of the Margaret-Pendrill Leaving Scholarship to Cambridge, endowed by Sir Pendrill Varrier-Jones, O.W., the President of the School, in memory of his mother. It is hoped that in the coming years, with help from various quarters, it may be found possible to extend very considerably the number and value of both entrance and leaving scholarships.

There is much more that might be told. No reference, for example, has been made to the Gilbert & Sullivan operas, nowadays an almost regular feature of Speech Days, or to the wide range of plays presented by the Dramatic Society. Little has been said of the School Journeys undertaken overseas so cheaply and successfully. In 1931 a party of 25 visited Greece, the total cost of twenty-two days' travel being less than £15. In 1933 86 Rovers and Scouts camped by the Mediterranean in Algeria, the cost of an expedition lasting fifteen days being just over £8 per head. In 1935 another party of 80 Scouts visited Rome, Naples, Florence and Milan, camping for four days also in Sicily, at a cost of £11 for sixteen days' travel. In 1936 a camp of 80 in Bavaria, with visits to Austria and North Switzerland, a tramp across the Black Forest, and a journey down the Rhine, came to less than £9. In 1937 a party of 31 Rovers and Scouts spent three days in Egypt and ten in Palestine, and travelled 6,000 miles, for just over £20 a head.

Enough has been said, none the less, to present a picture of steady and at times exhilarating development. Many problems lie ahead of the public boarding-schools of Britain. The increasing efficiency and competition of schools largely maintained at the cost of the State and the rates, the threatened fall in the birth-rate, social changes and international complications, must make every prophet hesitate to commit himself.

THE CHAPEL AND MEMORIAL SPIRE

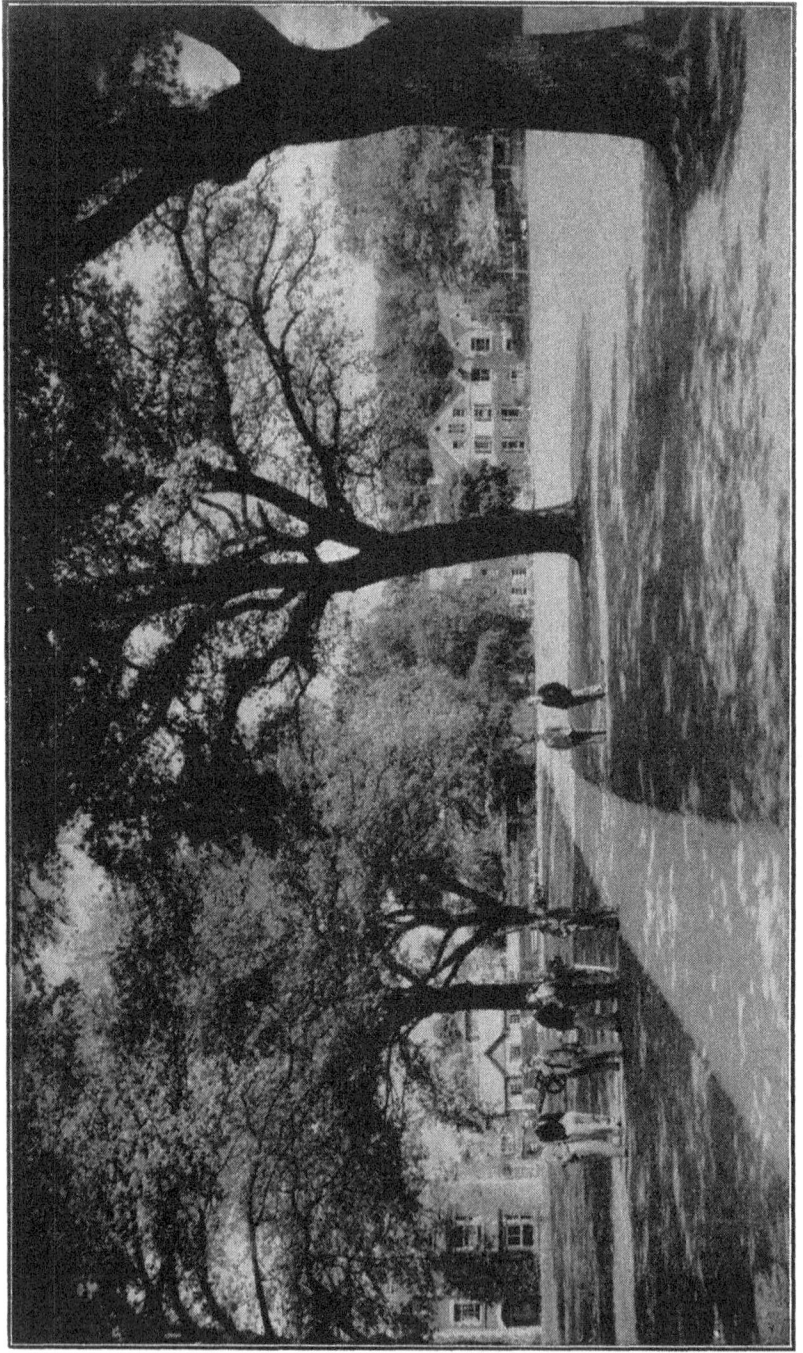

UNDER THE OAK TREES ON A MAY MORNING

THE SCHOOL HOUSE FROM THE TERRACE
(The shy mulberry is slow to put forth its leaves)

SENIORS AND PROBATIONERS, 1895.

W. N. Bubb, W. L. Phillimore, J. H. L. Vellacott, W. S. Butt, W. M. Howell,
E. A. Duncalf, W. I. Evans, F. R. Beacham, J. B. Albury, C. E. Stanier, C. E. Gane, E. P. Hulbert, H. J. Brookes, P. W. Blatherwick,
E. R. Graham, B. T. W. Jones, A. K. Coomaraswamy, H. H. Smith, Somerville Hastings, J. D. Phillips,
W. H. Langley-Smith, H. J. Trump, G. E. Wood, E. D. Evans, H. Barnes.

We do not ask to see the distant scene, nor know what the end shall be, and yet, as we look back over more than fifty eventful years, we can at least feel that Providence has been very good to Wycliffe, and hope that, with the loyal and devoted aid of so many of its sons and friends, it may long keep its old traditions of kindliness and wholesomeness and service, so proving that here too the best is yet to be.

REGISTER OF OLD WYCLIFFIANS

ABBREVIATIONS

R.	= Ryeford Hall (Preparatory School)	C.	= Cotswold, including The Grove, Cambray, Elmsleigh
S.H.	= School House	D.B.	= Day Boy
H.	= Haywardsfield	"Star"	= "Wycliffe Star"
Spr.	= Springfield	"W. & W."	= "Wycliffe and The War"
dau.	= daughter	h.	= Home Address

Abbott, John Goodreid, 89 *Queen's Hill Crescent, Newport, Mon.* (S.H.), 1910–1912. Form IV. 2nd XI Football. North Somerset Yeomanry and Machine Gun Corps. Bank Clerk. Married.

Acomb, Leonard Ernest, 11 *Clytha Park Road, Newport, Mon.* (H.), 1893–1896. Form IV. Late House Surgeon, Middlesex Hospital. Hon. Anaesthetist, Newport and County Hospital. Deputy Medical Officer of Health for Newport. Medical Officer of Military Hospital, Newport. Hon. Surgeon, Royal Gwent Hospital. Married.

Adams, Crofton Gordon Avery, 12 *Pembridge Gardens, Bayswater, London, W. 2.* (Spr.), 1927–1933. Upper Remove. Printing Trade.

Adams, Deryck Underwood, 18 *Tewit Well Road, Harrogate,* (H.), 1929–1933. Matric. Form. Vice-Pres. of League. Pres. of Jun. Debating Society. Captain 2nd XV Rugby. Athletic Team. Prize for Public Service. Theological Student at Didsbury College, Manchester.

Adams, John Newton, *Oakdene, 233 East Lane, N. Wembley, Middlesex.* (H.), 1925–1929. Upper V. Assistant and Sub. Librarian. P.L. and 1st Class Scout. School Certificate. Tennis Team. Captain Royal Artillery (Territorial). Bank Clerk, National Provincial Bank.

Adams, William Davy, 48 *Cecil Avenue, Bournemouth* (h.) *Fairleigh, 7 Woodstock Road, Redland, Bristol.* (S.H.), 1927–1935. Modern VI. Prefect. Sec. of Boat Club. Sub. Librarian. P.L. and 1st Class Scout. School Certificate. 1st XV Rugby. Junior Athlete. Prize for Music. Pilot Officer in R.A.F.

Addicott, Arthur Stanley, (Spr.), 1904–1907. Form V. Senior. House Prize. 1st XI Cricket and Football. Cadet Pilot R.A.F. Building Contractor. Married.

Adkins, Edward Francis John, *The Mill House, Broom, Bidford-on-Avon.* (S.H.), 1919–1924. Form IV. Miller.

Affleck, David, 6 *High Street, Chippenham, Wilts.* (S.H.), 1931–1936. Prefect. King's Scout. 1st XV Rugby. 1st IV. Foster Rifle.

Affleck, John, 6 *High Street, Chippenham, Wilts.* (S.H.), 1924–1927. Upper V. Boat Capt. 2nd XI Football. Senior Cambridge. Bank Clerk.

Affleck, Stuart, *High Street, Chippenham, Wilts.* (S.H.), 1926–1929. Upper IV. House Monitor. P.L. Scouts. King's Scout.

Albury, the Hon. Joseph Baird, *Box 1, Nassau, N.P., Bahamas.* (H.), 1893–1896. Form VI. Senior. Pres. of Lit. Soc. London Matric. M.R.C.S., L.R.C.P. House Prize. 2nd XI Football. Natural Science Scholarship. Biology Prize and Demonstratorship in Biology at St. Mary's Hospital. Capt. N. P. Defence Force. Physician. Member of the Legislative Council of the Bahama Islands. Justice of the Peace. Chairman, Board of Management, Boys' Industrial School. Chief Medical Officer, 1914–1918.

Albury, Robert William, *Nassau, N.P., Bahamas.* (H.), 1881–1885. Senior. Pres. of Lit. Soc. and Field Club. Music and Excellence in Public Speaking Prizes. 1st XV Football. Degree of D.D.S. University of Pennsylvania. Surgeon in B.R.C.S. Italy. Dental Surgeon. Married.

Alcock, Christopher Arthur, *The Lodge, Brockworth, Glos.* (H.), 1929–1932. Upper IV. Engineer.

Alcock, Frank, *Forthampton, Tewkesbury, Glos.* (S.H.), 1898–1900. Form III. Farmer in Canada.

Alger, Clifford Henry, 50 *Oakfield Road, Newport, Mon., and* 56 *Warwick Road, Earl's Court, S.W.5.* (S.H.), 1923–1927. Upper V. House Monitor. Sub.-Librarian. Sec. of Boat Club. 1st Class Scout. P.L. Pioneers. Boat Capt. Pilot. School Certificate. 2nd XI Football 1927. Member of House Shooting Team. Electrical Engineer.

Alger, T. H., 50 *Oakfield Road, Newport, Mon.* (S.H.), 1927–1929. Form V. House Monitor. 1st XV. Refrigeration Engineer.

Allen, Hubert Richard, *Albany Road, Cardiff.* (H.), 1907–1910. Form IV. 2nd XI Football. Music Prize. L/Cpl. 53rd Div. Signal Co. R.E. L.D.S., R.C.S. (Eng.). Dental Surgeon. Married.

Allen, Newstead Adams, 79 *Columbia Avenue, Montreal, Canada.* (D.B.), 1900–1901. Form V. Mus.B., A.R.I.B.A. Architect. Married.

Allen, Percival John, 28 *King Edward's Avenue, Gloucester.* (S.H.), 1915–1918. Form IV. Probationer. Chief Assistant Manager (Wagons Dept.) Gloucester Ry. Carr. and Wagon Co. Married.

Allinson, Adrian Pulvermacher, 22 *Christchurch Avenue, N.W.* 6 and *The Old Cottage, Burleigh, Brimscombe, Nr. Stroud.* (S.H.), 1901–1905. Form V. Slade Scholar of London University. Exhibitor at New English and Royal Academy. Artist. Married : (1 son).

Allwood, Eric Sanders, 32 *Mansfield Road, Ilford.* (S.H.), 1908–1910. Form VI. Senior. Sec. of Lit. Soc. Cambridge Jun. II Honours. 2nd XI Football and Cricket. Chaplain to the Forces. Missionary in India 1917–1934. Methodist Minister. Married : (1 dau., 1 son).

Allwood, Leslie Holman, *East Dereham, Norfolk.* (S.H.), 1917–1923. Form VI. Senior. Pres. of Lit. Soc. London Matriculation. " Herbert Park " Literature and Public Speaking Prizes. Solicitor. Married : (1 dau.).

Ambrose, Gilbert. (S.H.), 1891–1893. Died September 30th, 1909, aged 31 years.

Anderson, John Henry, *St. Cyril's Road, Stonehouse, Glos.* (D.B.), 1898–1900. 9th Glos. Regt. Married : (1 son).

Anderson, Joseph Stewart, 161 *Golfdale Road, Toronto, Canada.* (D.B.), 1901–1905. Form VI. Senior. London Matric. 1st XI Football. House Prize. Sergt. D.C.M. 1st Can. M.G. Batt. Chartered Accountant. Treasurer of Western Canada Flour Mills Co. Ltd. Married : (1 dau.).

Andrew, Derek Ronald, 2 *St. Mary's Terrace, London Road, Worcester.* (S.H.), 1932–1935. Matric. Form. Jun. Librarian. Oxford and Cambridge School Certificate. Articled to Chartered Accountant.

Angel, T. Huber, 94 *Parkside Way, N. Harrow, Middlesex.* (S.H.), 1916–1919. Form IV. Probationer. B.Sc. Swansea University College. Ph.D. (Wales). Research Chemist, Venesta Ltd. Married : (2 sons).

Anstey, Major Henry Charles, 29 *St. James Street, London,* S.W. 1 (h.) *and Panton House,* 25 *Haymarket, London, S.W.* 1. (H.), 1892–1893. Form VI. Senior. Meteorological Secretary. 2nd XI Cricket and Football. Major, the Royal Warwickshire Regt. 25 years' war service— the South African War and the Great War (Divisional Staff in France and Headquarter Staff at home). Invalided out August 17th, 1921. H.M. Vellum Certificate of Honour. Solicitor of the Supreme Court of Judicature. Married.

Anstey, T. F., *High Street, Thornbury, Glos.* (H.), 1891–8986. Form V.

Anthony, Arthur Parnell, *The Rosary, Beeches Green, Stroud, Glos.* (S.H.), 1896–1898. Form III. Draper. Married.

Anthony, Gerald Hayne, 45 *Devizes Road, Swindon.* (D.B. and Spr.), 1902–1904. Form I. House Furnisher. War Service : Royal 1st Devon Yeomanry. 5th (P.O.W.) Batt. Devonshire Regiment 1915. Served India, Palestine, France, Germany. Awarded M.C. Married : (2 sons, 2 daus.).

Anthony, Gerald Parnell, *The Rosary, Beeches Green, Stroud, Glos.* (D.B.), 1915–1918. Draper. Married.

Antill, Charles Isaac (D.B.). Mechanical Engineer.

Antill, Stanley Morris, *Strathmore, Mangotsfield Road, Staple Hill, Bristol.* (D.B.), 1918–1924. Form V. Probationer. Manufacturer's Agent. Married.

Apperly, Arthur Lancelot. (D.B. and S.H.), 1885–1891. Form III. Trained as Chartered Accountant. Went to S. Africa, and for eight years was Bursar of St. Andrew's College, Grahamstown. On return to England became Co-Director of Dudbridge Mills and other Companies. Commission in Gloucestershire Regiment 1916. Killed in Battle of the Somme, August 1916. (" W. & W." 12).

Apperly, Charles Alfred, *Villa Sphinx, Valescure, St. Raphael, Var. S. France.* (D.B. and H.), 1882–1888. House Prize. J.P. for Gloucestershire. Married.

Apperly, Ernest Paice, *Springvale, Huddersfield, Yorks.* (D.B. and H.), 1882–1889. War Service : Flanders 1916–1917. Captain R.E. Woollen and Worsted Cloth Manufacturer. Married : (1 dau., 7 grd. ch.).

Apperly, Henry David, 4 *Mandeville Place, Cavendish Square, London, W.* (S.H.), 1885–1893. Form VI. Senior. Pres. of Lit. Soc. L.D.S., R.C.S. (Eng.), 1899, F.Z.S. 1907. Dental Surgeon. Married. Died 1937.

Apperly, Dr Raymond Ebenezer, 15 *Burgess Hill, Hampstead, London, N.W.* 2. (D.B.), 1893–1902. Form VI. Senior. House Prize. 1st XI Football. Lyell Gold Medal and Scholarship in Practical Surgery, Middlesex Hospital. M.R.C.S., L.R.C.P. Anaesthetist. Past Pres. of Anaesthetic Section of British Medical Association and of Royal Society of Medicine. Late Captain R.A.M.C. (T.), 1915–1919. Married : (1 son, 1 dau.).

Appleby, Alfred Wesley, *Hengrove Road, Knowle, Bristol.* (H.), 1924–1929. Upper V. School Certificate. 1st XI Colours 1927–1929. 2nd XV Football 1927–1928. 1st XI Cricket. Married : (2 sons).

Appleby, Donald, *Dunmovin,* 69 *Beach Road, Weston-super-Mare.* (H.), 1922–1928. Upper V. School Certificate. 1st XI Cricket Colours 1928. 2nd and 1st Football XI Colours 1927–1928. 2nd XV Rugby 1928. 1st Class Boatman. House Shooting and Relay Teams. Music Prize.

Appleby, George Samuel, *Queen's Avenue, Bristol.* (H.), 1915–1919. Form VI. Senior. 1st XI Football. Provision Merchant. Married.

Archard, D. E., (S.H.), 1885–1887. Probationer. Curator of Field Club. Died while returning from India 1900.

Archbold, W. A. Jobson, *Selwyn Croft, Cambridge.* (S.H.), 1882–1884. Senior. Whewell Scholar of Cambridge University. M.A., L.L.B. Scholar of Peterhouse. For some years head of Government College in Bengal.

Arkell, Frank Joseph. (S.H.), 1907–1909. Form V. Senior. Hons. Senior Cambridge. Vice-President of League. 1st XI Cricket and Football. Articled to Solicitors in Cheltenham. Joined 2/5th Gloucesters in 1914. Missing after March 21st 1918. (" W. & W." 13).

Arkell, Henry, *Butler's Court, Nr. Cheltenham.* (H.), 1899–1901. Form VI. Farmer. Married : (2 sons, 2 daus.).

Armstrong, Ralph Joseph, *Tudor House, Red Hill, Worcestershire.* (S.H.), 1892–1896. Form V. 1st XI Cricket. 1st Prize and Bronze Medal, Swindon Engineering Soc., 1911. Divisional Supt. Locs., Carriage and Wagon Dept., G.W.R. On Council of Governors of Wycliffe College. Married : (1 dau.).

Arnott, A. Howard. (H.), 1896–1898. Died of pneumonia 1919.

Arnott, Edward Whiston, *Wraystone, Reigate, Surrey.* (H.), 1893–1902. Senior. Pres. of Lit. Soc. Sec. of Field Club. London Matric. House Prize. 1st XI Cricket. Captain 1st XI Football. M.A. St. John's College, Cambridge. Barrister.

Arnott, Leslie Ivan, *The Garth, Monmouth.* (H.), 1920–21. Probationer. London Matric. Rowell Cup. Prizes for Improvement, Music and Merit. Pembroke College, Oxford 1922–1926. Company Director and Secretary. Married : (1 son).

Arnott, Ronald Whiston, *Oakdene, Redbrook Road, Monmouth.* (H.), 1916–1918. Senior. Senior Cambridge. St. John's College, Cambridge, 1919–1921. War Service—Artists' Rifles. Public Works Contractor. Married : (1 son).,

Arnott, Trevor, *The Garth, Monmouth.* (H.), 1916–1920. Senior. Vice-Pres. of League. Pres. and Sec. of Lit. Soc. Capt. 1st XI Cricket. 1st XI Football. Senior Tennis Singles Championship. Rowell Cup. Captain of Glamorgan County C.C. 1922–32. Welsh Cricket XI. Lord Tennyson's Jamaica Tours 1927–1928. Sir J. Cahn's Argentine Tour. Gentlemen v. Players. Auctioneer, Estate Agent and Valuer. Married.

Ashley, John Tankard. (D.B.), 1922.

Ashton, John Ralph, *Cainscross Villa, Cainscross, Stroud, Glos.* (D.B. and Spr.) 1925–1933. Form VI. Prefect. Vice-Pres. of League. Sec. of Sports Committee. Sergeant at Arms and Treas. of Lit. Soc. P.L. and King's Scout. House Musical Director. School Certificate. 1st XI Colours 1931–34. Foster Rifle (twice). Jeune Cup 1933. High Jump Record (Spring 1933). Prizes : Music and Public Service. With E. S. & A. Robinson, Bristol.

Aston, H. Woodward, 46 *Eagle Wharf Road, London, N. 1.* (D.B. and S.H.), 1896–1902. Form VI. Senior. Sec. of Lit. Soc. and Field Club. London Matric. Managing Director of the Aston Construction Co. Director of Sussex Brick & Sussex Wagon Co., Southwater Brick and Tile Co., Smith Walker Ltd. Member of the Institute of Struct. Engineers. Married : (2 daus.).

Attwell, Harry Fison (S.H.), 1882–1884. Senior, Football XV. Studied milling in Liverpool. Went to Capetown (1890) and became partner with G. B. Attwell (Broker and Accountant). Married in 1895 and died after two days' illness in 1905.

Aurelius, T. J. Died in 1896.

Axton, John Charles, *Millbrook Lodge, Millbrook Road, Southampton.* (S.H.), 1924–1928. Upper V. School Certificate. House Cricket Team.

Ayers, Kenneth Donald, 23 *Lansdown, Stroud.* (D.B.), 1927–1930. Clerk.

Bailey, Frederick George, *Hillcrest, Dursley, Glos.* (D.B.), 1912–1917. Form IV. Probationer. Bristol Univ. O.T.C. Editor of Gazette Series of Newspapers, Dursley, Glos. Married : (2 sons).

Bailey, James Drover, *C/o Thos. Cook and Son, Collins Street, Melbourne, Australia.* (H.), 1918–1923. Form V. 2nd XI Cricket. Farming.

Bailey, Keith Cyril, *Standeford, Langland, Swansea.* (H.), 1932–1936. Camb. School Certif. Form.

Bailey, Wilfred Hughes. (D.B.), 1902–1907. Probationer. Junior Athlete. Cloth Trade. Deceased.

Baker, Cyril Bennett. (H.), 1899–1904. Form VI. Senior. Capt. 2nd XI Cricket. 1st XI Football. Major R.A.F. Belgian Croix de Guerre.

Baker, Gordon Maurice, *Tall Chimneys, St. Wilfrid's Road, Bessacarr, Doncaster.* (Spr.), 1921–1925. Form VI. Senior. Senior Camb. 1st XI Football and Cricket. House Cricket Capt. 1924 and 1925. Solicitor's Articled Clerk.

Baker, Hedley Augustus. (H.), 1899–1904. Form VI. Senior. London Matric. House Prize. Electrical Engineer in New Zealand.

Baker, Hugh A. G. (H.), 1914–1917. Form V. Senior. Pres. Sec. and Treas. of Lit. Soc. 1st XI Football. 2nd XI Cricket. Sub-Lieut. R.N.V.R. Assistant to Messrs Birkmyre Bros., Jute Merchants, Calcutta. Drowned April 10th, 1927. ("Star," August 1927).

Baker, Hugh Ivimy, *Hazeldene, Tewkesbury, Glos.* (H.), 1923–1928. Upper V. House Monitor. P.L. Scouts. School Certif. Bank Clerk.

Baker, Ivan Arnott Gothard. (H.), 1902–1905. Form VI. Senior. Vice-Pres. of League. Hons., Camb. Locals. Died 1918. ("Star," Aug., 1918).

Baker, Kenneth Erskine, *Kirkgate House, Redhill.* (H), 1902–1906. Form VI. Senior. Vice-Pres. of League. London Matric. Capt 2nd XI Cricket. Chartered Accountant.

Baker, Martyn Wilfrid, *Kirkgate House, Redhill.* (H.), 1899–1902. Form VI. Senior. Pres. of Lit. Soc. London Matric. House Prize. Capt. 1st XI Cricket. 1st XI Football. M.B., B.C., M.A. Cantab., M.R.C.S., L.R.C.P. Consulting Surgeon and Vice-Pres. East Surrey Hospital. War service : 1915–1918, Egypt and France. Captain R.A.M.C. Married (1 son).

Baker, Walter. (H.), 1905–1909. Form III. Was in business in Birmingham and London. Commission in the Gloucesters. Served in France. Became Captain and won M.C. Mortally wounded October 1917. ("W. & W." 14).

Balleny, William H., 12 *Bower Street, Fulwell, Sunderland.* (S.H.), 1905–1908. Chemist.

Banks, Herbert Leonard, 44 *Friern Road, London, S.E.* 22. (S.H.), 1913–1916. Form V. Civil Service. Accountant-General's Dept., G.P.O. London. Married : (3 daus.).

Banks, John de Carle, *Elgin Lodge, Stonehouse, Glos.* (h.) 23 *Dunmow Road, Andover, Hants.* (D.B.), 1916–1920. Form III. Electrician.

Bannister, Frank Alexis Charles, *Stoneleigh, Stafford Road, Bloxwith, Staffs.* (H.), 1922–1926. 2nd XI Cricket. Pharmacist (M.P.S.). Optician (F.S.M.C.).

Bannister, Frederick William. (H.), 1897–1903. Form VI. 2nd XI Football. Sergt. A.S.C. Mentioned in despatches. Ship Broker. Married.

Bannister, Thomas Donovan Wood, *Bellevue, Stroud, Glos.* (h.) ; *Shanghai Club, Shanghai, China.* (D.B.), 1900–1906. Form V. 1st XI Cricket and Football. Leeds Univ. (Textile Dept.). Woollen Manufacturer's Agent. Married : (1 son.).

Bannister, Thomas Geoffrey, *Stoneleigh, Stafford Road, Bloxwich, Staffs.* (H.), 1922–29. Middle V. 2nd XI Cricket and Football. Passed Chemist and Druggist Exam. 1933. Pharmacist. M.P.S.

Bannister, W. W. (S.H.), 1883–1885. 1st XI Cricket. 2nd XI Football. Went to America in 1887.

Barber, S. J.

Barber, Edgar Maurice, *Ingledene, Staple Hill, Bristol.* (S.H.), 1922–1927.

Bardrick, John Alexander. (S.H.), 1899–1903. Probationer. Lieut. M.G.C.

Barling, S.

Barnard, Alfred Yockney, *Siangoba, Mazabuka, N. Rhodesia.* (H.), 1910–1915. Form V. Pte. Oxford and Bucks. L.I. Birmingham Univ. Boxing Club, Lightweight, 1921–1923. Farming in N. Rhodesia.

Barnard, Cyril. (H.), 1910–1913. Form V. Took up fruit farming in S. Africa. Came home and joined Tank Corps at beginning of the War. Was fatally wounded on the Western Front in September 1917. ("W. & W." 15).

Barnes, Alexander Frederick. (H.), 1902–1908. Form V. Junior Athlete. Railway Engineer.

Barnes, Harold G. (D.B.), 1891–1895. Form VI. National Provincial Bank.

Barnett, Anthony M., 131 *Old Bath Road, Cheltenham.* (H.), 1929–1933. Science VI. Prefect. Pres. of League and Lit. Soc. Capt. 1st XI Cricket. 1st XV Football. School Shooting Team. Camb. School Cert. (Hons.). Medical Student at St. John's College, Cambridge. Treasurer Camb. Univ. Medical Society. Medical Student, St. Thomas' Hospital, London.

Barnett, Arthur Peter, *Bramleigh, Priors Road, Cheltenham.* (H.), 1920–1924. 1st XI Cricket. 2nd XI Football. At Cavendish House, Promenade, Cheltenham.

Barnett, Charles John, *Cowcombe House, Chalford, Nr. Stroud.* (H.), 1921–1925. Form Lower V. Probationer. 1st XI Cricket and Football. West of England Scout Swimming Championship. Junior Tennis Doubles. Professional in Gloucestershire Cricket Team. Has played for England v. West Indies and in M.C.C. Indian Tour. Member of the M.C.C. Team in Australia 1936–37. Married: (2 sons, 1 dau.).

Barnett, Charles Sherborne, *The Cross, Tewkesbury.* (H.), 1899–1900. Form VI. Senior. Capt. 1st XI Cricket and Football. Lieut. 4th Batt. Gloucestershire Regt. Gloucestershire County Cricketer. Purveyor. Married: (2 sons).

Barnett, Donald, 2 *Montpellier, Cheltenham and South Lawn, Church Road, St. Marks, Cheltenham.* (H.), 1913–1915. Form IV. 1st XI Cricket. 2nd XI Football. Lieut. R.A.F. Purveyor. Married: (2 sons).

Barnett, Edgar. (H.), 1899–1901. Form VI. 1st XI Cricket and Football. Captain 1st XI 1901, when he made 539 runs (average 44.9). Studied Dentistry at Guy's Hospital, and won the Inter-Hospital Lightweight Boxing Championship (1905–1907). Played for Gloucestershire at Assoc. Football, and for fifteen years in the Gloucestershire Cricket Team. Distinguished himself in Amateur Theatricals and as a Freemason and member of the Cheltenham Rotary Club. Died of meningitis in January 1922 ("Star," April 1922).

Barnett, Leslie, 2 *Ebor, High Street, Cheltenham.* (H.), 1913–1917. Form IV. Probationer. 1st XI Cricket and Football. Newman Cup. Boxing and Wrestling Championship. Cadet, R.A.F. Purveyor. Married.

Barnett, Percy Playle, 121 *Leckhampton Road, Cheltenham.* (H.), 1902–1905. Form IV. 1st XI Cricket and Football. Gloucestershire County Cricketer. Land Agent in Canada. Married.

Barnett, Victor, 121 *Whitegate Drive, Blackpool, Lancs.* (H.), 1900–1902. 1st XI Cricket. Purveyor. Married.

Bartlett, Bernard Yorke, 24 *Upper Belgrave Road, Clifton, Bristol.* (S.H.), 1922–1926. 2nd XI Cricket. Stockbroker.

Barrett, A. N., *Sydney House, Littleover, Derby.* (Sp.), 1934–1935. Lower V.

Barton, Alfred Kenneth, *The Cottage, Bower Hill, Melksham, Wilts.* (S.H.). 1916–1920. Form III. Building Manager. Married : (1 son, 1 dau.),

Barton, Eric Dawson, *Sarnia, Blacksmith's Hill, Sanderstead Village, Surrey.* (S.H.), 1913–1920. Probationer. Manager Flooring Company.

Barton, John Francis Kenyon, 14 *Ferrymead Gardens, Westridge Estate, Greenford, Middlesex.* (S.H.), 1916–1922. Form V. Prizes for Lower School and Exams. Engineer, A.I.Mech.E. Factory Manager. Married : (1 dau.).

Batchelar, Hubert Walters, *The Limes, Rickmansworth, Herts.* (S.H.), 1911–1916. Senior. Vice-President of League. Pres. and Treas. of Lit. Soc. 1st XI Football. Senior Athlete. House Prize. Pte. R.A.S.C. (M.I.) Solicitor. Member of Council of Governors, Wycliffe College.

Bateman, Ernest Hugh, 87 *High Avenue, Letchworth, Herts.* (Spr.), 1915–1917. Probationer. Camb. Sen. Hons. II. Scholar of Trinity College, Cambridge. 1st Class Mechanical Science Tripos. Engineer. Married.

Bateson, A. Campbell. (S.H.), 1885–1887. Deceased.

Bateson, J. Severs. (S.H.), 1882–1884. Died while studying medicine at Edinburgh in 1889.

Bayley, Archie Clarence. (S.H.), 1902–1904. Chartered Accountant. Went to Canada. In 1914 enlisted in 16th Canadian Scottish, and was killed in action in October 1916. (" W. & W." 16).

Bayley, George Luke, *Le Karaka, Gisborn, New Zealand.* (S.H.), 1897–1899. Probationer. Farming.

Bayley, Leslie William, 11 *Pittville Villas, Cheltenham.* (S.H.), 1900–1902. Probationer. 2nd XI Cricket. B.R.C.S. att. 8th French Army. Director Chelt. and Glouc. Building Society. Chairman Bristol and District Branch Auctioneers' and Estate Agents' Institute. Auctioneer and Surveyor. F.A.I. Married.

Bayley, Wilfrid Alec, *Makauri, Gisborne, New Zealand.* (S.H.), 1902–1905. Form V. Senior. Cpl. N.Z. Forces. Farming.

Bazeley, Edward Stuart, 145 *Gloucester Terrace, W.* 2 *and* 56 *Southampton Row, W.* 1. (S.H.), 1914–1920. Senior. Vice-Pres. of League. Cotton growing in Bahamas. Manager Milk Bar, 56 Southampton Row. Married : (1 son).

Bazeley, Gordon, 193 *Forest Hill Road, Toronto, Ontario, Canada.* (S.H.), 1918–1920. Senior. Final exam. Ontario Architects Registration Board 1934. Member Ontario Assoc. of Architects and of Royal Architect. Inst. of Canada. Late Member Brit. Water Colour Soc. Lived in Nassau, Bahamas (1926–1929) and Toronto (1929–1936). Married : (1 dau.).

Bazeley, Henry Paulle, 2 *Westfield Hall, Hagley Road, Birmingham.* (S.H.), 1917–1923. Senior. Pres. of League. Sec. and Treas. Lit. Soc. Sen. Camb. Hons. II. London Matric. Capt. 2nd XI Football. B.A. St. John's Coll., Cambridge. A.C.A. Stockbroker. Married.

Bazzard, Wyndham Norris, *High Street, Amersham, Bucks.* (S.H.), 1921–1926. Senior. Vice-Pres. of League. Pres. of Lit. Soc. Capt. 1st XI Cricket and Football. Jeune, Woodley and Batchelar Cups. Boxing Shield. House Prizes. Cambridge School Certif. Solicitor.

Beacham, Arthur Conway, 84 *Wellington Street, W. Toronto, or* 120 *Duvernet Avenue, Toronto.* (H.), 1895–1896. 1st XI Football. Director S. Allcock & Co. Agent for Dominion of Canada representing manufacturers of Fishing Tackle, Sports Goods, Toronto. 1914–1919 Manager of Factory working on contracts for War Office and Ministry of Munitions. Freemason Lodge 2804 Seymour, Warwickshire. Married : (3 sons, 1 dau.).

Beacham, Cecil James. (H.), 1897–1898. After leaving school joined firm of Messrs Abel Morrall of Redditch, and became a most successful representative of that and other firms in many parts of the world. Was in Canada at the outbreak of War. Trained with the Artists' Rifles, and received a commission in June 1917. Fell in action near Ypres in October 1917. (" W. & W." 17).

Beacham, Francis Robert. (H.), 1891–1895. London Matric. Senior Athlete and Capt. 1st XI Football. Joined Standard Bank of South Africa, and spent nearly twenty-three years in their London Headquarters. Died of pleurisy and pneumonia in 1925.

Beale, Miles Complin, *The Yews, Minchinhampton, Glos.* (D.B.), 1887–1889. Married.

Beavan, A. E.

Beavan, William Gordon, *Hill Crest, Dinas Powis, Glam.* (S.H.), 1907–1909. Probationer. Capt. The Welsh Regt. M.C. Coal Factor. Married.

Beddoe, Fred. L. (S.H.), 1888–1890. Twice Senior Athlete. Pte. R.A.S.E. Sec. for Wales of British Legion. Deceased.

Behr, George Lovell de. (D.B.), 1902–1908. Senior. Bank Clerk.

Bell, Rev. R. W. Minister in U.S.A. Methodist Episcopal Church. Married.

Bellamy, Robert W., *Penalt, Fawley, near Hereford.* (S.H.), 1909–1912. Form IV. Egypt and Palestine 1917–1919.

Bellingham, J. E., *Sunnyside, Twyford Gardens, Banbury, Oxon.* (H.), 1930–1931. Form IV.

Bellows, John Karl, 18 *Beech Road, Bournville, Birmingham.* (S.H.), 1926–1929. Prefect. School Certif. (Hons.), Downing College, Cambridge 1929–1932. Mechanical Science Tripos Class II. B.A. Assistant Surveyor to the Bournville Village Trust, Bournville Estate Office, Birmingham.

Bence, Percy. (Spr.), 1900–1902. Actor. Married.

Bennett, Alan Davenport, *Rosedene, Hareshill Lane, Leeds 8, Yorks.* (S.H. and G.), 1923–1933. House Monitor. London Matric. Customs and Excise Officer.

Bennett, Charles Wilfrid. Has died.

Bennett, John West, *Rosedene, 32 Harehills Lane, Leeds 8,* (S.H.), 1923–1926. Representative of Electrical Wholesalers, Yorkshire.

Bennett, John W. (S.H.), 1882–1884. Probationer. 1st XI Cricket. Capt. 1st XV Football. Fruit Grower. Married.

Bennett, Leonard Joseph, *The Court, Cromhall, Charfield, Glos* (h.). 23 *Dutton Lane, Eastleigh, nr. Southampton.* (S.H.), 1925–1930.

Bennett, Raymond Victor Mitchell, *St. Catherine's,* 336 *Old Bath Road, Cheltenham.* (H.), 1916–1918. Probationer. A.S.M. 2nd XI Cricket. Editor Proprietor " The Cheltenham Circular." Married.

Bennett, Robert Montague, 180 *Redland Road, Bristol 6* (h.), *and* 12 *St. Stephen's Street, Bristol.* (D.B.), 1900–1905. Form VI. Senior. Senior Hons. London Matric. House Prize. A/Sergt.-Maj. R.A.M.C., 3rd South Midland Field Ambulance, 61st Division. Chartered Accountant. Married : (1 son, 2 daus.).

Berry, Oliver, 65 *Bath Road, Cheltenham.* (S.H.), 1900–1904. 2nd XI Football and Cricket. War Service 1915–1919. Electrical Engineer.

Best, Arthur Pickup, *Courtfield, Park Lane, Great Harwood, Lancs.* (Spr.), 1925–1930. · B.Sc.(London), 1st Class Hons. Neil Arnott Studentship. at University College, London.

Best, William John, *Courtfield, Park Lane, Great Harwood, Lancs.* (Spr.), 1924–1930. Sub-Librarian. Foster Rifle. City and Guilds of London, 1st Class Honours in Textiles. Secretary to Cotton Manufacturing Co.

Bethley, Allan Frederick, 6 *Chadwick Road, Westcliff-on-Sea, Essex.* (H.), 1933–1934. Builders' Apprentice.

Bevan, Corby Garland. (S.H.), 1897–1898. Senior. Pres. of League. A.M.I.C.E. Civil Engineer.

Bevan, David E. 1899. Electrical Engineer.

Bevan, Eric Grover. (S.H.), 1898–1899. Form IV. Probationer. Farming in British Columbia.

Bevan, John George Moore. (S.H.), 1908–1911. Form VI. Senior. Pres. of Lit. Soc. Vice-Pres. of League. 1st XI Cricket. Admiralty Designer. Was in Federated Malay States.

Bevan, Rowland Vincent, *Glen Horton, Sketty Road, Swansea.* (S.H.), 1921–1923. Form IV. Bank Clerk.

Bidlake, Alec Danvers Guyer, 2 *Cloister Crofts, Leamington Spa, Warwickshire.* (S.H.), 1904–1912. Form VI. Probationer. Music Prize. 2nd XI Football. Lieut. R.E. Served in France and Palestine 1914–1919. Cloth Factor. Married.

Bidlake, Arthur Danvers Melancthon, *Houndscroft, Amberley.* (D.B.), 1892–1893. Form VI. M.A. Cantab. In Holy Orders.

Bidlake, Christopher A., *Inchdene, Woodchester.* (H.), 1913–1917. Form VI Senior. Pres. of Lit. Soc. Vice-Pres.. of League. House Prize. Music and Public Speaking Prizes. Midshipman R.N.V.R. Mediterranean Representative of Apperly, Bidlake & Co., Cloth Merchants.

Bidlake, Luther, *The Elms, London Road, Reigate, Surrey.* (D.B.), 1884–1890. Senior. 1st XI Cricket. 1st XV. Tennis Champion. Guy's Hospital. L.D.S., R.C.S.(Eng.). Dental Surgeon.

Billington, Jack William, *West House, Bredon, Tewkesbury.* (D.B.), 1917–1923. Form V. Probationer. House Prize. Senior Cross-Country Championship (twice). Jeune Cup. 2nd XI Football. Farmer.

Binding, Leonard Hubert, *Howe Manse, Castle Street, Torrington.* (D.B.), 1921–1926. Lower V.

Binning, Rex Austin, 18 *Brunswick Square, Hove, Sussex.* (Spr.), 1922–1928. Form VI. Prefect. Pres. of League and Lit. Soc. King's Scout. School Certif. 1st M.B. Parts, I, II, III. Capt. 1st XI Football. 1st XV Football. 1st XI Cricket. Batchelar Cup. Heavyweight Boxing Championship 1928. House and Hearson Prizes and for Public Speaking and Prop. Rep. Essay. B.A. Cantab. Scholarship at St. George's Hospital 1931. M.R.C.S.(Eng.), L.R.C.P.(Lond.) Casualty Officer, House Surgeon and Physician, St. George's Hospital. Physician. Married : (1 son).

Bird, Eric Leslie, 19 *Ealing Village, London, W.* 5. (H. and Spr.), 1904–1911. Form VI. Senior. Pres. of Lit. Soc. and League. London Matric. Camb. Senior (Hons.), Capt. 2nd XI Cricket. 2nd XI Football. House Prize. Associate of R.I.B.A. Architect. Journalist. Technical Editor of " Journal " of Royal Inst. of Brit. Architects. Housemaster, Architectural School of Architecture. Capt. M.G.C. M.C. Married : (2 sons, 1 dau.).

Bird, George Harold, 1 *Berkeley Villas, Lower Street, Stroud.* (D.B.), 1903 Form I. F.R.C.O. Organist and Teacher of Music. Married : (2 sons, 1 dau.).

Bird, Harold Gordon, 61 *Canford Lane, Westbury-on-Trym, Bristol.* (H. and Spr.), 1916–1921. Form VI. Senior. Camb. Senior. Sec. and Treas. of Lit. Soc. 2nd XI Football. Capt. 2nd XI Cricket. Branch Manager of Elder, Fyffe Ltd., Shipping Fruit Importers. Married : (1 dau., 1 son).

Bird, Harry Joseph, 1 *Pittville Terrace, Cheltenham.* (D.B.), 1901–1906. Form IV. Bank Clerk. Married : (1 son).

Bird, Kenneth Collingwood, *Ryeford Hall, Stonehouse, Glos.* (Spr.). 1916–1922. Senior. Pres. of League. Treas. of Lit. Soc. Junior Cross Country Championship (twice). Batchelar Cup. 1st XI Cricket. Capt. 2nd XI Football. M.A. Lincoln College, Oxford. Schoolmaster. Headmaster of Ryeford Hall.

Bird, Rex William. (H. and Spr.), 1902–1910. Form VI. Assisted Mr W. A. Sibly in establishing Springfield. Senior. Pres. of League and Lit. Soc. Sen. Camb. (Hons.), and London Matric. 1st XI Cricket and Football. House Prize and for Public Speaking. Articled as Architect. Joined 12th Gloucesters 1914. Commission in 1st Wiltshires, and later Captain. Killed on the Somme in August 1916, being recommended for the D.S.O. on the day he died. (" W. & W." 18).

Bird, Stanley, *Eastholm, Churchdown, near Gloucester.* (S.H.), 1931–1935. Art Student.

Bird, Tom L. (S.H.), 1882–1887. Curator of Field Club. 2nd XV, Studied at Royal Agricultural College, Cirencester. After three years farming in Canada was invalided home with malaria, followed by more serious disease. Died in mid-Atlantic on his way back to Canada.

Bishop, Arthur Rowsell, *Dumbleside, Burton Joyce, Notts.* (H.), 1925–1931. Form V. 1st XV. Junior Tennis Singles and Senior Tennis Doubles. Electrical Engineer.

Bishop, Frederick Edward, *Ffordffawr, Hay, Brecon.* (h). *Mill Half Farm, Whitney-on-Wye, Hereford.* (R. and H)., 1929–1934. Form IV Farming.

Bishop, John Harold, *Dumbleside, Burton Joyce, Notts.* (h). *Universities' Mission, Delhi.* (H.), 1921–1926. Form VI. Senior. Nottingham University 1926–1927. Durham University 1927–1930. B.A. Master at Ryeford 1930–1933. Clerk in Holy Orders. Ordained Deacon to St. Stephen's, Gloucester in 1935. Priest June 21, 1936.

Black, William Alderson, *Clach-na-Faire, Pitlochry, Perthshire, Scotland* (h). *c/o Messrs Read, Ward & Co., P.O. Box 577, 6 Lyons Range, Calcutta, India.* (H.), 1907–1910. Form VI. Senior. Camb. Sen. London Matric. 2nd XI Cricket and Football. Stock and Share Broker. Past District Grand Senior Warden, Bengal. General Service with India Defence Force. Married : (1 dau.).

Blackall, Claude Trelawney, 21 *Southville Road, Thames Ditton, Surrey.* (H.), 1908–1912. Form VI. Senior. A.S.M. Lieut. 1st Batt. Monmouthshire Regt. Chartered Surveyor. P.A.S.I., F.A.I. Middlesex County Council, Valuation Dept., 10 St. George St., Westminster, S.W. 1. Married : (1 dau.).

Blackmore, Arthur S. (S.H.), 1899–1904. Form IV. Probationer. Capt. 1st XI Football. Engineer.

Blackmore, Percy William. (S.H.), 1895–1900. Form IV. Optician. Married.

Blackwell, Edward S., *Hullacey House, Tarlton, near Cirencester.* (D.B. and Spr.), 1898–1904. Form II. Glos. Regt. Farming. Married : (1 son).

Bladwell, Ernest Wilfred, *Kingsley House, Upper Oldfield Park, Bath.* (S.H. and Spr.), 1908–1912. Form VI. Senior. Vice-Pres. of League. Treas., Sec. and Pres. of Lit. Soc. Sen. Camb. Hons. II. London Matric. Captain 2nd XI Cricket. 2nd XI Football. Senior Cross Country Championship. Sergt. R.E. B.Com. Birmingham University. Builders' Merchant. Married : (1 son, 1 dau.).

Bladwell, Leonard J. (S.H. and Spr.), 1906–1909. Form VI. Senior. Cambridge Sen. Hons. II. London Matric. Pres. of League and Lit. Soc. Along with Mr G. W. Sibly, Mr W. A. Sibly, F. G. Luker, R. W. Bird, he took part in the 1st Wycliffe Continental ("Star " Dec. 1909). Obtained Engineering Scholarship and B.Sc. degree at Birmingham University (1914). Enlisted in Public School Corps, transferred to R.E. special brigade in 1915, and served in France for two and a half years. Early in 1918 was sent home for training, and in the summer returned to the Front as a R.E. officer. Was killed in action on October 14th, 1918. " W. & W." 22).

Bladwell, Stanley F. (Spr.), 1912–1917. Form VI. Senior. 1st XI Football. Swimming Champion (twice). Clever artist. Left to join Bristol O.T.C. and passed thence to R.A.F. Was killed in a flying accident in November 1918, and buried in the English portion of the Vendôme cemetery. (" W. & W." 24).

Blake Herbert Edwin, *The Pines, Nailsworth, near Stroud.* (h.)   66 *Marlborough Mansions, Cannon Hill, Hampstead, N.W.* 6. (D.B. and H.), 1923–1930. Upper V. House Monitor. School Certificate. 2nd XV. Insurance Clerk.

Blake, Thomas Arnold, *Dept. of Agriculture, Wellington, N.Z.* (D.B.), 1894–1899. Probationer. M.R.C.V.S. Capt. New Zealand Forces. Belgian Croix de Guerre. Veterinary Surgeon.

Blakemore, Frederick Samuel. (S.H.), 1883–1884. During War was Lieut.-Col. in the A.P.C. and obtained the O.B.E. Died in October 1924.

Blakemore, Noah, *Leek, Staffs.* (S.H.), 1882–1884. 2nd XI Cricket 1884. Ironmonger. Married.

Blampied, John Francis Buttfield de Blampied, *7 Elizabeth Place, Parade, St. Helier, Jersey.* (h.). *and Jersey Farm, Northam, Rustenberg Cotton Area, Transvaal, South Africa.* (Spr.), 1928–1934. School Certif. House Monitor. 1st XV. 1st XV Colours 1934–1935. School Swimming Team. Jeune Cup. Foster Rifle. Connaught Shooting Team. Bank Clerk in Johannesburg.

Blanch, Arthur Thomas Henry, *71b Sinclair Road, Kensington, London, W.* 14. (D.B.), 1909–1914. Form VI. Senior. London Matric. Capt. 1st XI Cricket. Rowell Cup. House Prize. Lieut. R.E. M.C. Mentioned in despatches. M.A. (Hons.), Christ Church, Oxford. Committee of O.U.D.S. The Stage. Artistic Staff of B.B.C. Married.

Bland, Arthur Henry. (S.H.), 1887–1889. Senior. 1st XI Cricket and Football. Deceased 1916.

Bland, George Heighington, *Heighton, Wotton, Gloucester.* (S.H.), 1887– 1888. Lieut. R.F.A. General Printer. Married.

Blatherwick, R. Pursey, *Westminster Bank, Ltd., Newark, Notts.* (S.H.), 1893–1896. Form V. Probationer. 2nd XI Cricket and Football. J.P. for the Borough of Newark, Chairman Newark Public Library. ex-President Chamber of Commerce. Bank Manager. Married : (1 son, 2 daus.).

Blatherwick, William Thomas, *Farnsfield House, Notts.* (S.H.), 1893– 1894. Form III. Farming. Married : (2 sons, 2 daus.).

Blick, Leopold Robert James, *Newlandene, St. Cyril's Road, Stonehouse.* (D.B.), 1900–1906. Form III. 1st Class in City and Guilds Building Construction Exam. Builder and Government Contractor. Despatch Rider 1914–1916 " Welsh Horse." 1916–1918 R.A.F. Married : (1 son).

Bloodworth, Raymond Ward. (S.H.), 1905–1907. Form VI. Senior. Sergt. R.A.F.

Boardman, James, *Brooklands, Park Lane, Great Harwood, near Blackburn,* Lancs. (R. and H.), 1928–1935. Matric. Form. Prefect. School Certificate. Textile Student at Blackburn Technical School.

Bomford, Benjamin Raymond. (S.H.), 1905–1908. Form IV. Joined firm of Messrs Bomford & Evershed, Engineers and Contractors. En-Listed in Royal Warwickshire Regt. in 1914, but owing to pneumonia and trench fever was discharged as medically unfit in August 1916. Died at home in December. (" W. & W." 26).

Bomford, Douglas R., *Bevington Hall, Evesham,* (S.H.), 1909–1913. Form VI. Senior. Pres. of League and Lit. Soc. London Matric. Sen. Camb. (Hons.). 2nd XI Cricket and Football. Capt. Worcester Regt. Farmer. Married.

Bomford, Ernest Raymond, *Pitchill, Evesham.* (S.H.), 1913–1915. Form IV. Farmer.

Bomford, Leslie R., *Tipton Warren, Whitchurch, Hants.* (S.H.), 1909–1914. Form VI. Senior. Pres. of League and Lit. Soc. Sen. Camb. (Hons.). 2nd XI Cricket and Football. Capt. Worcester Regt. D.S.O., M.C. and Bar. Farmer. Married : (1 child).

Bomford, Raymond Bradshaw, *The Manor, Stoulton, Worcester.* (S.H.), 1915–1917. Form VI. Probationer. Farmer.

Bond, Henry Gilbert. 1902–1903.

Bond, James Douglas, *Lester Lodge, Birchwood Road, Parkstone, Dorset* (h.) c/o Nat. Prov. Bank, Westbourne, Bournemouth. (Spr.), 1900–1904. Form IV. Probationer. House Prize. 1st XI Cricket. 2nd XI Football. Pay-Lieut. R.N.R. Married : (2 daus., 1 son).

Boswell, Richard Arthur. (S.H.), 1900–1902. Probationer. 1st XI Football. Stockbroker.

Boucher, Eric Gazzard. (D.B.), 1907–1908. Form II. Capt. 2nd Mon. Regt.

Boughton, Hubert Brian. (H.), 1904–1906. Form V. Senior. 1st XI Cricket. Capt. 2nd XI Football. On leaving took up farming. Lieut. in Gloucester Regt. Deceased.

Bowen, Clifford Alfred. (S.H.), 1887–1892. Form IV. Probationer. Capt. 1st XI Cricket and 1st XV Football. Capt. Devonport Albion and Devon County XV. Welsh Rugby International. Metal Broker. Married : (1 dau.). Died in 1929.

Bown, John Henry Edgar, *Lansdown, Stroud, Glos.* (H.), 1929–1933. Form VI. Senior Prefect. House Musical Director. School Certificate. Capt. 1st XV. 1st XI Cricket. Senior Athlete. Tennis Team. Gymnastic Championship. Middle Weight Boxing Championship. Secretary R.F.C.; St. John's College, Cambridge. Motor Agent.

Bowron, Henry, 15 *Compton Road, Addiscombe, Croydon.* (S.H.), 1901–1903. Probationer. Capt. R.A.S.C. O.B.E. (Mil.). Tea Merchant.

Boyce, F. J. Deceased.

Boyd, Gerald Victor A., *The White House, Church Road, Ballybrack, Killiney, Co. Dublin, I.F.S.* (H.), 1917–1918. Senior. 1st XI Football. Senior Athlete 1918. Manufacturing Chemist, Messrs Boileau & Boyd, Dublin.

Bozworth, E. R. W., *Chavenage, Tetbury, Glos.* (S.H.), 1909–1912. Form III. Farmer.

Brace, Ivor Llewellyn, *Crown Counsel, Lagos, Nigeria.* (S.H.), 1910–1914. Form VI. 1st XI Football. 2nd XI Cricket. R.F.A. Barrister-at-Law.

Bradbeer, Arthur George, *Brook House, Water Lane, Brislington, Bristol* 4. (H.), 1923–1929. Middle V. Foster Rifle. Engineer.

Bradford, Bruce E. (S.H.), early eighties. Farmed at Hown Hall, Taynton, Glos. Died of typhoid at Falmouth in December 1910.

Bradford, John Howard Penny. (S.H.), 1895–1899. Senior. 1st XI Cricket and Football. Senior Athlete. M.I.C.E. Chartered Civil Engineer. Married.

Bradford, Thomas W. H. (S.H.), 1884.

Bradley, Walter H. (S.H.), 1901–1902. Deceased.

Braine, H. Alexander. (H.), 1896–1897. Lieut. R.E. Architect.

Braithwaite, Charles Douglas, 118 *Hagley Road, Edgbaston, Birmingham* 16. *Little Sunte, Haywards Heath, Sussex* (h.). (Spr.), 1925–1934. Form VI. Prefect. Treas. of Lit. Soc. School Certificate and Higher Certificate. 1st Class Scout. Prize for Speaking. Training for business.

Bramley, James. (S.H.), 1882–1883. Senior and 1st XI Cricket. B.A. London. Master at Wycliffe. Master at Prince Albert's College, Adelaide, S. Australia, and at Victoria College, Congleton. Died of consumption at Knutsford in 1890.

Branch, Gilbert Peter, *All Ways, Wickwar, Glos.* (D.B.), 1932–1935. 1st XV Football. Foster Rifle (twice). Electrical Engineer.

Brentnall, Percy Smith, 23 *Cholmeley Park, Highgate, N.6.* (h.). 19 *St. Dunstan's Hill, London, E.C.* 3. (H.), 1888–1890. Senior. London Matric. 1st XV Rugby. Ambulance duty during War. Solicitor. Married : (1 son, 2 daus.).

Bretherton, Leonard Francis, *Killarney, Petts Wood Road, Petts Wood, Kent.* (H.), 1918–1927. Prefect. Pres. of League and Lit. Soc. London Matric. 1st XI Cricket and Football. Tennis Team. Jeune Cup. Foster Rifle. House Prize. Camb. Univ. B.A. (Hons.). Engineering. Assoc. Member of I.C.E. Municipal Engineer. Married.

Bretherton, Wilfrid George, *Hillesley, Green Lane, Hucclecote, Gloucester.* (H.), 1917–1925. Senior. Vice-Pres. of League   Sec. of Lit. Soc. London Matric. House Prize. M.A. Lincoln College, Oxford. Solicitor.

Brett, Robert A. Marriott, *Bleasley Manor, Nottingham.* (H.), 1900–1902. Form V. Farmer. Married.

Brewer, A. Percy. (S.H.), 1897.

Brewer, Edmund Derrick, *Fairfields, Hartpury, Gloucester.* (S.H.), 1931–1934. Middle IV. Farming.

Brewer, Jack (D.B.), Served as Pte. and Lieut. in Marshall's Horse throughout the Boer War. Died of blackwater fever at Victoria Falls, S. Africa.

Brigden, Frederick William. (S.H.), 1896–1898. In business in Canada. Married.

Brighton, Ronald W., 12 *Cyril Street, Northampton.* (S.H.), 1921–1924. Probationer.

Brighton, William Charles, *Trebartha, Alvreton, Penzance.* (H.), 1913–1917. Form VI. Horticulturist. Married.

Brimacombe, William. Died at his farm at Marsland, N. Devon, about 1908.

Britton, Arthur Richard, *Teucer, Lugtrout Lane, Solihull, Warwicks.* (S.H.), 1919–1924. Officer in Mercantile Marine. Motor Tyre Distributor. Married : (1 son).

Britton, Frederick John, *Bank House, Frogmore Street, Abergavenny.* (S.H.), 1914–1917. Probationer. Officer in Royal Mail Steam Packet Co. Married.

Broadhurst, Douglas Stewart, *Box 51, Kisumu, Kenya Colony.* (S.H.), 1905–1910. Form IV. Canadian Forces 1914–1916. 2nd Lieut. Northumberland Fus. 1916–1917. Lieut. R.A.F. 1917–1918. Managing Director. East African Industrial Equipment Co. Ltd., Kisumu, Kenya. Married.

Broadhurst, Francis Arkle, *City Treasurer's Office, Pietermaritzburg, Natal, South Africa.* (S.H.), 1899–1902. Lieut. Indian Volunteer Force. Engineer. A.M.I.E.E., A.M.I.Mech.E. East African Industrial Equipment Co., Kisumu, Kenya. Married : (1 son).

Broadhurst, Dr Henry Cecil, *Palm Cross Green, Modbury, Devon.* (S.H.), 1905–1907. Form V. Senior. M.B., B.Sc. Durham 1916. Demonstrator Physiology Sheffield Univ. 1919–1920. Beit Memorial Research Fellow 1920. District Medical Officer Kingsbridge. Temp. Surgeon R.N. Married : (2 sons, 3 daus.).

Brookes, Henry Josiah, 10 *Melville Road, Edgbaston, Birmingham.* (S.H.), 1895–1897. Senior. Brass Founder.

Brookes, Sydney Payne, 10 *Melville Road, Edgbaston, Birmingham* (S.H.), 1886–1890. Probationer. 2nd XI Cricket. Bedstead Manufacturer.

Brookes, William Arthur, 10 *Carisbrook Road, Edgbaston, Birmingham.* (S.H.), 1886–1892. Senior. Pres. of Lit. Soc. Capt. 1st XI Cricket. House Prize. Bedstead Manufacturer.

Brooks, C. H. (H.), 1885–1887. Married.

Brooks, Frank T. H. (H.), 1885–1886. Married.

Brough, W. Oldfield (*was at the Hippodrome, Gloucester*). (S.H.), 1885–1888. Theatrical Manager.

Brown, Clifford James. (H.), 1885–1887. Ironmonger. Married.

Brown, Rev. James Henry, *Indiana, U.S.A.* (D.B.), 1891–1892. Minister in Methodist Episcopal Church, U.S.A.

Brown, George Gordon, *Tigh Sheag, Ballater, Scotland and Chartered Bank of India, Australia and China* 18 *The Bund, Shanghai.* (D.B. and Spr.), 1918–1922. Bank Accountant.

Browne, Arthur Heber, *The Bishop's Lodge, Bermuda.* (S.H.), 1882–1884. Senior. Pres. of Lit. Soc. First Editor of the " Wycliffe Star." M.A., D.D.(Oxon.), LL.D. (Trin. Coll., Dublin). Bishop of Bermuda. Married.

Bruce, Frederick W. (D.B.), 1902–1904. Form IV. Engineer.

Bryant, Leonard Webber, 77 *Eaton Crescent, Uplands, Swansea.* (S.H.) 1923–1927. Form VI. Senior. Vice-Pres. of League. Treas. and Pres. of Lit. Soc. House Musical Director. School Certificate. 1st XI Football and 2nd XI Cricket. Prize for Public Speaking.

Bubb, Anthony Henry, *Orchard Lea, Orpington, Kent, Bank of England, E.C.* 2. (H.), 1921–1923. Form VI. Senior. 1st XI Football. 2nd XI Cricket. Prize for Public Speaking. Bank Clerk.

Bubb, Arthur Percy, *Beaulieu, Ridgeway Road, Torquay, Devon. Bank of England, E.C.* 2. (H.), 1888–1893. Form VI. Senior. Pres. of Lit. Soc. Sec. of Field Club. Capt. 1st XI Cricket. Senior Athlete House Prize 1892–1893. A Principal in Bank of England. Married : (1 son).

Bubb, Charles H., O.B.E., *Saniikoti, Bude, Cornwall.* (H.), 1889–1894. Form VI. Senior. 1st XI Cricket. M.D., L.D.S. Dental Surgeon. Married.

Bubb, Ernest Edward, 9005 *Jos Campan, Hamtranck, Michigan, U.S.A.* (D.B.), 1890–1891. University of Michigan. Dentist. Married.

Bubb, G. Cooper, *last known address—Frampton-on-Severn, Glos.* (D.B.). Farmer.

Bubb, Henry Charles. (D.B.), 1885. Motor-cycle Agent. Married. Deceased July 1936.

Bubb, John Durham, *Oakdene,* 233 *East Lane, N. Wembley, Middlesex.* (H.), 1928–1932. Upper V. 2nd XV Cols. Imperial Tobacco Co. (Wills, London).

Bubb, Norman Edward, *Donoon,* 86 *Lynton Road, West Acton, W.* 3. (H.), 1919–1923. Form V. Probationer. Prize for Public Speaking. In National Provincial Bank. Married.

Bubb, William Norman, *Oakdene, N. Wembley, Middlesex.* (H.), 1886–1895. Form VI. Senior. 1st XI Cricket and Football. Placed 3rd in Final Exam. of Society of Accountants and Auditors 1900. Member of the Council of the Soc. of Incorporated Accountants and Auditors. Incorporated Accountant at 5, Philpot Lane, E.C.3. Member of Council of Governors of Wycliffe College. Widower : (2 sons).

Buckle, Percy, *The Ridge, Bourton-on-the-Water, near Cheltenham.* (D.B.), 1903–1908. Form V. Senior. 2nd XI Cricket and Football. Lieut. R.E. A.M.Inst.M. and Cy.E. Divisional Surveyor Glos. County Council.

Budgett, F. George, *Rockleaze Point, Sneyd Park, Clifton, Bristol.* (S.H.), 1883–1886. Tea Specialist.

Budgett, William J. (S.H.), 1885–1887. Died 5th June 1936.

Bunt, Leslie Howard, 13 *Mount Park Crescent, Ealing, W.* 5 (h.), *and Calle Madero* 4, *Pachuca, Mexico.* (H.), 1914–1919. Probationer. 1st XI Football. Ranch Manager. Married : (1 son, 1 dau.).

Burgess, Ernest Barron. (H.), 1906–1909. Form III. 2nd XI Football. Architect and Surveyor.

Burgess, Harold Edward. (H.), 1907–1909. Form II. Dental Surgeon.

Burnett, Cuthbert Neville, *St. Catherine's, Clifton Road, Shirley, Southampton* (h.) *c/o British Cigarette Co., Shanghai, China.* (S.H.), 1924–1928. Prefect. 1st XI Cricket.

Burnett, David, *Slymbridge, Glos.* (D.B.), 1916–1918. Form II. Farmer.

Burnett, William J. (D.B. and H.), 1904–1907. Form IV. Worked as engineer at Dudbridge Iron Works, and afterwards in Australia and Brussels. Joined R.N.A.S., and in 1917 received commission. On September 26th 1917 he started with twelve others on a flight from which none of them returned. (" W. & W." 26).

Burtt, John Bevington, *Little Orchard, Stonehouse, Glos.* (R. and D.B.), 1932–1936. Form V. School Certificate. Scholarship to Leighton Park School. Reading.

Buston, J. P. (S.H.), 1921. Form I.

Butler, Arthur Leslie, 150 *Church Street, Kensington, W.* 8. (S.H.), 1913–1917. Lce-Cpl. Scottish Engineers O.T.C. A.R.C.A. 1922. Commercial Artist.

Butler, Francis George, 96 *Elgin Avenue, Maida Vale, W.* 9. (Spr.), 1924–1929. Upper IV. Café Manager.

Butlin, William. Deceased.

Butt, Anthony Eastcott, *Marshfield Farm, Epney, near Gloucester.* (S.H.), 1930–1932. Lower III.

A SUMMER AFTERNOON AT WYCLIFFE
(Haywardsfield and the Memorial Spire in the background)

MASTERS' GROUP, 1902

Mr. F. H. Sherwell, Dr. F. A. Sibly, Miss K. E. Jackson, Mr. J. S. Evans, Mr. E. F. Hugill, Mr. M. Müller (Hastings).
Mr. R. V. Ward, Mr. Sibly, Mr. J. Bramley.

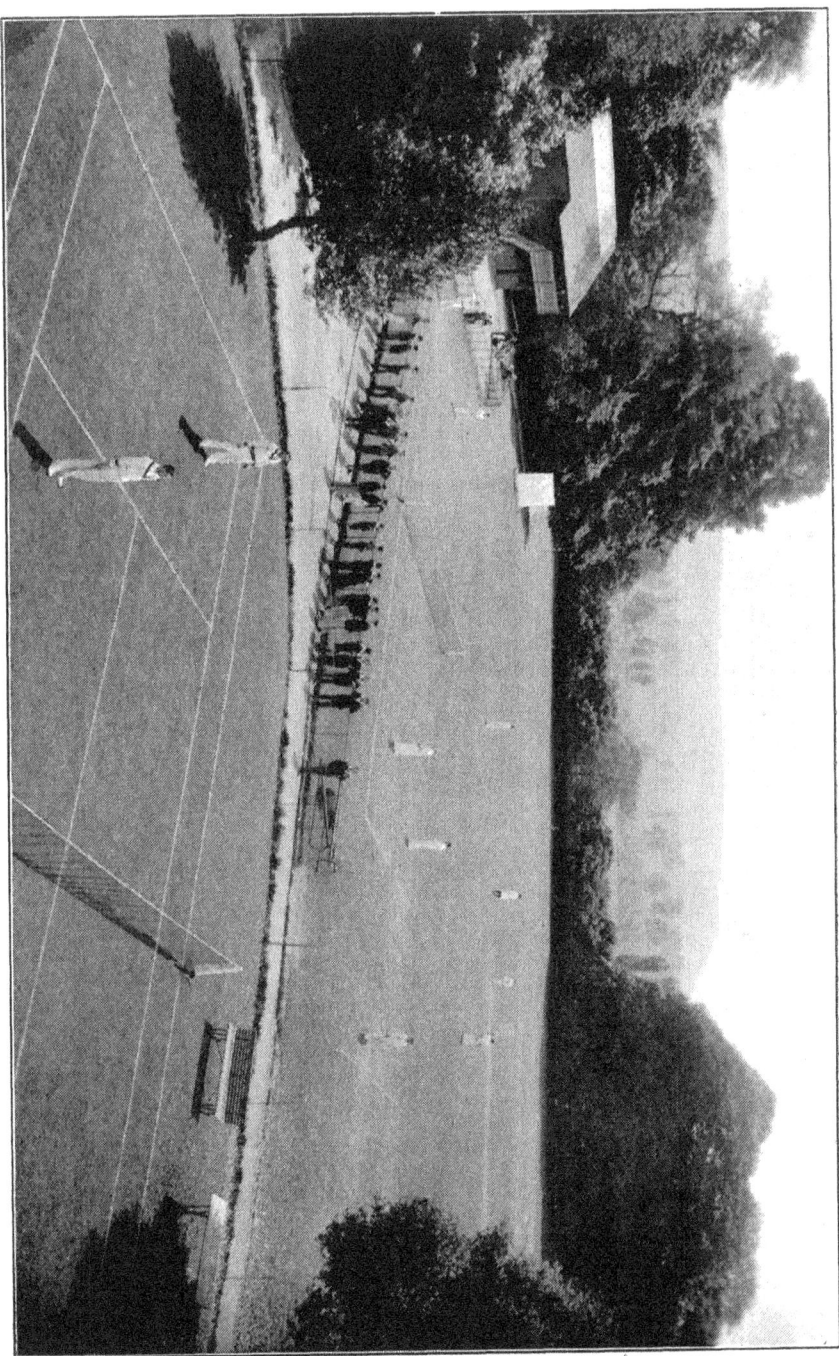

LOOKING SOUTH-EAST ACROSS THE MAIN CRICKET FIELD

SENIORS AND PROBATIONERS, 1909.

P. M. Jones, R. E. Lones, E. D. McCrea, K. E. Howell, A. Strachan, G. L. Elliott, F. Evers Swindell, M. Chamberlayne, W. W. Thomas,
W. H. B. Stride, W. R. K. Skinner, R. L. Thomas, E. S. Allwood, K. A. Cleland, W. A. Black, J. F. Lawson, H. S. Park, F. C. Leather, J. G. M. Bevan.
E. L. Bird, R. B. Hayward, G. A. Higgs, P. B. Jarvis, N. D. Hill, L. J. Bladwell, F. G. Luker, L. Dudbridge, N. H. Langley-Smith, R. W. Bird,
A. D. C. Herne, E. W. Bladwell, F. J. Arkell, W. R. Gibbons, G. A. Beavan, W. W. Morgan.

Butt, Gilbert Fryer. (Spr.), 1907–1909. Form IV. Lieut. Indian Cavalry. Farmer. Managing Director of Wickwar Cider Co. Married. Deceased 1935.

Butt, Leslie, *Wallclose Villa, Weston-super-Mare.* (Spr.), 1903–1906. Form I. Lieut. E. Yorks Regt.

Butt, Robert Arthur, *Wallclose Villa, Weston-super-Mare.* (S.H.), 1896–1900. Form V. Capt. Sherwood Foresters. Chartered Accountant.

Butt, Wilfrid S. (D.B.), 1891–1896. Form VI. Senior. House Prize. Held a post at Lodgemore Mill, but died in August 1898.

Cadman, H. (S.H.), 1884–1886. Mining Engineer.

Cadman, Henry Melville, *Oonanagalla Estate, Madulkelle, Ceylon.* (S.H.), 1917–1920. Upper III. Tea Planter. Married.

Cadman, Joseph. (S.H.), 1883–1886.

Cadman, T. F. (S.H.), 1885–1886.

Cadwallader, John Archer. (D.B.), 1912–1913. Form I.

Callard, J. Vinson. (S.H.), 1886–1889. Manufacturing Chemist.

Calvert, E. C. T. (S.H.), 1883–1884. Journalist.

Calvert, Eric Ruegg. 1902–1906. Form VI. Senior. Clerk in Capital and Counties Bank. Joined Inns of Court O.T.C. and held commission in Royal Sussex Regt. (1916) and went to the Front in January 1917. Was killed on August 8th by a shell, and buried in Dickerbosch Cemetery. ("W. & W." 28).

Cambray, Robert, *Baunton Farm, Cirencester.* (S.H.), 1919–1924. Form IV. 1st XI Football.

Camm, Gerald Gordon, *Rookhill House, Keynsham, Bristol.* (S.H.), 1927–1930. Form VI. House Monitor. School Certificate. Clerk at E. S. & A. Robinson. Captain of Keynsham Badminton and Tennis Clubs, and Sec. Rugby.

Canfor, Arthur Robert, 36 *Beaconsfield Road, Ealing, London, W. 5.* (S.H.), 1932–1936. Modern VI. Prefect. Treasurer of Lit. Soc. Higher Certificate. 1st XV Football. Prizes for Improvement in and Good Speaking, Harmston Piano, Prop. Representation Essay, Modern Languages, Good work in VI Form and Dramatic Society. Bank Clerk. (Barclay's Bank, West End Trustee Dept.).

Cardall, Laurence Yates, 17 *Summerland Street, Exeter.* (H.), 1907–1908. Form V. Probationer. R.A.F. Automobile Engineer.

Carder, Arthur Thomas, *Wycliffe, Magdalen Road, Exeter.* (H.), 1915–1917. Form VI. Senior. Prize for Public Speaking. Sub.-Lieut. R.N.V.R. Confectioner. Manager of Barnstaple Bakeries Ltd. Married: (3 sons).

Carlile, G. Stanley C., *Redland Supply Stores, Blackboy Hill, Bristol.* (H.), 1898–1899.

Carr, John Wooltorton, *Silverwood, Branksome Park, Bournemouth.* (Spr.), 1930–1935. Form VI. Prefect. School Certificate. 2nd XV. Connaught Shooting Team. Jeune Cup (twice). Undergraduate at St. John's College, Cambridge. Cambridge University Small Bore Club Colours. R.A.F. Pilot Reserve. Cambridge Univ. O.T.C. (R.E. section).

Carter, Charles Roger, *Ridgmont, near Stroud, Glos.* (H.), 1916–1924. Form VI. Senior. Vice-Pres. of League. School Certificate. Capt. 1st XI Cricket. 1st XI Football. Music Prize. Sec. Lit. Soc.

Carter, Hugh John, 10 *Fields Road, Newport, Mon.* (H.), 1931–1933. Upper Remove. Scouts Swimming Team. 1st XV.

C

Carter, Robert Stuart, 10 *Fields Road, Newport, Mon.* (H.), 1931–1935. Lower V. School Certificate. 2nd XV Football and 2nd XI Cricket. Swimming Team.

Case, Basil Leonard Sully, 284 *Newport Road, Cardiff.* (H.), 1923–1927. Upper IV. 2nd XI Football. 1st XI Cricket. Winner of Junior Cross Country 1925.

Cash, Oscar Henry Gilbert, 133a *Ashley Road, Burton-on-Trent.* (S.H.), 1915–1919. Form V. Probationer. Bank Clerk. Married.

Caunt, Frederick William, *Torquay.* (S.H.), 1903–1904. Form III. Confectioner and Caterer. Married.

Chamberlain, John. (D.B.), 1909–1910. Form III.

Chamberlayne, Howard, *Oldlands Farm, Berkeley, Glos.* (D.B.), 1925–1931. Lower Remove. Farmer.

Chamberlayne, J. A., *Oldlands Farm, Berkeley, Glos.* (D.B.), 1925–1929. Middle V. Insurance Inspector.

Chamberlayne, Maurice, *The Home Farm, Prestbury, Cheltenham.* (D.B.), 1907–1909. Form IV. Probationer. Royal Gloucester Hussars (Yeomanry). Farmer.

Champion, H. Stafford. (D.B.), 1892–1894. Form IV. In business in Australia.

Champion, J. Norman, *Glenholm Ranch, Priddes, Alberta, Canada.* (D.B.), 1893–1896. Form IV. Farmer. Married.

Chandler, Edward, *Etloe House, Newnham, Glos.* (D.B.), 1891–1893. Farmer.

Chandler, George Cooper, *The Chestnuts, Haresfield, Glos.* (D.B.), 1908–1912. War Service 1915–1918. Five years overseas (France and Belgium). Farmer. Married : (3 children).

Chandler, George James. (D.B.), 1883–1888. Died in 1925.

Chandler, George Surman. (D.B.), 1892–1896. Form III. Helped to manage Court Farm, Stonehouse, except during the War, when he served with the Royal Gloucestershire Hussars and was wounded. A kick from a horse, followed by pneumonia. led to his death in March 1926. ("Star," Apr. 1926).

Chandler, J. R., 8 *Harlington Park, Redland Green, Bristol.* (S.H.), 1925–1928. Form II.

Chandler, Robert Arkell. (D.B.), 1883–1889. Managed a farm at Standish Died in 1928.

Chandler, Sidney J., *Court Farm, Stonehouse, Glos.* (D.B.), 1891–1895. Form III.

Chaplin, Peter John, *Merrie Towers, Cooks Folly, Bristol* (h.). *Bloomsbury House Club, Cartwright Gardens, London, W.C. 1.* (S.H.), 1931–1935. Form V. Wholesale Produce Merchant.

Chapman, T. E.

Charles, Frank Pendril J. (S.H.), 1896–1899. Form V. Probationer. Sec. of Lit. Soc. 1st XI Football and 2nd XI Cricket. Articled to Solicitor at Neath. Went to South Africa as Lieut. in 1st Welsh Regiment Volunteer Coy. Was shot by the Boers while guarding a drift on the Klip River, and died in Netley Hospital in 1902.

Chatham, Charles Henry, *Manor Farm, Tredington, near Tewkesbury.* (H.), 1924–1926. Form V. 1st XI Cricket. 2nd XI Football. Farming.

Chirgwin, Richard. (S.H.), 1912–1918. Form VI. Senior. Pres. of League. Sec. of Lit. Soc. House Prize and Public Speaking. 1st XI Football. Capt. 2nd XI Cricket. Merchant. Died of pneumonia on January 18th 1930. (" Star," Apr. 1930, p. 6).

Chivers, Alban Percy, *The Cottage, Writhlington, Bath.* (S.H.), 1902–1905. Form VI. Senior. 1st XI Football. Senior Athlete. Newman Cup. R.N.A.S. Colliery Secretary. Married : (2 sons, 1 dau.).

Chivers, Philip Roy, *The Cottage, Writhlington, Bath.* (S.H.), 1926–1933. Form VI. Prefect. Treas. of Lit. Soc. School Certificate. School Shooting Team. Senior Cross Country 1931. Mile Record. Half Mile Record. Battery Sgt.-Major, Artillery Unit, London O.T.C.

Chivers, Ralph Stevens, *Hillside, Radstock, Bath.* (S.H.), 1899–1901. Form V. Senior. Capt. 2nd XI Football. Worcester Regt. Bank Cashier.

Church, Frederick George, *Northgate Mansions, Gloucester.* (Spr.), 1904–1906. Form VI. Senior. Lieut. R.E. A.M.I.M.E. Consulting Engineer.

Ciclitira, Dennis John, 109 *Chalkwell Avenue, Westcliff-on-Sea, Essex.* (H.), 1933–1935. Lower VI. 1st XV Football. Electrical Engineering. Studying in Greece, preparatory to joining his father's business.

Clack, Leslie Alan. (H.), 1910. Form III. Oxfordshire Yeomanry. Farming.

Claridge, Kenneth Thomas, *Wycliffe,* 157 *Beechwood Avenue, Coventry.* (S.H.), 1926–1929. Upper V. Prefect. 1st XV Football and 1st XI Cricket. Working for a Solicitor's Final.

Clark, A. G.

Clark, Arthur John, *Dalmally, Midanburg Lane, Bitterne Park, Southampton.* (S.H.), 1921–1926). Upper V. Prefect. School Certificate. 1st Class Scout. House Shooting Team.

Clark, Eric Reeves, *Thorold Lodge, Bitterne Park, Southampton.* (S.H.), 1925–1931. Form VI. Prefect. Vice-Pres. of League. Cambridge School Certif. London Matric. 1st XV Football. Articled Clerk to Solicitor and Notary Public.

Clark, John Henry, *Cerne Abbas, Frome Park Road, Stroud.* (H.), 1916–1924. Form V. Prefect. 1st XI Cricket and Football. Music Prize. Draper.

Clark, Norman Reeves, *Thorold Lodge, Bitterne Park, Southampton.* (S.H.), 1928–1933. Matric. Form. Prefect. School Certificate. 1st XV. Farming.

Clark, Ronald Alfred, *Tree Tops, Chine Avenue, Bitterne Park, Southampton.* (S.H.), 1923–1929. Matric Form. Prefect. School Certificate. 1st XV Colours 1928–1930. Boxing Championship 1929. Builder. Married.

Clark, William Douglas. (S.H.), 1913–1915. Form III. Served in the King's Royal Rifles. Was taken prisoner. His health suffered in consequence, and he died in Cheltenham in March 1922.

Clay Richard Roy. *The Sao Paulo Railway, Alto da Serra, Sao Paulo, Brazil, South America.* (Spr.), 1907–1911. Form IV. 2nd XI Football. M.I.Loco.E. Railway Mechanical Engineer. War Service R.F.C. and R.A.F. Married : (1 son, 2 daus.).

Cleland, Alan Ian Henry. (H.), 1910–1914. Form VI. House Prize. Farmed in Scotland. Joined Artists' Rifles in 1915. Was reported wounded and missing at Marcoing in December 1917. (" W. & W." 29).

Cleland, Kenneth Andrew, 8 *Bath Road, Bedford Park, London, W.* 4. (H.), 1904–1911. Form VI. Senior. Vice-Pres. of League. Pres. of Lit. Soc. House Prize. 5th Glos. Regt. Coal Factor and Merchant. Married.

Cleveland, Grahame, 50 *Thornbury Avenue, Southampton* (h.). 11 *Cargate Avenue, Aldershot.* (S.H.), 1923–1927. Upper IV. Bank Clerk, Lloyds Bank, Aldershot.

Clifford, Herbert. (H.), 1905–1906. Form III.

Clift, John Webb, *Milestone Cottage, Rodborough Common, Stroud.* (D.B.), 1927–1934. Science VI. Prefect. School Certif. 2nd XV Football. Prize for Public Service. Aircraft Draughtsman.

Clinton, Geoffrey Osbert. (S.H.), 1924–1926. Form I.

Clinton, Henry George. (S.H.), 1918–1920. Form II. Farming in Canada.

Clissold, Frank Willoughby, *Mildwaters, Watledge, Nailsworth.* (D.B.), 1912–1913. Form III.

Clissold, George, *Windsmeet, Nailsworth, Glos.* (D.B.), 1884–1885. Engineer. Married : (2 sons, 1 dau.).

Clissold, Harry. (S.H.), 1882–1885. Scholarship at Clifton College and leaving scholarship to Trinity Coll., Cambridge. 1st Class Natural Science Tripos 1891. Master at Marlborough College for two Terms. Returned to Clifton as Science Master in 1894, and in 1912 became House Master. Was C.O. of the Clifton College O.T.C. and in September 1914 was appointed to command new field company of the South Midland Royal Engineers. Was twice mentioned in despatches, awarded the D.S.O. and became Major. Was killed in action on September 28th, 1917. ("W. & W." 30).

Clissold, Kenneth George, *Windsmeet, Nailsworth, Glos.* (D.B.), 1909–1912. Form V. R.M.A., Woolwich. R.A. Served in France 1917–1918. Married : (1 dau., 1 son).

Clissold, Rev. William John, *Firle, Painswick.* (D.B. and H.), 1893–1899. Form VI. Senior. B.A. (Cantab.), Missionary in charge of Molepolola, Bechuanaland. Archdeacon of Kirongwe, Tanganyika (1930) Rector of Margaret River, S.W. Australia (1933).

Cloke Douglas, *Moorend, Slimbridge, Glos.* (D.B.), 1911–1916. Form IV. Farmer. Married.

Cloke, Eric H., *Moorend, Slimbridge, Glos.* (D.B.), 1911–1917. Form II. Farmer. In the Argentine 1926.

Cloke, Ernest, *Upleadon, Newent.* (S.H.), 1896–1898. Form III. Farmer.

Cloke, Ernest Palmer, *Hacketts, Colwall, Malvern.* (Spr.), 1909–1911. War Service 1915–1918. Discharged with a Life Pension. Farmer. Married : (1 son, 1 dau.).

Cloutman, Norman Froyne, *Sutton Farm, Bishop Sutton, near Bristol.* (S.H.), 1907–1911. Form IV. Lieut. 6th Glos. Regt. Served in France 1916. Married.

Clutterbuck, J. (D.B.), 1891–1892.

Coates, Alan David, *Stort Lodge, Bishop's Stortford, Herts.* (R. and H.), 1927-1932. Upper III. Advertising: with First International Agency Ltd.

Coates, David Wilson, *Stort Lodge, Bishop's Stortford, Herts.* (H.), 1896–1902. Form VI. Senior. Pres. of Lit. Soc. London Matric. House Prize. M.A., LL.B., St. John's College, Cambridge. F.C.A. Formerly partner Elles, Salaman, Coates & Co., and D. W. Coates, West Grimwood and Co. War Service. Successively Chief Accountant, Financial Secretary and Financial Adviser to Mines Dept. of Board of Trade 1917–1921. C.B.E. Member of Council of Governors of Wycliffe College. Married : (3 sons, 2 daus.).

Coates, Lewis James Montcrieff, *Badger's Mount House, Halstead, Kent.* (H.), 1893–1896. Form IV. Senior. War Service : Private, Artists Rifles, 2nd Lieut. I.W. & D.R.E. Silk Manufacturer (retired). Married.

Coates, Peter John Hurst, *Stort Lodge, Bishop's Stortford, Herts* (h.). 4 *Wharton Terrace, Heaton, Newcastle-on-Tyne.* (H.), 1927–1931. Form V. Engineering Student at C. A. Parsons & Co. Ltd.

Coates, W. H. Brunton, 86 *Queen's Gate, London, S.W.* (H.), 1895–1900. Form V. Probationer. Sec. of Lit. Soc.

Cocker, Jack E. (H.), 1889–1890. Worked on a ranch in Arizona. Later went to S. Africa and joined Thorneycrofts' Mounted Infantry. Took part in relief of Ladysmith, and received S. African medals and clasps. Became an artist and journalist in New York. His health breaking down, he returned home to Merthyr Tydvil, where he died in January, 1907.

Codrington, W. S., *Claremont, Merlin Haven, Wotton-under-Edge.* (S.H.), 1910–1912. Form II. Veterinary Surgeon.

Cole, Herbert, 331 *Bay Street, Toronto, Canada.* (S.H.), 1904–1907. Form VI. Probationer. Major, M.G.C.

Cole, Hugh Thomas Llewellyn, *Templeslowe Estate, Rozelles, Ceylon.* (H.), 1930–1934. Matric. Form. Senior. 1st XI and 1st XV 1934. School Athletic Team. Tea Planter in Ceylon.

Coleman, Val, 51 *Bath Road, Swindon.* (L.B.) 1927. Form IV.

Coles, Bernard Arthur, *Hartley Wintney, Winchfield, Hants.* (H.), 1899–1901. Form V. Probationer. R.A.F.

Coles, Frederick, *Thornton Heath, Surrey.* (S.H.), 1885–1887.

Coles, Ralph John, *Hartley Wintney, Hants.* (H.), 1905–1908. Probationer. Form IV. 1st XI Football. Capt. 11th Suffolk Regt. Mentioned in despatches. Draper. Married.

Coley, Carl Leslie Joseph. (D.B.), 1908. Form II. In Australia.

Coley, H. Rex. (D.B.), 1908. Form IV. Went to Australia in 1912 with his brother Leslie. On the outbreak of war joined the 12th Australian Light Horse, and was killed in action at Beersheba in 1917. (" W. & W." 32).

Coley, James Perrin, 26 *Cole Park Road, Twickenham.* (D.B.), 1923–1926. Upper III.

Colledge, Arthur Vincent. (S.H.), 1906–1907. Form I. Fell fighting with the North Russian Relief Force in August 1919. (" W. & W." 33)

Collihole, Philip Hunter, 43 *High Street, Glastonbury, Som.* (S.H.), 1924–1930. Form VI. Prefect. Vice-Pres. of League. London Matric. School Certif. Shopfitting.

Collingwood, Deryck Cuthbert, 45 *Fairdene Road, Coulsdon, Surrey.* (Spr.), 1928–1935. Modern VI. Senior Prefect. Pres. Treas. and Sec. of Lit. Soc. Pres. of League. London Matric. 1st XV Colours 1934–1935. School Chess Team. School Athletic Team. Prizes for Speaking and Public Service. Theological Student, Headingley, Leeds.

Collingwood, John Gildas, 45 *Fairdene Road, Coulsdon, Surrey.* (Spr.), 1929–1936. Form VI. Prefect. Pres. Lit. Soc. London Matric. Higher Certificate. 1st XV Football. Student at London University.

Collins, John Francis, *Bredon View, Benge Hill, Evesham, Worcs.* (S.H.), 1918–1925. Form V. Probationer. With Messrs Collins, Bros., Provision Manufacturers.

Collins, Leonard Walter Graham, *Rosewood, The Grange, Guernsey, C.I. and Waldorf, Stratford Road, Stroud, Glos.* (h.). (D.B., O.B. and S.H.), 1927–1930. Lower V. House Monitor. School Certif. Secretary of the " Star" Press, Guernsey.

Collins, Peter John, *Woodlands, Cefn Coed Road, Cardiff.* (H.), 1928–1933. Commercial VI. House Monitor. School Certif. 1st XI Colours 1932–1933. Draper.

Colquhoun, Ernest Ivor, *Newport, Mon.* (H.), 1885–1887. Architect.

Colquhoun, Robert S. (S.H.), 1883–1885. Salesman. Married. Died in 1932.

Collhurst, J. C. (S.H.), 1886. Farming in Australia.

Connell, William Allan, 208 *Infirmary Road, Sheffield* and *Balijan Tea Estate, Assam, India.* (H.), 1909–1914. Form III. R.N.V.R. Engineer

Cook. Alexander Anthony, 14 *Pemberton Avenue, Burry Port, Carmarthenshire.* (S.H.), 1926–1930. Matric. Form. House Monitor. School Certificate.

Cook, Alwyn, *High Street, Berkeley, Glos.* (S.H.), 1922–1924. Form I. Farmer.

Cook, C. Richard Vallance, *St. Peter's Vicarage, Upton Park, London E.* (S.H.), 1912–1915. Form IV. Lieut. R.A.F.

Cook, John Alastair, 14 *Pemberton Avenue, Burry Port, Carmarthenshire.* (S.H.), 1929–1933. Form V. House Monitor. School Certificate. 1st XV Football. Apprenticed to Leyland Motors.

Cooke, E. J. Has died.

Cooke, Francis Gordon. (S.H.), 1905–1908. Form IV. Probationer. Staff Sergt. R.A.S.C. Glos. C.C. Main Road Surveyor. Married.

Cooke, Martin Alfred, 201 *Church Road, Upper Norwood, London, S.E.* 19. (D.B.), 1883–1887. M.R.C.S., L.R.C.P., L.S.A., St. Bartholomew's Hospital. Surgeon. Norwood Cottage Hospital and L.C.C. Throat Clinic. Twenty years' service with Territorial R.A.M.C., London Associated Biigade Field Ambulance and Oak Grove Military Hospital, Tooting. Awarded Military O.B.E. Medical Practitioner. Married : (1 son, 1 dau.).

Cooke, William Henry Howard, 30 *Zion Road, Rathgar, Dublin, Ireland.* (D.B.) 1893–1899. Form V. Probationer. Placed third Civil Service exam for H.M. Office of Works. A.R.I.B.A. Senior Government Architect. Hon. Sec. Board of Architect. Education since 1928. President Architect. Assoc. Ireland 1929–1930. Member of Council R.I.A.I. since 1929. Hon. Treas. and Fellow R.I.A.I. 1931–1934. Married : (1 son, 1 dau.).

Coomaraswamy, Dr. Ananda K. *Museum of Fine Arts, Boston, U.S.A* (S.H.), 1889–1895. Form VI. Senior. London Matric. and Inter. Arts. 1st XI Football. D.Sc. London. Fellow for Research in Indian, Persian and Muhammadan Art in the Museum of Fine Arts, Boston, U.S.A. Hon. Member Bhandarkar Oriental Research Institute, Poona.

Copp, Harold Ernest, *Addison House, Sutton-on-Hull.* (H.), 1887–1891. Form VI. Senior. Chartered Civil Engineer. M.I.C.E. President of Institution of Gas Engineers 1930–1931. Pres. of First International Gas Conference 1931. Married.

Corbett, Ernest W. W. (H.), 1900–1902. Form II, On Canadian Pacific Railway.

Corbett, Victor S., *Cheltenham.* (H.), 1901–1902. Form II. Cpl. Canadian Infantry.

Cornock, Charles John, *Fairview, Painswick, Glos.* (H.), 1910–1911. Form IV. Devon Regt. Actor and Singer. (Repertory Company, Oxford).

Cornock, John Norman, *The Elms, Rudgeway, near Almondsbury.* (Spr.) 1910–1913. Form IV.

Cornock, Walter Beale, *Uplands Cottage, Birdlip, Glos.* (H.), 1902–1907. Form V. Probationer. 1st XI Cricket. Captain 30th Punjabis (Regular) retired 1922. War Service in Gallipoli, France and on N.W. Frontier. Director Gloucester and Three Counties Photo Engraving Co., Quay Street, Gloucester, and of Hygienic Laundry, 169 Southgate Street, Gloucester.

Cornwell, A. Bryan, *The Homestead, Ellenborough Park, Weston-super-Mare.* (H.), 1915–1916. Form IV.

Cory, C. 1906. Form I.

Cosslett, Jestyn A. (Spr.), 1913–1914.

Cotton, Frederick W., *Tapsays, Marnhull, Dorset.* (H.), 1891–1892. Form VI. Senior. London Matric. Lieut.-Col. R.A.M.C. (Regular). Now on retired pay. Medical Practitioner. Married.

Cotton, Henry Eric, *Coxbridge, West Pennard, Glastonbury, Som.* (H.), 1915–1917. Form VI. Senior. Vice-Pres. of League. 2nd XI Football. Farmer.

Cotton, Ronald Worgan, *Coxbridge, West Pennard, Glastonbury, Som.* (H.), 1920–1924. Form V. Probationer. Farmer.

Couch, George Kynaston. (H), 1910–1912. Form IV. Was in service with Atlantic Transport Co. During the War served in Belgium and France. Was invalided home with lung trouble in 1917. Died in January 1920. ("Star," Apr. 1921).

Couzens, Alfred John, 6 *Wimpole Street, London W.* (S.H.), 1883–1886. Probationer. 1st XV Football. Surgeon. F.R.C.S.

Cowlin, Conrad Kingsley, *The Elms, Nailsea, Som. and c/o William Cowlin and Son, Stratton Street, Bristol.* (S.H.), 1896–1899. Form IV. 2nd Lieut. A.S.C. Served in France with 27th Heavy Artillery Brigade. Builder and Contractor. Married.

Cox, Edward Percival. (D.B.), 1909–1911. Form III. Farmer. Married

Cox, Francis John Beattie (D.B.), 1907–1909. Form III. Royal Glos. Hussars. Sometime farmer in Canada.

Cox, Reginald Harry, 4 *Granville Villas, Bisley Road, Stroud.* (D.B.), 1895–1900. Form VI. Senior. London Matric. 1914–1919 Rifle Brigade and R.A.F., Egypt. Coal Merchant. Married : (3 sons).

Cox, Stanley E. (D.B.), 1897–1900. Form IV. Entered Baptist Ministry and became President of the Glos. and Hereford Assoc. 1925. Died in May 1926.

Cridland, Charles E. T. *Was in Cheltenham.* (S.H.), 1911–1915. Form V. 1st XI Cricket. Married.

Crocker, Rex Parry. (Spr.), 1922–1925. Form V. Wine and Spirit Merchant.

Crockett, Herbert. *Pontypridd, Glamorgan.* (S.H.), 1890–1893. Solicitor. Married.

Crockett, J. E. Capt. 1st XI Football 1885. Has died.

Cross, F. C. (S.H.), 1884–1885.

Cross, Lionel Douglas, 11 *Bergholt Crescent, Stamford Hill, N. 16.* (S.H.), 1883–1885. Retired from Public Works Dept., India. Married.

Cross, T. D.

Crouch, Arthur J. (H.), 1899–1901. Form III.

Crouch, Stanley Edward. (S.H.), 1893–1894. Form II.

Cullen, Charles Geoffrey, 72 *Pinner Court, Pinner, Middlesex.* (Spr.), 1911–1913. Form V. Senior. 1st XI Cricket and Football. Lieut. 1st Batt. Suffolk Regt. France and Belgium 1916–1918. Sales Manager. Married.

Cullen, James Attenborough, *Chief Native Commissioner's Offices, Salisbury, S. Rhodesia.* (H.), 1904–1905. Form V. Probationer. 1st XI Cricket and Football. War Service—S.A. Rebellions and S.W. Africa 1914–1915 (1st Rhodesia Regt.), France 1917–1918 R.G.A. 7th Siege Battery. Lieut. Chief Clerk, Native Affairs Dept., Salisbury. Married: (1 dau.).

Cullimore, Godfrey Ernest, *Newhouse, Cambridge, Glos.* (R. and D.B.), 1929–1935. Matric. Form. 2nd XI Cricket. 2nd XV Rugby. Farmer.

Cullimore, Martin Henry, *Kilcrevan, Downfield, Stroud, Glos.* (D.B.), 1918–1926. Upper V. Senior. Vice-Pres. of League. 1st XI Cricket. 1st XI Football. 1st XV Rugby. Senior Tennis Singles. House Prize.

Culverwell, George Lane, *Lowden Manor, Chippenham, Wilts.* (H.), 1901–1906. Form V. Senior. Pres. of League and Lit. Soc. 1st XI Cricket. 2nd XI Football. Served with Exp. Force in Palestine and Egypt 1915–1919. F.S.I., F.A.I. Auctioneer and Valuer. Mayor of Chippenham (1937). Married.

Culverwell, John, *Lloyds Bank House, Henleaze, Bristol.* (S.H.), 1929–1931. Form VI. House Monitor. School Certificate. 1st XI Cricket. 1st XV Rugby. With Bristol Waterworks Co.

Culverwell, John Reginald Stanley, *Tresco, 53 Stoke Lane, Westbury-on-Trym, Bristol.* (Spr.), 1902–1903. Form IV. Lieut. R.F.A. 1914–1919. Managing Director Clifton Laundry Ltd., Bristol. Married : (1 son, 1 dau.).

Culverwell, Vernon Bernard, 27 *St. Oswald's Road, Redland, Bristol.* (Spr.), 1902–1906. Form V. Probationer. House Prize. 2nd XI Cricket and Football. Produce Broker. Married : (1 son).

Culverwell, William Henry. (H), 1901–1908. Form VI. Senior. Pres. of Lit. Soc. Vice-Pres. of League. 1st XI Cricket and Football. Farmed in S. Africa. Served with South African Field Forces in German East Africa. In September 1923 was knocked down by a train and fatally injured. (" Star," Apr. 1924).

Cummin, John Thomas, 43 *Rue d'Isly, Algiers, North Africa.* (Spr.), 1929–1934. Form V. Prefect. School Certificate. 1st XV Rugby. School Swimming Team. Undergraduate at Oxford preparing for Holy Orders. Undergraduate, St. Catherine's College, Oxford.

Cummin, Reginald Comyn, 43 *Rue d'Isly, Algiers, North Africa.* (Spr.). 1929–1936. Science VI. Prefect. Pres. Lit. Soc. Vice-Pres. League. London Matric. Capt. 1st XV. Prize for Public Service. Medical Student.

Curtis, Charles Kingsley. (D.B.), 1887–1891.

Curtis, Eustace Carter. (D.B.), 1888–1893. Form III. Dairy Farmer. Married.

Curtis, H. A. (D.B.), 1886–1889. 2nd XV Football. Married.

Curtis, Thomas Britt. (D.B.), 1909–1911. Began journalistic career with " Gloucestershire Chronicle" Volunteered with 1/5th Gloucesters. Obtained commission in the Cheshires. Was mortally wounded in France, October 1917. (" W. & W." 34).

Curtis, William Clissold. (D.B.), 1885–1889. Senior. M.A. Cantab. Clergyman.

Daggett, Harry Norman. (D.B.), 1905–1907. Form III. Australian Forces.

Dakers, Herbert Hugh, *Penycraig, Glamorgan.* (H.), 1892–1893. Form IV. 1st XI Football. Colliery Manager.

Dakers, John Edward Sydney, *Park Row, Tredegar.* (H.), 1892–1893. Form V. Colliery Manager. Married.

Daniel, Archibald, *The Redlands, Pontypridd.* (S.H.), 1888–1891. Senior Form VI. Pres. of Lit. Soc. London Matric. House Prize. 1st XV Football. Capt. 2nd XI Cricket. Ex-President Pontypridd and Rhondda Law Society. Vice-Pres. Pontypridd Y.M.C.A. Trustee Pontypridd Boys' Club. Served with Special Service Volunteers Home Defence. Capt. 6th Vol. Batt. Welch Regt. Solicitor. Deputy Coroner for East Glamorgan. Married : (3 sons).

Daniel, John Arthur, *Cathedine Hill, Bwlch, Breconshire.* (S.H.), 1896–1901. Form VI. Senior. Pres. of Lit. Soc. London Matric. House Prize. Public Speaking Prize. Cpl. R.G.A. Solicitor. Married.

Daniell, John Francis. (S.H.), 1903–1905. Form IV. Farmer.

Daniels, Frederick Lionel, *Stringers Court, Rodborough, Stroud.* (D.B.), 1887–1893. Form VI. Senior. Fellow of Geological Society. M.I.P.E. M.I.W.E. Pres. of Western Section of Inst. of Production Engineers. Member of Council of Governors of Wycliffe College. Married.

Daniels, Frederic William, *Stringers Court, Rodborough, Stroud.* (D.B.), 1914–1923. Form V. Electrical Engineer. Business Manager.

Daniels, John Stuart, *Whitecroft, Nailsworth.* (D.B.), 1884–1888. Probationer. Engineer.

Daniels, John William. (D.B.), 1903–1904. Form III. Engineer. Deceased.

Daniels, Joseph Harold. (D.B.), 1892–1898. Probationer. Engineer. Deceased Feb. 9th, 1937.

Daniels, Joseph Lionel, *Innisfree, Rodborough, Stroud.* (D.B.), 1915–1924. Form VI. Senior. Vice-Pres. of League. Cambridge Senior. House Prize. Hearson Science Prize. B.Sc. Birmingham University in Mechan. Engineering. A.M.I.Mech.E. Chartered Mechan. Engineer and Director T. H. & J. Daniels Ltd. Married : (2 sons).

Daniels, Sidney Reginald, *Elcot Lodge, Boar's Hill, Oxford.* (D.B.), 1883–1888. Form VI. Cambridge Sen. Hons. I. 2nd place in Hons. London Matric. Indian Civil Service. Judge of the High Court (retired). Deputy Chairman of the Proportional Representation Society. Liberal Candidate for Bath 1929, 1931 and 1935. Married. Died Aug., 1937.

Dann, Henry Norman Groves. (D.B.), 1908–1913. Form V. On leaving school spent some months in his father's stick factory at Chalford. Joined Artists Rifles, and obtained a commission in the R.F.C. A few weeks after his arrival on the Western Front his machine was brought down and he was killed. Buried with full military honours at St. Omer. (" W. & W." 35).

D'Arcy, Edwin. (D.B.), 1882. London Matric.

Darke, Harold Jack. (D.B.), 1902–1906. Form V. Apprenticed to Apperly, Curtis & Co. While taking part in some local sports in August 1907 he sustained what appeared to be a harmless fall, but it resulted in his dying suddenly in his sleep a week later while on a visit to Weston-super-Mare.

Darke, William Henry. (D.B.), 1900–1904. Form V. 1st XI Cricket and Football. R.G.A. Bank Manager. Married.

Dash, Douglas Beavis, *Cherwell, Rodborough Avenue, Stroud.* (D.B. and H.), 1919–1927. Lower VI. House Monitor. School Certificate. London Matric. 2nd XI Football. 1st XV Rugby 1927 and 1st XI Cricket. With Messrs Townsend & Co., Stroud.

Dash, Eric Edward, *Cherwell, Rodborough Avenue, Stroud.* (D.B. and H.), 1931–1934. Lower Remove. 2nd XI Cricket. House Rugby Team. Building Trade.

Dashwood, Vivian de Courcy, *The Elms, Stratford Road, Stroud.* (D.B.), 1914–1921. Form V. Probationer. 1st XI Cricket. Automobile Agent. Married.

Davidson, Hunter Fulton. (Spr.), 1905–1906. Form III. Fruit-Farming in Canada.

Davies, Andrew Arthur Cecil. (S.H.), 1882–1887. Probationer. Civil Engineer. Married. Died May 24th, 1935.

Davies, Dr A. H., *Vancouver, British Columbia.* (S.H.), 1886–1887. Class I Nat. Science Tripos, Cambridge, M.R.C.S., L.R.C.P., Guys. Surgeon in Boer War. Physician and Surgeon. Married.

Davies, Arthur Llewellyn B., *Ellensburg, Washington, U.S.A.* (S.H.), 1884–1887. Senior. Capt. 1st XV Football. 1st XI Cricket. Senior Athlete. House Prize. Officer in U.S. Army. Vice-President Washington National Bank of Ellensburg.

Davies, C. Ivor. (S.H.), 1912–1914. Probationer. Warwickshire Regt. Shortly before he was due at the Front he was attacked by bronchial pneumonia, but was temporarily patched up and served behind the lines in France. He was never really fit, and after being demobilised showed symptoms of tuberculosis. He got gradually worse, and passed away in February 1932.

Davies, D. C. (S.H.), 1889. Died in South America.

Davies, David L., *Glanwern, Radyr, near Cardiff, Glam.* (S.H.), 1901–1907. Capt. 1st XI Football. Senior Athlete.

Davies, Edward Arthwel Richards, *Gorwel, Sketty, Swansea.* (H.), 1927–1933. Modern VI. Prefect. School Certificate. 1st XV Rugby. 2nd XI Cricket. Senior Athlete. Hundred Yards Record 1933. Undergraduate Oxford University.

Davies, Ernest Albert John, 35 *Ormonde Gate, Chelsea, S.W.* 3. (Spr.), 1914–1920. Form VI. Senior. Vice-Pres. of League. Sec. of Lit. Soc. London Matric. Prize for Public Speaking. Diploma in Journalism, Univ. Coll. London. Sec. of Fabian Nursery 1920–1922. Treas. of Univ. Lab. Federation. Director of First Co-operative Investment Trust. Editor of " The Clarion " 1927–1932. Director and Associate Editor of " The New Clarion " 1932–34. Married : (3 sons).

Davies, Ernest Morton Gwynne, *Manorafon, Pontardawe, Swansea.* (Spr.), 1927–1934. Prefect. School Certif. 1st XV Colours 1932–1934 (Capt. 1934). 2nd XI Colours 1932–1933. Clerk.

Davies, Ernest W. Parry, 270 *Baring Road, Grove Park, S.E.* 12. (S.H.), 1901–1907. Form VI. Senior. Treas. and Sec. Lit. Soc. 2nd XI Cricket. Lieut. in R.A.S.C., transferred to 18th and 24th Batts. Welch Regt. Dried Fruit Merchant. Married : (1 dau.).

Davies, Evan. (H.), 1908–1911. Probationer. Lieut. the Welch Regt. Newsagent.

Davies, Frederick Herbert, *Varteg, Mon.* (S.H.), 1882–1885. Probationer. 1st XV Football. J.P. for Monmouthshire. Colliery Director and Agent. Married.

Davies, Geoffrey Hier, *Rosemont, Clytha Park, Newport.* (H.), 1901–1903. Form VI. Capt. Mon. Regt. Probationer.

Davies, George Howard, 12 *Park Avenue, Porthcawl.* (H.), 1897–1898. Form IV. Probationer.

Davies, Griffith T. (S.H.), 1890–1893. Form VI. Senior. London Matric. M.A. Oxon. Solicitor. Died in 1935.

Davies, Griffith Thomas. (H.), 1900–1901.

Davies, Harold Gwynne Grenham. (S.H.), 1886–1889. Stockbroker. Married.

Davies, Haydn P. (S.H.), 1901–1902. Form VI. Probationer. Prize for Music.

Davies, Hubert Edwin, *Hill Crest, Park Drive, Uplands, Swansea.* (H.), 1923–1928. Form VI. Prefect. Vice-Pres. of League. 1st XI Football. 1st XV Rugby. 1st XI Cricket.

Davies, Hubert Ellis, 153 *Hedge Lane, Palmers Green, N.* 13. (S.H.), 1919–1921. Form III. Mechanical Engineer with The Metal Bottle Co. Married.

Davies, Hugh John, *North Neeston, Milford Haven, Pembrokeshire.* (H.), 1932–1935. Lower V. School Certif. Farmer.

Davies, James Alun, *Penmorlan, Caswell Road, Mumbles, Swansea.* (S.H.), 1923–1928. Upper V. House Monitor. Treas. of Lit. Soc. Capt. 1st XI Football. 1st XV Rugby. 1st XI Cricket. Woodley Cup. Married.

Davies, Dr. Joe J. (S.H.), 1891–1893. Form VI. Probationer. 1st XI Football. Deceased.

Davies, John Howard, *Manorafon, Pontardawe, Swansea.* (Spr. and H.), 1931–1936. Modern VI. Prefect. Vice-Pres. of League. School Certif. and Supplementary Higher Certif. 1st XV Rugby. 1st XI Cricket. Middle Weight Boxing 1936. Prize for Public Service

Davies, Max Emil, 8 *Stoneygate Road, Leicester.* (Spr.), 1924/1930. Form VI. Prefect. Treas. of Lit. Soc. School Certif. Batchelar Cup. Excellence in Speaking Prize. B.A. University College, Oxford. Steel Salesman. Married.

Davies, Ronald Martyn, *R.A.M.C., c/o Glyn Mills & Co., Holts Branch, Kirkland House, Whitehall, S.W.* 1. (H.), 1897–1901. Form VI. Senior. Pres. of Lit. Soc. 1st XI Cricket and Football. M.B., B.Sc., Durham University. Lieut.-Colonel R.A.M.C. War Service in France 1915–1919. Married.

Davies, William Brynmor, *Maes Gwyn, Porth, Rhondda.* (H.), 1903–1905. Form III. Mining Engineer. A.M.I.C.E.

Davies, William E. (S.H.), 1896. Form III.

Davis, Archibald Gordon, *Heron's Pool, Amberley, Glos.* (D.B.), 1896–1897. Form V. Lieut. 5th Glos. Regt. Transport Officer. Served in Egypt, Gallipoli and on Western Front 1915–1918. Retired Tea Planter.

Davis, Arnold Percivale, 59c, *Compayne Gardens, N.W.* 6. (D.B.), 1897–1900. Form IV. St. John's College, Oxford. Diploma in Forestry (Oxford Univ.). Bursar of St. Andrew's University. Lieut. 2/70th Burma Rifles. Indian Forest Service, Burma 1909–1932. Retired. Married : (1 dau.).

Davis, A. T.

Davis, Bernard Charles, *Whitecroft, Greenway Lane, Charlton Kings, Cheltenham.* (D.B.), 1913–1919. Form VI. Senior. London Matric. House Prize. Bank Clerk. Married.

Davis, Charles, *Highfield, Abergavenny, Mon.* (H.), 1927–1933. Form V. House Monitor. P.L. Scouts. School Certif. 2nd Lieut. 3rd Batt. Brecon & Monmouthshire Regt. (T.A.). Grocer and Provision Merchant.

Davis, Grahame Edward. (S.H.), 1907–1911. Hons. Cambridge Locals London Telegraph Training College (1912). Wireless operator on liner to New York. Continued to act in same capacity in other lines. During the War made a number of trips to the Far East, mostly in the service of the P. & O., afterwards to South Africa. Contracted malaria fever, from which he died on July 9th, 1917. (" W. & W." 36).

Davis, Howard Henry, *Little Stoke, Patchway, Glos.* (S.H.), 1912–1914. Form V. Probationer. R.G.A. Farmer.

Davis, John, *Highfield, Abergavenny, Mon.* (h.), *and Godfrey Davis Ltd., 7 Eccleston Street, Victoria, W.* 3. (H.), 1924–1931. Form VI. House Monitor. School Certif. 2nd XV Rugby. Motor Salesman.

Davis, Norman de Lancy. (D.B.), 1895–1900. Form VI. London Matric. Senior. Prize for Public Speaking. Exhibitioner of Jesus College, Oxford. Degree in Modern History 1905. Commenced reading for the Bar. For two years Secretary of University Settlement at Toynbee Hall. In 1909 became Assistant Commissioner in Brit. East Africa, and for three years administered a district almost as large as Wales. Died suddenly of blackwater fever on August 29th, 1911. (" Star " Dec., p. 128).

Davis, Percival James. (D.B.), 1909–1912. Form VI. Probationer. Joined Phoenix Insurance Co., and thence passed into the Royal Fusiliers. Mortally wounded in the advance on Combles on October 16th, 1916, and died in hospital at Rouen some weeks later. (" W. & W." 37).

Davis, Reginald Alfred, *Peak Villa, Cam, Glos.* (D.B.), 1910–1914. Form V. Probationer. R.G.A. Hons. Diploma in Philosophy Bristol University 1923. Board of Education Teachers' Certif. (Distinction) in Principles and Practice of Teaching. Member of Inst. of Hygiene. Held Appointments as Temperance Official 1923–1930. President National Fraternal Assoc. of Band of Hope Union Officials 1934–35. Author of works on Temperance Teaching and Sunday School Work. Departmental Temperance Lecturer.

Davis, Wilfred Chester. *Was at Tetbury.* (S.H.), 1903. Form I. R.N.V.R.

Davis, Wilfred Ernest. (S.H.), 1895–1897. Swimming Championship. Automobile Engineer.

Dawson, Gilbert James Cameron, 44 *Victoria Road, Swindon* (h.). (H.), 1914–1915. Form V. Probationer. Lieut. 9th Manchester Regt. Engineering Draughtsman in Australia.

Dawson, John Douglas, *Dekhari Tea Co., Dekhari, Ragmai P.O. Sebragoe, Assam.* (H.), 1914–1917. Form IV. Probationer. Engineer. Engineer to above Company.

Dawson, Leonard Watkins. (D.B.), 1894–1895. Form IV.

Day, Frank Henry, 38 *Monpelier, Weston-super-Mare, Som.* (h.) *and St. John's College, Durham University.* (R. & H.), 1931–1935. Form V. School Certif. Prizes for Piano and Organ. Theological Student.

Deacon, Arthur William, *Stonecote, Kington, Herefordshire.* (S.H.), 1924–1930. Upper V. House Monitor. School Certif. 1st XV Rugby. Swimming Championship. 2nd West of England Scout Swimming Championship 1928. Connaught Shield Shooting Team. National Diploma, London School of Building. Building Contractor.

Deacon, John Ernest Arnold, *Stonecote, Kington, Herefordshire.* (R. and S.H.), 1928–1934. Science VI. House Monitor. School Certif. 2nd XV Rugby.

Deakin, Hamish Vipond Ieuan, *Parkend House, Parkend, near Lydney. Glos.* (S.H.), 1931–1936. Science VI. Prefect. Vice-Pres. of League. School Certif. 1st XV Rugby. Capt. 1st XI Cricket. Tennis Team, Prize for Public Service. Timber Trade. With Messrs Meggitt & Jones, Cardiff.

Denley, Montague Charles, *Wyesham, London Road, Cheltenham.* (S.H.), 1930–1933. Lower V. 2nd XV 1933. King's Scout. Prelim. and Intermed. Exams. A.C.A. Accountancy.

Dennis, George V., *Airdale, Busselton, W. Australia.* (H.), 1895–1899. Form III. Sub.-Lieut. R.N.V.R.

Dennis, Preston, *Brookfields, Ross-on-Wye.* (D.B.). 1909–1910. Form III. Captain Indian Army S.C. Salonica 1917–1918. Married : (1 dau.).

Denniss, William Calvert. (H.), 1892–1895. Form VI. Probationer. Member of the '94–'95 " invincible " Football XI. Joined a Bank in India, and later became a planter in " British East." In 1914 joined King's East African Rifles, and was killed in action early in 1916. (" W. & W." 37).

Desprez, Charles Stanley, 91 *Hampton Road, Redland, Bristol.* (S.H.), 1901–1905. Form IV. Lieut. R.A.S.C. Engineer.

Dew, Reginald Keith, *Fritwell, near Bicester, Oxon.* (H.), 1929–1931. Upper IV. 2nd XV Rugby.

Dewey, Arnold S. (S.H.), 1893–1895. Form III.

Dickenson, Ernest Arthur, *Down Farm, near Stroud.* (D.B.), 1902–1907. Form III. Royal Glos. Hussars. Served in Gallipoli and Palestine. Farmer. Married (1 son).

Dickenson, Robert J., *Abbotsville, Abbotsham Road, Bideford, North Devon.* (S.H.), 1904–1907. Form III. Royal Fusiliers. Lloyds Bank. Married : (1 son, 1 dau.).

Dickins, Charles Henry, 3 *Cheapside, Fishponds, Bristol.* (Spr.), 1910. Form II. War Service : two years with Infantry in France ; later Lieut. R.A.F. (Pilot). Tobacconist. Married : (2 sons, 2 daus.).

Dickins, Frank Albert, *Thorsby, Evesham Road, Cheltenham.* (H.), 1911–1917. Form V. Batchelar Cup. Boxing and Wrestling Shield. Bristol Univ. O.T.C. Tobacconist. Married.

Didier, Donovan Simon, *Lima Villa, Roseau, Dominica, B.W.I.* (S.H.), 1913–1916. Form VI. Senior. 1st XI Football. 2nd XI Cricket. Coffee Planter.

Dimmock, A. E. (D.B.), 1888–1892.

Dimmock, C. W. (S.H.), 1885–1890. Senior. London Matric. Went to India, where he died of fever in 1908.

Dimmock, William A. (D.B.), 1888–1891. Married.

Dix, Graham Cameron, *Park View House, Stratford Road, Stroud.* (H.), 1927–1934. Science VI. London Matric. Prizes for Music, Exams. and Upper Remove Form Prize. School Certif. Articled to Chartered Accountant.

Dix, John Hardcastle. (S.H.), 1882. Form VI. Senior. Became solicitor and joined his father, Alderman J. W. S. Dix, in practice in Bristol. He died in 1904.

Dixon, Arthur Perrin, *Black and White House, Upton St. Leonards, Glos.* (S.H.), 1897–1898. Form III. Played Water Polo for Somerset. Held one mile swimming record for Bath and West of England 1904–1905. Late Superintendent of Zoological Society of Scotland. F.Z.S. F.R.P.S.E. Lieut. Royal Scots. Married.

Dodds, Gordon de Malpas Kearney, 41 *Blenheim Gardens, N.W.* 2.   (D.B.), 1935–1936. Lower Remove.

Donaldson, George Ian, *Uplands, Aylestone Hill, Hereford.* (Spr.), 1930–1936. Science VI. Prefect. London Matric. School Certif. Dux and Science Prizes. Articled to Borough Engineer, Weston-super-Mare.

Doret, Peter Francis, *The Rocks, Maidstone, Kent.* (Spr.), 1931–1936. Form VI. House Monitor. School Certif. Prize for Excellence in Speaking. Student at London University.

Downey, Harold, 67 *Berrylands, Surbiton, Surrey.* (S.H.), 1891–1892. Form IV. 1st XI Cricket. Sergt. R.A.M.C. in S. African War. Married: (1 son).

Downing, Clifford L., *Brewery House, Anchor Brewery, Mile End Road, E.* 1. (D.B.), 1910–1914. Form VI. Probationer. 1st XI Cricket. Lieut. 5th Glos. Regt. Brewer.

Downing, Dennis James. (D.B. and H.), 1914–1921. Form V. Probationer. 2nd XI Cricket. Went to South Africa and was in business in Durban. He died on February 4th, 1927.

Downs, Henry Summers, *c/o H. W. J. Smith, Esq., Dunedin, Charlton Road, Keynsham, Som.* (Spr.), 1904–1909. Form V. Cambridge Senior. 2nd XI Cricket and Football. Prize for Public Speaking. Inns of Court O.T.C. Capt. York Regt. 1915–1919. R.A.F. Imperial Tobacco Co., Cigar Box Factory, Old Street, E.C. 1.

Drew, George Henry. (D.B.), 1900–1903. Form III. Corn Merchant in Canada.

Drew, Gerald H., *Leighterton Farm, Tetbury, Glos.* 17th Lancers.

Drew, John Wilfred, *West End. Abingdon-on-Thames.* (D.B.), 1902–1904. Form III. Bucks Yeomanry. Timber Merchant.

Drew, William Farinton. (S.H.), 1896–1898. Form V. Fellow of Inst. of Builders. Builder and Contractor.

Drew, William Tyndale, *Leighterton Farm, Tetbury, Glos.* (D.B.), 1907–1909. Form II. R.A.F.

Driffield, Ernest. (H.), 1887. Curator of Field Club. Draper.

Duck, Frederick Arthur, *c/o R. W. Duck & Co., Chemists, St. John Sq., Cardiff* (h.). *Maypole Cottage, Collier Row, Romford, Essex.* (S.H.), 1909–1912. Form III. 2nd XI Football. R.F.A. 1915–1917. Poultry Farmer.

Dudbridge, Leonard, *Fir Tree Cottage, Rodborough, Stroud.* (D.B.), 1904–1910. Form VI. Senior. London Matric. House Prize. 1st XI Football. 2nd XI Cricket. Senior Cross Country Championship. Winner of 100 yards in all six classes. Gloucestershire and Barbarians Rugby Football. Capt. 5th Glos. Regt. M.C. and Bar. Married : (3 daus.)

Dudbridge, Morton, *Magdala, Uplands, Stroud.* (Spr. and D.B.), 1908–1915. Form VI. Senior. Vice-Pres. of League. A.S.M. Cambridge Senior. House Prize. 1st XI Football. Lieut. R.F.C. Automobile Engineer. Married.

Dudbridge, Norman, *The Uplands, Stroud.* (D.B.) 1914–1921. Form V. Probationer. Accountant. Member West of England District Soc. of Incorp. Accountants, and, of Stroud Urban District Council. Vice-Chairman Stroud and Tetbury Boy Scouts. Treasurer Stroud Rugby Football Club. Married.

Dugdale, Edward Beaumont. (H.), 1914–1917. Form V. Probationer. Flour and dust from milling brought on lung trouble. Did light work on his father's farm, and acted as Secretary to the Tewkesbury Branch of the Gloucestershire Farmers' Union. Died in March 1922. (" Star," Apr. 1922).

Dugdale, John Hogg, *Woodend Farm, Grassendale, Liverpool.* (S.H.), 1932–1934. Dairy Farmer.

Dugdale, Richard Osborne, *The Old Thatch, Deerhurst, near Gloucester.* (H.), 1923–1926. Form V. Probationer. Cert. Assoc. Inst. of Bankers. Bank Clerk.

Duncalf, Edwin Allen. (S.H.), 1892–1895. Form VI. Senior. London Matric. 2nd XI Cricket and Football. Lieut. 12th London Regt. Sometime Sec. and Manager of Investment Registration Committee, Guest, Keen and Nettlefold Ltd. He died in 1931.

Duncalf, William John, 1 *Pembroke Road, Clifton, Bristol.* (S.H.), 1892–1894. Form VI. Senior. London Matric. 1st XI Cricket and Football. L.D.S. (Eng.). Dentist. Married.

Dunsford, Gordon, *Harnham, Hewlett Road, Cheltenham* (h.). (D.B.), 1902–1904. S.A. Field Artillery. Merchant.

Durden, Arthur Henry, 30 *Cwrt-y-vil Road, Penarth, Glam.* (S.H.), 1898–1902. Form VI. Probationer. 2nd XI Cricket and Football. Sergt. Middlesex Imperial Yeomanry and 23rd Batt. Middlesex Regt. Member of S. Wales Inst. of Engineers. Engineer. S. Wales representative of Urquhart and Linsay, Engineers, Dundee. Married.

Duthie, Robert Alan, 2 *St. Aidan's Road, Carlisle, Cumberland.* (Spr.), 1929–1933. Science VI. School Certif. (Hons.). Prizes: Dux and Mathematics. Accountant.

Dyer, E. (S.H.), 1913–1915.

Earle, E. E. (D.B.), about 1904. Berks. Regt.

Eaton, George John, *Ballards, Hinton, Evesham, Worcs.* (H.), 1933–1936. Lower V. 2nd XI Cricket 1936.

Edkins, Arthur Norman, *Manor Farm, Great Alne, Alcester, Warwicks.* (S.H.), 1916–1920. Form VI. Senior. London Matric. Farming.

Edwards, Arthur Stuart, 5 *Forrest Gardens, Norbury, S.W.* 16. 9 *Brigstock Road, Thornton Heath, Surrey.* (H.), 1913–1915. Form IV. Probationer. F.A.I. Auctioneer and Estate Agent. War Service, M.G.C. Married: (1 dau.).

Edwards, Charles Ernest, *Palace Road, Llandaff, Cardiff.* (S.H.), 1883–1889. Senior. Pres. of Lit. Soc. Treas. of Field Club. London Matric. 1st XI Cricket. 1st XV Rugby. Solicitor. Married.

Edwards, Charles Henry Budgett, *The Old Vicarage, Midsomer Norton, Som.* (H.), 1922–1928. Upper V. House Monitor. London Matric. School Certif.

Edwards, E. S. (S.H.), 1891–1892. Upper III.

Edwards, Francis George, *Waterley, Hucclecote, Gloucester* (h.). (H.), 1928–1932. Modern VI. Prefect. School Certif. 1st XV Rugby. Tennis Team. 2nd XI Cricket. Senior Athlete. Played regularly for Gloucester XV. County Rugby Cap. Representative for Messrs E. S. & A. Robinson in North Wales. Played in English Rugby Trial at Twickenham, Dec., 1936.

Edwards, Frank Howard, 18 *Montpellier Terrace, Cheltenham.* (Spr.), 1906–1909. Form V. Probationer. War Service 1914–1918. N.C.O. 2/5th Gloucesters. Lieut. 3rd Wiltshire Regt. Capt. 6th D.C.L.I. M.C. and Bar. Gentlemen's Outfitter. Married: (1 son 1 dau.,).

Edwards, Herbert Archer, *Burnholme, Furze Hill, Boreham Wood, Herts.* (S.H.), 1895–1896. Form III. Emery Cloth Manufacturer. Married.

Edwards, James Herbert, *Woodside, Cranham, near Gloucester.* (S.H.), 1884–1890. Form VI. Senior. Pres. of Lit. Soc. London Matric. 1st XI Cricket. 1st XV. Rugby. Managing Director of Electric Light and Power Co. Chairman of Council of Governors of Wycliffe College. Married,

Edwards, John Richard, *Waterley, Hucclecote, Gloucester.* (H.),1924–1928. Lower IV. Batchelar Cup (Gardening). Assistant Auctioneer and Estate Agent.

Edwards, L. D. 1891–1892. Upper III.

Edwards, T. J., *St. Margarets, Llandaff.* Architect.

Eeles, George Proctor. (H.), 1901–1904. Farming in Canada.

Elder, John Howard, 3 *Padderswick Road, Hammersmith, W. 6. 21 Oxford Street, Oldham* (h.). (Spr.), 1926–1931. Matric VI. House Monitor. Connaught Shooting Team. London Matric. 1st XV Rugby. Foster Rifle. Jeune Cup. 150 yards Swimming Record. Winner of Swimming Championship 1931. Harmston Music Prize. Prize for Public Service. Mersey Swimming Championship Certif. 1933. Metropolitan Police Force.

Elliott, Arthur E. B. (D.B.), 1898–1902. Form V.

Elliott, E.

Elliott, George Laurent. (H.), 1906–1909. Senior. Sec. of Lit. Soc. 1st XI Cricket and Football. Capt. R.F.A. Goldsmith, Silversmith and Medallist. Married.

Elliott, Herbert, W. (D.B.), 1898–1902. Form III.

Ellis, John James. (S.H.), 1913–1914. Form V. Welch Cyclists Regt. Joined the 14th R.W.F. in France. Shot by a sniper Aug. 31st, 1916, and buried in Ypres. (" W. & W." 35).

Ellis, Kenneth Ernest, 104a *Sinclair Road, Kensington, London, W. 14.* (S.H.), 1905–1907. Form III. Prize for Public Speaking. Soloist for Royal Choral Society, Royal Albert Hall. Pioneer Vocalist in Broadcasting. Queen's Hall Promenade Concerts. Celebrity Concerts. War Service : Member of concert parties in France, Belgium, Malta and with Mediterranean Fleet; in Italy from August 1914 until after the Armistice. Vocalist. Teacher of Singing and Voice Production. Royal Opera House, Covent Garden, Autumn 1936. Married : (1 son).

Ellis, Thomas Wilson, 108 *Cambridge Gardens, London, W. 10.* (S.H.), 1914–1919. Form IV. Probationer. 2nd XI Cricket. Civil Engineer.

Esnouf, Greville Gascoyne, *The Glen, Saundersfoot, Pembrokeshire.* (H.), 1934–1935. Upper IV.

Essex, J. W. L. (D.B.).

Evans, Albert Edward. (S.H.), 1893–1898. Probationer. 1st XI Cricket and Football. Cambridge University Blue (Rugby). Half Blue, Tennis.

Evans, Arthur John (I). (H.), 1889–1893. Form V. Probationer. 1st XI Football. Capt 2nd XI Cricket. Became an Architect and Surveyor at Whitchurch, Glam. Died in 1912.

Evans, Arthur John (II). (H.), 1893–1898. Became a Solicitor at Pontypridd. Died in 1912.

Evans, Ben C. (*was at Chief Lake, B.C., Canada*). (H.), 1891–1892. Probationer. 2nd XI Football. Canadian Forces. Musquash Fur Farmer. Married.

Evans, Caryl Albert Gear, 15 *Portsmouth Road, Woolston, Southampton.* (S.H. and Spr.), 1911–1913. Form IV. Married.

THE TOWER OF THIS CHAPEL IS DEDICATED TO THE MEMORY OF THE OLD BOYS OF WYCLIFFE COLLEGE WHO GAVE THEIR LIVES FOR ENGLAND IN THE GREAT WAR 1914 — 1918.

GREATER LOVE HATH NO MAN THAN THIS THAT A MAN LAY DOWN HIS LIFE FOR HIS FRIENDS

THESE SERVED AND DIED IN THE DEATHLESS CAUSE OF RIGHT AND LIBERTY THEIR NAMES ARE WRITTEN IN THE BOOK OF LIFE AND ARE ENGRAVEN HERE THAT WE WHO READ WITH WHAT A GREAT PRICE FREEDOM STILL IS BOUGHT MAY PAY OUR TRIBUTE OF REVERENCE GRATITUDE AND AFFECTION AND GIVE ALL PRAISE TO GOD.

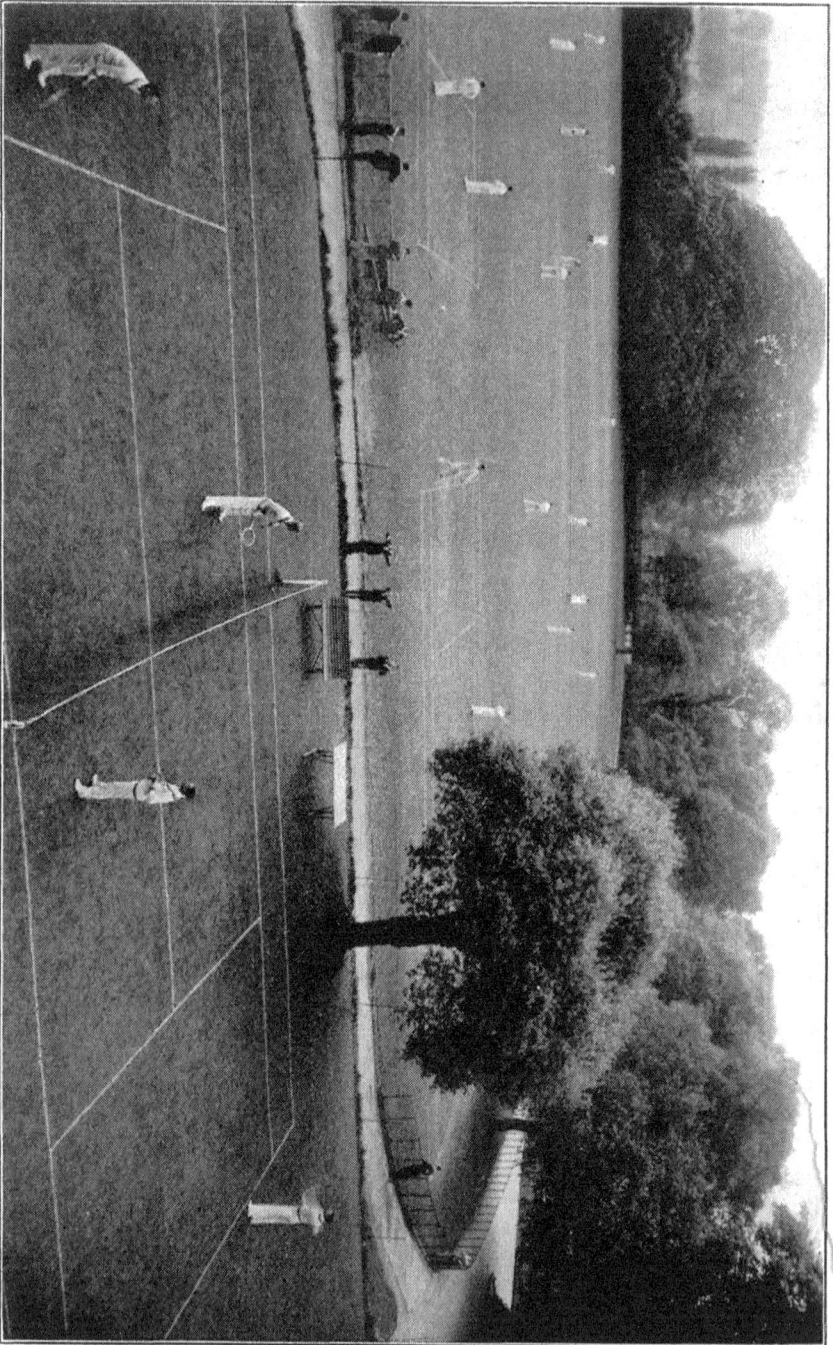

LOOKING SOUTH-WEST ACROSS THE MAIN CRICKET FIELD

THE FIRST O.W. GATHERING AFTER THE WAR, 1919

SENIORS AND PROBATIONERS, 1920.

W. Sharrock, T. Giles, P. Stanfield, H. Hutchen, E. M. Williams, S. Livsey, E. Barton, P. Bazeley, A. Hancox, J. Johnceline, J. Wainwright, M. Hampton, U. Gardiner, N. Fearis, R. M. Reece, N. Dudbridge, G. Richards, N. Williams, E. A. Smith, J. Powell, R. George, E. Maze, H. Withey, H. Keene, N. Edkins, G. Bird, L. Arnott, G. Lloyd, J. Tancock, K. Bird, A. Poole, F. Timmins, D. Hart, J. Newth, K. Humpidge, D. Shaw, E. Hart, N. Wiggins, T. Arnott, A. Grey, A. Hutchen, M. Jones, S. Bazeley, G. Bazeley.

Evans, Edward D. (S.H.), 1892–1897. Form VI. Senior. London Matric. 1st XI Cricket and Football. Cambridge University Blue (Rugby). Half Blue (Tennis). Civil Engineer. Married.

Evans, Edward Thomas, *Middle St. Farm, Eastington.* (D.B.), 1901–1904. Form II. Farmer.

Evans, G. G. *In Canada.*

Evans, Harold S. (H.), 1884–1885. Woollen Manufacturer. Married.

Evans, Ifor Leslie, *University College of Wales, Aberystwyth.* (H.), 1908–1912. Form VI. Senior. Cambridge Senior Hons. I. Sec. of Lit. Soc. Imprisoned at Ruhleben 1914–1918. M.A. (Cantab.). Economics Tripos, Class I. Historical Tripos, Class I. Fellow of St. John's College. Lecturer in Economics at Cambridge 1923–1924. Principal of University College of Wales since 1934. Member of Council of Governors of Wycliffe College.

Evans, Kenneth Halbeck Louis, *Kentsford Farm, Watchet, Taunton, Som.* (R. and H.), 1929–1935. Upper V. House Monitor. School Certif. 1st XV Rugby. 2nd XI Cricket. School Athletic Team. Aircraftsman.

Evans, Melville Gear, *The Mount, Orme Road, Peterborough.* (Spr.), 1914-1921. Form V. Probationer. 1st XI Cricket and Football. Tie Record High Jump (5 ft. 2½ ins.). Senior Athlete. Senior Tennis Doubles. Eastern Counties' Representative of Bulmers', Hereford. Married.

Evans, Philip James. (D.B.), 1883–1885. Married.

Evans, Prosper Gear. (Spr.), 1913–1917. Form VI. Senior. Pres. of League. Cambridge Senior. House Prize. 1st XI Football. Capt. 1st XI Cricket. Senior Athlete. Senior Tennis Singles. Rowell Cup. Medical Student at Bristol University for which he played Cricket, Golf, Rugby and Soccer. In Sports won 220, quarter, half and mile on same day. Played Rugby for Bristol and Gloucestershire and in Welsh Trials. Was a first-class Golfer. Was Medical Officer of Health at Wensley Sanatorium, near Bath, and later practised in Peterborough; after being in poor health for some years died at Bridgend, October 1936.

Evans, Trevor Morse, *Parc, Bridgend, Glam.* (H.), 1892–1898. Form VI. Senior. 1st XI Football. Capt. 2nd XI Cricket. B.A. (Cantab.) Capt. R.F.A. Barrister. Married.

Evans, William Bernard. (H.), 1899–1904. Form VI. Senior. Vice-Pres. of League. London Matric. Capt. 2nd XI Cricket. B.Sc. London. Civil Engineer and Surveyor in Nelson, British Columbia.

Evans, William Henry, *Alkerton Court, Eastington, Glos.* (D.B.), 1900–1904. Form II. Farmer.

Evans, William Ivor. (S.H.), 1892–1895. Form VI. Senior. London Matric. 1st XI Cricket and Football. M.A. Cantab.

Evans. William P. 1889–1894. Form III. Farmer. Died in 1902.

Evered, Derrick Albert, *Moor Hill, Little Kimble, Princes Risboro', Bucks.* (R. and S.H.), 1927–1932. Upper III.

Evered, Henry Freeman, *Moor Hill, Little Kimble, Princes Risboro', Bucks.* (S.H.), 1924–1932. Form VI. Prefect. London Matric. 2nd XV Rugby.

Evers-Swindell, Arthur E., *Stillingfleet, Lower Hutt, Wellington, New Zealand.* (D.B.), 1904–1905. Form VI. Farming. Married.

Evers-Swindell, Ernest Frederick. (H.), 1906–1910. Form IV. Probationer. Took up farming in New Zealand. In 1914 joined New Zealand Infantry, but was killed in France in October 1917. ("W. & W." 39).

Exell, Francis John, *White House Farm, Cam, Glos.* (D.B.), 1920–1923. Form IV.

Eyles, Henry Gordon, 4 *Paulton Drive, Bishopston, Bristol.* (H.), 1918–1921. Form IV. Probationer. 1st XI Cricket and Football. Wholesale Fruit Merchant. Married : (1 dau.).

Eynon, Henry Hadyn, *Oxford Street, Mountain Ash.* (Spr.), 1907. Form II.

Eyre, Charles Malton Le Grice, 12 *Esmond Road, Bedford Park, London, W.4.* (H.), 1922–1927. Matric. Form. Prefect. Vice-Pres. of League. London Matric. 1st XV Rugby. 1st XI Cricket. Foster Rifle.

Fabien, Ernest Percival, *Stamford, Wood Lane, Hemel Hempstead, Herts.* (S.H.), 1929–1936. 1st XV. Lower Remove. In Royal Air Force.

Fabien, John Gravely, *Stamford, Wood Lane, Hemel Hempstead, Herts.* (S.H.), 1929–1933. 2nd XV. Lower Remove. In Metropolitan Police.

Fanner, George Clifford, *Darwin Station, Puerto San Julian, Santa Cruz, Argentina.* (Spr.), 1921–1926. Senior. Vice-Pres. of League. 1st XI Football. Maiden Sculls (Gloucester Regatta). Sheep Farming.

Farmer, Geoffrey John, 62 *Lonsdale Road, Barnes, London, S.W. 13.* (S.H. and Spr.), 1909–1913. Form IV. Artists Rifles 1915. Commissioned to Queen's Westminster Rifles 1916. R.F.C. 1917. Served with 13th Squadron as Observer and Pilot till 1919. Architect. Married : (1 dau.).

Farmer, Philip A., *c/o Lake of the Woods Milling Co., Winnipeg, Manitoba* (permanent). 301 *Manitoba, W. Moose Jaw, Sask., Canada.* (Spr.), 1916–1920. Form IV. Saskatchewan Representative to the Canadian Rugby Union. President Moose Jaw Rugby Clubs. Married : (1 son, 1 dau.).

Farr, Frank J., *Brentry Lodge, Westbury, Bristol.* (S.H.), 1910–1916. 2nd Lieut. R.A.F. Chemist.

Farr, William Bryant, *Langton, Mount Nebo, Taunton, Som.* (S.H.), 1910–1912. Form V. Imperial Tobacco Co. Despatch Rider. Corporal R.E. France 1915–1919. Representative of W. D. & H. O. Wills. Married : (1 son, 1 dau.).

Farrer, Frederick Gordon. (D.B.), 1902–1903. Form III.

Faulkner, H. F. W. (D.B.), 1891.

Faulkner, Ronald, *Cranham, Brooklands Road, Brooklands, Cheshire.* (Spr.), 1921–1928. Form VI. Prefect. Vice-Pres. of League. Sec. of Lit. Soc. Editor of " Star." Winner of Senior Cross Country. Capt. Tennis Team. Junior and Senior Tennis Singles and Doubles. 1st XI Cricket. 2nd XI Football. Prize for Public Speaking. Contractor.

Fawkes, Brian, *St. Cyril's Road, Stonehouse.* (H.), 1914–1915. Form I.

Fawkes, Clifford Tennyson, *Royal Stock Farm, Leonard Stanley.* (D.B.), 1920–1925. Form II. Poultry Farmer. Married : (1 son).

Fawkes, Frederick Stuart Estcourt, *Haresfield, Packhorn Road, Bessels Green, Kent.* (D.B. and H.), 1910–1916. Form VI. Artists Rifles. A.C.A. Accountant to the Goldsmiths Company. Married : (1 son, 1 dau.).

Fawkes, George Arthur. (D.B.), 1911–1913. Form IV. R.F.C. Leading Aircraftsman. Farmer. Married.

Fawkes, Kingsford Sidney, 39 *Free Street, Brecon.* (D.B.), 1899–1900. Form, III. Cpl. R.E.

Fawkes, Stanley Victor, *Rubens, Park Road, Camberley, Surrey.* (D.B.), 1921–1925. Form V. Probationer. 2nd XI Football. Higher Certif. in Gas Engineering (Inst. of Gas Engineers). Chief Asst. Engineer to the Yorktown (Camberley) and District Gas and Electricity Co. Married.

Fearis, Edward Norman, *Temperley, Hucclecote, Gloucester.* (H.), 1918–1921. Form VI. Senior. Capt. 1st XI Football. 1st XI Cricket. Swimming Championship. Woodley Cup. Open Tennis Doubles. House Prize. Assist. Managing Director, Fearis & Co. Married : (2 sons)

Felton, John Herbert. *Was at Cheltenham.* (S.H.), 1907–1909. Form IV. Despatch Rider, R.E. Wine and Spirit Merchant.

Fenn, Harold George, 3 *Audley Road, Ealing, London, W. 5.* (S.H.), 1898–1901. Form III. On the Somme. R.F.C. 1916–1918. Commercial Traveller. Married : (1 son).

Field, Charles Lindon Robert Edward. 1911. Died at sea.

Field, Gerald Richard. (D.B.), 1912–1919. Form IV. Woollen Manufacturer.

Filer, Kenneth James, *Woodlands,* 1 *Arbutus Drive, Combe Dingle, Bristol* (h.) and *c/o E. S. & A. Robinson Ltd.,* 114 *Portland Street, Manchester.* (Spr.), 1928–1934. Senior Prefect. Pres. of League and Lit. Soc. School Certif. 1st XV Rugby. Batchelar Cup. School Shooting Team. Prizes for Singing, Public Service and Excellence in Public Speaking. Representative of Messrs E. S. & A. Robinson in Manchester.

Fish, Arthur Charles, *The Chalet, Compton Dando, near Bristol.* (S.H.), 1898–1901. Form VI. Senior. 1st XI Football. Capt R.F.A. Officer in Command Anti-Gas School 1916–1919. Road Transport Contractor (retired). Married.

Fish, Howard Macdonald, 7 *Henleaze Road, Westbury-on-Trym.* (S.H.), 1901–1904. Form IV. Probationer. War Service : Road Transport. Managing Director of Road Transport Firm. Married : (1 son, 1 dau.).

Fish, Joseph, *Toronto, Canada.* (S.H.), 1894–1895. Form IV. 1st XI Football. Married.

Fish, Thomas Percival, 90 *Southam Road, Hall Green, Birmingham.* 43/46, *New Street, Birmingham* 2. (S.H.), 1898–1901. Form VI. Senior. Pres. of Lit. Soc. London Matric. 1st XI Football. District Surveyor (Midlands and N. Wales). Married.

Fisher, Hubert Frank. (H.), 1895–1898. Form III. Took engineering course at King's College, London, and in 1903 or 1904 went out to the Argentine, where he became chief engineer and manager to an important firm. On the outbreak of war trained as an aviator, and became a Major in the R.A.F. After being wounded in France, he was appointed Chief Instructor and Lecturer in Aeronautics at the University of Toronto. Obtaining sick leave after the Armistice, he returned to England, but developed pneumonia and died at the R.A.F. Hospital on March 22nd, 1919. (" W. & W." 40).

Fisher, Robert John Bertram, 96 *London Road, E. Grinstead, Surrey.* (H.), 1891–1896. Form VI. Senior. 1st XI Football. Hurdles Record 1896–1911. Sergt. R.A.F. Caterer and Confectioner. Married.

Flambert, Anthony Geoffrey. (S.H.), 1920–1924. Lower V. Probationer. After farming at home, joined Lloyds Bank (Aldershot and Southampton). Met with a serious motor accident on September 26th, 1927, and died the same day in the Andover Memorial Hospital. (" Star," Dec. 1927, p. 14).

Ford, Alfred Rogers, *Meriland, Weston-super-Mare.* (D.B.), 1883–1886. Senior. London Matric. Hons. in Solicitors Final Exam. Solicitor. Married.

Ford, Francis Walter, *The Hollies, Bushton, Wootton Bassett, Wilts.* (D.B.), 1885–1892. Form VI. Senior. Solicitors Final Exam. Practised for five years. Afterwards farmed in Alberta and British Columbia, 1904–1911. Married.

Ford, Gerald, 14 *Bassett Road, Kensington, W.* 10. (H.), 1890–1894. Form V. Probationer. 1st XI Cricket and Football. Imperial Yeomanry in South African War. Chief Local Officer, Apprentice Training Dept., Ministry of Labour. Married : (2 daus.).

Ford, Harold R. (D.B.), 1891–1893. Form VI. Became wholesale stationer in Gloucester. Died in 1917.

Ford, Malcolm Stephen, 6 *Stow Park Crescent, Newport, Mon.* (Spr.), 1927–1930. Lower V. 1st XV Rugby. Three years Royal College of Art. Artist.

Ford Percy Hadley. (D.B.), 1891–1893. Form V. Probationer. 1st XI Cricket. Became a Director of Messrs Ford & Branch, Printers and Stationers, Gloucester. Played for Gloucester City and Gloucestershire at cricket for many years. During the War was a Captain in the Bedfords. Died of pneumonia in December 1919. (" Star," April 1920).

Ford, Philip, *Oakdene, Slad Road, Stroud.* (D.B.), 1925–1930. Lower IV. Builder.

Ford, Richard Jellard. (H.), 1888–1890. Was ranching in Texas, when the S. African War broke out, but returned to England and joined Kitchener's Horse. Eventually he became a Captain in the Worcestershire Regt., one of the first to be sent to the Front in 1914. For six months he was almost continually in action. He was mentioned in despatches and received the Military Cross for the part he played in the recapture of Gheluvelt. He was killed at Neuve Chapelle on May 9th, 1915. (" W. & W." 14).

Ford, William Henry Rogers, *Municipal Buildings, Calcutta.* (D.B.), 1882–1886. Chief Accountant to the City of Calcutta. Married.

Foster, Edward C. M. (S.H.), 1890–1895. Form VI. Senior. Capt. 1st XI Cricket and Football. M.R.C.S., L.R.C.P. Medical Field Service in S. African War. Major R.A.M.C. Surgeon and Demonstrator in Anatomy at Oxford University. Married.

Foster, D. Norman K. (S.H.), 1891–1895. Form V. M.B., B.S. (London). Physician.

Foster, Walter, *The Chestnuts, Bourton-on-the-Water, Glos.* (H.), 1926–1932. Form VI. House Monitor, School Certif. Capt. 2nd XV Rugby. School Chess Team. Undergraduate at Bristol University. President S.C.M. and Treasurer of Wills Hall. 1st XV Rugby and 1st VI Tennis. B.A. Bristol Univ. (Hons. in History). Preparing to serve as a Missionary in India (Baptist Missionary Society). Mansfield College, Oxford.

Foster, William Wasbrough, 4815 *Belmont Avenue, Vancouver, B.C.* (D.B.), 1887–1889. Past Pres. Alpine Club of Canada and National Parks Assoc. Member Alpine Club (Eng.). First ascent Mt. Robson and Mt. Logan. F.R.G.S. Director Canadian Geog. Soc. Hon. A.D.C. to Governor General of Canada. Pres. Pacific Engineers Ltd., 1st Vice-Pres. Canadian Legion B.E.S.L. Hon. Colonel 15th Batt. C.A. Brigade Commander (Brevet-Col.) C.E.F. D.S.O. and two Bars. V.D. French and Belgian Croix de Guerre. Married : (3 sons, 2 daus.).

Fothergill, George Leonard. (S.H.), 1905–1910. Form II. R.A.F. Engineer.

Fothergill, Roger Lyall, *Newlands, Natland, near Kendal, Westmorland* (H.), 1933–1935. Lower Remove.

Foweraker, Richard Maxwell, 33 *Redland Grove, Redland, Bristol.* (S.H.), 1925–1929. Upper V. School Certif. Connaught Shooting Team.

Fowler, E. R. (D.B.). Engineer.

Fox, Edwin James. (D.B.), 1887–1888. Schoolmaster. Married.

Foyster, Eric Ross, *Weston Kingskerswell, South Devon.* (h.). *c/o National Provincial Bank Ltd., Castle Circus Branch, Torquay.* (S.H.), 1904–1906. Probationer. Lieut. 8th Batt. the Hampshire Regt. Bank Accountant. Married.

Foyster, Philip Albert, 14 *Belmont Road, Ilfracombe.* (Spr.), 1911–1914. Form VI. Senior. Senior Cambridge. Literature and Music Prizes London Rifle Brigade. Served in Palestine 1918. Atth. 1/10th London Regt. Priest (C. or E.).

Francis, Allan Walter Goodwin. (D.B.), 1902.

Francis, Robert David, *South View, Bath Road, Melksham, Wilts.* (S.H.), 1926–1929. Upper V. House Monitor. School Certif. Prize for Organ. Advertising Representative of Wilts United Dairies Ltd.

Franklin, Albert George, *Dunselma, Cirencester Road, Charlton Kings, Cheltenham.* (H.), 1911–1914. Form IV. 2nd Lieut. R.F.C. and Gloucestershire Regt. Master Butcher. Married : (1 dau.).

Frearson, Richard Charles, *Freefolk Manor, Whitchurch, Hants.* (H.), 1916–1922. Form V. Probationer. Farming.

Freeman, Arthur Hubert. (Spr.), 1906–1908. R.A.F.

Freeth, C. J. Has died.

Friedenson, Thomas Stuart, *Highways, Corfe Castle, Dorset.* (Spr.), 1924–1931. Form VI. Prefect. Pres. of League and Lit. Soc. Capt. 2nd XV. Editor of " Star." School Certif. and Higher Certif. School Chess Team. Prizes for Public Service, Proportional Representation Essay and Excellence in Public Speaking. Journalist. On Relief Committee for Victims of Fascism. Married.

Fryer, Alan Astley, 31 *Collington Road, Brislington, Bristol.* (S.H.), 1902–1904. Form I.

Gabb, Cyril Reginald, *Doverow House, Stonehouse, Glos.* (D.B.), 1909–1911. Form II. R.H.A. Farming. Married.

Gabb, Henry Samuel Darke, 5 *Spa Road, Gloucester.* (D.B.), 1909–1911. Form V.

Gainer, Robert Harold, *British Columbia.* (D.B. and H.), 1892–1898. Form VI. Fruit Farmer. Married.

Gainer, William George Cullum, *British Columbia.* (D.B.), 1896–1897. Form V. Canadian Exped. Force. Fruit Farmer. Married.

Galvayne, Alfred Eustace Leslie. (Spr.), 1918–1919. Form V. Estate Agent.

Galvayne, Vernon Frederick Attride. (S.H.), 1913–1915. Form VI. Probationer. Passed Chartered Accountant's Prelim. On the outbreak of war volunteered for service with the R.N.A.S. Was an exceptionally skilful pilot. Took part in the long distance reconnaissance over the Heligoland Bight on March 21st, 1917, but met his death off Terschelling on June 4th, 1918. (" W. & W." 42–44).

Gammidge, Leonard Norton (" Dick "). (H.), 1906–1910. Form VI. 2nd XI Football. Articled to a London firm of Estate Agents. Joined the Civil Service Rifles in 1914. Was killed on September 25th, 1915 while conveying bombs to a forward battalion near Loos. (" W. & W.") 44).

Gane, Crofton Endres, 24 *Downs Park West, Bristol* 6. (H.), 1889–1894 Form VI. Senior. Pres. of Lit. Soc. 1st XI Cricket and Football. Served in Friends Ambulance Unit attd. French Army. French Croix de Guerre with palm. Chairman Furnishing and Decorating Co. Rotarian. Married : (2 children). Member of Council of Governors of Wycliffe College.

Gane, Leslie Harold, 1126 *Dallas Road, Victoria, B.C., Canada.* (H.), 1898–1901. Form IV. War service (Staff Sergt.), with Canadian Expeditionary Force 1914–1917. For some years Director of P. E. Gane Ltd., Bristol.

Gapp, Cecil Brady, 11 *Stewart Avenue, Ealing, W.* 5. (H.)., 1906. Auctioneer.

Gapp, Frank W., 57 *Chatsworth Gardens, Acton.* (H.), 1900–1902. Form IV. Lieut. R.N.V.R. Auctioneer and Surveyor. Married.

Gardiner, Urmston, *Walls Quarry, Brimscombe, Glos.* (h.). 3 *Elm Way, Neasden, London, N.W.* 10. (D.B.), 1914–1920. Form V. Probationer. Bank Clerk.

Gardner, Charles Eric, 41 *Compton Road, Winchmore Hill, N.* 21. (S.H.), 1891–1897. Form VI. Senior. Prefect. 1st XI Football. 2nd XI Cricket. Capt. Bristol Ariel Rowing Club 1906, member of crew that won West of England Challenge Vase in record time (1912). Sec. and Treas. of Soc. of Bristol Gleemen. Joined 6th Batt. Glos. Regt. (1914) and R.A.F. Joined Royal Flying Corps in 1915, retired with rank of Major. Was Staff Major (acting Colonel) on the S.E. Area of R.A.F. Mentioned in Despatches. Fellow Royal Empire Soc. Director George Brodie & Co., Stockbrokers, and Representative for Marsh & Baxter Ltd. Married : (2 sons).

Gardner, C. H., *Woodside, White Knight's Road, Reading.*

Gardner, Fernley, 37 *West Hill Avenue, Epsom, Surrey.* (S.H.), 1887–1894. Form VI. Senior. Excellence in Public Speaking Prize. Music Prize. Company Director and Produce Broker. J.P. Member of Council of Governors of Wycliffe College. Married : (2 sons, 2 daus.).

Gardner, Hedley Pratt, 7 *Marlborough Road, Richmond, Surrey.* (D.B.), 1907–1912. London Matric. 2nd Lieut. R.A.F. Inspector of Taxes.

Gardner, John Leonard, *Cheyne House, Cheyne Road, Stoke Bishop, Bristol.* (H.), 1894–1899. Form V. Brush Factor. Married.

Gardner, Kenneth, *Trevose, Cainscross Road, Stroud.* (D.B.), 1926–1929. Painters and Decorators, London Road.

Gardner, Michael Eric, 28 *Orpington Road, Winchmore Hill, N.* 21, (R. and S.H.), 1928–1936. Upper V. School Certif, (J.B.). On staff of Pearl Insurance Co., High Holborn.

Gardner, Owen David Fernley, 37 *West Hill Avenue, Epsom, Surrey.* (S.H.), 1932–1936. Science VI. Prefect. Higher Certif, distinction in Mathematics. Prizes for Public Service, Proportional Representation Essay. Leather Factor.

Gardner, Richard Spencer, *Beresford House, Uplands, Swansea.* (H.), 1928–1933. Form VI. House Monitor. School Certif. 1st XV Rugby. Lightweight Boxing Championship. Scout Swimming Team. Law Student at Swansea University.

Gardner, Samuel Norton. (H.), 1890–1892. Form V.

Gardner, Thomas Edward, *Trevose, Cainscross Road, Stroud.* (D.B.), 1918–1922. Form VI. Senior. 1st XI Football. 2nd XI Cricket. Foster Rifle. Open Tennis Doubles. House Prize. Builder. Married. Painters & Decorators, London Road.

Gardner, William, *Beresford House, Uplands, Swansea.* (H.), 1928–1930. Form II.

Gardner, Wintour Banks. (S.H.), 1899–1902. Form III. Despatch Rider R.E. Ironmonger.

Garlick, Charles Sidney. (H.), 1912–1914. Form VI. Senior. Prizes for Public Speaking and Music Essay. 1st place in Lit. Exam. Bristol Univ. O.T.C. Commission in King's Royal Rifle Corps. Mortally wounded in the Battle of the Somme, July 1916. (" W. & W." 45).

Garner, A. F. (D.B.), 1894–1897. Died in 1905.

Garner, Frederick John Murcott, *Greengates, Hatton, Warwick.* (H.), 1926–1929. Upper V. . Prefect. 1st XV Rugby. School Tennis Team, Bank Official.

Garner, George Robert Withey, *Roundaway Down, Crescent St., Launceston, Tasmania.* (S.H. & D.B.), 1890–1896. Form III. 2nd Lieut. King's Shropshire L.I. A.M.I.Mech.E. Consulting Engineer. Married : (2 daus.).

Gass, Martyn, 14 *Holland Road, Kensington, W. 14.* (Spr.), 1917. Form I. At Waring & Gillows, 1927.

Gauntlett, David, *Little Bedwyn, Marlborough, Wilts.* 8 *Worcester Terrace, Clifton, Bristol* 8. (Spr.), 1926–1934. Modern VI. Prefect. School Certif. 1st XV. Connaught Shooting Team. With Messrs E. S. & A. Robinson, Bristol.

Gauntlett, William Tanner, *Little Bedwyn, Marlborough, Wilts.* (Spr.). 1923–1931. Form VI. Prefect. Vice-Pres. of League. School Certif. 1st XV Rugby 1929–1931. Batchelar Cup. Certificate in Agriculture, Reading University. Farming.

Gayner, Ronald Court, 29 *Withdean Court Avenue, Brighton 6, Sussex. High Street, Thornbury, Glos.* (h.). (H.), 1906–1908. Form VI. Senior. 2nd XI Football. Sergt. R.A.S.C. Bank Accountant. Married.

Gazard, Henry John. (D.B.), 1885. Glos. Swimming Champion 1892. Swindon Amateur Heavy-weight Boxing Champion 1896. Works Manager. Married.

George, Charles Evelyn, *Fayland, Hambleden, Henley-on-Thames.* (H.), 1897–1900. Form IV. Partner in Messrs Roberts & George, Engineers. Director : The Light Production Co. ; The London Piston Ring Co., all three of 60/66 Rochester Row, Westminster, S. W. 1. Married : (3 sons).

George, Ellis Paul, 18 *Combe Park, Bath* (h.). (Spr.), 1911–1919. Form VI. Senior. Pres. of Lit. Soc. London Matric. Prizes for Literature and Public Speaking. 1st XI Cricket and Football. London representative of Messrs E. S. & A. Robinson.

George, Rowland David, *Stoke Meadow, Stoke Poges, Bucks.* (Spr.), 1914–1922. Form VI. Senior. London Matric. Music and Literature Prizes. B.A., Lincoln College, Oxford. Member of the Great Britain Olympic Coxless Four 1932. With Messrs E. S. & A. Robinson. Married (2 sons).

Gibbons, Charles Philip, *Sunnymede, Avon Road, Keynsham, Som.* (S.H.), 1909–1915. Form VI. Probationer. Camb. Senior. Lieut. Tank Corps. M.C. Company Director. Married : (2 daus, 2 sons).

Gibbons, George Lyde, *Model Farm, King's Langley, Herts.* (S.H.), 1908–1910. Form IV. Despatch Rider R.E. Farmer.

Gibbons, Philip Arnold. (S.H.), 1903–1908. Form VI. Senior. Vice-Pres. of League. London Matric. Casberd Scholar, St. John's College, Oxford. Gladstone Prize Essay. B.A. Oxon. Lieut. Bedfordshire Regt. Became History Master at Bradford Grammar School, but died in December 1927.

Gibbons, Ralph, 2 *Garston Drive, Watford, Herts.* (S.H.), 1910–1913. R.F.A. War Service 1914–1919 R.F.A. France 1915–1917 ; Italy 1917–1919. Driver B Battery, 48th Div. Electrical Engineer and Contractor. Married : (1 son).

Gibbons, William Robert, *Rostrevor, The Glen, Saltford, near Bristol.* (S.H.), 1903–1909. Senior. Vice-Pres. of League. London Matric. Prizes for Music and Excellence in Public Speaking. 2nd XI Football. Sergt. N. Som. Yeomanry. Lieut. att. 7th Hussars 1st Battle of Ypres and Mesopotamia 1914–1919. Married : (1 son, 1 dau.).

Gibbs, John Lancaster. *In Australia.* (S.H.), 1912–1917. Form V. Probationer. 2nd XI Cricket and Football. Farming.

Gibbs, Percival Victor. *In Australia.* (S.H.), 1911–1914. Form IV. Artists' Rifles. Farming. Married.

Gibbs, Peter Houlder, *Broomshill, Stroud, Glos.* Form VI. Prefect. 1st Class Scout. Oxf. and Camb. Joint Board School Certif. London Matric.

Gifford, Clive Stanley Edward, *Ashton Lodge, Selhurst Road, S. Norwood, S.E.25.* (Spr.), 1927–1935. Science VI. Prefect. A Cub-Master Ryeford. School Certif. (Hons.), London University. Medical Student.

Gifford, Vernon Alexander James, *Ashton Lodge, Selhurst Road, S. Norwood, S.E. 25.* (Spr.), 1925–1932. Science VI. Prefect. London Matric. 2nd XV Rugby. Batchelar Cup. Prizes for Music. British Empire Scholarship to Loughborough Engineering College. President Loughborough College Students Representative Council. Electrical Engineer.

Giles, Cecil Attwell, *Plough Farm, Stonehouse, Glos,* (H.), 1911–1913. Form V. Probationer. Student of Surveyors' Inst. of Great Britain 1915. War Service 1916–1919 with 2/4th Hampshires. India 1916–1917. Egyptian Exped. Force 1917–1918. Staff Corpl. at Prisoners of War Camp 1918–1919. Dublin July to Sept. 1919. Independent.

Giles, Henry Hartley, *Kemyell, Paul, Penzance.* (S.H.), 1914–1917. Form VI. Senior. London Matric. Bulb and Flower Grower.

Giles, Percy Kenneth Townsley, *Sea View, Carnglas Road, Sketty, Swansea.* (S.H.), 1909–1912. Form IV. Lieut. R.F.A. and R.H.A.. France 1915–1917. Wounded and gassed 1919. Invalided out of service 1918. Transport Contractor. Married : (2 sons).

Giles, Thomas Trevor, *Kemyell, Paul, Penzance.* (S.H.), 1916–1921. Form V. Probationer. 2nd XI Football. Bulb and Flower Grower.

Gillman, Charles Alfred. (D.B.), Accountant in Canada. Married. Deceased 1936.

Gillman, William Norris. (D.B.), In business in Australia.

Gladman, Donald Arthur, *Westgrove, Bath Road, Stroud, Glos.* (D.B., R. and H.), 1927–1933. Lower V. Tennis Singles 1932. Piano Manufacturer.

Glasbrook, Thomas Gordon. (Spr.), 1931–1934. Form V. 2nd XV Rugby. Joined the Police Force, but was fatally injured by a collision of his motor-cycle with a fallen tree on the night of January 9th, 1936. (" Star," Apr. 1936, p. 28).

Glasbrook, Thomas James, *Bangeworth Fields, Evesham.* (Spr.), 1905–1907. Form IV. Probationer. 1st XI Football. 2nd XI Cricket. Rowed in winning Pairs and Fours in many Regattas. Market Gardener and Fruit Grower. Married : (1 son, 2 daus.).

Gledhill, George Peter, *Royd House, Holmfirth, nr. Huddersfield.* (S.H.), 1931–1934. Upper Remove. Textile (Woollen) Trade.

Gobey, Stanley Clarke, *Lloyds Bank House, Sherborne, Dorset* (h.) and 274 *Maryvale Road, Bournville, Birmingham.* (R. and H.), 1928–1934. Form V. Prefect. 1st XV Rugby. 1st XI Cricket. Senior Athlete. Throwing Cricket Ball Record. Athletic Sports Team. With Cadbury Bros., Bournville.

Goddard, William, *Washwell Farm, Painswick, Glos.* (H.), 1891–1892. Form III. Farmer. Married.

Godfrey, Ivo Humphries, 9 *Abbotsford Grove, Timperley, Cheshire.* (H.), 1908–1913. Senior. 1st XI Cricket and Football. With Y.M.C.A. in France 1915–1919. Cotton Goods Salesman. Married : (2 daus, 1 son).

Godsell, Richard Thomas. (S.H.), 1891–1893. Form III. Afterwards at Clifton College and Cambridge, where he gained a Cricket Blue. Gloucestershire County Cricketer. In America.

Goldsworthy, Augustus William, *Dalry, Cefn Coed, Brecknock.* (S.H.), 1900–1903. Form VI. Senior. London Matric. 1st XI Football. Lieut. 1st Monmouthshire Regt. Mentioned in Despatches. Solicitor. Commissioner of Cefn Coed Boy Scouts Assoc.

Goldsworthy, Walter Hannah, *Garngoch Common, Fforestfach, Swansea.* (S.H.), 1903–1906. Form VI. Senior. Capt. R.E. M.C. Mining Engineer. Married : (1 dau, 1 son).

Golledge, Stephen W., *Ditcheat, Evercreech, Somerset.* (H.), 1887–1889. Sec. of Field Club. Farmer. Married.

Gooch, George Ernest, *Bremen House, Edgerton, Huddersfield, Yorks.* (D.B.), 1918. Form IV. Lieut. 5th Batt. Duke of Wellington's Regt. Cloth Manufacturer. Married : (1 son).

Goodwin, Frederick Pryse, *Sheep House, Hay, Hereford.* (H.), 1899–1900. Form III. Sometime rancher in Mexico. Married.

Goold, Harold.

Gore, Thomas Alfred Hoskins. (S.H.), 1911–1914. Form I.

Gough, H. J. (S.H.), 1887–1888.

Graham, Derek Sydney, *Fountains Farm, Kirdford, Billingshurst, Sussex.* (Spr.), 1925–1928. Form VI. House Monitor. School Certif. 2nd XV Rugby. Light-weight Boxing Winner 1926–1927. Studied at Birmingham and Oxford. Fruit Grower. Married.

Graham, Ernest Rendell, 215 *Bristol Road, Birmingham.* (S.H.), 1892–1895. Senior. 1st XI Football. 2nd XI Cricket. Pole Jump Record (8 ft. 3½ ins.). At one time Civil Engineer in Singapore and Hong Kong. Joint Managing Director of T. J. Graham & Sons (retired in 1934). Married.

Graham, James Bruce, 15 *Cliff Terrace, Hartlepool.* (Spr.), 1926–1934. Modern VI. Senior Prefect. Vice-Pres. of League. Pres. of Lit. Soc. School Certif. and Prelim. Exam. for Chartered Accountants. 1st XV Rugby. 1st XI Cricket. Heavy-weight Boxing. Tennis Team. Senior Tennis Singles. Prize for Public Speaking. 2nd Lieut. Royal Artillery. Articled to Chartered Accountant.

Graham, Leslie Irwin. (D.B.), 1908–1911. Form V. Probationer.

Gray, George Leslie. (Spr.), 1910–1915. Form V. Apprenticed to drapery firm in London, but on reaching military age enlisted in the Queen's Westminster Rifles. Was sent to France in 1918, and fought through the Hindenburg line, but was killed in action on October 11th at the age of nineteen. (" W. & W." 46).

Gray, Harry. (H.), 1904–1907. Form III. Naval Architect. Marine Surveyor and Engineer. Became Director of the firm of Dudgeon & Gray. Member of the Inst. of Naval Architects. Died from a sudden heart attack on August 5th 1932.

Greaves, Edwin. (D.B.), 1898–1904. Form III. Went to India in 1911, and held important business appointments there. Rendered arduous service in the Indian Defence Corps, and became a most popular and efficient Lieut.-Colonel. Came home in 1929 suffering from heart trouble, and died on January 23rd, 1930 at the home of his parents in Malvern. Married.

Greaves, Gordon, *Conderton, near Tewkesbury, Glos.* (S.H.), 1926–1929 Form V. House Monitor. 1st XI Cricket and Football. 1st XV Rugby. School Certif. *Farmer.*

Greaves, Samuel Jack. (S.H.), 1925–1927. Upper V. School Certif. 1st XI Football 1927 1st XV Rugby. 2nd XI Cricket. Junior Athlete. Winner of Gym Competition and Middle-weight Boxing Competition 1926. House Cricket, Relay, Shooting Teams. *Farmer.*

Greaves, Trelawney. (D.B.), 1899–1906. Form III. Contracted infantile paralysis in India, and all his life was more or less a cripple ; but with the assistance of his family and brother in India he ran a sort of Eastern curio business on a small scale. In his later years he lived with his family in comparative retirement at Malvern, and died from heart failure following influenza early in 1925.

Green, A. J. A. (D.B.), 1925–1928. Form IV. 2nd XI Cricket.

Green, E. E.

Green, Hubert Lloyd, *Kingston, Longford, Gloucester.* (S.H.), 1914–1915. Form III. R.A.S.C. *Gunmaker and Sports Outfitter.*

Green, Wallace Swanton, *Sands, Shellingford, Faringdon, Berks.* (H.), 1918–1921. Form III. *Farming.*

Greenway, Frederick Charles Garton. (Spr.), 1911–1912. Form V. Probationer. Joined Staff of Land Valuation Dept. Enlisted in the 6th Gloucestershire Regt., and in 1916 obtained a commission in the Leicestershire Regt. Was killed on the Somme in July 1916 just after his twentieth birthday. He has left behind him at Wycliffe one worthy memorial at least, for it was through him that the Chapel received its main foundation stone. (" W. & W." 47).

Greer, Arthur Laurent. (H.), 1908–1912. Form IV. 2nd XI Football. *Flight-Lieut. R.A.F.*

Greer, Samuel Laurent, 23 *Lancaster Road, Birkdale, Southport, Lancs.* (h.), and c/o *Keystone Paint and Varnish Co., Scott Street, Hull.* (H.), 1905–1908. Form IV. 2nd XI Football. 1914–1919 Major Royal Flying Corps. Squadron Leader R.A.F. Air Force Cross. *Manager Keystone Paint and Varnish Co.* Married : (1 dau.).

Greer, William Henry, 30 *Coleherne Court, London, S.W.* 5. (H.), 1901–1905. Form VI. Senior. Pres. Lit. Soc. 1st XI Cricket and Football. Junior Athlete. Has played Rugby for Midland Counties' and in Irish Trials. Capt. R.A.F. Served with the Grand Fleet at various Seaplane Stations. Later, attached to Admiral Sims' Staff (U.S. Navy)., and in Washington D.C. to Admiral Benson's Staff (C. in C. of American Navy). Married.

Gregor, George Trevor. (S.H.), 1885–1887. Probationer and member of the 1st XI Cricket. He became in time senior partner in the firm of Gregor Bros., Timber Importers at Swansea, and in 1914 was President of the Bristol Channel Timber Importers Association. He was an enthusiastic volunteer and an officer in the Welsh Garrison Artillery, holding the

Victorian Decoration. When the first O.W. Register was published (1912), he was the Major commanding the 1st Glamorgan Battery. During the War he was transferred to the R.F.A. and went to France. He had only been there a fortnight when he was killed during a tour of inspection of the batteries near Ypres in July 1917. ("W. & W." 48).

Gregor, John Bernal, 40 *Whatley Road, Clifton, Bristol.* (S.H.), 1884–1885. 2nd XV Football. Manager Messrs J. Lysaghts Ltd., Spelter Works, Bristol. Munition Work. Director Gregor Bros., Timber Importers, Swansea ; Brodo Timber & Saw Mill Co., Fishguard ; Savoy Cinema Co., Shirehampton, Bristol. Analytical Chemist (retired). Married : (2 daus.).

Greswell, Richard Frederick Clement Karslake, *Salisbury Lodge, Ham, Berkeley, Glos.* (S.H.), 1926–1929. Upper V. House Monitor.

Grey, Charles Brian, *Lime Tree Cottage, Nonington, near Dover.* (S.H.), 1919–1922. Form V. Probationer. 1st XI. Cricket. With Messrs John Harvey, Seed Merchants, Nonington. Married.

Grey, David Alan, *Bryn Eithin, 2 Arran Place, Cardiff.* (S.H.), 1917–1920. Form VI. Senior. Vice-Pres. of League. London Matric. House Prize. 1st XI Cricket. 2nd XI Football. Foster Rifle. Jeune Cup. Bank Clerk. Local Head Office Staff of Barclay's Bank Ltd. Married.

Grey, Ivor William Samuel, *Cotham, 84 Cassis Road, Watford, Herts.* (Spr.), 1922–1927. Form VI. Senior. Capt. 1st XI Cricket. 1st XV. Rugby. Treas. Lit. Soc. School Certif. Prize for Public Speaking. Bank Clerk. (Barclays Bank, Watford).

Griffin, Allan Goulstone. (S.H.), 1915–1918. Form VI. Senior. School Certif. 1st XI Cricket and Football. Went into the corn trade in Bristol. Was attacked by appendicitis in January 1921, and after an operation died in a nursing home in Clifton.

Griffin, Richard Parker, *Manningford Bohuna, Marlborough, Wilts.* (S.H.), 1917–1920. Form V. Probationer. 2nd XI Football. Farmer.

Griffin, Stuart Hellier, *Churt, near Farnham, Surrey.* (H.), 1890–1891. Form V. Probationer. Senior Camb. Retired Produce Broker, Married.

Griffiths, Dr. Arthur D. (S.H.), 1887–1888. Senior. 1st XV and in 1888 tied for the 100 yards' record. Took his M.R.C.S. and L.R.C.P. at London and his M.D. at Brussels. Practised in South Wales, becoming Medical Officer of Health for Bridgend. As Medical Referee to the Glamorgan Coal Owners' Assoc. and as District Superintendent of the Welsh Division of the St. John Ambulance Brigade did much useful work. He died in 1905 as a result of overwork in a typhoid epidemic in South Wales.

Griffiths, Haydn. (S.H.), 1913–1914. Form II.

Griffiths, Reginald Hopkins. (H.), 1913–1914. Form II. Obtained commission in the Welch Regt. and went out to France in January 1918. He received the Military Cross for his work near Cambrai in March— was three times recommended for the M.C. Returning home in June 1918, he transferred to the R.A.F. and went out again in September. On the 17th of October his machine was brought down and both he and his pilot were killed. ("W. & W." 48).

Griffiths, W. Trefor, 2 *Highcroft, North Hill, Highgate, N. 6.* (Spr.), 1910–1917. Form VI. Senior. Pres. of Lit. Soc. London Matric. Capt. 1st XI Football. 1st XI Cricket. Long Jump Record. Lieut. Tank Corps. Studied Medicine at Welsh National School of Medicine, Cardiff, and St. Bartholomew's Hospital from 1919–1923. Took up Law instead of Medicine. Barrister at Law. Civil Servant. Legal Department of Ministry of Health. Married.

Grimes, J. B. Died in America in 1906.

Grist, Digby Berkeley. Member of two Government Commissions to the Balkans. Lieut. A.S.C. Married.

Grist, George Alexander, *U.S.A.* (D.B.), 1883–1884. Government Official.

Grist, Lionel. (H.), 1891–1893. Flock Manufacturer. Married.

Grist, Samuel Harry, *The Croft, Rodborough Common, Stroud, Glos.* (H.), 1891. Form III. Ten times finalist for the King's Prize at Bisley. Shot for England (Mackinnon Cup) 1908, 1909, 1921, 1927, and for National Trophy 1908, 1909, 1911, 1921, 1926, 1927. Adjutant English Teams National Trophy 1931, 1932. Capt. English Team (Mackinnon Cup) 1935. Capt. English Team National Trophy 1936. Company Director. Married : (1 son, 1 dau.).

Grose, William Frederick. (Spr.), 1914–1918. Form VI. Probationer. 1st XI Football. In Canada.

Groundwater, Stanley Thompson, *Trevidren, Winchester Close, Esher Place, Esher, Surrey.* (H.), 1910–1914. Form VI. Senior. Vice-Pres. of League. 1st XI Football. Capt 2nd XI Cricket. House Prize. Lieut. R.F.A. 1916–1919. Capt. 2/7th Burma Rifles 1919–1921. Agency Inspector and Surveyor, Insurance Company. Married : (1 son). Deceased. (" Star," Dec. 1936, p. 29).

Grover, John Messent, *Culverend, Amberley, near Stroud.* (H.), 1927–1934. Form VI. House Monitor. School Certif. Articled to Solicitor.

Grover, Richard Steele, *Farthingloe, Theescombe Lane, Amberley, Glos.* (H.), 1921–1928. Form VI. House Monitor. Chartered Estate Agent and Surveyor. Piano Manufacturer with Stroud Piano Company.

Groves, Kenneth James Llewellyn, *Iken, Woodbridge, Suffolk.* (D.B. and H.), 1931–1935. Matric. Form. House Monitor. School Certif. Insurance Agent.

Guest, Gordon Cardo, 124 *Southam Road, Hall Green, Birmingham.* (Spr.), 1929–1936. Prefect. London Matric. Prizes for Junior and Senior Lit. Competition. Articled to Solicitor.

Guilding, Lyndon John, *The Greens, Bushley, Tewkesbury.* (S.H.), 1924–1926. Lower V. House Chess Team 1926. Farming.

Guilding, Walter John, *Africa Inland Mission, Machekos, Kenya.* (D.B.), 1901–1903. Form IV. House Prize. Junior Athlete. 2nd XI Football. Cpl. R.E. Missionary. Married.

Guilding, William Edwin. (D.B.), 1898–1902. Senior. Vice-Pres. of League. 1st XI Cricket and Football. He built up a successful practice as a Dentist in Clapham, where he also did much religious work. He died of neurasthenia in 1923.

Gunson, John Farquhar, *c/o Meredith, Esq., 2 Courtland Terrace, Merthyr.* (S.H.), 1908. Form I.

Gunter, Harry A., *Goodrich, Ross-on-Wye.* (S.H.), 1907–1910. Form II.

Guy, Leonard Northwood, *The Caves, Banwell, Som.* (S.H.), 1930–1933. Form V. House Monitor. School Certif. 2nd XV Rugby. Bank Clerk.

Gwillim, W. Roger, 4 *Shootup Hill, Brondesbury, N.W.* 2. (H.), 1926–1931. Matric. Form. Prefect. London Matric. 1st XV. Rugby.

Hackforth, Philip, 79 *Petersfield Road, Hall Green, Birmingham.* (S.H.), 1918–1921. Form IV. Commercial Traveller. Married.

Hadley, Arthur Edward, *Ham Farm, Coaley, Dursley, Glos.* (D.B.), 1922–1926. Probationer.

Hadley, Bernard. (D.B.), 1890–1891. Lived for many years at Silver Street Farm, Coaley. During S. African War volunteered for service in the Imperial Yeomanry (Royal Gloucestershire Hussars). Died of enteric fever while on active service.

Hadley, Bernard Charles, *Forthay, Dursley, Glos.* (h.). 9a *Weald Parade, Harrow Weald, Middlesex.* (D.B.), 1919–1922. Form V. Probationer. Camb. Senior. Final Exam. of Institute of Bankers. Bank Clerk. Cert. A.I.B. Married.

Hadley, Charles A., *Nelsonia, Johannesburg.* (D.B.), 1887–1889. Fought with Remington's Guides in S. African War.

Hadley, Edward Morton. (D.B.), 1882–1884. In the S. African War fought with the Imperial Yeomanry. Died at Johannesburg in 1910.

Hadley, George. (S.H.), 1904–1909. Form IV. 1st XI Football. Royal Navy. F.A.I. Auctioneer.

Hadley, Joseph Ernest, *Ham Farm, Coaley, Glos.* (D.B.), 1919–1923. Probationer. Farming.

Hadley, Raymond, *Silver Street, Coaley, Glos.* (D.B.), 1889–1892. Form III. Farmer.

Haines, Alfred James Farmer, *Ashcroft, Bengeworth, Evesham,* (Spr.), 1905–1906. Form II. Evesham Rowing Club Four. Victorious in eleven regattas 1911. 2nd Lieut. Fruit Farmer.

Hall, Arthur James. (H.), 1906–1907. Form IV. Probationer. 2nd XI Cricket. Bank Clerk.

Hall, Frederick Geoffrey, *Springdale, Rodborough Avenue, Stroud, and* 12 *King Street, Stroud.* (D.B.), 1921–1927. Stamp Merchant.

Hall, Hartley Percival. *In New Zealand.* (S.H.), 1903–1906. Form III. 2nd XI Cricket and Football. L/Cpl. Cheshire Yeomanry. Farmer, Married.

Hall, John Milner, *Springdale, Rodborough Avenue, Stroud.* (D.B.), 1921–1923. Form V. Probationer. School Certif. Associate Auctioneers' & Estate Agents' Inst. Estate Agent. Died October 4th, 1937.

Hamar, Arthur Samuel T., *Builth.* (Spr.), 1907.

Hammer, Reginald Bigwood, (H.), 1902–1904. Marine Engineer.

Hammond, F. W., *Gwenhalden, St. Lawrence Road, Chepstow, Mon.* (H.), 1883–1884. House Prize. Civil Engineer.

Hampton, Arthur Mervyn, *Bracebridge,* 16 *Woodland Avenue, Coventry.* (S.H.), 1917–1921. Form V. Probationer. Caterer. Married.

Hampton, Frank Edmund, *Southwood, Prestatyn, N. Wales.* (S.H.), 1883–1884. General Manager, Iron Steel & Brass Foundries. John Sumners & Sons Ltd., Shotton, Chester.

Hampton, H. L. (S.H.), 1887–1889.

Hanby, Cecil J., *Upper Butters End, Hartpury, Glos.* (S.H.), 1911–1913. L/Cpl. 9th Worcs. Regt. Farmer. Married : (2 sons, 1 dau.).

Hancox, Avery Stallard, *Great Alne, near Alcester, Warwicks.* (Spr.), 1915–1922. Form VI. Senior. 2nd XI Cricket. 1st in England City & Guilds Milling Exam. Flour Miller.

Hanks, Geoffrey G., *Manor House, Naunton, Glos.* (S.H.), 1930–1932. Upper III. 2nd XV Rugby.

Hanman, A. H. 1892.

Hannah, Clive Hawkridge, *Buckhurst, Hamilton Road, Sherwood Rise, Notts.* (H.), 1905–1907. Cpl. Despatch Rider, R.E. 1914 Star. Wholesale General Dealer.

Hannah, Frank Egbert, *Gwynfryn, Tylorstown, Glam.* (S.H.), 1898–1900. Probationer. 2nd XI Cricket and Football. Capt. R.F.A. Colliery Manager.

Hannah, Walter William *Pochin, Tredegar, Mon.* (S.H.), 1899–1903. Senior. Vice-Pres. of League. Sec. of Field Club. London Matric. 1st XI Football. Sergt. R.E. Electrical Engineer. Married.

Hansard, Archie. (S.H.), 1910–1911. Probationer. 2nd XI Football. Entered Lloyds Bank. Died of pneumonia 1915.

Hansard, Trevor Thomas, *Maesffrwd, Merthyr Tydvil.* (S.H.),1911–1913. Probationer. 2nd XI Football. Capt. 5th Welch Regt. (T.A.), Lieut. Labour Corps. France 1917–1919. Mentioned in Despatches. Mineral Water Manufacturer. Married : (1 son).

Hansen, Paul, *Blaagaardsgade 4, Copenhagen N., Denmark.* (S.H.), 1929–1930. Lower Remove.

Hansen, Svend Christian, *Anglaesvei 30, Ringsted, Box 45, Denmark.* (Spr.), 1930–1931. 2nd XV Rugby. " Business Leader."

Hardess, Arthur John, *Eastgate, Gloucester.* (S.H.), 1905–1906. Form III. 2nd Lieut. Berks Regt. In Belgium.

Harding, Edgar John. *In Canada.* (S.H.), 1891–1895. Form V. A.C.A. J.P. for Province of Saskatchewan. Lieut. R.A.F. Chartered Accountant.

Harding, L. Nelson, *Dumas House, Berkeley, Glos.* (h.). *British Bank of America, Sao Paulo, Brazil, South America.* (S.H.), 1905–1907. Form IV. S. African Mounted Rifles, Horse Artillery and R.N.R. Bank Official. Married : (1 son).

Harding, Norman. (H.), 1916–1917. Form I. Died March 1917. ("Star," April 1917).

Harding, Philip William. (S.H.), 1891–1897. Form VI. Senior. Pres. of Lit. Soc. London Matric. First President of League. Went out to Cape Town in the service of the National Bank of Africa, took his B.A. at the University there, and became an Inspector of the Bank, and Lecturer on Banking at Pretoria University. He was on holiday with his family in England when he was taken ill and died on July 2nd 1925 in a nursing home at Paignton. (" Star," Aug. 1925).

Hardwick, W. H. (H.), 1883–1884. 1st XV Rugby. Farmer. Deceased, Dec. 1922.

Hardy, Alphonse. (Spr.), 1915–1917. War Refugee. Returned to his native Belgium.

Harmer, Reginald Harry, 57 *Chancery Lane, London, W.C.* 2. (Spr.), 1907–1915. Form VI. Senior. Cambridge Senior. 1st XI Football. Capt. 2nd XI Cricket. Lieut. R.A.F. 1918. Western Front 1916-1918. Battles of the Somme ; German Offensive. Wounded Apr. 1918. Consultant, Printing and Advertising. Married.

Harmston, Archibald Harry. (S.H.), 1905–1906. Form II.

Harmston, Roy Meadows, *Glenvellyn, Pontypool, Mon.* (S.H.), 1922–1928. Prefect. Capt. 1st XV Rugby. 1st XI Football. Senior Athlete. School Certif. Solicitor.

Harper, J. F. (S.H.), 1892–1893. Lieut. in the Imperial Yeomanry, and volunteered for service in S. Africa, where he was killed.

Harper, Thomas Arthur, 68 *Woodland Road, Northfield, Birmingham.* (S.H.), 1888–1889. Needle Manufacturer. Married.

Harries, Ivor Ewart, 38 *Grange Road, Ealing, London, W.* 5. (S.H.), 1912–1918. Form VI. Senior. 1st XI Football. M.R.C.S. (Eng.), L.R.C.P. (Lond.). Doctor. Married : (2 sons, 2 daus.).

Harries, W. W. (S.H.), 1889. Sometime tutor in Montreal.

Harris, A. E., 198 *Cathedral Road, Cardiff.* (S.H.), 1893.

Harris, C. Howard. (H.), 1911–1913. Form IV. 2nd XI Football. Held an appointment in the Government Land Valuation Dept, and then entered Lloyds Bank. In 1914 joined the Bankers' Battalion of the Royal Fusiliers. Spent six months in the front line in France ; was badly wounded in the Battle of the Somme on October 8th, 1918 and died in the Field Ambulance two days later. ("W. &W." 49).

Harris, Donald Frank, 50 *Broad Street, Bristol.* (H.), 1904–1906. Form IV. Probationer. Capt. Glos. Regt. Solicitor.

Harris, Edward P., *Rydal Mount, Bodenham Road, Hereford.* (H.), 1925–1926. Form II.

Harris, James Edward, *St. Leonard's, Horcott, Fairford, Glos.* (D.B.), 1916–1921. Form V. Probationer. Bank Clerk. Married.

Harris, Joseph Robert. (S.H.), 1888–1890. Miller.

Harrison, James Alfred, *Clinton House, Thrupp, Stroud.* (D.B.), 1907–1909. Form IV. Lieut. 1st Dorset Regt. Bank Clerk.

Harrison, Maynard Colchester, *Dynas,* 24 *Fields Park Road, Newport, Mon.* (S.H.), 1891–1892. Form V. Probationer. 1st XI Football and 1st XV Rugby. Member of Inst. of Civil Engineers and of Structural Engineers. Fellow of Royal Soc. of Arts. Civil Engineer. Divisional Docks Engineer (G.W.R.) Past Chairman S. Wales Branch of Inst. of Civil and of Structural Engineers. Married : (1 son, 2 daus.).

Harrison, Robert Thomas, *Lloyds Bank House, Newnham, Glos.* (H.), 1905–1908. Form V. Senior. Vice-Pres. of 'League. Capt. 1st XI Cricket. 1st XI Football. Lieut. R.F.A. Bank Manager. Married : (1 son).

Harroway, E. A., *Woodside, Stonegate Rd., Moortown, Leeds, Staffs.* (S.H.), 1914–1916. Form V. Married.

Hart, Edmund Scambler, *Dinglewood,* 34 *Eagle Brow, Lymm, Warrington.* (Spr.), 1916–1920. Form VI. Senior. Pres. of Lit. Soc. London Matric. Prize for Public Speaking. 1st XI. Football. B.Sc. (London). A.R.S.M. A.I.M.M. Works Manager. Married : (1 dau.).

Hart, Edward Dunstan, 16 *Glebe Crescent, Hendon, N.W.* 4. (Spr.), 1916–1921. Form VI. Senior. Pres. of Lit. Soc. London Matric. Prize for Public Speaking. Exhibitioner and Winner of Open Scholarship at Royal College of Music. A.R.C.M., L.R.A.M. Public Singer and Exponent of Voice Production. Touring Australia. Married : (1 son, 1 dau.).

Hart, Edward Goyen. *In South Africa.* (Spr.), 1902–1904. Form IV.

Hart, Miles Goyen. *In South Africa.* (Spr.), 1900–1902. Form III. Bank Clerk. Served in South African Forces.

Hart, Vincent Edward Lloyd, *The Cross, Nailsworth, Glos.* (S.H.), 1917–1927. Form VI. Prefect. Pres. of Lit. Soc. Editor of " Star." School Certif. Heavy-weight Boxing Champ. 1st XI Cricket. 2nd XI Football. 1st XV Rugby. Medical Practitioner. L.R.C.P., M.R.C.S. Emergency Officer, House Physician of the Cardiac Dept. and Receiving Food Officer at the London Hospital.

Hartland, Henry Bernard, *Culver Lodge, Waterloo, Poole.* (H.), 1904–1907. Upper III. Flour Milling.

Hartland, Philip Gerrard, *Birnbeck, Cheriton Road, Alresford, Hants.* (H.), 1906–1911. Form IV. War Service 1915–1919, Corpl. R.E. Despatch Rider, France and the East. Builder. Married : (1 dau.).

Hartland, Wilfred, *Endsleigh, Connaught Place, Weston-super-Mare.* (H.), 1905–1909. Form III. 2nd XI Football. Sergt. R.E.

Hartley, Arthur Everett, *Fairmount, Red Hill, Castleford, and Barclay's Chambers, Castleford, Yorks.* (H.), 1901–1905. Form VI. Senior. Vice-Pres. of League. Pres. of Lit. Soc. House Prize. 1st XI Cricket and Football. Capt. R.A.F. Solicitor and Notary. Married : (2 daus, 1 son).

Hartley, James F. (D.B.), 1893–1899. Form VI. Woollen Manufacturer.

Hartley, John Poles, *Lynch Farm, Alwalton, Peterborough.* (H.), 1901–1902. Form III. Farmer. Married : (1 son).

Harvey, Frank Emery, *Norton Hall, Norton-on-Tees, Co. Durham.* (S.H.), 1919–1925. Form VI. Senior. Pres. of League and Lit. Soc. London Matric. Capt. 1st XI Cricket and Football. Senior Athlete. Woodley Cup. Foster Rifle. Jeune Cup. House Prize. Univ. of Bristol, B.Sc. Ph.D. Technical Chemist. I.C.I. (F. & S.P.), Billingham.

Hastie, Thomas David. (D.B.), 1918. Died of pneumonia in February 1922. ("Star," Apr. 1922).

Hastings, Dr. Somerville, 43 *Devonshire Street, Portland Place, London, W. 1.* (D.B.), 1890–1896. Form VI. Senior. London Matric. House Prize. M.B., M.S. (Lond.), F.R.C.S. (Eng.), Capt. R.A.M.C. Labour M.P. for Reading and Private Sec. of Minister of Education in Government 1924, 1931. Surgeon to Ear and Throat Dept., Middlesex Hospital. Ear, Nose and Throat Surgeon. Chairman, Hospital and Medical Services Committee, London County Council 1934–1936. Member of Council of Governors of Wycliffe College. Married : (1 son, 1 dau.).

Hatcher, Vernon Bennett *Silver Wells, Ingestre Street, Hereford.* 35 *Carnarvon Road, Redland, Bristol* 6 (h.). (Spr.), 1922–1924. Form IV. Accountant (Insurance).

Hatherell, Benjamin Robert, *Calcot, near Tetbury, Glos.* (H.), 1907–1910. Form IV. Cpl. Tank Corps. D.C.M. and M.M. Farmer.

Hatherly, Rev. Arthur Wilfrid. (D.B.), 1887–1889. Senior. London Matric. House Prize. Sometime Mansel Exhibitioner, St. John's College, Oxford. M.A. Oxon. Priest (C. of E.).

Hatherly, Rev. Norman, *Crick Rectory, Rugby.* (D.B.), 1886–1887. Sometime St. Andrew's Scholar at Oxford. M.A. Oxon. Rector of Crick, Northants. Rural Dean of Haddon P. 1936. Married : (1 son).

Hathway, Frank Edwin, 58 *Woodlands Road, Ilford, Essex.* (R. & H.), 1929–1936. Science VI. House Monitor. School Certif. 1st XI Cricket. 1st XV. Speaking Prize. Now at Port au Prince, Haiti.

Hawkin, Robert Michael Pearse, 30 *Hampstead Way, N.W.* 11. (Spr.), 1925–1928. Form II. University College, Oxford 1935.

Hawkin, Martin Driffield, 30 *Hampstead Way, N.W.* 11. (Spr.), 1925–1928. Form IV. Queen's College, Cambridge 1932–1935. B.A. Journalist ("Bystander.").

Hawkins, Charles S. (S.H.), 1890–1891. Form III.

Hawkins, Hengler Joseph. (S.H.), 1905–1907. Form III. Royal Glos. Hussars. Farmer. Has died.

Hawkins, Hugh Harry, *The Villa, Harescombe, Glos.* (S.H.), 1891–1893. Form I. Farmer.

Hawkins, H. J. 1891–1893. Form II.

Hawkins, John Sylvester, *Westminster Bank House, High Street, Southend-on-Sea, Essex.* (S.H.), 1929–1932. Matric VI. House Monitor. Cambridge Senior. 2nd XV Rugby. Auctioneer and Surveyor.

Hawkins, Montague James. (D.B.), 1897–1899. Form III.

Hawkins, Thomas George, *Bridge Farm, Frocester, Glos.* (D.B.), 1890–1892. Form III. Farmer. Married : (1 son, 2 daus.).

A LOWER SCHOOL GAME IN THE 'MIDDLE FIELD,' WITH HAYWARDSFIELD AS SEEN FROM THE S.W.

THE 1ST ELEVEN, AUTUMN, 1924

B. Woodman   W. Jackson   J. Clark   N. Bazzard
W. Wakefield   R. Carter   G. D. Lloyd (Capt.)   F. Harvey   W. Lockey
M. Cullimore   D. G. Williams

IVY GROVE
(as it was before the addition of the new Sanatorium)

A MASTERS' GROUP, MAY, 1924.

Mr. Webb, Mr. Dixon, Mr. Caudle, Mr. Bevan, Mr. Timpson, Mr. French.
Mr. Thuyn, Mr. Ward, Mr. T. M. Sibly, The Headmaster, Mr. Reade, Mr. Hugill, Mr. Pryce.

Hayes, Christopher Walter. (H.), 1899.

Hayes, George Forbes Raymond, *Saltaire, Porthcawl, Glam.* (H.), 1926–1935. Matric. Form. House Monitor. London Matric. School Certif. Harmston Music Prize. Undergraduate at Trinity College, Cambridge.

Hayes, John Cecil, *Boundary Court, Selsley, near Stroud, and* 44 *Bedford Row, London, W.C.* 1. (H.), 1905–1908. Form VI. 1st XI Football. Senior Athlete. Lieut. M.G.C. Member of Council of Governors of Wycliffe College. Paper Manufacturer.

Hayes, John William Gordon, *Wyndonin, Sketty Green, Swansea.* (S.H.), 1918–1922. Form V. Probationer. Morris Distributor. Company Director. Chairman West Wales Division of the Motor Agents' Association. Married : (1 son, 1 dau.).

Hayes, Raymond Stanley, *Saltaire, Porthcawl, Glam.* (H.), 1892–1896. Form IV. J.P. for Glamorgan. Member of S. Wales Inst. of Engineers. Owner-Director of Engineering Works. Member of Council of Trinity College, Carmarthen. Member of Council of Governors of Wycliffe College. Married :(5 sons, 1 dau.).

Hayman, Leonard Augustus, 610 *Kelowna, B.C., Canada.* (H.), 1892–1896. Form IV. Master's Certificate for minor inland waters of Canada. Captain. Married.

Haynes, William Brewster. (H.), 1900–1904. Form VI. 1st XI Football. House and Music Prizes. Lieut. R.F.A. Mentioned in Despatches Farmer.

Hayward, Alec William Morley, *Trafalgar House, Tewkesbury* (h.). *Watledge House, Tewkesbury.* (S.H.), 1914–1917. Form IV. 1st XI Football. 2nd XI Cricket. Music Prize. 4th Dorset Regt. Ironmonger. Married.

Hayward, Cecil Norman, *Watledge House, Tewkesbury.* (S.H.), 1903–1906. Form V. Senior. London Matric. Vice-Pres. of League. 1st XI Football. 2nd XI Cricket. Borough Chamberlain and Treasurer to Corporation of Tewkesbury. Head of Haywards Ltd. (Tewkesbury). Q.M.S. Royal Glos. Hussars (Yeomanry). Lieut. R.F.A. Served in France. Ironmonger and Electrical Contractor. Married : (1 son, 2 daus.).

Hayward, Charles Edward Ronald, 42 *Church Road, West Drayton, Middlesex.* (S.H.), 1920–1922. Form VI. Senior. London Matric. 2nd XI Football. Area Lands Officer, Air Ministry. Chartered Surveyor (P.A.S.I.). Married : (2 daus.).

Hayward, Reginald Brydes. (S.H.), 1906–1909. Form VI. Senior. Vice-Pres. of League. London Matric. House Prize. 1st XI Football. 2nd XI Cricket. Officer of Customs and Excuse. Married. Died in Aug., 1928.

Headly, Harold J. (S.H.), 1906–1908. Form V.

Headly, John Alexander, *Ganges Harbour, Salt Spring Island, British Columbia, Canada.* (H.), 1900–1902. Form IV. Farmer.

Healey, Robert Geoffrey, *Moorcroft, Haywood, Lancs.* (Spr.), 1923–1933. Modern VI. Head Prefect. Pres. of Lit. Soc. Higher School Certif. Prizes for Excellence in Public Speaking and P.R. Essay. B.A. (Econ.), St. John's College, Cambridge. Rope and Twine Manufacturer.

Healey, Stuart Mason, *Selsley, Manchester Road, Heywood, Lancs.* (Spr.), 1916–1924. Form VI. Senior. Vice-Pres. of League. Pres. of Lit. Soc. House Prize. M.A. Lincoln College, Oxford. Assoc. Manchester College of Technology. Rope and Twine Manufacturer. Married : (1 dau.).

E

Hearson, Henry John Spencer, *Stepstone Lane, Knowle, Braunton, Devon.* (Spr.), 1917–1922. Form V. Journalist. Married.

Heath, George Alexander, *Bradley House, Wotton-under-Edge, Glos.* (h.). *and Kenya, E. Africa.* (Spr.), 1907–1911. Form V. Probationer. 2nd XI Football and Cricket. Capt. R.A.F. and Glos. Regt. Hon. Game Warden of Kenya. Mine Owner, Kenya, E. Africa. Married : (1 son).

Heath, J. G. Form III.

Heath, John Long, *Bradley House, Wotton-under-Edge, Glos.* (h.). (Spr.), 1906–1907. Form II. War Service in Australian Navy. Western Australian Government. Married.

Heath, Reginald Ivan, *Bradley House, Wotton-under-Edge, Glos.* (h.). (Spr.), 1906–1908. Form V. Officer in R.A.F. Superintendent Utica Air Force, U.S.A. Married : (1 son, 1 dau.).

Hedges, Ernest C., *14 Ravensbourne Gardens, W. Ealing, W.* 13. (H.), 1893–1896. Form IV. Merchant. Married.

Hemmens, Joseph Anthony, *Bank House, Hurle Road, Clifton, Bristol* 8. (H.), 1927–1930. House Monitor. P.L. and 1st Class Scout. Pioneer and Rover. School Certif. Articled Clerk.

Hemsted, John Rustat, *52 Springvale Terrace, Glasgow, N.* (Spr.), 1931–1936. Form VI. Senior Prefect. Pres. Lit. Soc. and League. 1st XI Cricket. 1st XV Rugby. Higher Certif. Open Exhibition and State Scholarship to St. Catherine's College, Cambridge. Undergraduate.

Henderson, Graeme Westwood, *Craig Rossie, Letham Road, Perth* (h.). *c/o Gen. Acc. Five & Life Assce. Corp. Ltd., 66 Cadzow Street, Hamilton, Lanarkshire.* (H.), 1929–1931. Matric. Form. Insurance Inspector with above Corporation. 2nd Lieut. (Queen's Own Royal Glasgow Yeomanry) Field Brigade, Royal Artillery, T.A.

Henly, Henry John, *Harnhill Manor, Cirencester, Glos.* (S.H.), 1932. Lower III.

Henly, Robert, *Harnhill Manor, Cirencester, Glos.* (S.H.), 1931–1932.

Heppell, Sidney Kirkness, *Marsden, Thompson's Avenue, Victoria Park, Cardiff.* (S.H.), 1899–1903. Form IV. 1st XI Football. Staff Sergt. R.E. Manager of Iron Foundry.

Heppell, Wilfred Harrison, *Galli Rise, Ystrad Rhondda.* (S.H.), 1900–1904. Form IV. 1st XI Football. Mining Engineer and Colliery Manager.

Herne, Alan Dudley Colrick. (Spr.), 1907–1911. Form VI. 1st XI Cricket. House Prize. Capt. 11th Welch Regt. Died in February 1928.

Herne, Arthur John, *15 Church Avenue, Penarth.* (S.H.), 1883–1884. Insurance Broker. Widower.

Herne, Edmund Donald Colrick. (S.H.), 1899–1905. Form VI. Capt. R.A.F. Salesman and Demonstrator for Cadiallac Motor Co.

Herne, Keith Colrick. (S.H.), 1901–1902. Form I. Practised as an auctioneer in Birmingham. Joined his old Territorial Unit, the Royal Glamorganshire Artillery, and obtained a commission in the Royal Warwickshire Regt. in which he became a Captain. On July 1st 1916 was badly wounded on the Somme, and afterwards invalided home with severe shell shock. He died of pneumonia in March 1919. (" W. & W." 54).

Herne, Leslie Colrick. (S.H.), 1908–1909. Form II. After leaving school went out with his people to Canada, and in 1914 enlisted in a British Columbia Regiment. Received a commission and served on the Western

Front from May 1915 to December 1917, when he was wounded for the second time. After the War he held a business appointment in India, but died from ptomaine poisoning, in Bombay on September 21st, 1927. (" Star," Dec. 1927, p. 14).

Herne, Roy Colrick. (Spr. and S.H.), 1907–1909. Form III. Cpl. Canadian Seaforths. Was in British Columbia. Married.

Heyward, Norman Grant, 18 *Downs Park East, Durdham Downs, Bristol.* (H.), 1920–1923. Upper V. Probationer. School Certif. Camb. Senior. Prize for Public Speaking.

Higgins, Percival Edward J., *St. Malo, Meridian Road, Redland, Bristol* (h.). 60 *Park Street, Bristol.* (H.), 1898–1901. Form VI. Probationer. Cpl. Royal Glos. Hussars. Director of Higgins & Sons, Ltd., Bristol. Married.

Higgs, George Alfred, 50 *Amherst Crescent, Hove* 4, *Sussex.* (S.H.), 1903–1909. Form VI. Senior. Pres. of Lit. Soc. Senior Cambridge. 1st XI Football. Sergt. Manchester Regt. Cadet Pilot, R.A.F. Dairy Analyst. Married.

Highfield, Rev. Henry, *Crabtree Butts, Pickering, Yorks.* (S.H.), 1883–1884. Senior. Pres. of Lit. Soc. 1st XV Rugby. M.A. London and Cambridge. Goldsmith Exhibitioner (Camb. 1893). 30 years Principal of Wesley College, Colombo. Married. Retired.

Hill, Evan John, 15 *Victoria Buildings, Commissioner St., Johannesburg, South Africa.* (D.B.), 1892–1896. Form V. Coal Merchant. Married.

Hill, Geoffrey Ashton. (D.B.), 1918–1922. Form III.

Hill, Herbert Edward. (H.), 1911–1913. Form III.

Hill, Herbert Hopson, *Fallows Green, Harpenden, Herts,* (D.B.), 1910–1915. Form V. Probationer. 2nd Lieut. R.A.F. Architect and Surveyor. Married : (2 sons).

Hill, John Holbrook, *St. Brendan's, Pencisely Road, Cardiff.* (S.H.), 1920–1925. Form V. 2nd XI Cricket and Football. Medical Student at Cardiff Royal Infirmary.

Hill, Joseph Hyde. (D.B.), 1893–1895. Form III. Farmer.

Hill, Maurice William, *Inland Revenue Office, Johannesburg.* (D.B.), 1892–1897. Form V. Senior. 1st XI Cricket. Union of South Africa Customs Office. Qualified as Residential Magistrate.

Hill, Mervyn Richard, *Pennall's End, Coaley, Glos.* (D.B.), 1906–1908. Farmer.

Hill, Norman Dan. (D.B. and S.H.), 1902–1909. Form VI. Senior. London Matric. 1st XI Cricket and Football. House Prize. Lieut. C.L.C. Officer of Customs and Excise. Married.

Hill, Reginald Charles, *Sherdale, Estcourt Road, Gloucester.* (D.B.), 1900–1905. Form VI. Probationer. Ex Salvage Engineer (R.N.). Associate Member of Soc. of Engineers (London). Clarke Premium and Diploma (for technical papers and lectures) 1922 and 1923. Hon. Sec. St. Mark's Church Council, Gloucester. Engineer-in-Charge, Gloucester Corp. Electricity Dept. Married : (1 dau.)

Hill, Reginald Thomas Murrell, *Elmsholme, Carmarthen Road, Westbury-on-Trym, Bristol.* (Spr.), 1923–1925. Form V. Timber Trade. Married : (1 dau.).

Hill, Stanley Joseph, 27 *Brocklehurst Gardens, Mill Hill, N.W.* 7. (D.B.), 1911–1915. Form IV. Bank Cashier.

Hill, Thomas Harry, *Ledbury, Herefordshire.* (H.), 1907–1909. Form V. 2nd XI Cricket and Football. Lieut. Worcs. Regt. M.C. Builder.

Hill, Tom Hawkins. (D.B.), 1892–1894. Form II. Farmer. Married. Died in 1932.

Hill, William Francess, *Queensland, Australia.* (S.H.), 1922–1923. Form I.

Hill, William Hopson, *Whitehall, Stroud.* (D.B.), 1889–1893. Probationer. Agricultural Implement Engineer. Married.

Hill, William Hopson (Jr.), *Five Willows, Hythe End, near Staines, Middlesex.* (D.B.), 1915. Form I. Estate Agent. Married.

Hillier, George Norman, *Mersa, Matruh, Western Province, Egypt.* (H.), 1902–1906. Form III. Major. Camel Transport Co. A.S.C. Sub-Inspector in Govt. Dept. of Agriculture, Egypt. Married.

Hillier, Kenneth John, *Nairobi, Kewstoke Road, Weston-super-Mare.* (R. and S.H.), 1923–1934. Form V.

Hillier, Dr. Thomas Lucas, *Tolcarne, Boscastle, N. Cornwall.* (H.), 1909–1913. Form VI. Senior. Pres. of League and Lit. Soc. A.S.M. Camb. Senior. House Prize. 1st XI Football. 2nd XI Cricket. B.A., M.B., B.Ch. (Cantab.), M.R.C.S. (Eng.), L.R.C.P. (Lond.). Surg-Lieut. H.M.S. " Magnolia " and " Resolution." Medical Missionary. Surgeon to China Inland Mission Hospital. Paoning, Sze, W. China. Now in practice in Cornwall. Married : (3 sons, 1 dau.).

Hince, John Ernest Foy, 429 *Stapleton Road, Eastville, Bristol.* (H.), 1932–1935. Matric. Form. 2nd XV Rugby. Bank Clerk.

Hobbs, Alfred Percy, *Waylands, R.R., 1 Royal Oak, Victoria, B.C. Canada.* (D.B.), 1890–1895. Upper III. Served in S. Africa in Imperial Yeomanry (1900–1901). Queen's Medal with bars. Sergt. 31st Canadians 1914–1918. 1915 Star. Victory and General Service Medals. Fruit Farming. Married : (1 dau.).

Hobbs, F. H. Form III.

Hobbs, Harold J., *La Matilde, Santa Inies, F.C.O., Argentine Republic, S. America.* (S.H.), 1931–1935. Form V. Prefect. 1st XV Rugby. 1st XI Cricket. Athletic Team. With the firm of Hopkins y Gardom, 185 Pasco Colon, Buenos Aires, engaged on railway construction.

Hobson, Alexander Petrie, *Mayfield, London Road, Cheltenham.* (H.), 1905. Form IV. Capt. Middlesex Regt. Served in France 1915–1920, and was on H.Q. Staff in Rouen. Widower : (1 son).

Hobson, Edmund Godfrey, *Hazelwood, The Camp, near Stroud.* (D.B.), 1928–1932. Form VI. Prefect. Vice-Pres. of League. Sec. and Treas. of Lit. Soc. Editor of " Star." Higher Certif. Senior Literature Competition and Public Speaking Prizes.

Hobson, R. A. Died at his home in Trinidad.

Hoddinott, Harvey Maurice, *Weton, Lechlade, Glos.* (S.H.), 1900–1902. Form III. Farmer.

Hodges, Edgar, *Nant Goch, Llwydcoed, Aberdare.* (H.), 1912–1918. Form VI. Senior. Vice-Pres. of League. Senior Camb. House Prize. 2nd XI Football. Clothier.

Hodges, William Jayne, *Bronwydd, Llwydcoed, Aberdare, Glam.* (H.), 1908–1912. Form VI. Senior. Pres. of Lit. Soc. London Matric. Public Speaking Prize. 1st XI Football. Lieut. 5th Batt. Welch Regt. In Gallipoli, Egypt and Palestine. Clothier. Married : (1 son, 1 dau.)

Hodgkinson, Douglas, 4 *Kirkmoor Terrace, Clitheroe, Lancs.* (S.H.), 1930–1935. Matric. Form. Prefect. Vice-Pres. of League. School Certif. 1st XV Rugby. Heavy-weight Boxing. 1st XI Cricket. Working for Matric at Blackburn. Clerk, County Bank.

Hodgkinson, Eric, 4 *Kirkmoor Terrace, Clitheroe, Lancs.* (S.H.), 1928–1932. Science VI. Prefect. School Certif. 1st XV Rugby. 1st XI Cricket. Intermed. Exam. of Inst. of Chartered Accountants 1935. Accountant.

Hodgkinson, George, 4 *Kirkmoor Terrace, Clitheroe, Lancs.* (S.H.), 1926–1928. Lower IV. 1st XI Football. 1st XV Rugby. 1st XI Cricket. Assistant Surveyor of the Erith Urban District Council.

Hodgkiss, Francis Hall, *Rua Venezuela* 15, *Jardin America, Sao Paulo, Brazil, S. America.* (S.H.), 1929–1933. Form VI. House Monitor. Scout Swimming Team. Connaught Shooting Team. 2nd XV Rugby.

Hodgkiss, James Hall, *Rua Venezuela* 15, *Jardin America, Sao Paulo, Brazil.* (S.H.), 1929–1933. Upper V. School Certif.

Hogarth, James Crosbie, *Kevoly, Llyswen Road, Cyncoed, Cardiff.* (S.H.), 1918–1923. Form VI. Senior. Vice-Pres. of League. Sec. and Treas. of Lit. Soc. Oxford Certif. Capt. Football and Cricket 1st XI's. Open Tennis Singles. Rowell Cup. Jeune Cup. Foster Rifle. House Prize. Commercial Traveller and Agent. Married : (1 dau.).

Hogarth, William Graham, *The Haining, Cyncoed Road, Cardiff.* (S.H.), 1922–1925. Form V. Probationer. 1st XI Cricket and Football. In business.

Holborow, Arthur Conrad, *Shanghai Club, Shanghai.* (D.B.), 1890–1896. Form V. Lieut. Glos. Regt. Solicitor.

Holborow, Guy Randolph, *Rosendale, 7 Somerdale Avenue, Bloomfield Road, Bath.* (D.B.), 1890–1896. Form III. Glos. Regt. Engineer.

Holborow, Henry Ratcliffe, *Randwick House, Pannel Ash Road, Harrogate.* (D.B.), 1890–1895. Form V. Company Director. Married : (4 sons. 2 daus.).

Holborow, Richard Wraxall, *Stafford House, The Chipping, Tetbury, Glos.* (R. and H.), 1930–1935. Matric. Form. School Certif. Articled to Architect. Returning to Building Trade,

Holborow, Robert John, *Glenure House, Cirencester Road, Charlton Kings, near Cheltenham.* (H.), 1931–1936. Lower V. Student at Reading University.

Holborow, Ulrich Norman, *Beachcroft, Trowbridge, Wilts.* (D.B.), 1887–1891. Probationer. Cloth Merchant. Married.

Holborow, Wilfred H. (D.B.), 1890–1895. Form VI. Probationer. Joined Messrs. Curtis, Jenkins, Chartered Accountants, Bristol. Just before his Final C.A. exam. he died from consumption in 1903.

Holbrook, Arthur Denton. (Spr.), 1904–1907. Probationer. 2nd XI Football. Engineer with White Star Steamship Co.

Holder, Harold J. (H.), 1899–1903. Form V. 1st XI Cricket and Football.

Holloway, Harold Hugh, *c/o United Drug Co.,* 21 *Trafalgar Road, Moseley, Birmingham.* (S.H.), 1900–1903. Form VI. Territorial Manager to English Branch of United Drug Co., Boston, Mass. Lieut. R.G.A. Married.

Holman, Frederick Lionel, 7 *Morrab Road, Penzance, ¦Cornwall.* (Spr.), 1928–1932. Lower V. Marine Engineer.

Holmes, A.

Holtham, George Frederick. (S.H.), 1900–1902. Form IV. Farmer. Married. Has died.

Holtham, Leslie Cyril. (Spr.), 1904–1909. Form IV. Served in the Army in 1915 and 1916, and was discharged as medically unfit. He died early in 1924.

Hooper, Ernest R. (D.B.), 1895–1899. Form V. Engineer. Married.

Hooper, Herbert Edward, 3 *Dyer Street, Cirencester.* (D.B.), 1885–1887. Married.

Hooper, Sidney Arthur. (D.B.), 1886–1887. Married.

Hope, Douglas Goodwin, *Rozel, West Bank, Dorking, Surrey.* (S.H.), 1918–1922. Form V. Probationer. Director and Secretary, C. J. Peirson & Co., Ironmongers and Heating Engineers. Married : (1 dau.).

Hopgood, Reginald Salisbury, *Hillbrow, Caswell Road, Mumbles, Glam.* (Spr.), 1900–1904. Form IV. Probationer. Vice-Pres. of League. 1st XI Cricket and Football. Lieut. Welch Regt.

Hopkins, Alfred Daniel, 3 *Kipling Road, Bexley Heath, Kent.* (S.H.), 1890–1891. Form IV. Probationer. 1st XI Cricket and Football. 1st XV Rugby. L.D.S., R.C.S. (Eng.) Guy's. Assistant Dental House Surgeon, Guy's Hospital. Dental Surgeon to Children's Welfare Centres, Plumstead and Woolwich. London County Council Dental Inspector various Schools. Married : (1 son, 1 dau.).

Hopkins, Donald, 53 *Westmoreland Road, Bromley, Kent.* (Spr.), 1933–1934. Form IV.

Hopkins, Edgar Lionel, *The Cottage, Lodge Park, Northleach, Glos.* (D.B.), 1902–1906. Form V. Gloucester Yeomanry, Egypt. Transferred to 2/5th Glos. Regt. (1st Lieut.). Finished with 1st Glos. Regt. and Army of Occupation (1914–1919). Married : (1 dau.).

Hopkins, E. W. 1886–1887. 2nd XV Football.

Hopkins, Lionel Gordon, *The Ash Grove, Westcliff-on-Sea.* (H.), 1887–1892. Form VI. Probationer. Pres. of Lit. Soc. House Prize. Speaking Prize. 1st XI Cricket. M.D. (London). J.P. County Borough Southend-on-Sea. Chairman of General Hospital, Southend-on-Sea. Surgeon and Physician. War Service 1914–1915 M.O. Rochford Aerodrome 1918. Med. Ref. Ministry of Pensions. Married : (1 son).

Hopkins, Michael John, 53 *Westmoreland Road, Bromley, Kent.* (Spr.), 1934–1935. Form IVA.

Hopkins, Percy Stanley. (H.), 1887–1892. Form V. Camb. Locals Hons. Surgeon on the Booth Line. Practised as a doctor at Westcliff-on-Sea. Died in 1923.

Hopkins, Thomas Eustace. (S.H.), 1905–1906. Form III.

Hopkins, T. Owen Llewellyn. (S.H.), 1904–1907. Form V. Probationer. In Mercantile Marine.

Hopkins, William Foster Morley, *Lennox House, Northlands Road, Southampton.* (D.B.), 1900–1904. Form VI. Senior. Cambridge Senior. 1st XI Football. Associate London Assoc. of Certified Accountants. Assistant Manager Lloyd's Bank, Southampton. Special Constabulary long service medal. Sometime Chairman Glos. & Dist. Centre Inst. of Bankers. Past Master St. George's Lodge of Freemasons, Tewkesbury. Capt. R.A.F. Married : (1 dau.).

Horder, Albert Samuel, 9 *High Street, Swindon.* (S.H.), 1915–1919. Form V. Senior. Vice-Pres. of League. Capt. 1st XI Football. 1st XI Cricket. Woodley Cup. Draper.

Horner, Edward Richard. (H.), 1902–1904.

Horsley, Alec Stuart, *Nigeria, W. Africa.* (Spr.), 1913–1914. Form III. B.A. Worcester College, Oxford. In British Colonial Office.

Horsley, George Maurice. *In the Transvaal. The Lawn, Belper, Derby* (h.). (Spr.), 1913–1914. Form III. Farming in the Transvaal.

Horstmann, Kenneth John, 2 *Newbridge Hill, Bath.* (S.H.), 1917–1920. Form III.

Hosegood, Alan John. *In Canada.* (H.), 1902–1905. Form V. Probationer. 28th Canadians. Farmer. Married.

Hosegood, Roland William. *In Canada.* (H.), 1904–1910. Form V. Probationer. 1st XI Football and Cricket. Lieut. 53rd Canadians. M.C.

Hosking, Donald Clifford. (S.H.), 1919–1921. Form III.

Houghton, Richard Aylmer. (H.), 1889–1896. Form V. Probationer. Junior Athlete. 1st XI Cricket and Football. As Assistant Overseer in the Western Telegraph Co. he was stationed at Rio de Janeiro, and went through the Revolution in 1907. He played Cricket and Tennis for the State of Rio, and Football for Brazil against Argentina. He died in 1924.

Howard, Charles Stavely. (S.H.), 1897–1899. Form V. Inspector of Agents for Scottish Accident Life and General Insurance Co.

Howell, Cedric Illtyd, 1 *Caerau Crescent, Newport, Mon.* (H.), 1923–1925. Form V. Probationer.

Howell, Charles Everard, *Burry Port, R.S.O.* (H.), 1893–1898. Form VI. Probationer.

Howell, Illtyd Mark, *Wildersmouth, Bassaleg Road, Newport.* (H.), 1915–1919. Form VI. Senior. Vice-Pres. of League. 1st XI Football. Senior Athlete. Senior Cross Country. Swimming Champ. Batchelar Cup. B.A. Cantab. Iron and Steel Merchant. Married.

Howell, Kenneth. (H.), 1907–1911. Form VI. Probationer. Lieut. I.C.O.T.C. Steel Merchant. While at Gibraltar in the summer of 1931 was attacked by fever and died there. ("Star," Dec. 1931, p. 16).

Howell, Richard John Garold. (S.H.), 1905–1911. Form III.

Howell, Stephen Naylor. (S.H.), 1908–1911. Form III.

Howell, Wilfrid Eric, 292 *London Road, Leicester.* (H.), 1907–1913. Form V. Senior. London Matric. Prize for Public Speaking. St. Bartholomew's Hospital. M.R.C.S. (Eng.), L.R.C.P. (Lond.). Lieut. M.G.C. India. Medical Practitioner. Married : (1 dau.).

Howell, William Mervyn, *Burry Port, R.S.O.* (h.). (H.), 1893–1896. Form VI. Senior. Solicitor and Notary. Married.

Howell-Davies, Mervyn M., 89 *Scalby Road, Scarborough, Yorks.* (h.). (D.B.), 1922–1929. Form VI. Prefect. Pres. of League and Lit. Soc. Higher Certif. Naval Cadetship. 1st XV Rugby. 1st XI Cricket. Tennis Team. Jun. (1927), Sen. Athlete (1929). Public Speaking Prize. Lieut. R.N.

Hucklesby, George Theodore. (D.B.), 1904–1906. Form VI. Senior. London Matric. Entered Baptist Ministry. Died from pneumonia and pleurisy, July 15th 1910.

Hudleston, Christopher Roy, *The Grove, Winterbourne, Glos.* (D.B.), 1915–1922. Form V. Probationer. Camb. Senior. Literary Editor "Bristol Evening Post." Hon. Sec. Bristol & Glos. Archaeol. Assoc. 1931. Married : (1 dau.).

Hudleston, John Neville, *Oxford Villa, Bisley Road, Stroud, Glos.* (R. and D.B.), 1927–1932. Lower IV. Articled to Harold F. Trew, F.R.I.B.A., who is the Consulting Architect to Wycliffe College.

Hudson, George Percival Leslie, *High Butts, Rodborough, Stroud.* (D.B.), 1910–1916. Form VI. Senior. Vice-Pres. of League. House Prize. Camb. Senior. 1st XI Cricket. 2nd XI Football. A.C.A. Chartered Accountant. Married.

Hughes, David Leslie, *Ashley House,* 74 *Draycott Av., Kenton, Middlesex.* (H.), 1926–1930. Form VI. Prefect. Pres. of Lit. Soc. School Certif. 1st XV Rugby. Middle-weight Boxing Champ. Swimming

Champ.   Prizes for Public Speaking and Senior Lit. Comp.   Veterinary Surgeon.   M.R.C.V.S.   House Surgeon at R.V. College 1934.   Research Scholar in Animal Health (Ministry of Agriculture) 1934–1937.

Hughes, Eric Lawrence Knutton, *Radnor House School, The Common, Redhill, Surrey.* (D.B.), 1917–1927. Form VI. Prefect. Vice-Pres. of League. School Certif. 1st XV Rugby. Schoolmaster.

Hughes, Fred Edwin. (D.B.), 1883–1888. Probationer. Capt. 2nd XI Cricket. Land Agent. Married. Has died.

Hughes, Harold Victor. (D.B.), 1887–1891. 1st XI Cricket. Journalist in Canada. Canadian Infantry. Killed at Passchendaele in November 1917. (" W. & W." 55).

Hulbert, Arthur George, 5 *Southwood Gardens, Newcastle-on-Tyne.* (D.B.), 1886–1889. Probationer. Wholesale Furniture Warehouseman. Married.

Hulbert, Edward William Restall. (D.B.), 1884–1887. Journalist : was for several years sub-editor of " Stroud News." Went to Canada in 1895, and became sub-editor of a Toronto paper, but died in 1898.

Hulbert, Ernest Percy, *Amberley, St. Columb Minor, Newquay, Cornwall, and 8 Central Square, Newquay.* (D.B.), 1889–1895. Form VI. Senior. London Matric. 2nd XI Cricket. Public Accountant and Auditor. A.A.I.A. Married.

Hulbert, Wilfred Harry, *c/o Alston Rivers Ltd., 18 York Buildings, Adelphi, W.C. 2.* (D.B.), 1889–1893. Form V. Director of above Firm of Publishers. Married.

Hume, John Lawrence, *c/o Lloyds Bank, 6 Pall Mall, London, S.W. 1.* (S.H.), 1923–1926. Probationer. School Certif. 1st XV Rugby. R.M.C., Sandhurst. Lieut. in the Army.

Humphreys, Ronald. (Spr.), 1902–1906. Form V. 1st XI Cricket. 2nd XI Football. Engineer.

Humpidge, Kenneth Palmer, *Churchfield House, Rodborough, Stroud* (h.). *c/o Public Works Dept., Nigeria.* (D.B.), 1913–1920. Senior. London Matric. House Prize. B.Sc. (Engineering) Bristol. A.M.Inst.C.E. Civil Engineer.

Humpidge, Vernon Henry Calley, *Churchfield House, Rodborough, Stroud.* (H.), 1913–1916. Form VI. Probationer. Matriculated at Bristol University. Fruit Grower.

Huntingdon, W. (S.H.), 1887–1888. Timber Merchant. Married.

Huntley, William Cary. (D.B.), 1894–1899. Form III. Completed education in Germany. Afterwards in Accountant General's Dept., Whitehall. Articled to Messrs G. K. Stothert & Co., Marine Engineers (Bristol). In February 1906 was attacked by muscular rheumatism. and then paralysis. Died on August 18th 1906, aged 21, and was buried at Stonehouse.

Hutchen, Alan Frank. *Dryden House, Rockingham Road, Kettering, Northants.* (Spr.), 1917–1920. Form VI. Senior. C.S.M. Hearson Prize. Engineer.

Hutchen, Joseph Frederick Holland, *c/o E. S. & A, Robinson Ltd., Victoria House, Southampton Row, W.C. 1.* (Spr.), 1918–1922. Form VI. Senior. Pres. of League and Lit. Soc. House Prize. Capt. Cricket and Football. Woodley Cup. Representative of Messrs. E. S. & A. Robinson Ltd., Bristol.

Hutchins, Derek Arthur, 61 *Pencisely Road, Llandaff, Cardiff.* (S.H.), 1931–1936. Matric. Form. House Monitor. 1st XV Rugby. Engineering. With Bristol Aeroplane Co.

Hutchison, Seton Marshall. (D.B.), 1903–1904. Form V. Was in Rhodesia, but came home in 1915 and obtained a commission in the Hampshires, but was later attached to the 2nd West India Regt. Died of pneumonia in German East Africa, January 1918. (" W. & W." 56).

Hutchison, William Gregor Maxwell, *The Rectory, New Milton, Hants.* (Spr.), 1903–1908. Form VI. Senior. Camb. Senior. M.A. (Oxon.). Priest (C. of E.).

Iles, Daniel. (H.), 1901–1903. In 1904 the horse which he was riding fell with him, and his leg was badly broken. Exhaustion followed, and he died when only sixteen years of age.

Iles, Stanley William. (S.H.), 1900–1902. Form V. Farming in New Zealand.

Inglis, John Priestley, *Drybridge, Hereford.* (H.), 1923–1927. Form III. Electrical Engineer.

Inglis, Robert Brander, *Drybridge, Hereford.* (H.), 1924–1932. Form VI. Prefect. Capt 2nd XV Rugby. School Certif. Connaught Shooting Team. School Chess Team. Land Agent.

Ingram, Philip James. (H.), 1900–1901. Form I. Pte. A.P.C.

Ingram, William James Norman, *Robinswood, Frome Park Road, Stroud.* (D.B.), 1914–1919. Form V. Engineer.

Ireland, Ernest Arthur.

Ireland, Humphrey John. (D.B.), 1911–1915. Form VI. Probationer. A.S.M. 1st XI Cricket and Football. Capt. R.F.A.

Ireland, James Balleny. (D.B.), 1911–1914. Form VI. Senior. Vice-Pres. of League. Pres. of Lit. Soc. A.S.M. Senior Camb. House Prize. Went up to Lincoln College, Oxford, in 1914, and at once joined University O.T.C. and obtained a commission in the Gloucesters. Took part in the landing at Suvla Bay (Gallipoli) and in the final evacuation at Cape Helles. Badly wounded in the attempt to relieve Kut. Finally sent to France with another battalion of the Gloucesters and killed by a shell on May 5th, 1917. (" W. & W." 56).

Isaac. Alfred, *West End, Wickwar, Glos.* (S.H.), 1915–1916. Form III. Farmer. Married : (1 dau.).

Isaac, George Thomas, 3 *Tydraw Road, Roath Park, Cardiff.* (H.), 1902–1903. Form IV. Married.

Isaacke, H.

Jackson, George Ernest. (S.H.), 1884–1885. Missioner. Married. Died in 1928.

Jackson, Kenneth Vernon, *Silbury House, Bath Road, Swindon.* (S.H.), 1926–1929. Matric Form. House Monitor. School Certif.

Jackson, Ronald Gibson, *St. Auvergne, Queen's Road, Cheltenham* (h.). (H.), 1921–1928. Lower IV. 2nd XV Rugby. Connaught Shooting Team. Manager for C. & H. Fabrics Ltd. (Silk Merchants).

Jackson, William E. (S.H.), 1884–1885. 1st XI Cricket and Football.

Jackson, William Guy, *Meadowlands, Keynsham, near Bristol,* (Spr.), 1907–1911. Form V. Probationer. 2nd XI Cricket. Lieut. R.E. M.C. Despatch Rider in France 1914–1916. Signal Officer. R.E. 1916–1918. Mons Star. Service and Albert Medals. Chairman Keynsham Branch British Legion. With E. S. & A. Robinson. Married : (2 daus.).

Jackson, William Henry Closs, *Portway Cottage, Upton St. Leonards, Glos.* (H.), 1919–1924. Form V. Senior. 1st XI Cricket and Football. Bank Clerk. Married.

Jacob, Fred William, *Ffrwdwyllt, Port Talbot.* (H.), 1906–1908. Form II. Lieut. M.G.C. In Tin Plate Business.

James, Cecil. (S.H.), 1906–1907. Form I.

James, Dudley George Walker, *Kennet House, Hungerford, Berks.* (S.H.), 1923–1930. Lower V. House Monitor. 2nd XV Rugby. 2nd XI Football.

James, Hubert Renshaw, *Bartestree, Fields Park Av., Newport.* (S.H.), 1907–1910. Form IV. R.A.F. A.M.I.E.E. Electrical Engineer in Civil Service. Royal Arsenal, Woolwich. War Service 1917–19. With Glamorgan Fortress Electric Light Co. Corpl. R.E. 1917–1919. 49th Squadron R.F.C and R.A.F. England and France. Married : (1 dau.).

James, Illtyd Edward, 6 *Park View, Port Talbot.* (H.), 1895–1899. Form VI. Senior. Sec. and Treas. of Lit. Soc. London Matric. 1st XI Football. Chief Electrical Engineer, Guest, Keen, Baldwin, Ltd., Iron and Steel Co., Port Talbot, Glam. Married : (1 son, 1 dau.).

James, John Percy, 3 *Glenfall Terrace, Cheltenham* (h.). 29 *Promenade.* (D.B.), 1896–1898. Form VI. Senior. Member of Pharmaceutical Society.

James, T. Stanley. (S.H.), 1902–1906. Form III.

Jamieson, Eric Gavin, *Woodcroft,* 20 *Lismore Road, S. Croydon.* (S.H.), 1925–1930. Form VI. Prefect. Vice-Pres. of League. School Certif. Capt. 2nd XI Cricket. 2nd XI Football. 1st XV Rugby. Connaught Shooting Team. School Chess Team. Prizes for Public Speaking and Public Service. Assoc. Chartered Insurance Institute.

Jarrett, Maurice, *Stonebury, Lydney, Glos.* (S.H.), 1904–1905. Form III. Probationer. 1st XI. Cricket and Football. Junior Athlete. Inns of Court O.T.C. Pin Manufacturer. Married : (2 sons).

Jarrett, Stanley, *Foxhill, Lydney, Glos.* (S.H.), 1906–1907. Form V. Senior. 1st XI Football. 2nd XI Cricket. Lieut. 1/1st Monmouths. Company Director. Married : (1 dau.).

Jarvis, Percy Bernard, 58 *Woodbastwick Road, Sydenham, London, S.E.* 26. (S.H.), 1904–1909. Form VI. Senior. London Matric. Treas. Lit. Soc. 2nd XI Football. Gunner, H.A.C. Customs and Excise Officer. Married : (1 dau., 1 son).

Jarvis, Raymond Sylvester. (S.H.), 1915–1920. Form IV.

Jarvis, Richard Cyril, *Chywoone, Paul, Penzance.* (S.H.), 1908–1914. Form IV. Despatch Rider R.F.C. Merchant.

Jayne, Frederick J., *Talgarth, Brecon.* (S.H.), 1888–1891. Form VI. Senior. Pres. Lit. Soc. 1st XV Rugby. M.B., C.M., Glasgow. J.P. for Breconshire. M.O.H. Married.

Jayne, Robert Frederick. (H.), 1912–1915. Form III.

Jeffes, Charles Edward Donald, *Hyde Farm, Chalford, Glos.* (D.B.), 1923–1930. Form VI. House Monitor. School Certif. With Messrs. Townsend & Co., Stroud.

Jeffes, Eric A. D., *Hyde Farm, Chalford, Glos.* (D.B.), 1930–1933. Lower Remove. Farming.

Jeffes, George Reginald Stanley, *Hyde Farm, Chalford, Glos.* (D.B.), 1925–1930. Lower IV.

Jeffes, Richard E. D., *Hyde Farm, Chalford, Glos.* (R. and D.B.), 1929–1934. Lower IV. Scholarship to the Royal Agricultural College, Cirencester. Farming.

Jeffes, Robert, *Hyde Farm, Chalford, Glos.* (D.B.), 1924–1926. Form II.

Jeffes, Robert Henry Francis, *Hyde Farm, Chalford, Glos.* (D.B.), 1922–1928. Form III. Farming.

Jefford, Lionel Barker. (S.H.), 1913–1914.

Jenkins, David Vivian, *Redcroft, Whitchurch, Glam.* (S.H.), 1930–1934. Lower V. House Monitor. 1st XV Rugby. Articled to Auctioneer and Valuer.

Jenkins, Ernest John, *Roker, Augusta Road, Penarth.* (H.), 1904–1911. Form V. Probationer. 1st XI Cricket and Football. A.S.M. Capt. R.G.A. Chartered Accountant. Married.

Jenkins, Frederick T., *8 Uplands Crescent, Swansea.* (H.), 1891–1892. 1st XI Cricket. 1st XV Rugby.

Jenkins, George T. 1886–1887. 1st XV. Rugby.

Jenkins, J. H. H. (S.H.), 1889.

Jenkins, James Thomas, *Redcroft, Whitchurch, Glam.* (S.H.), 1898–1899. 1st XI Football. Architect & Surveyor. Married : (2 sons).

Jenkins, T. T.

Jenkins, Thomas Jacob, *Glanwern, Radyr, near Cardiff.* (S.H.), 1899–1903. Form V. 1st XI Football. A.S.C. Timber and Slate Merchant.

Jenkins, William Alan, *27 Grange Road, Rotherham.* (Spr.), 1920–1926. Form VI. Pres. of League and Lit. Soc. 1st XI Football. 1st XV Rugby. 2nd XI Cricket. Winner Junior and Senior Cross Country. House Prize. Public Service Prize. Sheffield University. Engineer. Married.

Jenner, Arthur Ernest Algernon. (S.H.), 1902–1908. Form VI. Probationer. Marine Engineer.

Jenner, Arthur E. (D.B.), 1916–1917. Form III.

Jenner, Henry John. (D.B.), 1912–1914. Form III.

Jenner, W.

Johnceline, John Raymond, *8 Warham Road, South Croydon.* (H.), 1919–1922. Form VI. Senior. London Matric. In Bank of England.

Johnson, Daniel Macfie, *17 Cockspur Street, London, S.W. 1.* (S.H.), 1901–1903. Form V. Senior. 1st XI Cricket and Football. Throwing Cricket Ball Record 1903. Senior Athlete. Public Speaking Prize. Assoc. Ontario Agric. Coll., Guelph. B.S.A. Univ. of Toronto. European Colonization Manager, Canadian National Railways, London. Married : (1 dau.).

Johnson, Douglas Craig. (H.), 1907–1910. Form III.

Johnson, Graham Christopher Colpoys, *Orchards, 1, Carbery Av., Southbourne, Bournemouth.* (H.), 1931–1933. Upper Remove. Junior Athlete. Registered Probationer of Royal Inst. of British Architects. Architect.

Johnson, Pearse Douglas Stuart, *Newcastle House, Bridgend, Glam.* (H.), 1929–1931. Form VI. House Monitor. School Certif. School Chess Team.

Johnson, W. Mountfort, *Leek, Staffs.* (H), 1887–1889. Manufacturer's Agent.

Johnston, Gilbert G., *Hillcrest, Crocketford Road, Dumfries.* (Spr.), 1929–1930. Form V.

Johnstone, Norman White, *25 Cuffe Parade, Colaba, Bombay* (h.). *c/o Kimberley Morrison, 55 Temple Row, Birmingham.* (H.), 1926–1931. Matric. Form. School Certif. House Relay and Swimming. Articled to Chartered Accountant.

Johnstone, Ronald David, 25 *Cuffe Parade, Colaba, Bombay, India.* (R. and H.), 1929–1936. Entrance Scholar. Modern VI. Oxford and Camb, Joint Board School Certif. and Higher Certif. London Matric. Diploma Univ. of Poitiers. Prefect. Treas. of Lit. Soc. 1st XI Colours 1934–1936. Undergraduate at St. John's College, Cambridge.

Jones, A. Stanley. Has died.

Jones, Alfred Denton. (D.B.), 1909–1913. Form IV. A.S.C.

Jones, Alun Morgan, 3 *Insole Gardens, Llandaff, Cardiff.* (S.H.), 1914–1919. Form IV. Probationer. Solicitor. Sec. for Wales, British Sailor Society. Married.

Jones, Bernard T. White. (S.H.), 1890–1895. Form VI. Senior. Pres. of Lit. Soc. 1st XI Cricket. 1st XI Football ("Invincibles" 1894–1895). M.A. St. John's College, Cambridge. Curate of St. Mary's Redcliffe and St. John's, Bedminster. Vicar of Amblecote, Stourbridge, Worcs. Died in 1912 after operation for severe appendicitis. ("Star," April 1913, p. 4).

Jones, Clifford Fernley, 54 *Clarendon Road, Redland, Bristol* (h.). (S.H.), 1916–1919. Form V. Senior. Pres. of League and Lit. Soc. Wesleyan Minister. Married.

Jones, Cyril C. (H.), 1886–1890.

Jones, Dan Powell. (H.), 1896–1902. Form V. Probationer. J.P. for Breconshire. Timber Merchant. Married.

Jones, Daniel Norman Wynne, 3 *Insole Gardens, Llandaff, Cardiff.* (S.H.), 1921–1925. Form V. 2nd XI Cricket. B.A. Univ. of Wales. Bank Clerk.

Jones, David, *Pytindu, Brecon.* (H.), 1900–1902. Form IV. Capt. S. Wales Borderers. Farmer.

Jones, David Bradwyn, *Richmond House, Fore Street and Pine Hurst, Haldon Avenue, Teignmouth.* (S.H.), 1909–1913. Form VI. Senior. 1st XI Football. 2nd XI Cricket. Senior Gymnastic Prize. Artists' Rifles 1915. King's Liverpool Regt. 1918. France 1918. Chartered Accountant. Married : (1 dau.).

Jones, David Leonard. (H.), 1897–1901. Form III. 2nd XI Cricket and Football. Provision Merchant.

Jones, David Trevor Austin. (S.H.), 1922–1926. Lower V. Probationer. 1st XI Football. 1st XV Rugby. 1st XI Cricket.

Jones, Edgar Cecil, *c/o Midland Bank Ltd., Tredegar, Mon.* (S.H.), 1916–1921. Form V. Probationer. 1st XI Cricket and Football. Rowell Cup. Open Tennis Doubles. Bank Clerk. Cert. A.I.B. Married.

Jones, Ernest Loveday, *The Bungalow, Piper's Hill Lane, London Road, Kettering.* (H.), 1919–1925. Form VI. Senior. London Matric. Prize for Public Speaking. Batchelar Cap. B.A. St. John's College, Cambridge. Solicitor.

Jones, Ernest William, 38 *Bernard Street and Albion Chambers, Swansea.* (S.H.), 1885–1887. Senior. Pres. of Lit. Soc. House Prize. 1st XV Rugby. Capt. 1st XI Cricket. Captained S. Wales v. Australians at Cricket 1908. Vice-Chairman S. Wales Federation of Port Labour Employers. Chairman Pilotage Authority. The Welch Regt. Capt. 4th V.B. Chartered Shipbroker. Widower : (1 son).

Jones, Felix Bassett, *Bona Vista, Grosvenor Road, Sketty, Swansea.* (H.), 1927–1931. Matric. Form.

Jones, Frank Powell. (H.), 1903–1905. Form II. Took up Sheep Farming in Australia and New Zealand, but has died.

Jones, Horace Birchall. (Spr.), 1905–1907. Form III. Was in business in Liverpool and London and then became a junior member of the Birmingham firm of W. T. Jones & Co. On the outbreak of War joined the Birmingham Univ. O.T.C. and then the 1st Birmingham City Batt., finally he was commissioned to the 1/6th Staffordshire Regt. He was killed on the opening day of the Battle of the Somme, July 1916. ("W. and W." 59).

Jones, Hugh. (S.H.), 1902–1905. Form VI. Senior. Vice-Pres. of League. 1st XI Cricket and Football. House Prize. After a year in Bristol entered his father's business at Lydney Docks. Played cricket for Gloucestershire. In 1914 joined 12th Gloucesters, was given a commission and promoted Captain. Received the Military Cross and was twice wounded. When recovered he was posted to the 3rd Gloucesters. Early in November 1918 he was attacked by influenza and died of pneumonia at Chatham on Nov. 10th. ("W. & W." 60).

Jones, John Lionel Stuart, *Fromedale, Stroud.* (D.B.), 1917–1923. Form IV. Probationer. 1st XI Football. 2nd XI Cricket. Open Tennis, Singles and Doubles. Has played tennis for Gloucestershire.

Jones, Kenneth Leslie, 18 Park Place, Cardiff. (S.H.), 1909–1915. Form VI. Senior. Pres. of League and Lit. Soc. Cadet Sergt.-Maj. House Prize. Capt. 1st XI Football. 1st XI Cricket. Junior and Senior Athlete. Open Tennis Doubles. Swimming Champ. Rowell Cup. 2nd Lieut. Welch Regt. M.C. Solicitor. Partner in firm of Yorath, Tudor & Jones, 18 Park Place, Cardiff.

Jones, Kenneth Pughe, *Deva, Coronation Lane, Calderstones, Liverpool.* (H.), 1917–1921. Form IV. 2nd XI Cricket and Football. Bank Clerk.

Jones, Maurice Henry, *P. O. Steynsrust, O.F.S., S. Africa.* (H.), 1918–1921. Form VI. Senior. Matric. 2nd XI Football. Married : (1 son).

Jones, Norman Arundel, *Yatesfield, Nailsworth, Glos.* (S.H.), 1905–1910. Form V. Probationer. 1st XI Cricket. 2nd XI Football. Bombardier, R.F.A. Coal Merchant.

Jones, Norman Hedley, *Dartmouth House,* 54 *Clarendon Road, Redland, Bristol.* (S.H.), 1916–1922. Form V. Senior. Music Prizes. Pianist.

Jones, Percy Lloyd, *c/o Ignamic Electric Co., Bedford.* (H.), 1914–1917. Form IV.

Jones, Percy Morgan Powell. (H.), 1903–1909. Probationer. Became a Timber Merchant at Abergavenny, and was an officer in the Brecknocks at the outbreak of war. He was reported missing in Mesopotamia in April 1916. ("W. & W." 64).

Jones, Richard Llewellyn. *Highmead, Pontypridd.* (H.), 1892–1895. Surgeon Dentist. L.D.S. (Eng.), Married.

Jones, Robert Norman, *Northfield, Cliff Terrace, Aberystwyth.* (S.H.), 1917–1923. Probationer. 1st XI Cricket and Football. Chartered Accountant. F.C.A.

Jones, William Kirby, 8 *Escombe Avenue, Parktown West, Johannesburg. P.O. Box* 44, *Steynsrust, O.F.S., South Africa* (h.). (H.), 1922–1929. Traveller for Manufacturers' Representative. Lieut. 52nd Anti-Aircraft Brigade. Lieut. Transvaal Horse Artillery.

Jowett, Christopher Hardy, 103 *Westbourne Grove, London, W. 2.* (Spr.), 1924–1930. Form VI. Head Prefect. Pres. Lit. Soc. and League. Higher Certif. 1st XV Rugby. Senior Cross Country. B.A. Lincoln College, Oxford. Departmental Assistant Asiatic Petroleum Co.

Jowett, Edward Pearse, 103 *Westbourne Grove, London, W. 2.* (Spr.), 1924–1931. Form VI. Prefect. School Certif. 1st XV Rugby. Junior Cross Country. B.A. St. John's College, Cambridge. Natural Science. Medical Student at St. Mary's Hospital, London, W. 2.

Joynes, Francis William, *Woodcote, Woodhill Road, Pinfold Lane, Penn, Wolverhampton.* (D.B.), 1888–1891. Senior. Capt. R.A.M.C., L.R.C.P. (Lond.) 1897. M.R.C.S. (Eng.). Married.

Joynes, Henry E. (D.B.), 1893–1898. In business in Brooklyn, N.Y. U.S.A.

Joynes, William James, *Old Kilpatrick, Dumbartonshire.* (D.B.), 1889–1893. In charge of Oil Fuel Depot. Married.

Judd, Wilfrid Pearce. *Was in Australia.* (H.), 1897–1898. 2nd XI Cricket.

Keene, Harold E. *Over, Gloucestershire.* (H.), 1918–1920. Form IV. Probationer. Corn Merchant. Married.

Keene, Rees, *Over, Gloucestershire.* (H.), 1919–1921. Corn Trade.

Keene, Roger Melville, *The Cayo, Llanvoucher, Magor, Mon.* (H.), 1924–1926. Form IV.

Keevil, Donald Haines, *Tetbury, Eiffel Flats, Gatooma, S. Rhodesia, S. Africa.* (S.H.), 1907–1909. Form IV. 2nd XI Cricket. Farmer. Despatch Rider. Observer. 1915–1917 in France. Flying Instructor R.F.C. Married : (1 son, 1 dau.).

Keevil, Frank Manning, *Kelowna, British Columbia.* (S.H.), 1900–1902. Form III. Married : (2 daus.).

Keevil, Wilfrid Sam, *Many Trees, Curridge, Newbury, Berks.* (S.H.), 1900–1903. Form IV. 2nd XI Cricket and Football. Farmer in S. Rhodesia and then in Gloucestershire. Officer with the Wessex Electricity Co. Married : (1 son).

Kenchington, Charles Richard, 4 *Mount Road, Wombourne, Staffs.* (H.), 1916–1923. Form VI. Senior. London Matric. Foster Rifle. M.B., Ch.B. (Birmingham). L.R.C.P. (Lond.). M.R.C.S. (Eng.). Medical Practitioner. Married.

Kenchington, Frederick William, *Thicknall Lane, Clent, Worcs.* (H.), 1919–1928. Form VI. Prefect. London Matric. 1st XV Rugby. High Jump Record 1927. Chartered Surveyor, Valuer and Auctioneer. Married.

Kenchington, John Mark, *Scarsdale, Farnham Royal, Bucks.* (H.), 1916–1924. Form VI. Senior. Sec. of Lit. Soc. London Matric. House Prize and Public Speaking. Batchelor of Commerce (Birmingham Univ.). Stockbroker. Married : (2 daus.).

Kenchington, Noel S., 331 *Pershore Road, Edgbaston, Birmingham 5.* (H.), 1924–1932. Form VI. Prefect. Pres. of League and Lit. Soc. Editor "Star." School Certif. Priz for Public Service. B.A. and 2nd M.B., St. John's College, Cambridge. Medical Student.

Kennan, Deric Williams, *Lakefield, Strand Road, Merrion, Co. Dublin.* (H.)., 1917–1919. Engineer with Westland Engine and Aircraft Co.

Kennan, Reginald Read, *Brookfield, Preston, Yeovil.* (H.), 1915–1917. Form V. Probationer. 2nd XI. Despatch Rider R.E. Member Inst. Brit. Engineers. Engineer Sales Manager. Peace Commissioner, Dublin City and County. Served on Western Front 1918 (198th Inf. Brig.). Married. Sales Manager, Messrs. Petters, Yeovil.

Kennish, Peter Forbes, *Woodcroft, Totteridge Green, London, N.* 20. (R. and H.), 1930–1934. Matric. Form. School Certif. Medical Student, University College, London.

Kerby, Norman Guy, 37 *Waverley Road, Redland, Bristol.* (Spr.), 1921. Form III. 2nd XI Cricket and Football. House Furnishing.

Kerr, Geoffrey Alexander Borthwick, *Wycliffe, Allyryn Av., Newport.* (H.), 1921–1923. Form V. Probationer. 1st XI Football. Clothier. Married : (1 dau.).

Kerr, Kenneth Borthwick, *Lyndhurst, Ridgeway Avenue, Newport.* (H.), 1921–1922. Form V. Tailor. Married : (1 dau.).

Keys, Alfred Ernest, *Alkerton House, Eastington, Stonehouse.* (D.B.), 1902–1905. Form IV. Probationer. London Matric. Chairman, Glos. County Branch, National Farmers' Union. Married.

Keys, Francis William. (D.B.), 1906–1908. Form IV. Took up farming but later gained an Honours B.Sc. degree at Bristol, and entered an Engineering Works. He died in 1920.

Khan, Abdul Mateen, *c/o Mrs Rina Khan, c/o Lloyds Bank, 6 Pall Mall, S.W. 1., and c/o Abdus Subhan Khan, Esq., Extra Assist. Commissioner, Government Engineering School, Nagpur, C.P., India.* (Spr. and G.), 1932–1933. Upper Matric. House Monitor. School Certif.

Kidd, Hubert. (H.), 1905–1906. Form III. Stockbroker.

Kimmins, Arthur James. *S. Africa.* (D.B.), 1891–1893. Form III. Farmer. Married.

Kimmins, Edward James, *Dersingham House, Armthorpe Road, Doncaster.* (H.)., 1917–1923. Form V. B.Sc. (Mining), Birmingham University. 1st Class Certif. of Competency (Board of Trade). Inst. of Mining Engineers Post Grad. Travelling Scholarship. Assoc. Member Inst. of Mining Engineers. Member Nat. Assoc. of Colliery Managers. Married: (1 son).

Kimmins, Edward Russell, *Cotswold Grange, Stonehouse, Glos.* (D.B.), 1891–1896. Form V. 1st XI Football. Engineer. Married: (2 sons, 1 dau.).

Kimmins, Gordon Stewart, 56 *Northville Road, Bristol 7.* (D.B. and Spr.), 1898–1908. Form VI. Senior. Camb. Senior. Swimming and Diving Championship. Birmingham University (Engineering). Tester of Aero Engines. Married : (1 son).

Kimmins, Howard Charles, 25 *Riverdale, Kroonstadt, Orange Free State, S. Africa.* (D.B.), 1889–1894. Form IV. Lieut. in S. African Forces. Farmer. Married.

Kimmins, Percy Alderson. (D.B.), 1893–1900. Form V. Probationer. 2nd XI Cricket and Football. Became a Chartered Accountant and also engaged in social and religious work. Died after an illness of several months and was buried in Stonehouse Churchyard. ("Star," Dec. 1907, p. 296).

King, Charles Edward, 18 *Ranmoor Cliffe Road, Sheffield 10.* (D.B.), 1888–1894. Form VI. Senior. London Matric. 1st XI Cricket. Consulting Engineer. Married.

King, George Aldred, *Cotswold, Thornton Avenue, Higher Bebington, Cheshire.* (Spr.), 1915–1917. Probationer. Bank Inspector. Married : (2 daus.).

King, Henry Aubrey. (S.H.), 1904–1906. Form VI. Capt. 2nd XI Football. Australian Army Corps. Farming.

King, Henry James Hubert, *Newmarket Court, Nailsworth.* (H. and D.B.), 1884–1891. Form VI. Senior. London Matric. 1st XI Cricket. 1st XV Rugby. County Councillor. M.Inst.Mech.E. Engineer. Married.

King, Mervyn, *Little Britain, Woodchester, Glos.* (D.B.), 1931–1932. Lower IV. Farmer.

Kingsley, Charles. (D.B.), 1919–1924. Form V. Probationer. B.A., Lincoln College, Oxford.

Kinnersley, Leslie Gordon, 106 *Redland Road, Bristol* 6. (S.H.), 1897–1901. Form IV. L.D.S. (Eng.). Dental Surgeon. Married : (2 daus.).

Kitchen, Alfred Tiley, *The Tannery, Leonard Stanley, Glos.* (D.B.), 1894–1896. Form III. A.B., R.N.V.R. Tanner and Leather Merchant. Served in India with Somerset L.I. 1914–1918.

Kitchen, Benjamin Bryant, *Seven Waters, Leonard Stanley, near Stonehouse.* (D.B.), 1897–1899. Form II. Tanner and Leather Merchant. Married : (3 children).

Kitchen, William. (S.H.), 1898–1902. A.B., R.N.D. Manager of Cloth Mill. Married. Died in 1927.

Knott, Arthur John, 46 *Redland Court Road, Bristol* 6. (S.H.), 1900–1903. Form V. Probationer. Sergt. S. African Heavy Artillery. A.R.I.B.A. Architect. Married.

Laidlaw, John Douglas, 11 *Catherine Place, Bath.* (D.B.), 1902–1908. Form IV. Senior. Tied as Senior Athlete. Capt. 1st XI Football. Rowell Cup. House Prize. Lieut. R.F.A. In Lloyds Bank.

Lakeman, John Pearse. (S.H.), 1909–1915. Form VI. Senior. Vice-Pres. of League. Pres. of Lit. Soc. 1st XI Cricket and Football. Joined Inns of Court O.T.C., and subsequently received commission in Northumberland Fusiliers. Served in France for three months ; wounded in the head in the Arras offensive and died in Le Touquet Hospital on April 20th, 1917. (" W. & W." 65).

Lalonde, Kenneth Blandford, 30 *Pembroke Road, Bristol.* (H.), 1920–1923. Form VI. Senior. Camb. Senior. 1st XI Football. 2nd XI Cricket. Woodley Cup. Auctioneer and Estate Agent. Married.

Lamb, Ernest Henry. *Vide* Rochester, Lord.

Lamb, Martin, *Cardington,* 11 *Avenue La Croix, Sea Point, Cape Town, S. Africa.* (Spr.), 1925–1927.

Lamb Walter, *Cardington,* 11 *Avenue La Croix, Sea Point, Cape Town, S. Africa.* (Spr.), 1925–1927.

Lambert, Henry T. (H.), 1894–1895. Form IV. 2nd XI Cricket. Mechanical and Electrical Engineer.

Lambert, Hubert Trotman. (H.), 1890–1893. Form III. 2nd XI Cricket. Trained as a Mechanical and Electrical Engineer, and obtained an appointment with the Harland Engineering Co. (Manchester), with whom he remained until his death in the summer of 1929. (" Star," Aug. 1929, p. 18).

Lambert, Leslie A. (D.B.), 1912–1915. Form VI. Senior. London Matric. Rejected by Inns of Court O.T.C. on account of age, he taught for two years in preparatory schools. In May 1917 joined the Civil Service Rifles ; after an attack of pleurisy he worked at Quedgeley Munition Works. In April 1918 was posted to the Grenadier Guards, but in July contracted influenza. Complications followed ; he was discharged and died five months later. (" W. & W." 67).

Lamplough, John Stewart, 17 *Fitzjohn's Avenue, Hampstead, N.W.* 3. (Spr.), 1927–1935. Science VI. Prefect. A.S.M. London Matric. 1st XV Rugby. Electrical Engineering Student.

RYEFORD HALL
(opened as a Junior School in 1928)

THE PREFECTS, 1926

N. E. Welch, R. A. Binning, M. H. Cullimore, J. H. Bishop, W. N. Bazzard, W. T. Woodley, L. W. Bryant,

THE GROVE, WITH DOVEROW HILL IN THE BACKGROUND

(In 1931 Mr. T. M. Sibly opened this House for fifteen Wycliffe and Ryeford boys).

SOME OF THE COUNCIL OF GOVERNORS IN 1932

Mr. S. T. Toogood (Secretary), Mr. A. S. F. Morris, Dr. Somerville Hastings, Mr. R. S. Hayes, Mr. H. L. Porcher, Mr. C. A. Carr, Mr. H. J. Trump, Mr. R. J. Armstrong, Mr. F. L. Daniels, Miss Sibly, The Headmaster, Mr. J. H. Edwards, The Bursar, Mr. W. N. Bubb, Mr. Fernley Gardner.

Lance, Albert Edward, *Waterloo House, Weston-super-Mare.* (S.H.), 1883–1884. Probationer. 1st XV Rugby. Managing Director of Lance & Lance Ltd.

Lance, Henry Joseph, *Waterloo House, Weston-super-Mare.* (S.H.), 1883–1884. Probationer. 1st XV Rugby. Managing Director of Lance & Lance Ltd.

Lance, Kenneth John, *c/o Miss Lance, The Oaks, Church Road, St. Mark's, Cheltenham.* (H.), 1915–1917. In China.

Lane, Brian H. (S.H.), 1894–1898. Form VI. 1st XI Cricket and Football. Joined Army Veterinary Corps in 1904, and rose to rank of Captain. Sustained concussion of the brain while riding in a steeplechase at Meerut, and died a few days later on November 5th 1911. (" Star," Dec. 1911, p. 129).

Lane Douglas Yockney, 46 *Prospect Road, Birmingham.* (D.B.), 1897–1898. Form I. Lieut. Dover Patrol. Corn Merchant. Married : (1 son).

Lane, Henry Fitzgerald William. (D.B. and H.), 1890–1894. Form VI. Probationer. B.A. Worcester College, Oxford. Played Chess for Oxford *v.* Cambridge and for combined English *v.* American Universities. Solicitor. Married.

Lane, Hubert, 2 *Oriel Villas, Oriel Road, Cheltenham.* (S.H.), 1894–1897. Form V. 1st XI Cricket and Football. K.R.R. Married.

Lane, Ivor Anthony, *Woodchester, Glos.* (D.B.), 1925–1928. Form II.

Lane, Laurie J. (D.B.), 1890–1894. Form IV. Wholesale Clothing Manufacturer. Married. Died in 1930.

Lane, Lawrence Alan. (D.B.), 1918–1922. Form III.

Lane, Sidney David, *Northmoor, Rendcomb, Cirencester, Glos.* (D.B.), 1896–1898. Form V. Late Capt. Gloucester Old Boys' R.F.C. and Gloucester Rowing Club. Paper Manufacturer. Married : (4 sons, 2 daus.).

Lane, William George. (H.), 1908–1909. Farmed at home until he joined the Worcestershire Yeomanry in 1914. He took part in the fighting in Gallipoli, and in battles at Katia, El Arish and Gaza. He received a commission just before the fighting near Beersheba, in which he was fatally wounded, and died in hospital a few days later. (" W. & W." 69).

Lane, William Woodhouse. (H.), 1895–1896. Form III. B.A. (Cantab.). Has played Chess for English *v.* American Universities.

Langdon, John Gordon, *Freetown, W. Africa ;* 2 *Acacia Road, St. John's Wood, London, N.W.* 8 (h.) ; 32 *Sussex Place, Regent's Park, London, N.W.* 1 (h.). (Spr.), 1926–1929. Upper III. With United Africa Co.

Langford, Frank Merrow, *Down Cottage, off Trodd's Lane, Guildford, Surrey.* (Spr.), 1912–1917. Form VI. Senior. London Matric. M.B., Ch.B. (Bristol). F.R.C.S. (Eng.). L.R.C.P. (Lond.). D.P.H. (Liverpool). Assistant Medical Officer of Health. Married.

Langford, George Edward. (D.B.), 1905. Form I. Engineer.

Langford, Karol Eric, 8 *Beaconsfield Road, Clifton, Bristol 8.* (Spr.), 1919–1924. Senior. 2nd XI Football. London Matric. A.M.I.C.E. Civil Engineer.

Langley-Smith, Edgar L. H., *Wotton Hill House, Gloucester.* (H.), 1892–1899. Senior. Capt. 1st XI Cricket. Capt. 2nd XI Football. Engineer. Married : (1 dau.).

Langley-Smith, Nelson Humphries. (H.), 1902–1911. Form V. Senior. Pres. of League and Lit. Soc. Capt. 1st XI Cricket and Football. House Prize. At Queen's College (Camb.) captained his College A.F.C. took

F

honours in Law, and his B.A. and LL.B. degrees just before the War. Passed his final Bar examination and was admitted at Gray's Inn. In October 1914 was serving in Public Schools Batt. (16th Middlesex), and later obtained commission in the Gloucesters. Served on the Western Front, and while leading his men in June 1915 was severely wounded and suffered from shell shock. After another severe illness in 1917 he was discharged. Having been called to the Bar in 1919 he joined the Oxford circuit, but in 1920 went to Shanghai as advocate to Messrs. Hansens. He also became Secretary of the China Association. He died there after an operation in February 1924. (" Star," April 1924, p. 16).

Langley-Smith, W. Harold Humphries, *Belmont, Kenilworth Avenue, Gloucester.* (H.), 1893–1896. Senior. 1st XI Cricket. Played Golf for Gloucestershire. Solicitor. Married : (1 son, 1 dau.).

Langley-Smith, William Humphries, *Westgate Chambers, Gloucester* : *Wotton Hill House, Gloucester* (h.). (H.), 1902–1907. Senior. 1st XI Cricket. M.T., R.A.S.C. Solicitor. Married.

Lanham, William Henry, 24 *Sefton Park Road, Bishopston, Bristol* 7. (S.H.), 1889–1892. Member of Supervisory Staff of J. S. Fry & Sons, Somerdale. War Service 1914–1919. In Belgium and France with 48th 61st and 56th Divisions. A.D.C. to G.O.C. R.A., 61st Division.

Larque, Leslie Digby. (D.B.), 1924–1928. Form II.

Larque, W. E. (D.B.), 1924–19—.

Laugher, Leonard. (S.H.), 1897–1898. Form IV. Played Hockey for Somerset. Lieut. R.A.S.C. Managing Director of Veronese Ltd., London.

Lawford, Llewellyn A. W. *India.* (H.), 1903–1904. Form III. Indian Army.

Lawrence, Jack. (S.H.), 1903–1905. Form IV. 1st XI Cricket and Football. Canadian Civil Service.

Lawson, John Sutton, *c/o Pretoria Club, Pretoria, Transvaal.* (D.B.), 1898–1905. Form VI. Senior. Pres. of League. Capt. 1st XI Cricket and 1st XI Football. House Prize. Capt 3/14th Cheshires. O.C. 86th T.M.B.

Lawson, Joseph Frank, *c/o G.P.O., Wellington, New Zealand.* (S.H.), 1902/1909. Form VI. Probationer. 1st XI Cricket and Football. Senior Athlete. Swimming Championship. A.M.S.I. Capt. Indian Cavalry.

Lawson, Vincent Wade, 51 *Tudor Close, London, S.W.* 2. (S.H.), 1896–1903. Form VI. Camb. Senior. London Matric. 1st XI Cricket and Football. Lieut. R.A.F. Actor. Theatrical Producer, Lyrist, Films and B.B.C.

Leach, Percy Hastings, *Venters Lodge, Rusper, Sussex.* (H.), 1897–1902. Form VI. Probationer. 1st XI Cricket and Football. Lieut. R.F.A. M.C. Married.

Leach, Samuel Bernard, *Southcroft, Sandhills Lane, Barnt Green, Birmingham.* (H.), 1899–1905. Form V. Cambridge Senior. 1st XI Cricket and Football. Birmingham University. Fishing Tackle Manufacturer. Married : (4 daus.).

Leather, Francis Copner. (Spr.), 1908–1909. Form IV. Probationer. House Prize. 16th Warwickshire Regt. Manufacturing Jeweller.

Lee, Archibald Ward. 1906. Form IV. Bank Clerk in Canada.

Lee, Denis George. (H.), 1915–1917. Form III. 2nd XI Football.

Lee, Gerald Richard. (H.), 1916–1918. Form III. 2nd XI Cricket. Farmer.

Lee, Leslie John. (H.), 1915–1921. Form V. Probationer. 2nd XI Cricket and Football. Farmer.

Lees, Robert Edwin, *Southfield, Charfield, Glos.* (D.B.), 1905–1907. Form V. Probationer. 2nd XI Football. Farmer.

Lester-Jones, William Poole, 67 *George Street, Baker Street, W.* 1. (H.), 1893–1896. Probationer. London Matric. Inns of Court O.T.C. 1916. Lieut. R.F.C. and R.A.F. 1917–1919. Served in France 1918.

Letcher, Harold Bertie, 62 *Malone Road, Belfast.* (S.H.), 1885–1890. Senior. London Matric. Inter. and Final B.A. (London) when at school. Pres. of Lit. Soc. Senior Athlete. Capt. 1st XI Cricket and 1st XV Rugby. House Prize. Played and acted as Hon. Sec. and Capt. Glamorgan County C.C. Resident Secretary, Scottish Provident Inst., Belfast. Married : (1 son, 1 dau.).

Letcher, Owen Jameson. (S.H.), 1882–1884. Came with Mr G. W. Sibly from Taunton. Senior. 1st XV Football ; afterwards played Rugby for Swansea. After some years in business entered Wesleyan Ministry (London, Leeds, Birmingham, Manchester). In 1915–16 acted as Chaplain to Sixth Division, and in 1917–1918 was deputy-assistant principal Chaplain to 1st Army Corps. Was awarded the D.S.O. for his work at the Battle of Cambrai (1917), and was four times mentioned in despatches. In 1919 be became Chaplain of the Portsmouth District, and in 1924 was transferred to Bristol. He assisted Dr T. Ferrier Hulme at the School Memorial Service in 1921, and started the Memorial Clock at 4 p.m. on July 11th of that year. He died of heart failure after an operation in November 1926. ("Star," Dec. 1926, p. 12).

Leven, Charles. (Spr.), 1906–1908. Form III.

Lewis, Cecil Stanley, *Tweedholme, Tyrfran, Llanelly.* (S.H.), 1910–1915. Form V. Probationer. 1st XI Cricket and Football. Lieut. Middlesex Regt.

Lewis, David Godfrey, *c/o Orr, Dignam & Co. Ltd., Standard Buildings, Calcutta, India.* (S.H.), 1903–1905. Form III. Lieut. Indian Cavalry (37th Lancers). M.C.

Lewis, Dudley George, *c/o Barclay's Bank, Circus Place, London Wall, E.C.2.* (S.H.), 1920–1929. Form VI. Vice-Pres. of League. Pres. of Lit. Soc. Capt. 1st XI Cricket. London Matric. Capt. 1st XV Rugby. 1st XI Football. School Tennis Team. Prize for Public Service. B.A. St. John's College, Cambridge. Flt.-Lieut. in Royal Air Force.

Lewis, Edward Harold, *Tweedholme, Tyrfran, Llanelly.* (S.H.), 1908–1912. Form IV. 2nd XI Football. 2nd Lieut. R.F.A. In Copper Miners' Tin Plate Co., Cwmavon.

Lewis, Henry Gethin, *Cliffside, Forest Road, Penarth.* (H.), 1909–1914. Form V. Probationer. M.A., Trinity Coll., Oxford. Played for O.U. A.F.C. v. Cambridge. Rowed 6 in Trinity College Eight, winners of Ladies' Plate, Henley 1923. 2nd Lieut. R.A.F. Barrister-at-Law (Inner Temple). Rolling Stock Contractor. Married. (2 daus, 1 son).

Lewis, Hubert Kenneth, 36 *Long Oaks Avenue, Uplands, Swansea.* (S.H.), 1927–1932. Matric. Form. Prefect. Vice-Pres. of League. School. Certif. 1st XV Rugby. Junior Athlete. Surveyor, Auctioneer and Estate Agent.

Lewis, Ivor Llewellyn, *Porthkerry, Barry, Glam.* (H.), 1912–1915. Form I.

Lewis, Jerrard Howell, *Enfield,* 36 *Coleshill Terrace, Llanelly.* (S.H.), 1915–1919. Form IV. Probationer. Draper.

Lewis, John Llewellyn, 15 *Howard Gardens, Cardiff.* (H.), 1895–1899. Form VI. Senior. Capt. 1st XI Football. 1st XI Cricket. Swimming Championship. Major R.E. (T.), War Service, August 1914–1919. Merchant. Married : (1 son, 2 daus.).

Lewis, Kenneth Purdon, c/o *R.A.F. Club,* 128 *Piccadilly, W. 1.* (D.B.), 1923–1924. Form IV. Ft.-Lieut. R.A.F.

Lewis, Percy Gething. (H.), 1896–1902. Form VI. Rolling Stock Manufacturer. Died in 1930.

Lewis, Robert Mervyn, *Fields Lodge, Milford Haven, Pem.* (H.), 1922–1925. Form V. Probationer. 2nd XI Cricket and Football. Timber Merchant.

Lewis, Ronald Harry, 22 *St. Peter's Road, Mumbles, Swansea.* (H.), 1914–1918. Form VI. Senior. 1st XI Cricket and Football. Senior Cross Country Cup. Clerk with Electrical Repair Firm.

Lewis, William Hayden. (H.), 1924–1931. Upper V. 1st XV Rugby. Drowned, while bathing near Bude on August 5th 1931.

Liley, John Edward, *Lynwood, Hampton, Evesham, Worcs.* (S.H.), 1922–1928. Form V. House Monitor. School Certif. 1st XI Cricket. Tennis Singles and Doubles. Married.

Linacre, John Howard T. (H.), 1901–1902. Form I.

Lister, Edward Ashton. (S.H.), 1905–1911. Form IV. On leaving school studied in Zurich and Düsseldorf, and returned to " go through the mill " in Messrs. R. A. Lister & Co.'s Engineering Works at Dursley. In 1914 joined the 5th Gloucesters, but was soon transferred to the R.F.C. Met his death while flying in France in July 1915. (" W. & W." 70).

Lister, George Ashton, *Dursley, Glos.* (S.H.), 1901–1903. Form I. Capt. Glos. Regt. Director of R. A. Lister & Co.

Lister, Robert Browning, *The Elms, Stone, Glos.* (S.H. and Spr.(, 1904–1911. Form IV. Probationer. 1st XI Football. Lieut. Army Signal Service. Director of R. A. Lister & Co., Dursley.

Little, Edward James, *Bartle House, Llanishen, near Chepstow, Mon.* (S.H.), 1925–1928. Upper V. Eight years in Australia and New Zealand. Farmer.

Livings, Montague. (S.H.), 1892–1896. Form V. Engineer.

Livingston, Arthur Burton. (S.H.), 1888–1889. 1st XV Rugby. Played Rugby for Swansea. Became Director of Messrs Livingston & Co., Coal and Patent Fuel Exporters. Died in October 1925, (" Star," Dec., 1925).

Livingston, Edward Llewellyn. (S.H.), 1888–1889. Capt in Mercantile Marine.

Livsey, Martin, 86 *London Road, North End, Portsmouth.* (Spr.), 1920–1927. Form V. House Monitor. Optician. Married.

Livsey, Stephen, *Chester Road, Holmes Chapel, Cheshire.* (Spr.), 1915–1922. Form VI. Senior. 1st XI Football. Head Designer, Holmes Chapel Branch of Wallpaper Manufacturers Co. Married : (1 dau.).

Llewellin, Herbert Clenyg Howard, *Hamilton Terrace, Milford Haven, Pem.* (h.). 25 *Brithdyr Street, St. Cathays, Cardiff.* (S.H.), 1928–1931. Form VI. House Monitor. School Certif. Chemist.

Lloyd, Geoffrey Herbert Thornley, *Inglewood, Melton Drive, Bridgend, Glam.* (H.), 1932–1936. Science VI. House Monitor. London Matric. Medical Student, Guy's Hospital.

Lloyd, George Arthur Lewis, 53 *Belper Road, Derby.* (Spr.), 1917–1921. Form VI. Probationer. London Matric. B.A., A.K.C. King's College London. Hon. Sec. for Debates and Vice-Pres. London University Union. Boxed for King's College. Lieut. London University O.T.C. Clerk in Holy Orders. Senior Curate, St. John with St. Savior, Fitzroy Sq., Succentor, Derby Cathedral. C.F. (R.A., R.O.). Married: (1 son, 1 dau.).

Lloyd, George David, *Lindula,* 23 *The Broadway, Thorpe Bay, Essex.* (H.), 1918–1924. Form VI. Senior. Pres. of League and Lit. Soc. Capt. 1st XI Football. 1st XI Cricket. Junior and Senior Athlete. Woodley Cup. Insurance Official with the National Mutual Life Assce. Society.

Lloyd, John Edward, 29 *Tyrone Road, Thorpe Bay, Essex.* (H.), 1914–1918. Form VI. Senior. Vice-Pres. of League. Pres. of Lit. Soc. A.S.M. Camb. Senior. Prize for Public Speaking. Capt. 1st XI. Cricket and 2nd XI Football. Camb. Univ. O.T.C. Capt. 6th Batt. Essex Regt. (T.A.). St. John's College, Cambridge. Chartered Accountant. Investment Trust Secretary. Married: (1 son, 1 dau.).

Lloyd, John Francis Peplow. (D.B.), 1916–1918. Form V. London University Diploma in Journalism. Journalist.

Lloyd, Philip Franklin, 3 *Park Lane Mansions, Croydon.* (H.), 1896–1900. Form VI. Senior. 1st XI Football. 2nd Lieut. R.E. Electrical Engineer. Married.

Lloyd, Thomas Owen Leeds. (S.H.), 1911–1917. Form V.

Locke, Gilbert Martin, 11 *Royal Crescent, Cheltenham.* (H.), 1902–1904. Form IV. Sergt. R.A.S.C. Bakery Manager. President of South Western Federation of Master Bakers and Confectioners. Married: (1 son).

Lockey, William Graham, 23 *Geraldine Road, Wandsworth Road, Wandsworth, S.W.* 18 (h.). *Osteraa* 6¹¹, *Aalborg, Denmark.* (S.H.), 1922–1925. Probationer. 1st XI Cricket and Football. Motor Engineer.

London, Douglas Norman. (H.), 1908–1912. Form V. 2nd XI Cricket. Sapper R.E. Licentiate of Society of Architects. Architect and Surveyor.

Lones, E. H. (S.H.), Form I.

Lones, Ralph Edward, *Oak House, Blaenavon, Mon.* (S.H.), 1908–1911. Form VI. Senior. Capt. 2nd XI Football. Lieut. 1st Mon. Regt. In Steel and Plate Industry.

Long, Geoffrey Robert Wallis, *Chitterne, Warminster, Wilts.* (O.B.), 1924–1925. Form III. Bank Official, Warminster.

Loosley, Stanley George Henry, 90 *Victoria Road N., Southsea, Hants.* (h.). *Wycliffe College, Stonehouse, Glos.* (H.), 1924–1929. Prefect. Pres. of League and Lit. Soc. Editor of "Star." Higher School Certif. 1st XI Cricket. 2nd XV Rugby. Chess, Shooting and Tennis Teams. Foster Rifle. Jeune Cup. Senior Doubles. Prize for Public Service. B.A., St. John's College, Cambridge. Mathematical Master at Chard School and (1934) at Wycliffe.

Lord, Harold Anthony, 60/64 *Fisherton Street, Salisbury.* (H.), 1896–1898. Form VI. Senior. Mech. Trans. A.S.C. Draper. Married: (2 sons).

Lorimer, John Scott. (D.B.), 1905–1907. Form III. On leaving Wycliffe attended Clayesmore School, Twickenham. In 1914 was in camp with the Artists Rifles, and in October was in France with the 1st Battalion. After three months, received commission in the Norfolk Regt. He became Captain and won the Military Cross. He was killed by a shell on the night of 4th–5th November 1917.

Lovell, Arthur Thomas, *Sunny Mead, Bishop Sutton, near Clutton, Bristol.* (S.H.), 1929–1930. Upper Remove. Grocer.

Lovell, John Allan, 380 *High Street, Cheltenham and Southover, Fairfields Park Road.* (S.H.), 1903–1904. Form VI. Senior. Rubber Merchant. Married : (2 daus.).

Lovell, George Harold, *Wydale, Fields Park Road, Newport, Mon.* (H.), 1911–1915. Form IV. A.S.C. Manufacturing Confectioner. Married.

Lovell, Tom, *Sunny Mead, Bishop Sutton, Bristol.* (S.H.), 1930–1932. Upper Remove.

Loxton, Ernest Adshead Dudley. (S.H.), 1904–1906. Form II. Took up farming and in 1911 sailed for Australia. Enlisted in 1914 in the Australian Light Horse and in April 1915 in the Infantry. He served for five months in Gallipoli, and in June 1916 in France. In the following September he was invalided home with dysentery. Returning to the Front at the end of 1917, he was engaged in heavy fighting in January, and on April 24th was mortally wounded by machine gun fire. He was buried at Caestre, near Hazebrouck.

Loxton, Edward William, *Virginia Farm, Queen Charlton, Keynsham, Som.* (Spr.), 1908–1909. Form IV. Lieut. E. Lancs. Regt. Commercial Traveller.

Loxton, Joseph Reginald, *Virginia Farm, Queen Charlton, Keynsham, Som.* (Spr.), 1903–1904. Form III. Dorset L.I. Farmer. Married.

Loxton, Wilfrid Paget, *Queen Charlton, Keynsham.* (Spr.), 1905. Form III. Farmer.

Luker, Cyril Tom, *Enfield, Cashes Green, near Stroud, Glos.* (H.), 1921–1931. Form VI. Prefect. Pres. of League. School Certif. 1st XV Rugby. 1st XI Cricket. Senior Tennis Singles. Junior and Senior Athlete. 100 yards record. Foster Rifle (twice). Prizes for Public Service and Harmston Music. B.A. St. John's College, Cambridge (Hons. Economics). With Jos. Lucas & Co., Birmingham.

Luker, Frederick George, *c/o Addison & Co. Ltd., Madras, India.* (D.B.), 1903–1910. Form VI. Senior. Pres. of Lit. Soc. Vice-Pres. of League. London Matric. 1st XI Cricket. Capt. 1st XI Football. Birmingham University Cricket and Football. B.Com. Inns of Court O.T.C. Member of the Legislative Council, Madras, 1932-1933. Chairman of European Assoc. S. Indian Branch 1934–1935. Director Madras Rotary Club 1933–1934. Director of Addison & Co. Married : (2 daus.).

Luker, Sidney Land, *Kuling, Strathfield, Sydney, N.S.W., Australia.* (D.B.), 1903–1907. Form VI. Senior. Pres. of Lit. Soc. Vice-Pres. of League. House Prize. B.Sc. Birmingham. President A.M.I.C.E. District Scout Commissioner. President Community Service League. Chartered Civil Engineer. Acting Chief Engineer, Dept. of Main Roads, N.S.W. War Service : 2nd Lieut. R.E. France and Flanders. Married : (2 sons, 2 daus.).

Luker, William, *The Tynings, Stonehouse, Glos.* (H.), 1924–1933. Form VI Commercial. House Monitor. London Matric. 1st XI Cricket. Student at London University.

Lulham, Archibald Robert, *Llanthony Abbey, Gloucester.* (H.), 1902–1903. Form III.

Lusty, A. R. D.B. for some years. On leaving school he went in for Journalism, and seemed to be doing well when he developed consumption. He died in 1909, when eighteen years of age.

Luttrell, William Fownes, *Inveresk, Bussage, Glos.* (Spr.), 1917–1919. Form I. Afterwards at Eton.

Lynham, George Allin, *Fernleigh, Heoldon, Whitchurch, Cardiff.* (S.H.), 1930–1935. Lower V. Architectural Student.

Mace, Albert Ernest, 44 *West Street, Chipping Norton.* (S.H.), 1883–1888. Solicitor (retired). Married.

Mace, Howard Kimberley, 27 *Grange Park, Ealing, Lomdon, W. 5.* (S.H.), 1903–1907. Form V. Senior. Artists' Rifles 1915–1916. Lieut. 12th Batt. London Regt. 1916–1919. Bank Manager, Lloyds Bank Ltd., Stamford Hill, 174 Clapton Common, E.C. 5. Married : (1 son).

Mace, John H. (S.H.), 1882–1884.

Macfarlane, Conrad Coulsting, *Clare House,* 12 *Beaconsfield Road, Weston-super-Mare.* (S.H.), 1899–1901. Form V. R.G.A. Wine Merchant. Married.

Mackenzie, A. Douglas. (S.H.), 1893–1894. Form IV. Has died.

Maddox, Donald Frederick, 17 *Pen Lea Road, Weston, near Bath.* (S.H.), 1918. Form IV. Building Contractor. Married.

Maggs, Charles, *Fairview, Nickerbah, Queensland.* (S.H.), 1899–1901. Form V. Farmer.

Maggs, Frank, *Pyt House, West Lavington, Wilts.* (S.H.), 1893–1895. Form IV. Chairman Devizes R.D. Council. Farmer. Married : (2 daus.).

Maggs, Frederick James, *Larcombe Farm, Exford, Somerset.* (S.H.), 1892–1894. Form IV. Farmer. Married.

Maggs, Joseph Herbert, *The Manor, Rushall, Marlborough.* (S.H.), 1888–1890. Probationer. Chairman United Dairies Ltd. Married.

Maggs, Leonard, *Bowerhill Lodge, Melksham.* (S.H.), 1900–1906. Form V. Senior. Capt. 1st XI, Cricket. 2nd XI Football. Pres. of Lit. Soc. Royal Garrison Artillery. Director of United Dairies Ltd.

Maidment, Stanley Charles. (S.H.), 1913–1914. Form IV.

Malings, Francis Rowland Fortnam, *Corndron, Dial Hill, Clevedon, Somerset.* (S.H.), 1931–1934. Modern VI. Prefect. School Certif. 1st XV Rugby. School Athletic Team. Apprentice to United Dairies Ltd., London.

Malings, William George Fortnam, *Cray Croft, Spa Road, Melksham, Wilts.* (S.H.), 1929–1930. Matric Form. School Certif. Bank Clerk.

Mander, Alfred Oswald. (H.), 1899–1902. Form III. Deceased 1935.

Mann, Francis Oswald Hasker, *Bellevue, Rodborough, Stroud.* (Spr.), 1927–1935. Science VI. Prefect. London Matric. Harmston Music Prize. Engineering Student at Queen Mary College, E. London.

Manning, Edward Vivian, 67 *Cranbrook Road, Redland, Bristol 6.* (S.H.), 1928–1935. Modern VI. Pres. of Lit. Soc. Vice-Pres. of League. Capt. 1st XI Cricket. 1st XV Rugby. A.S.M. Senior Tennis Doubles. Prizes for Excellence in Speaking and Public Service. With E. S. & A. Robinson, Bristol.

Manning, R. 1892–1893. Form II. Has died.

March, Hermann George, *The Red House, near Sandy, Bedfordshire.* (Spr.), 1919–1923. Form VI. Senior. Pres. of Lit. Soc. 1st XI Football. B.A. (Hons.), Lincoln College, Oxford. Chartered Accountant.

Marchant, G. T. H. Form III.

Marfell, H. W.

Marks, Gordon C., 8a *Merchant's Place, Reading.* (S.H.), 1890–1891. Probationer. 1st XI Football. A.M.I.M.E. Engineer. Married.

Marmont, Arthur J. B. (D.B.), 1886–1893. Form IV. 1st XI Football. Joined a wholesale house in London to gain experience for his father's business of pin manufacturer. Did a good deal in organizing Association Football in Mid-Gloucestershire. At the age of eighteen developed heart trouble and died in December 1896.

Marmont, Cuthbert B., *Verity House, Firs Glen Road, Bournemouth.* (D.B.), 1890–1899. Form VI. Senior. 1st XI Football Joint Senior Athlete with Bryan Fisher. Served three years with 26th Batt. Royal Fusiliers. Chief Cashier, Lloyds Bank Ltd., Bournemouth.

Marmont, Richard Haile, 51 *Bloxcidge Street, Langley, Birmingham.* (D.B.), 1926–1929. Upper III. Horticulture.

Marmont, Stanley, (D.B.), 1892–1898. Form V. Senior. 1st XI Football. Died in 1919.

Marsden, Charles Alan, c/o *Hinton & Son, Funchal, Madeira.* (Spr.), 1921–1926. Form V. Was farming in South Africa.

Marsden, Cyril, *Ashtree, Magdala Road, Nottingham.* (Spr.), 1902–1904. Form VI. Senior. B.Sc. Engineer.

Marsden, Harry. (H.), 1909–1912. Form V. Probationer. Joined his uncle's firm (J.D. Marsden) in Nottingham, and then the Sherwood Foresters. On the outbreak of the Sinn Fein rebellion saw active service in Ireland in 1916. Went to France as a Lewis gunner in 1917, and received wounds, subsequently fatal, in one of the great attacks near Ypres. Sept. 26th 1917. (" W. & W." 73).

Marsden, Laurence, 42 *Mayo Road, Sherwood Rise, Nottingham.*

Marsden, Thomas Haynes, 7 *Grosvenor Avenue, Nottingham.* (Spr.), 1902–1904. Form VI. London Matric. Secretary and Director, J. D. Marsden Ltd., Grocers. Married.

Marsh, Norman Baylis, *Exbridge House, Exbridge, near Tiverton.* (S.H.), 1889–1891. 1st XV Rugby. Timber Merchant. Married.

Marsh, William, *Ontario, Canada.*

Marshall, Allan Shirley, 3 *Devonshire Road, Westbury Park, Bristol.* (D.B.), 1893–1896. Form V. Horticulturist.

Marshall, John. (D.B.), 1898–1902. Form III. Deceased.

Marshall, John Percival. (Spr.), 1909–1912. Form VI. Senior. Entered Humber Works at Coventry and then took his Matric (London). Entered Woolwich in 1914, and in 1915 obtained commission in the R.F.A. Died of gas poisoning in Nov. 1917. (" W. & W." 74).

Marshall, Lenton Woodward, *Sharem Cottage, Charlton Horethorne, Som.* (D.B.), 1896. Major, Glos. Regt. Bank Cashier (retired). Married.

Marshman, T. Wallis, *Imber, Devizes, Wilts.* (H.), 1922–1925. Form V. Probationer. Miller.

Martin, Alfred, 31 *Victoria Embankment, Nottingham.* (Spr.), 1910–1914. Form V. Probationer. 2nd XI. Served in the Infantry, 1915–1918. Capt. and Adjutant. Company Director. Married : (2 sons, 1 dau.).

Martin, Bernard. (Spr.), 1910–1915. Form V. Probationer. Lieut. R.A.F. Served in France and Italy. At the age of eighteen brought down two German single fighting planes and attained rank of Acting Flight Commander. After the War became a pilot Instructor and in 1924 took part in the King's Cup race. In 1926 was appointed Chief Inspector of the Curtis-Reid Aircraft Co.'s Flying School at Montreal.

In October 1931 he was engaged by Canadian Airways as an air-mail pilot, and took part in the Trans-Canada Air Pageant. He was killed in June 1933, when testing a new aeroplane. ("Star," Aug. 1933, p. 32).

Martin, Laurence Alfred Dunkley, *Woodend, Warren Drive, Kingswood, Surrey.* (Spr.), 1914–1918. Form VI. Senior. Pres. of League. London Matric. 1st XI Cricket and Football. Prize for Public Speaking. Sergt.-Major, Inns of Court O.T.C. LL.B. (Hons.) London. Solicitor. Married : (1 son).

Martin, Richard William. (S.H.), 1896–1897. Form V. Settled down as ironmonger at Castle Cary, Somerset. Was Vice-Pres. of local Liberal Club, and engaged in various forms of public work. Was killed in a traffic collision on January 7th 1917. ("Star," April 1917, p. 48).

Martin, Robert Thomas Butt, *The Croft, Westrip, Stroud.* (D.B.), 1921–1928. Upper IV. House Monitor. Farmer.

Martyn, Henry Kenneth Graham, 25 *Tolcarne Road, Newquay, Cornwall.* (H.), 1915–1920. Form VI. Senior. 2nd XI Football. Accountant. A.C.A.

Mascall, Robert, *Ingleneuk, 2 Phillips Avenue, Linthorpe, Middlesbrough.* (S.H.), 1904–1907. Form VI. Senior. Vice-Pres. of League. Capt. 1st XI. Cricket. 1st XI Football. Amateur Assoc. International. Lieut. R.G.A. Treas. and Pres. of Middlesbrough Rotary Club 1934. Treas. and Pres. of North of England Branch of National Federation of Slate Merchants. Pres. of Middlesbrough Round Table (1935). On Board of Management of Middlesbrough Musical Union and also of Y.M.C.A. Tiling Contractor and Merchant. Married : (1 son, 1 dau.).

Mascall, Vallance Cook, *Beechlyn, Wesigaier Road, Linthorpe, Middlesbrough.* (S.H.), 1910–1914. Upper IV. Probationer. 1st XI Cricket. 2nd XI Football. Artists' Rifles. 2nd Lieut. N. Lancashire Regt. attached 7th S. Lancashires (Cambrai, Passchendaele). Slate Merchant. Married : (1 son, 1 dau.).

Mascall, William Neville, 97 *Grosvenor Road, London, S.W.* 1 (h.). 149 *Harley Street, W.* 1. (S.H.), 1914–1919. Form VI. Senior. Vice-Pres. of League. Capt. 1st XI Football. 2nd XI Cricket. M.A., Pembroke College, Cambridge. M.R.C.S. (Eng.), L.R.C.P. (Lond.). House Physician and Obstetrical Registrar, St. Thomas's Hospital. Assistant M.O.H., Rotherham. Consultant in London.

Maslin, Charles Edward, 21 *High Street, Clacton-on-Sea, Essex.* (S.H.), 1907–1911. Form V. 2nd XI Football. Junior Athlete. Capt. R.A.F. 120 yards Hurdles Champion. F.M.S. and Straits Settlements. Draper. Married : (1 son, 1 dau.).

Maslin, Jack Marcus Frank. (D.B.), 1915–1916. Form III.

Mason, Charles Leo, *Conniscliffe, Coronation Avenue, Heywood, Lancs.* (S.H.), 1920–1925. Form V. Probationer. Senior Camb. Assoc. of Chartered Insurance Inst. S.M. 4th Heywood Scouts. Resident Inspector Insurance.

Mastin, Leslie Arthur Cyril, *Connage, Bath Road, Stroud.* (D.B.), 1910–1916. Form III. Royal Warwickshire Regt. Commercial Traveller. Married : (1 child).

Matcham, Reginald Charles, 23 *Balmoral Road, St. Andrews, Bristol.* (S.H.), 1910–1912. Form III. Probationer. War Service 1916–1920, Egypt and N.W. Frontier of India. Afghan War 1919. Accountant, Auctioneer, Estate Agent and Quarry Owner. Married : (1 son, 1 dau.).

Mathias, Frederick William. (S.H.), 1901–1902. Married.

Mathias, R. Evan, *Ty-r-haul, Pontypridd.* (Spr.), 1908–1910. Form IV. Lieut. Welch Regt. Civil Engineer.

Mathias, W. Douglas, *Ty-r-haul, Pontypridd.* (Spr.), 1909–1911. Form III.

Matthews, Gerald Royston Morgan, 51 *Glanmor Road, Swansea.* (Spr. and H.), 1926–1931. Form V.

May, John Allan, 18 *Chepstow Villas, London, W.* 11. (Spr.), 1927–1931. Form VI. Pres. of Lit. Soc. Higher Certif. 1st XI Cricket. 2nd XV Rugby. Light- and Middle-weight Boxing Champ. Prize for Public Speaking. On Staff of " Christian Science Monitor." Married.

Maxey, H. M. 1891. Form I.

Maze, Douglas, *High Hopes, Yateley, nr. Camberley, Surrey.* (Spr.), 1917–1921. Form V. Probationer. Music Prize. Bank Clerk.

Maze, Eric, *Burghfield, nr. Reading.* (Spr.), 1917–1920. Form V. Probationer. Bank Cashier. Married : (1 dau.).

McCall, William Anderson. (H.), 1888–1890. Was associated with McCall Bros., Cloth Manufacturers, Trowbridge. He died in February 1926. (" Star," April 1926, p. 18).

McCormack, Dermot Patrick Hugh, *Midhill, Chalford, Glos.* (O.B., H. and D.B.), 1915–1917. Form III. Electrical Engineer. With Messrs. Walker Sons & Co., Electrical Engineers, Talawakele, Ceylon.

McCormack, James Denis, *Midhill, Chalford, Glos.* (D.B.), 1913–1928. Lower V. In charge of the Dye House at Marling & Evans, Stanley Mills.

McCrea, Edward D'Arcy, *The Cottage, Worsley, near Manchester.* (S.H.), 1905–1911. Form VI. Senior. Cambridge Senior. 2nd XI Football. Junior Athlete. Trinity College, Dublin, and Emmanuel College, Cambridge. M.D., M.Ch. (Dublin). F.R.C.S. (Eng. & Ire.). Research Fellow, University of Manchester. Hon. Surgeon Salford Royal Hospital. Lawn Tennis Half-Blue, Cambridge. Represented Ireland and Gt. Britain at Tennis. Olympic Games (for Ireland) 1924. Capt. R.A.M.C. Married : (1 son, 1 dau.).

McCrea, Philip C. S., 12 *Milner Street, Grahamstown, S. Africa.* (S.H.), 1910–1916. Probationer. 2nd XI Football. Lieut. R.A.F.

McFarlan, James William, *The Acacias, Stonehouse, Glos.* (D.B.), 1926–1934. Form VI. House Monitor. School Certif. Prize for Public Speaking. Undergraduate at Hertford College, Oxford.

McLannahan, George Goodhart, *The Mount, Stonehouse, Glos.* (D.B.) 1921–1924. Form II. Flying Officer R.A.F. Civil Aviation.

Meek, Arthur John, *Beechurst, Stockwood Crescent, Luton, Beds.* (S.H.), 1932–1936. Form VI. House Monitor. Oxford and Cambridge School Certif. Articled to Town Clerk, Luton.

Meldrum, Ian Haworth, *St. Mary's Gronant, Prestatyn, N. Wales.* (Spr.). 1929–1932. Upper V. Light-weight Boxing Champ.

Menedez, Frank Tremar Sibly, *Pendrea, Eton Av., Sudbury, Wembley,* (H.), 1909–1912. Form VI. Senior. 2nd XI Cricket and Football. Lieut. R.A.F. M.C. Civil Servant. Married.

Menedez, William Joseph, 170 *Marion Street, Toronto, Canada.* (H.), 1889–1893. Form VI. Sec. and Treas. Lit. Soc. 1st XI Cricket. 1st XI and 1st XV Football. Master at Wycliffe 1895–1896. Imperial Lighthouse Service 1907–1920. War Medal and Mercantile Marine Medal. Bahamas Hardware Merchant 1923–1930. Married : (1 son, 2 daus.).

Merrett, H. T., *Bath Road, Stonehouse, Glos.*

Metcalfe, Claude Jess, *Kimsbury,* 12 *Neville Road, Kersal, Manchester.* (S.H.), 1917–1925. Form V. Senior. Vice-Pres. of League. 1st XI Cricket. Music Prize. Solicitor. Married.

Michell, Jack, *Ravendene, Clements Road, Polwithin, Penzance.* (S.H.), 1917–1921. Probationer. Jeweller.

Michell, Tom Bennetts, *Mythyon, Heamoor, Penzance, Cornwall.* (S.H.), 1915–1918. Form IV. Senior. 1st XI Football. Jeweller. Married.

Miller, Cyril Ruegg, *Cyprus Villa, Chalford Hill, Glos.* (D.B.), 1919–1923.

Miller, James Alexander. (H.), 1893–1896. Worked with his father in salmon fisheries till the outbreak of war, when he served as Captain with the Middlesex Regt. in France and Italy, and was mentioned in despatches. He was subsequently in charge of the Foyle, Bann and Portrush Fisheries. He died in July 1925. ("Star," Dec. 1925).

Miller, Leslie William Spencer, *Cyprus Villa, Chalford Hill, Glos.* (D.B.) 1915–1919. Architect.

Miller, Lionel Stewart, *c/o J. A. Miller, The Old Rectory, Culmore, Co. Derry.* (H.), 1894–1896. Form III.

Milligan, Kenneth, *Southcroft, Caswell Road, Mumbles, Glam.* (H.), 1927–1932. Upper V. School Certif. B.Sc. Swansea University. With Messrs. Siemens Bros. (Woolwich).

Minors, Leslie E. S., 36 *Baldwin Street, Bristol.* (Spr.), 1904–1906. Sergt. A.S.C. British-American Tobacco Co.

Moffatt, Allen Brookes, 22 *Cumberland Place, Southampton.* (D.B.), 1920–1923. Probationer. Senior Camb. B.Sc., M.B., Ch.B. Manchester. M.D. Hon. Ophthalmic Surgeon, Free Eye Hospital. Late Resident Surgical Officer, Manchester Royal Eye Hospital. Member Oxford Ophthalmic Congress.

Mogridge, E. C., *Benin City, S. Nigeria, W. Africa.* Form I. Capt. Suffolk Regt.

Monaghan, Denis Laurence. (D.B.), 1899–1902. Form III. He afterwards went to Uppingham and University College, London, where he took up engineering and became an A.M.I.C.E. He was for a time associated with the Brecon and Merthyr Railway, and played Rugby for Middlesex and Cheshire. He obtained a commission in the Royal Irish Rifles, and was wounded in the Battle of the Somme. He transferred to the Tank Corps, and was killed on November 24th by a stray shell in Bourlon Wood. ("W. & W." 76).

Monaghan, R. (S.H.), 1883. Died in America in 1903.

Monaghan, Trenly. (D.B.), 1883.

Moncrieff, J. Scott.

Montrésor, Charles Egerton. (H.), 1904–1906. Form II.

Moody, Norman Herridge, *The Bungalow, Poulmer Road, Ringwood, Hants.* (H.), 1911–1915. Form VI. Senior. Vice-Pres. of League. 2nd XI Football. Royal Flying Corps 1915–1917. Music Prize. R.F.C. Poultry and Dairy Farmer. Married.

Moon, Arthur Letcher, *c/o Barclays Bank (D.C. & O.), Verulam, Natal.* (H.), 1893–1895. Form VI. Probationer. Associate of Inst. of Accountants (Natal). Bank Manager. Widower : (2 sons).

Moon, John Stafford, *Yew Tree Cottage, Church Lane, Chessington, Surrey.* (S.H. and Grove), 1928–1933. Science VI. House Monitor. School Certif. University of London 1933–1937.

Moore, J.

Moore, Lawrence Charles Lyndon, *Elmscott, Prince of Wales Road, Dorchester.* (S.H.), 1905–1908. Form V. Probationer. Capt. 2nd XI Cricket. 2nd XI Football. War Service 1914–1918 France, Egypt, Salonica and Army of Occupation. Partner in M. H. Tilley & Son, Gold and Silversmiths, 7 Cornhill, Dorchester. Married : (2 sons, 1 dau., 2 step-daus.).

Moorman, Frederick William. (D.B.), 1882–1884. B.A. (London) and Ph.D. (Strasbourg). Was Professor of English Literature at Leeds University. He wrote several books on English Poetry. He was drowned while bathing in the Wharfe.

Mordle, Percy M. (S.H.), 1887–1891. Form VI. Senior. London Matric. Prize of 1st Class Camb. Jun. Solicitor and Civil Servant. He died in 1927.

More, Alexander Wilfred Strickland, 9 *Birdhurst Road, S. Croydon.* (Spr.), 1927–1929. L wer V.

Morgan, D. I. Freeman. (H.). He entered the Merchant Service and became an officer in the P. & O. Line, gaining a 1st Class Officer's Certificate. During the War he became a Lieut. in the R.N.A.S., but died on May 9th 1915 at the age of 28. (" W. & W." 27).

Morgan, Edward Stanley. (D.B.), 1902–1906. Form V. Qualified as an Auctioneer with a Gloucester firm. In 1907 he became a Lieut. in the R.A.F., and won the Distinguished Flying Cross. On Sept. 7th 1918 he and his observer were both killed when his plane crashed into the sea off the Belgian coast. (" W. & W.", 81).

Morgan, Godfrey, *Churchend, Slimbridge, Glos.* (D.B.), 1901–1904. Form III.

Morgan, Ivor Stather, *Trosnant Villa, Pontypool, Mon.* (Spr.), 1925–1929. Lower IV.

Morgan, John Hywel. (S.H.), 1897–1903. Form V. Was for five years in the service of the Bank of Bengal. In 1915 he obtained a commission in the Duke of Cornwall's Light Infantry, and was at first sent to India. Ultimately he served in Palestine, where he died of wounds received in action on November 22nd 1917. (" W. & W.", 77).

Morgan, Ralph Gwyn. (S.H.), 1903–1905. Form VI. Mercantile Marine. Lieut. R.N.V.R. H.M.S. " Intrepid." Service in Russia ; then Gunnery Officer, Flagship of Light Cruiser Squadron ; later Lieut. Navigator of Submarine. Married. Died August 9th 1932.

Morgan, Richard Godfrey. (S.H.), 1903–1906. Form VI. Senior. Treas. of Lit. Soc. 2nd XI Football. On leaving school he entered the service of the Capital & Counties Bank and took the final certificate of the Institute of Bankers. During the War he first served in India with the East Surrey Regt. Later he obtained a commission in the East Yorkshire Regt. and in 1916 was sent to France. He took part in the opening of the Somme offensive. On November 13th 1916 he was reported missing, and it was not until March 11th 1917 that his body was recovered, and he was laid to rest on the battlefield of Serre, where he had fallen. (" W. & W.", 79).

Morgan, Thomas John, 12 *Archer Road, Penarth.* (H.), 1896–1899. Form V. Senior. 1st XI Football. Sergt. Canadian Army. Solicitor.

Morgan, Wilfrid Wynter, *Churchend, Slimbridge, Glos.* (D.B.), 1904–1910. Form VI. Senior. Capt. Glos. Regt. M.C. Married.

Morris, Arthur Russell, *Comrie,* 4 *Russell Road, Buckhurst Hill, Essex.* (Spr.), 1927–1932. Form VI. Prefect. Treas. of Lit. Soc. School Certif. 1st XV Rugby. Speaking Prize. B.A., St. John's College, Cambridge. In Publishing Firm.

Morris, Charles Ambler, *Lansdown, Tiverton, Devon.* (H.), 1912–1915. Form III. Editor of " The Tiverton Gazette." Married : (1 son, 1 dau.).

Morris, Donald Sinclair, *Comrie, 4 Russell Road, Buckhurst Hill, Essex.* (Spr.), 1929–1935. Science VI. Prefect. Vice-Pres. of League. Pres. of Lit. Soc. School Certif. 1st XV Rugby. Athletic Team. High Jump Record. Speaking Prize. Medical Student, St. Bart.'s Medical School.

Morris, Frank. (D.B.), 1899–1901. Form III. Engineer.

Morris, Graham Tregithim, *The Glyn, Westcross, Swansea.* (H.), 1906–1912. Form IV. Probationer. 1st XI Cricket and Football. Lieut. M.G.C.

Morris, Luther P. (Spr.), 1904–1905. Form III. 1st XI Football. 2nd XI Cricket. R.E.

Morris, Richard S. (H.), 1886–1887. Probationer. House Prize. Lieut. A.S.C. Surveyor and Estate Agent. Married. Died in 1926.

Morse, Cecil Charles William, *Field Court Farm, Quedgeley, Glos.* (D.B.), 1902–1906. Form III. Glos. Regt. Married. Farmer.

Mortimer, Percival Barling. (D.B.), 1894–1897. Form IV. Ih Canada. Married.

Mortimer, T. Leslie. (D.B.), 1894–1898. Form VI. Senior. Capt. R.A.S.C. O.B.E. Bank Inspector. Married.

Morton, Charles Frederick Alexander, *21 Suffolk Road, Barnes, London, S.W. 13* (h.). *c/o G. Mills & Co., Kirkland House, S.W. 1.* (H.), 1912–1916. Senior. Pres. of League. Capt. 2nd XI Football and Cricket. Junior Athlete. House Prize. 2nd Lieut. London Regt. Member of the H.A.C. Director of National Wine & Distilleries Stores, Ltd. Married.

Morton, Edward Henry. (Spr.), 1903–1904. Form IV.

Morton, John Williamson, *Rulow Lodge, Buxton Old Road, Macclesfield.* (S.H.), 1928–1931. Lower V. House Monitor. Flour Miller. Under-Manager Hovis Ltd. (Lincoln).

Morton, Oliver Sifford. (H.), 1899–1900. Form V.

Muir, James Moffat. (S.H.), 1900–1901. Civil and Mining Engineer.

Muller, Eugen Jorgen Bror Chatelain, *Roseview, Warkworth, New Zealand.* (Spr.), 1920–1925. Form I. Swimming Champ. 1922, 1923, 1924. Farming. Married : (1 son).

Mullins, Eric William. (S.H.), 1914–1916. Form III.

Mullins, George Edward, *2 New Street, Wells, Som.* (h.). (S.H.), 1905–1907. Form V. Senior. Pres. of Lit. Soc. Senior Athlete. 2nd XI Cricket and Football. House Prize and for Public Speaking. Surgeon R.N. Sometime House Surgeon at Queen's Hospital, Birmingham. M.R.C.S., L.R.C.P. (London). Hon. Medical Officer to Wells Division and Public Vaccinator. Surgeon Wells Division St. John's Ambulance Brigade. R.S.O. and R.M.O., Children's Hospital, Birmingham. General Medical Officer. Married : (1 son, 4 daus.).

Mullins, John Arthur. (S.H.), 1915–1916. Form III.

Mullins, Vincent Kenneth, *Regent House, Stonehouse, Glos.* (D.B.), 1918–1925. Form III.

Mullins, William John, *Regent House, Stonehouse, Glos.* (D.B.), 1919–1927. Upper V. Prefect. Vice-Pres. of League. School Certif. 1st XI Football and Cricket. 1st XV Rugby. Tennis Team. Outfitter.

Muncaster, T. James. (D.B.), 1888–1890. Probationer.

Muriset, Olivier Armand James Needham, *Church Street, Rushden, Northants.* (S.H.), 1897–1899. Form II. M.B., Ch.B. (Edinburgh), 1910. M.O.H. Rushden U.D.C. Medical Officer P.O. Hon. Capt. R.A.M.C. Fellow Royal Society Medicine. Late Resident Physician Royal Victoria Hospital for Consumptives, Edinburgh. Chief Tuberc. Officer, Northants C.C. Married.

Murley, John Roy Patterson, *Belgrave Court, Walter Road, Swansea.* (S.H.), 1930–1934. Lower VI. House Monitor. London Matric. 2nd XV Rugby. Medical Student at Guy's Hospital.

Mutton, Bernard W. G. (S.H.), 1917–1919. Form IV.

Nash, Albert Edward, *The Pines, Downwoods Drive, Toronto, Canada.* (H.), 1893–1895. Form IV. Alberta Lawn Tennis Champion 1910–1911. Lieut.-Col. commanding (in 1936) " The Mississauga Horse." War Service : Lieut. 19th Alberta Dragoons 1915. Capt. 1917. Major 1918. Trans. to 218th Inf. Batt. to 8th C.R.T. Western Front 1917–1918. Battles of Messines, Passchendaele. M.C. Chartered Accountant. Married : (3 daus.).

Nash, H. B. N. *vide* **Norton-Nash.**

Nash, Albert Henry, 30 *Howley Place, Paddington, W.* (S.H.), 1893–1895. Form IV. Draper.

Neale, Jack Warner, *Brook End, Berkeley, Glos.* (S.H.), 1922–1925. Form I. Farmer.

Neary, D. A. (Spr.), 1925. Form III. Died April 1926.

Netherway, Stanley P., *Fernbank, Mountain Ash, Glam.* (S.H.), 1903–1905. Form IV. 1st XI Football. 2nd XI Cricket. Senior Athlete. 1st Prize for Gymnastics. War Service : 23rd Sanitary Section R.A.M.C. In France May 1915–December 1918. Assistant Surveyor to Mountain Ash U.D. Council. Married : (1 son, 1 dau.).

New, G. E., *Westbury-on-Severn, Glos.* 1892–1893. Form III. Provision Merchant. Married.

Newcomen, Arthur B., *Nodens, Aylburton Common, Lydney, Glos.* (D.B.), 1898–1900. Form IV. Probationer. Manufacturing Chemist.

Newcomen, Thomas Guy, 39 *Hornsey Lane, London, N. 6.* (D.B.), 1898–1899. Form II. Chartered Civil Engineer. Married.

Newham, Clifford Howard, 106 *South Madison Avenue, La Grange, Illinois, U.S.A.* (H.), 1897–1902. Form IV. 1st XI Cricket and Football. Senior Athlete. Drury College. Springfield, Missouri, U.S.A. Northwestern University, Garrett Biblical Institute, Chicago. Army Service : Graduate of the Chaplain's Training School. Commissioned 1st Lieut. Chaplain. Minister of the Methodist Episcopal Church, U.S.A. Married.

Newham, Theodore Nelson, *Rock Holme, Quarry Road, Hastings.* (H.), 1897–1900. Form IV. 1st XI Cricket. Architect.

Newill, Edward Norman. (H.), 1911–1914. Form IV. Probationer. Music and Literature Prizes. Auctioneer and Valuer. Died in 1935. ("Star," August, 1935, p. 37).

Newman, Arthur Dudley, *Chestnut Hill, Nailsworth, Glos.* (D.B.), 1887–1892. Form VI. Senior. London Matric. House Prize. 1st XI Cricket. Junior Athlete. Engineer.

Newman, Charles Percy, *The Knoll, Amberley, Glos.* (S.H. and H.), 1887–1890. Company Director. Married.

Newman, Douglas Henry, *Cotswold, Mayfield Avenue, Prymble, Sydney, N.S.W.* (H.)., 1912–1916. For, III. Probationer. 2nd XI Football. Colonial Wool Merchant. Married : (2 sons, 1 dau.).

Newman, Francis, Bernard, *Newmarket House, Nailsworth, Glos.* (D.B.), 1885–1891. Form VI. Senior. House Prize. 1st XI Cricket. Colonial Wood Merchant.

Newman, Francis Lindsay. (D.B.), 1894–1898. Form VI. Senior. One of the managing directors of the Woodchester branch of the United Brass Founders & Engineers Co. He died of appendicitis, September 1921. (" Star," Dec. 1921).

Newman, Henry St. Elmo. (S.H.), 1896–1898. Form IV. Wool Merchant.

Newman, Herbert Mayo, *Rockness, Nailsworth, Glos.* (D.B.), 1883–1886. Form VI. Senior. London Matric. Capt 1st XI Cricket. 1st XV Rugby. Colonial Wool Merchant. Senior Vice-Pres. Colonial Wool Buyers' Association. J.P. Glos. War Service : Distributor of Colonial Wool in West of England under War Office. Married : (2 sons, 2 daus.).

Newman, Horace Sidney, *Garden House, London Road, Newcastle, Staffs.* (S.H.), 1897–1900. Form V. Bronze Medallist. Engineer and Manager Bullers Ltd. Married.

Newman, James Frederick, *Lassington, Streetly, Staffs.* (Spr.), 1926–1931. Form VI. House Monitor. London Matric. Harmston Music Prize. Medical Student, Birmingham University.

Newman, Julian Bedford, *Worley, Nailsworth, Glos.* (D.B.), 1884–1887. Senior. House Prize. 2nd XV Rugby. War Service : Acted under Government Scheme of Wool Control. Wool Broker (retired). Married : (3 sons, 1 dau.).

Newman, Reginald Mayo, *Theescombe Hill, Amberley, Glos.* (H.), 1909–1915. Form VI. Senior. Senior Camb. 2nd XI Cricket. Lieut. R.G.A. Mentioned. Colonial Wool Trade. Married : (2 sons, 1 dau.).

Newman, Samuel John. (S.H.), 1887–1892. Form VI. Senior. 2nd XI Cricket. Director of Newman, Hender & Co., Brassfounders. Married. Died in 1935. (" Star," August 1935, p. 37).

Newson, Frederick W. Died in America, where for several years he was a Bank Cashier in Vermont, New England.

Newth, Jack Douglas, *Briardene, Bois Lane, Chesham Bois, Bucks.* (D.B. and Spr.), 1914–1921. Form VI. Senior. Pres. of League and Lit. Soc. London Matric. House and Speaking Prizes. Capt. 1st XI Cricket. 2nd XI Football. Senior Cross Country Championship. B.A. (Hons.) and Stillingfleet Prizeman, Lincoln College, Oxford. Director of A. & C. Black, Ltd., Publishers. Member of Council of Governors of Wycliffe College. Married : (1 dau.).

Niblett, Edwin Paul. (D.B.), 1901–1902.

Nicholls, Albert Edgar. *Stalheim, Meole Brace, near Shrewsbury.* (S.H.), 1897–1903. Form VI. Senior. Vice-Pres. of League. Pres. of Lit. Soc. London Matric. Music and Speaking Prizes. 2nd XI Football. M.R.C.S., L.R.C.P. West Midland Medical Board. Medical Practitioner. Married : (several children).

Nicholls, Clifford, 14 *Taff Mead, Emblett, Cardiff.* (H.), 1898–1900. Sergt. Canadian Army. Wine and Spirit Merchant. Married : (2 sons).

Nicholls, Frank Edwin, *Normanhurst, Bridge Road, Epsom.* (H.), 1898–1900. Form V. Probationer. Capital & Counties Bank.

Nicholls, Theodore, c/o Dr A. E. *Nicholls, as above.* (S.H.), 1898–1903. Form V. Probationer. Sec. of Lit. Soc. Chef de Cuisine (Gold and Silver Medals).

Niles, William Leonard. (Spr.), 1906–1907. Form III. 1st XI Football. Cpl. Canadian Army.

Noakes, Philip Reuben, *Fernbank, How Lane, Chipstead, Surrey.* (H.), 1930–1934. Form VI. Prefect. Pres. of League and Lit. Soc. 2nd XI Cricket. Capt. 1st XV Rugby. Higher School Certif. Scholarship to Queen's College, Cambridge. Prizes for Lit. Comp. and Public Speaking. Undergraduate at Queen's College, Cambridge. Secretary of Union Society 1937.

Norman, Denis Charles, 190 *Middleton Hall Road, King's Norton, Birmingham.* (Spr.), 1926–1932. Modern VI. Prefect. Higher School Certif. School Chess Team. Printer.

Norman, Rowland Bruce, *Royal Automobile Club, Pall Mall, S.W. 1.* (S.H.), 1906–1907. Form VI. Senior. Cambridge Senior. Lieut., Lancs. Fusiliers. Bank Manager.

Norman, Wilfred R. (S.H.), 1890–1893. Form VI. 1st XI Football. In U.S.A.

Norman, William Gerald, *Cannard's Grave, Shepton Mallet, Som.* (S.H.), 1926–1928. Form V. House Monitor. Farming.

Norris, Charles Grayson, 56 *Carbery Avenue, W. Southbourne, Bournemouth.* (D.B.), 1910–1916. Form VI. Senior. Vice-Pres. of League London Matric. House Prize. 1st XI Cricket and Football. Senior Cross Country Record. R.F.A. Cadet. Solicitor. Married : (2 sons, 1 dau.).

Norris, Donald Lapage, *Field House, Minchinhampton, Glos.* (D.B.), 1916–1921. Form V. Probationer. Solicitor. Married : (1 son).

Norris, F. Joined Strathcona's Horse and was killed in action in the South African War.

Norris, J. Died in Canada in 1905.

Norris, John Sidney Lapage, 52 *F.O. Quarters, Europa, Gibraltar. Poplar Gate. Stonehouse* (h.). (D.B.), 1909–1915. Senior. 2nd XI Cricket and Football. Capt and Adjutant R.A. M.C. Married : (2 daus.).

North, John Howard, *Highfield Lodge, Stroud, Glos.* (D.B.), 1920–1927. Form V. Merchant Venturers Technical College, Pharmacy Dept. Passed Chemist and Druggist Qualifying Exam. Chemist and Druggist. M.P.S.

Norton-Nash, Henry Beddoes, 12 *Fields Park Road, Newport, Mon.* (S.H.), 1893–1895. Form III. F.S.I. Chartered Surveyor. Civil Servant, Valuation Office, Inland Revenue. Married.

Nott, John Arkell, *St. Ives, Naunton Park Road, Cheltenham.* (S.H. and D.B.), 1928–1933. Science VI. Prefect. Higher Certif. B.Sc. Engineering (1st Class Hons.). Member I.E.E. Electrical Engineer.

Ockenden, W. (S.H.), 1885–1888.

Offord, John Jeffcoat. (H.), 1901. He died of scarlet fever at Ealing in January 1902, when fourteen years of age.

Offord, Norman. (H.), 1902–1907. Form VI. Probationer. Lieut. R.A.F. Automobile Engineer and Coach Builder. Married.

Okey, Harold George. (S.H.), 1899–1902. Form III. He was in business in Plymouth when the War broke out, and after many rejections was finally accepted for the R.A.M.C. The strenuous work involved in the great push revived an old weakness, and after an operation he died at Devonport in September 1916. ("W. & W.", 82).

A SYLVAN SCENE ON DOVEROW : LOOKING WEST TO THE SEVERN AND THE HILLS OF THE FOREST OF DEAN

WINDRUSH

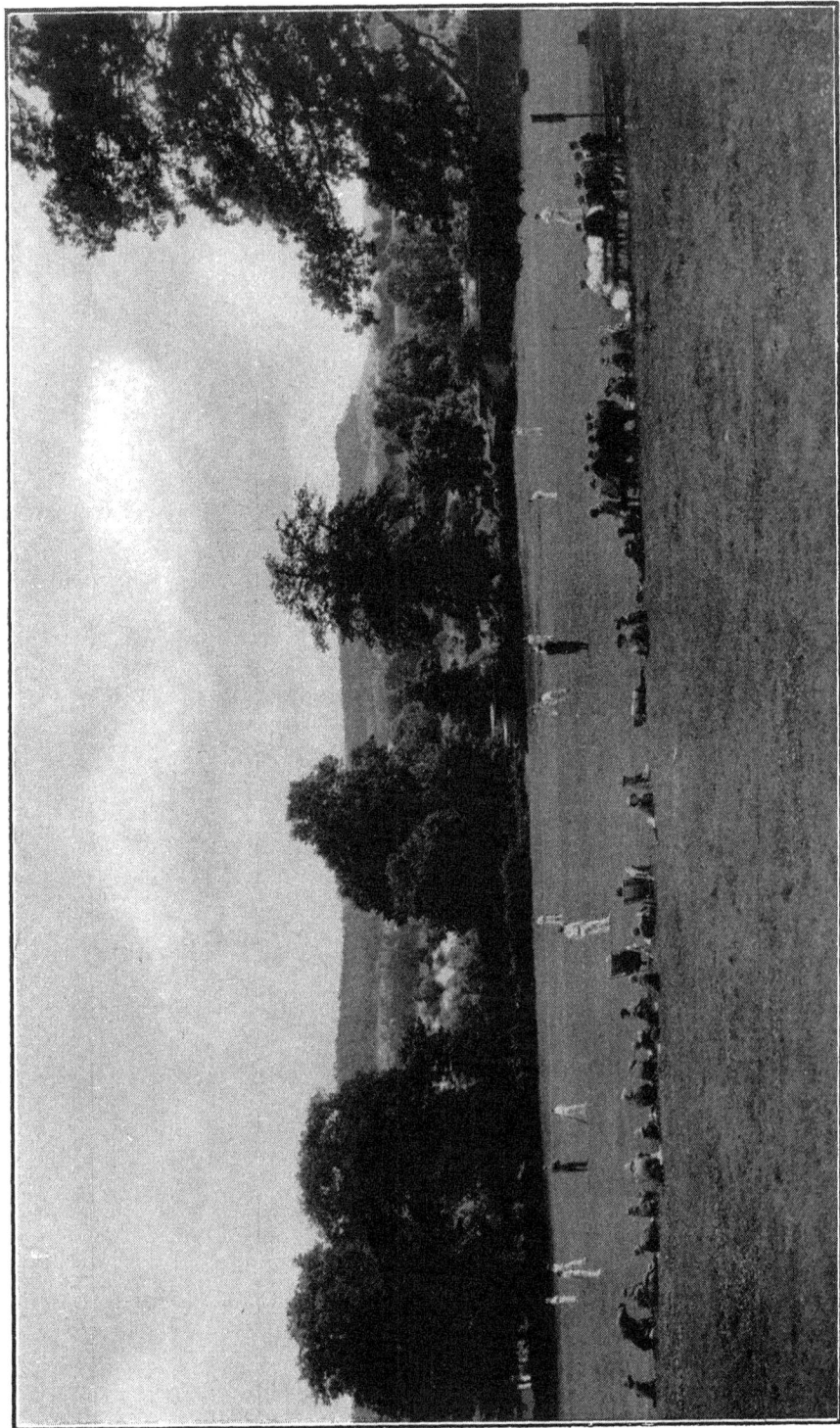

ONE OF THE JUNIOR SCHOOL PLAYING FIELDS

THE SANATORIUM

(This serves the needs of both Wycliffe and Ryeford, and contains 10 isolation rooms with accommodation for nearly 30 beds. The Office of the School Secretary is in the old Jacobean house which adjoins it).

Osborn, Edward Kelvin, 21 *Kimberley Road, Cardiff.* (Spr.), 1922–1927. Form VI. Prefect. Vice-Pres. of League. Sec. of Lit. Soc. Higher Certif. Middle-weight Boxing Champ. 2nd XI Football. Batchelar Cup. Public Speaking Prize. M.A. Cantab. (Christ's College). Modern Language Master at Solihull School 1932–1936, now at Bishop Wordsworth's School, Salisbury.

Osborne, J. Tysoe. (H.), 1889. He became partner in the flour mills at King's Langley, Herts., and was killed by the fall of a limb of a tree while playing golf at the West Herts. Club, Cassiobury Park, November 1923. ("*Star,*" Dec., 1923, p. 13).

Osborne, Robert J., *Kersoe, Elmley Castle, Pershore, Worcs.* (H.), 1930–1933. Upper V. School Certif. Birmingham School of Architecture. Farmer (student).

Osborne, William Peacey. (H.), 1923–1926. Form IV. Batchelar Cup.

Ovens, Edward A., 11 *The Avenue, Cirencester.* Furnisher. Married.

Overton, Edward Ernest, 14 *Hampton Terrace, Southsea.* (Spr.), 1922–1924. Upper IV.

Owens, Thomas Robert. 47 *Monk's Avenue, New Barnet, Herts.* (H.), 1900–1904. Form VI. Senior. Pres. of Lit. Soc. Sec. of Field Club. War Service 1914–1919. Lieut. Som. L.I. Ypres Salient and Somme. Solicitor. Married : (2 sons).

Paddon, Geoffrey Christopher, 21 *Portland Road, Oxford.* (S.H.), 1915–1919. Form IV. Probationer. 2nd XI Cricket.

Paget, Eric William, 2 *West Croft, Westbury-on-Trym, Bristol.* (Spr.), 1911–1916. Form V. Probationer. 2nd Lieut. R.A.F. Grain Trade. Married : (1 son).

Paine, David Baumann Easterbrook, 36 *Hauteville, St. Pierre Port, Guernsey, C.I.* (Spr.), 1925–1932. Modern VI. Senior. Prefect. Pres. of League and Lit. Soc. Editor of "Star." Higher School Certif. 1st XI Cricket. Capt. 1st XV Rugby. Tennis Team. Senior Doubles. School Chess Team. Prizes for Senior Lit. Comp., Public Service, Excellence in Public Speaking. B.A. St. John's College, Cambridge. Vice-Capt. St. John's College R.U.F.C. LX Club Colours. Student at Carnegie Physical Training College, Leeds.

Paine, Yerrick Schumn Easterbrook, 36 *Hauteville, St. Pierre Port, Guernsey, C.I.* (Spr.), 1923–1930. Form VI. House Monitor. London Matric. 1st XI Football. 2nd XV Rugby. Senior Tennis Doubles. Diploma in Automobile Engineering. A.M.I.M.T. Automobile and Electrical Engineer.

Palmer, H. D., *The Cedars, Bath Road, Stroud.* (D.B.), 1883–1888. Cloth Manufacturer. Married.

Palmer, Samuel John, *High Street, Stonehouse, Glos.* (Spr.), 1933–1936. Modern VI. Prefect. London Matric. Law Student in Gloucester.

Park, Herbert Sidney. (D.B. and H.), 1904–1910. Form VI. Senior. London Matric. On passing the 2nd Class Civil Service Competitive Exam., he was appointed to a post in the National Health Insurance Audit Dept. in London. In 1916 he joined the Artists' Rifles, and later obtained a commission in the Border Regt. He was killed in France by the explosion of a bomb in October 1917, and was buried at Bailleulmont. (" W. & W." 83).

Parker, David. (Spr.), 1933–1934. Middle IV. Died 1935. ("Star," Aug. 1935, p. 36).

G

Parker, Frank Cother, 20 *Cwrt-y-vil Road, Penarth.* (S.H.), 1931–1934. Form IVb.

Parker, Reginald George, *Unicorn House, St. Ives, Hunts.* (H.), 1931–1935. Form V. Senior Camb. 2nd XI Cricket. 2nd XV Rugby.

Parkin, Benjamin Theaker, *Elmsleigh, Pearcroft Road, Stonehouse.* (D.B.), 1915–1924. Form VI. Senior. Pres. of Lit. Soc. Vice-Pres. of League. Sec. of Field Club. London Matric. Prizes for Speaking and Literature (H. Park). Strasbourg University. M.A., Lincoln College, Oxford. Modern Languages Master at Wycliffe. Married : (2 sons).

Parkinson, David, 868 *Chester Road, Erdington, Birmingham.* (Spr.), 1932–1936. Matric Form. Prefect. P.L. Scouts. Cambridge School Certif. School 2nd XV Rugby 1935–1936. House 1st XV Rugby 1934–1936. Architectural Pupil at Birmingham School of Art.

Parr, Malcolm, *Holy Trinity Vicarage, Leamington Spa.* (D.B.), 1898–1899. Form II. B.A. London. Vicar of Bishop Latimer Memorial Church, Birmingham 1922–26. Vicar of Redford, Coventry 1926–1929. Vicar of Holy Trinity, Leamington since 1929. Married.

Parr, Reginald F. (D.B.), 1898–1899. Form I.

Parsons, Alden. (S.H.), 1913–1914. Form IV. Lieut. R.A.F. Boot and Shoe Factor.

Partridge, Anthony George. (Spr.), 1907–1910. Form I. Cpl. R.G.A. Market Gardener.

Pascoe, Clifford, 44 *Eaton Crescent, Swansea.* (H.), 1908–1911. Probationer. 1st XI Football. Auctioneer and Surveyor.

Pascoe, John Barron, 44 *Eaton Crescent, Swansea.* (H.), 1901–1905. Form V. Probationer. 1st XI Football. Secretary to Swansea and Gower Permanent Building Society. F.C.S.I., F.A.I. Auctioneer, Chartered Surveyor and Estate Agent. Married : (2 sons, 1 dau.).

Pascoe, Thomas Tonkin, 1 *Richmond Terrace, Swansea.* (H.), 1902–1905. Form III. 2nd XI Football. Sergt.-Major M.S.M. Coal Exporter. Director of T. T. Pascoe Ltd. Married : (1 son, 2 daus.).

Passey, George Arthur, *Achill, Prestatyn, Radnorshire.* (S.H.), 1919–1923. Form IV. Probationer. Farmer.

Pattison, Cresswell Lee, *The Bungalow, King Edward VII Hospital, Rivelin Valley Road, Sheffield.* (S.H.), 1902–1905. Form VI. Senior. Vice-Pres. of League. London Matric. M.B., B.S. (Lond.), M.R.C.S., L.R.C.P. Medical Superintendent, King Edward VII Hospital. Surgical Tuberculosis Officer City of Sheffield. Medical Officer in charge of Orthopaedic Clinics of the Child Welfare Centre, Sheffield. Consulting Surgeon, Rotherham Borough Council. Lieut. R.A.M.C. Married : (1 son, 1 dau.).

Pattison, Peter, *The Bungalow, King Edward VII Hospital, Rivelin Valley Road, Sheffield.* (R. and S.H.), 1928, 1932, 1936. Matric Form. Prefect. School Certif. 1st XV Rugby. Capt. 2nd XI Cricket. Senior Athlete (2). Medical Student at Sheffield University.

Payne, Alan Frederick Richard, *The Curtal, Rodborough, Stroud.* (D.B.), 1925–1926. Middle I.

Payne, Arnold Cyril, 19 *Cranmere Avenue, Northampton.* (Spr.), 1913–1915. Form VI. Senior. Pres. of League and Lit. Soc. London Matric. House Prize. Speaking and Literature Prizes. 1st XI Cricket and Football. A.C.A. Chartered Accountant. Northamptonshire County Cricket Committee. Married.

Payne, Christopher William, *The Curtal, Rodborough, Stroud.* (D.B.), 1919–1926. Lower V. Probationer. 2nd XI Football.

Payne, James Vernon, *Harlestone, Allington Park, Bridport, Dorset.* (Spr.), 1915–1919. Form VI. Senior. Pres. of League and Lit. Soc. London Matric. House Prize. Speaking and Literature Prizes. 1st XI Cricket and Football. Chartered Accountant. Borough Accountant, Rating and Valuation Officer, Bridport. Married. (1 dau.).

Payne, Spencer Robert, 41 *Garden Suburb, Dursley, Glos., and St. Peter's Hill, Caversham, Reading* (h.). (Spr.), 1910–1917. Senior. Vice-Pres. of League. London Matric. Engineer with R. A. Lister Ltd., Dursley. Burma Rebellion 1930–1932. Awarded Indian General Service Medal with clasp " Burma."

Payne, Sydney Howard, 117 *The Drive, Northampton.* (Spr.), 1919–1923. Form VI. Senior. Vice-Pres. of League. London Matric. House Prize. House Furnisher.

Payne, Thomas Algernon. (H.), 1906–1909. Joined the Marconi Co. and served throughout the War in the Royal Naval Reserve in the West Indies, Irish and North Seas, off the Coasts of Africa and S. America, A week after being demobilised he died of pneumonia on February 20th. 1919. (" W. & W.").

Peacey, Arthur Frederick, *Larkham, Matson, Glos.* (H.), 1912–1915. Probationer. 2nd XI Cricket. Capt. R.A.F. D.F.C. Farmer. Married.

Peacey, Howard George. (H.), 1904–1905. Form III. Farmed in Saskatchewan. On the outbreak of war joined the Royal Gloucester-shire Hussars, and became a sergeant. He was killed in Egypt on Easter Sunday 1916.

Pearce, Arthur Orlando, *Downfield, Stroud.* (D.B.), 1905–1910. Form IV. House Prize. 2nd XI Football. Lieut. Tank Corps.

Pearse, William, *Trevescan, Keynsham Road, Cheltenham.* (H.), 1928–1931. Form V. Motor Salesman.

Peet, Howard Augustus, 82 *Breedon Street, Long Eaton, Notts.* (H.), 1913–1916. Hampshire Regt. British Army of Occupation on the Rhine. Married.

Penwarden, Herbert, *The Rise, Hillingdon, Middlesex.* (Spr.), 1903. Civil Servant 1927. Research work at Admiralty Engineering Labora-tory, West Drayton. Married.

Penwarden, William Francis. (Spr.), 1908–1910. Form IV. Proba-tioner. He had just finished his time as a farm pupil when he joined the Royal Gloucestershire Hussars. He afterwards obtained a com-mission in the Royal Fusiliers and went to France in August 1916. He was killed on August 31st, 1917, while leading his platoon into action, and was buried near Ecoust.

Parrett, Albert Tremaine. (S.H.), 1912–1914. Form V. Probationer. 3rd Glos. Regt. In U.S.A.

Perry, Kenneth Mitchell, c/o *White Star Line, Liverpool.* (Spr.), 1913–1916. Form V. Literature Prize. Marine Engineer. Married.

Perry Samuel Dennis, *Winson, Bibury, Glos.* (S.H.), 1933–1934. Form IV.

Pethybridge, Harford Montgomery. (H.), 1920–1927. Form VI. House Monitor. 1st XV Rugby. Swimming Championship, Mile and Half-Mile. House Prize. B.Sc. (Hons.) Bristol University. President Mortimer House, Bristol University. Bristol University 1st Eight. Engineer. Died at Montana, Switzerland on February 1st 1936.

Pethybridge, Harford William, *Treyeres, Bodmin, Cornwall* (h.). *Wycliffe House, 58 Lewisham Park, S.E.* 13. (H.), 1920–1926. Form VI. Senior. Pres. of Lit. Soc. London Matric. 2nd XI Football. Foster Rifle. Chartered Accountant.

Pethybridge, John Henry, *Heather Ley, Bodmin, Cornwall.* (H.), 1919–1925. Form VI. Senior. Pres. of Lit. Soc. Excellence in Speaking Prize. M.A., Lincoln College, Oxford. Solicitor. Returning Officer, Bodmin Constituency.

Pethybridge, Walter Heather, *" Waihi," Chaddesden Lane, Chaddesden, Derby.* (H.), 1918–1925. Form VI. Senior. London Matric. B.Sc. University of London. Dyehouse Chemist with British Celanese Ltd. Married : (1 dau.).

Petty, John Mortimer, *Glenthorne, Glanmor Park, Swansea, Glam.* (H.), 1930–1935. Science VI. Prefect. Vice-Pres. of League. A.S.M. London Matric. 1st XV Rugby. Scout Swimming Team. Studying for B.Sc. (Engineering) Swansea University.

Phelps, Ernest Laurence, 9 *Halesworth Road, S.E.* 13. *London Road, Stroud* (h.). (S.H.), 1922–1930. Form VI. Prefect. Sec. and Treas. Lit. Soc. School Certif. London Matric. Inter. B.Sc. (Econ.). 1st XI Cricket. 2nd XI Football, 2nd and 1st XV Rugby 1928–1930. Jeune Cup. Bank Clerk.

Phennah, Reginald James. (S.H.), 1909–1911. Form III. Capt. Glos. Regt. Mentioned in Despatches. Auctioneer and Estate Agent.

Phillimore, Edward Brooke, *Cleve House, Brimscombe, Glos.* (D.B.), 1893–1895. Form III.

Phillimore, Lionel James Daniel, 73a *Tweedy Road, Bromley, Kent, or Bank of England, E.C.* 4. (H. and D.B.), 1916–1922. Form V. Probationer. Cambridge Senior. 1st XI Cricket. In Bank of England.

Phillimore, Walter Geoffrey, *Cleve House, Brimscombe, Glos.* (D.B., H. and Grove), 1927–1935. Science VI. House Monitor. School Certif. 2nd XI Cricket. Bank Clerk in National Provincial Bank, Ltd.

Phillimore, William Lionel, *Cleve House, Brimscombe, Glos.* (S.H. and D.B.), 1892–1895. Form VI. Senior. 1st XI Cricket. Durham College of Science, Newcastle-on-Tyne. Manager, G. Waller & Sons, Brimscombe, 1913–1920. War Service : Munitions. Engineer. Married: (2 sons).

Phillips, A. Edwin. (Spr.), 1932–1933. Died 1935. (" Star," Aug. 1935, p. 37).

Phillips, B. Islwyn, *Clydach, Swansea.* (S.H.), 1892–1897. Form V. Probationer. 1st XI Cricket. Sanitary Engineer.

Phillips, Cuthbert E. Vaughan, *Headingley Terrace, Leeds.* (Spr. and S.H.), 1906–1908. Form V. Probationer. 2nd XI Cricket and Football. P.A.S.I. Assoc. Estate Agents' Inst.

Phillips, David Allison, 3 *St. Annes Road, Liverpool* 17. (S.H.), 1892–1894. Form IV. Cotton Merchant. Married : (2 sons, 2 daus.).

Phillips, Gregory James, *The Limes, Kemble, near Cirencester.* (S.H.), 1931–1935. Modern VI. London Matric. 2nd XI Cricket. 1st XV Rugby. Agricultural College, Cirencester.

Phillips, Harold Louis, 11 *Croxteth Road, Liverpool.* (S.H.), 1892–1894. Form IV. Corn Merchant and Flour Importer.

Phillips, John D. (S.H.), 1892–1895. Form VI. Senior. 1st XI Cricket. 2nd XI Football.

Phillips, John Linton, 1a *Priory Road, Tyndalls Park, Bristol,* 8. (S.H.), 1900-1906. Form VI. Senior. 1st XI Cricket and Football. Junior Athlete. Devon County Hockey. Corp. R.G.A. In business. Married: (1 son).

Phillips, Roy Linton, 1a *Priory Road, Tyndalls Park, Bristol,* 8. (S.H.), 1929-1931. Matric. Form. House Monitor. Bank Clerk.

Phillips, Sydney Vernon. (H.), 1901-1904. Form VI. Probationer. Studied surveying and became a Fellow of the Surveyors' Institute and obtained a place on the permanent staff of the Inland Revenue Board. In 1915 he joined the Artists' Rifles, and obtained a commission in the 7th Leicesters. He went to France in August 1916, and a few days later was killed by the explosion of a German mine. (" W. & W.", 87).

Phillips, Thomas E. (S.H.), 1892-1893. 2nd XI Football.

Pike, Neville Ward, 30 *Carnarvon Road, Clifton, Bristol.* (S.H.), 1918-1924. Form V. 2nd XI Cricket.

Pine, Arthur Stanley. (S.H.), 1899-1900. Form IV. In Australia.

Plested. Eric Ingram, *Nastend Court, Stonehouse, Glos.* (D.B.), 1923-1928. Form V. House Monitor.

Pocock, Bernard M. (H.), 1886-1889. Probationer.

Pocock, James Herbert, *St. Dunstan's, Sutherland Avenue, Wahroonga, N.S.W.* (S.H.), 1889-1891. Form VI. Senior. London Matric. Engineer.

Pole, Norman H (Father Fabian), *Ealing Priory, Ealing, W.* 5. (H.), 1895-1898. Form VI. Senior. London Matric. 1st XI Cricket. L/Cpl. K.R.R.C. Priest (R.C.) and Schoolmaster.

Pole, Reginald Frank. (H.), 1891-1892. Trained for Methodist ministry, but compelled to open-air life. Died 1932. (See " Star," Jan. 1933).

Pool, Edwin, *Oakleigh, Hartley Wintney, Hants.* (H.), 1898-1903. Fruit Farmer.

Pool, Stanley, 8 *Tryew Road, Truro, Cornwall.* (H.), 1896-1899. Form IV. Probationer. 1st XI Cricket. Sergt. R.E. County Architect.

Poole, Arthur Frederick, *Savernake, Hurst Road, Sidcup, Kent.* (H.), 1917-1921. Lower VI. Senior. Vice-Pres. of League. Pres. of Lit. Soc. Cambridge Senior. 1st XI Cricket. Capt. 2nd XI Football. House Prize and for Public Speaking and " My System." Capt. Royal Artillery (T.A.). Now on T.A. Reserve of Officers. Assistant Transport Manager, B.I. Transport Co., E.C. 3. Married : (1 dau.).

Porcher, Henry Jestyn Hugh, *Cefn Coed, Lan Park Road, Pontypridd.* (H.), 1925-1931. Form VI. House Monitor. School Certif. School Chess Team. Medical Student at University College Hospital, London.

Porcher, Henry Leonard, *Cefn Coed, Lan Park Road, Pontypridd.* (H.), 1896-1899. Form VI. Senior. Pres. of Lit. Soc. London Matric. 1st XI Football. 2nd XI Cricket. House Prize and for Public Speaking. Ex-Pres. Soc. of Clerks of U.D.C.s and of Pontypridd and Rhondda Law Society. Governor of University College of South Wales. Member of Council of Governors of Wycliffe College. Solicitor and Clerk to Pontypridd Council. Married : (1 son).

Porter, William Wadsworth. (D.B.), 1903-1904. Form Ib. 2nd Lieut.

Pottenger, John William. (Spr.), 1904-1906. Form V. Probationer. 2nd XI Football. Farmer.

Poulton, Geoffrey Herbert, *The Beeches, Thrupp, Stroud, Glos.* (H.), 1926-1931. Upper Remove.

Powell, Alfred T., *Upton Court, Upton Bishop, near Ross.* (S.H.), 1910–1913. Form IVb. Inns of Court O.T.C. Farmer.

Powell, Arthur Falkenberg. (H.), 1898–1899. Form VI. Probationer. In 1899 he passed into the "Britannia," and in 1901 was appointed to H.M.S. "Magnificent." He was promoted to Lieutenant in 1906. He served on the China Station in H.M.S. "Merlin" and "Monmouth" 1912–1914. When war broke out he was Navigator of the "Queen." By May 1919 he had become a Commander, and Navigator of H.M.S. "Angus," but in June he died from septicemia. ("W. & W.", 88).

Powell, Ernest Perkins, 55 *The Ridings, Surbiton, Surrey.* (D.B.), 1909–1911. Form VI. Senior. Cambridge Senior. Day Boys' Prize. War Service: Home Service 1916–1918. Bank Manager. Married: (1 son).

Powell, John Douglas, 46 *Severn Avenue, Weston-super-Mare.* (H.), 1917–1922. Upper VI. Senior. Vice-Pres. of League. Sec. and Treas. of Lit. Soc. 1st XI Cricket and Football. Senior Athlete. House Prize and for Public Speaking. St. John's College, Cambridge. Medical Practitioner. Married.

Poynton, Raymond Edward, *Hillcrest, Caerleon, Mon.* (H.), 1925–1927. Upper IV. Gardening Cup.

Pratt, Herbert Burford, *The Farm, Westmancote, Bredon, near Tewkesbury.* (H.), 1907–1911. Form V. Probationer. King's Liverpool Regt. Farmer.

Pratt, Richard Thomas Charles, *The Drift House, Wothorpe, Stamford, Lincs.* (D.B.), 1927–1928. Form III. Left for Cheltenham College and Oxford.

Preston, Richard Aubrey, *Barrington, Ashcroft, Cirencester.* (S.H.), 1931–1933. Lower V. Assoc. of the Grocers' Inst. Grocer and Provision Merchant.

Price, A. E.

Price, Alfred Reginald, *Westcroft, Nailsworth, Glos.* (S.H.), 1906–1911. Upper IV. 5th Glos. Regt. M.M. Grocer. Married: (1 son).

Price, Edward C. (S.H.), 1895–1896. Form II. Organist and Teacher of Music.

Price, Harold George, 32 *Chancellor Road, Southend-on-Sea.* (S.H.), 1923–1925. Lower III. 2nd XI Cricket.

Price, John William. (D.B.), 1900–1901. Form III. Official of Canadian Pacific Railway. Married.

Price, Stanley Dean Higgins, *Beau Site, Tuffley, Glos. Barclays Bank House, Tenbury Wells.* (H.), 1922–1925. Lower IV. Probationer. Cambridge Senior. Certif. Assoc. Inst. of Bankers. Bank Cashier.

Prichard, Reginald Moreton. (S.H.), 1906–1908. Form VI. Probationer. Lieut. Cheshire Regt. M.A., St. John's College, Cambridge. Clerk in Holy Orders. Chaplain to the Bishop of Bradford. Married. Deceased.

Pridham, Arthur Inglis, *Tipper Down, South Harting, near Petersfield.* (D.B.), 1915–1923. Lower VI. Senior. Pres. of League. Sec. of Lit. Soc. London Matric. House and Speaking Prizes. With Shell Mex B.P. Ltd. Married: (1 son, 1 dau.).

Pridham, Charles William, *Brockley House, Lansdown, Stroud.* (R. and D.B.), 1929–1933–1936. House Monitor. 2nd XI Cricket. 2nd XV Rugby.

Pridham, John Collier, *Brockley House, Lansdown, Stroud.* (D.B.), 1921–1928. Form VI. Prefect. School Certif. 2nd XV Rugby. City Surveyor's Dept., Gloucester Corporation 1931–1936. Town Planning Dept., Worcester County Council. Town Planning Assistant. A.M.I.M. and Cy. E.

Primavesi, Fedele, 790 *Holdenhurst Road, Bournemouth.* (D.B.), 1919–1925. Lower V. Probationer. 2nd XI Cricket and Football. Junior Athlete. With Messrs. Elder & Fyffe.

Proger, John Guy. (H.), 1909–1911. Form V. Lieut. R.A.F. Sanitary, Heating and Ventilating Engineer.

Prout, Edward. (D.B.), 1898.

Prout, Edward Percival. (D.B.), 1917–1919. Form II. Took up farming at Haresfield, but was killed in a motor cycle accident.

Prout, Harold Martin, *Malthouse, Haresfield, Glos.* (D.B.), 1897–1898. Farmer. Married.

Prout, James Leonard, *Spring Farm, Frocester, Stonehouse, Glos.* (D.B.), 1931–1933. Lower IV. Farmer.

Prout, Robert Michael, *Haresfield, Glos.* (D.B.), 1906–1907. Form II.

Prout, Sidney Harold, *Elmcote, Coaley, Glos.* (D.B.), 1906–1907. Form II.

Prout, William Edward, *Kamsack, Saskatchewan, Canada.* (D.B.), 1892–1893. Form II. Farmer. Married.

Pullin, Arthur Reginald. (H.), 1906–1907. Form II.

Pullin, Francis Hamblett, *The Hayes, Brookthorpe, near Gloucester.* (D.B.), 1906–1909. Lower III. Farmer.

Pulsford-Browne, Walter, *Avoca, Westby Road, Bournemouth.* (Spr.), 1903–1904. Form I. Married.

Pyman, Walter A. E. (S.H.), 1888–1889. With Messrs. Pyman, Watson and Co., Shipowners, Cardiff.

Quartly, John H. (S.H.), 1889–1893. Form V. Probationer. In Saskatchewan.

Ractliff, Arthur Henry, *The Bungalow, Bisley Road, Stroud.* (D.B.), 1897–1899. Form I. Fellow Inst. Motor Trade. Ass. Member Inst. of Brit. Engineers. Director of Wycliff Motor Co. War Service 1915–1919. Commission in September 1917. Served in Italy, the Balkans, Mesopotamia, Persia and India.

Ractliff, Gilbert Charles, *Hotel Riviera, Torquay.* (D.B.), 1896–1901. Form III. Hotelier. Proprietor of Hotels Riviera, Torquay and Sidmouth, and of Crofton Hotel, Queen's Gate, S.W. 7. Chairman Torquay Hotels Assoc. Member Torquay Corporation Publicity Committee. Member Executive Council Residential Hotels Assoc. of G.B. Vice-President Torquay Athletic R.F. Club. Supervisor F.P.D. Ministry of Agriculture. Married : (2 sons).

Rawlings, Horatio, 35 *Mount Carmel, near Derby.* (Spr.), 1902–1903. Form II. Staff Major (1st Class) i/c Euphrates Area, Mesopotamia. Chief Constable of Derby. Married.

Raymer, Charles Robert Peyton, 124 *Warwick Road, Acocks Green, Birmingham.* (Spr.), 1927–1931. Form VI. School Certif.

Raynes, Frederick Paul Meredith, *Oxford House, Bath Road, Swindon.* (Spr.), 1922–1930. Form V. House Monitor. Auctioneer and Estate Agent.

Reade, George Lewis, *Wycliffe College, Stonehouse, Glos.* (H.), 1906–1914. Form VI. Senior. Pres. of League and Lit. Soc. London Matric. Capt. 1st XI Football. 1st XI Cricket. Record for Hurdles (old height). Capt. The Rifle Brigade. M.C. M.A., St. John's College, Cambridge. House Master of Haywardsfield 1922–1933. Master of the Middle School.

Reddy, Claude Butler, *Beaumont, Combe Down, Bath.* (S.H.), 1906–1911. Form VI. Probationer. 1st XI Cricket and Football. Senior Athlete. Sometime holder of Quarter-Mile and Cross Country Record. Sugar Merchant. Married : (1 dau.).

Redman, Harold Claude, *Station Road, Yate, Glos.* (H.), 1921–1924. Form III.

Reece, Philip John Marsden, 1 *Granville Villas, Bisley Road, Stroud.* (D.B.), 1917–1925. Form V. Probationer. Electrical Engineer.

Reece, Richard Marsden, 85 *Victoria Road, Cirencester.* (D.B.), 1914–1921. Form VI. Senior. Vice-Pres. of League. London Matric. 2nd XI Football. House Prize. Married. Bank Clerk.

Rees, Edward Davies, followed Mr G. W. Sibly from Taunton (1883–1884). Gained the L.S.A., M.R.C.S., and L.R.C.P. at King's College, London. Practised for thirty years at Caersws. His bardic name was " Ap Gwyddon," and he was a familiar figure at the National Eisteddfod. At Bangor in 1914 he was Herald Bard in the Inner Circle, and was Director of the Ceremonies when the late King was admitted to the mystic circle. He was a Governor of the National Museum of Wales at Cardiff. He died in February 1925. (" Star," April 1925, p. 7).

Rees, Justin David Reynolds. (H.), 1902–1904. Form VI. Senior. Pres. of Lit. Soc. Lieut. Welch Regt. M.C. Solicitor.

Rees, W. F. (D.B.), 1886–1887.

Renshaw, Anthony Stephen, 30 *St. Mary Abbot's Terrace, Kensington, W.* 14. (Spr.), 1932–1936. Matric. Form. Swimming Champion. In R.A.F.

Revell, Charles John Meredith, *The Granvilles, Bisley Road, Stroud.* (S.H.), 1917–1922. Form IV. Boot and Leather Trade. Married.

Revell, Edward Walter Millard, *c/o Posts & Telegraphs Dept., Nigeria.* c/o W. M. Revell, Esq., The Granvilles, Bisley Road, Stroud. (S.H.), 1911–1919. Form VI. Senior. Sec. of Lit. Soc. London Matric. House Prize. B.Sc. (Engineering) Bristol University. A.M.I.E.E. Telegraph Engineer. Married.

Revell, Leslie Shaylor, *Elmwood, Briton Ferry, Glam.* (S.H.), 1927–1931. Upper V. School Certif. Articled to Solicitor.

Reynolds, Arthur, *Tregleman, Croesgoch, Letterston, Pembroke.* (S.H.), 1897–1901. Probationer. 1st XI Football. 2nd XI Cricket. Lieut. A.V.C. Veterinary Surgeon. Married.

Reynolds, Arthur John Scale, *Millbrook, Carbeston Road, Pembroke.* (S.H.), 1897–1901. Form V. Probationer. 1st XI Football. 2nd XI Cricket. Lieut. A.V.C. Veterinary Surgeon. M.R.C.V.S. (London). Married.

Reynolds, David. (S.H.), 1894–1899. Form VI. Senior. Farmer. Was a prominent Agriculturalist and supporter of the N. Pembrokeshire Farmers' Club. Married : (2 daus.). Died on May 31st 1931. (" Star," Dec. 1931, p. 16).

Reynolds, Philip ap John, *Treglemais, Croesgoch, Haverfordwest, Pem.* (S.H.), 1894–1899. Form IV. 2nd XI Cricket. Farmer. Married : (2 daus.).

Rich, Jack. (S.H.), 1898–1901. Form VI. Probationer. Became a Bank Cashier. Deceased.

Richards, Archer Kenneth, *Carramore, Radyr, Glam.* (H.), 1918–1920. Form V. Probationer. 2nd XI Football. Ass. Member Inst. of Civil Engineers and of Municipal and County Engineers. Chartered Civil Engineer and Professional Civil Servant. Married : (1 son, 1 dau.).

Richards, Aubrey Mark, *New House Farm, Hawling, Andoversford, Glos.* (S.H.), 1921–1923. Form I. Farmer.

Richards, Bleddyn Cule, (S.H.), 1902–1903. Form III. Motor Engineer. Deceased 1930.

Richards, George, *Pensylva, Cecil Road, Weston-super-Mare.* (H.), 1884–1887. Form VI. Senior. London Matric. Pres. of Lit. Soc. Capt. 2nd XV Rugby. B.A. (Lond.). Three Scholarships and a Fellowship at Cooper's Hill R.I.E. College. Chief Engineer with the Railway Board of India. Member of the Inst. of C.E. War Service : Simla Rifles. Mesopotamian Transport Commission ; two medals for service in Mesopotamia. Married : (1 son, 2 daus.).

Richards, John Trevor, " *Wycliffe,*" *Park Road, Penycraig, Rhondda.* (S.H.), 1902–1905. Form VI. Senior. 1st XI Football. Senior Cross Country. House Prize. Lieut. Welch Regt. Member Pharmaceutical Society. Fellow of Spectacle Makers' Co. and Inst. of Opticians. Freeman of the City of London. Pharmacist and Optician. Married : (1 dau.)

Richards, Thomas Bertram, *Hexham, Shepton Mallet, Somerset.* (H.), 1884–1887. House Prize. J.P. for Somerset. Farmer. Married.

Richardson, Harry Lionel, *Glenthorne, Hayward's Heath, Sussex.* (S.H.), 1896–1899. Form IV. Probationer. 1st XI Football. M. of Inst. of Municipal and County Engineers. Lieut. R.E. Civil Engineer and Town Planning Consultant. Married : (1 son, 3 daus.).

Richardson, M. Hubert. (S.H.), 1896–1899. Form I.

Richardson, Ralph Nelson. (S.H.), 1896–1899. Form I. Joined the Brtish South African Police, and in 1906 was shot by Kaffirs when on duty in the Transvaal.

Rieppel, Maximilian Franz Wolfgang, *Bad Wiessee am Tegernsee, Gut Robognerhof, Bavaria, Germany.* (S.H.), 1934–1935. Modern VI. House Monitor. Since leaving has studied engineering at Zurich and is now preparing for Diplomatic Service.

Rivers, Henry Paul, *Notley, Hucclecote, Gloucester.* (H.), 1921–1926. Lower VI. Probationer. School Certif. Solicitor.

Rivers, Michael, *Notley, Hucclecote, Gloucester.* (H.), 1923–1929. Upper III. 2nd XI Cricket and Football. Junior Cross Country. Motor Engineer with Alvis Engineering Co.

Rivers, William James, *Notley, Hucclecote, Gloucester, and P.O. Box 372, Kingston, Jamaica, B.W.I.* (H.), 1920–1923. Form VI. Senior. Vice-Pres. of League. London Matric. 1st XI Cricket and Football. Senior Athlete. Egyptian 400 metres. Champion 1930–1932. 400 Metres Hurdles Record for Egypt 1931. Chartered Accountant. Chief Accountant for the Shell Co. (West Indies) Ltd., and the Shell Co. (Porto Rico), Ltd.

Roberts, Brian Meiric, 49 *Penylan Road, Roath Park, Cardiff.* (S.H.), 1930–1935. Modern VI. Prefect. London Matric. 1st XV Rugby. Winner of " My System " Comp. Articled to Civil Surveyor of Cardiff.

Roberts, Charles Keith, 13 *Broad Street, Ottery St. Mary, Devon.* (S.H.), 1926–1930. Lower Remove.

Roberts, Humphrey Davies, *Maesyrhedydd, Aberystwyth.* (H.), 1915–1918. Form V. Probationer. B.Sc., LL.B. (Hons.), University of Wales. Solicitor.

Roberts, Philip George, 13 *Broad Street, Ottery St. Mary, Devon.* (S.H.), 1925–1928. Upper IV. Cider Manfacturer.

Roberts, Reginald Roderick, 13 *Church Street, Camberwell, S.E.* (H.), 1904–1908. Form VI. Senior. London Matric. Pres. of Lit. Soc. Capt. 1st XI Football. 1st XI Cricket. Sergt. Gordon Highlanders. Chemist.

Roberts, V. Lloyd, *Lloyds Bank, Melksham, Wilts.*

Robbins, Cyril, *Blakemore, Ebley, near Stroud.* (D.B.), 1912–1915. Lower III. Lce/Cpl. R.E. Cider Manufacturer.

Robinson, Thomas Lloyd, 233 *Bristol Road, Edgbaston, Birmingham.* (H.), 1925–1930. Form VI. Pres. of League and Lit. Soc. Capt. 1st XI Cricket and 1st XV Rugby. School Certif. Connaught Shooting Team. School Tennis Team. Prizes for Public Service and Speaking. Messrs. E. S. & A. Robinson's Representative in Birmingham.

Robson, Eric, *Boveney Court, Boveney, Bucks.* (Spr.), 1917–1920. Form IV. Estate Agent. Secretary to Sir Reginald Kennedy-Cox.

Robson, Paul Stewart, *Castlefield, Cambridge Road, Walton St. Mary, Clevedon.* (S.H.), 1919–1925. Upper V. Probationer. Clerk.

Rochester, The Rt. Hon. Lord (Ernest Henry Lamb), *Park Hill Crest, Croydon, Surrey.* (S.H.), 1888–1889. C.M.G. (1907). J.P. Surrey. Knighted 1914. M.P. (L.) for Rochester 1906–1910 and 1910–1918. Member of the City of London Corporation and of the National Liberal and Guildhall Clubs. Paymaster-General 1931–1935. Represented Ministry of Labour in House of Lords 1931–1935. One of H.M. Lieutenants for the City of London. Member of the Port of London Authority. Chairman of the Distress Committee of the Central (Unemployed) Body for London 1920–1930. On Ministry of Transport Panel of Experts since 1920. National Trustee of the Crystal Palace. Vice-Pres. of the B. and F. Bible Society, and of the National Children's Home and Orphanage. For 22 years Connexional Treasurer of the Wesleyan Temperance and Social Welfare Dept. of the Methodist Church. Chairman and Governing Director of Lamb, Sons & Co. Married : (3 sons, 3 daus.).

Rodd, A. R. Minister. Married.

Rogers, Alan Stuart, *Ardmore,* 3 *Seymour Park Villas, Mannamead, Plymouth.* (S.H.), 1902–1903. Form VI. Probationer. Shipbuilder. Married.

Rogers, Denis R., *Wycliffe House,* 58 *Lewisham Park, S.E.* 13 *and Ardmore,* 3 *Seymour Park Villas, Mannamead, Plymouth.* (S.H.), 1927–1931. Upper V. School Certif. Shipping Clerk and Customs Agent.

Rogers, John Frederick, *Ardmore,* 3 *Seymour Park Villas, Mannamead, Plymouth* (h.). *Westminster College,* 130 *Horseferry Road, S.W.* 1. (S.H.), 1925–1930. Upper V. House Monitor. School Certif. B.A. London. At Westminster Training College.

Rogers, Norman. (S.H.), 1903–1904. Form VI. Probationer. Shipbuilder. Married. Deceased.

Roope, William James, *c/o W. A. Loxley & Co., Hong Kong, China.* (H.), 1907–1908. Form VI. Probationer. Staff Lieut.

Roseveare, Leslie, *Wearde, Bedfordwell Road, Eastbourne.* (S.H.), 1891–1892. Form VI. A.M.Inst.C.E., A.M.Inst.M.E. Major R.E. O.B.E. (Mil.). Borough Engineer. Pres. Town Planning Institute. Married.

Ross, A. Gordon. (D.B.), 1904-1905.

Ross, Norman Myrtle. (D.B.), 1898. Form I.

Ross, Richard Harold. (D.B.), 1898. Form I.

Round, Reginald Francis. (S.H.), 1895–1899. Form IV. Lieut. R.A.F. Died some years ago.

Rouse, Richard Henry. (S.H.), 1883–1887. Senior. Capt. 1st XI Cricket. Capt. 1st XV Rugby. Senior Athlete. Somerset Rugby Cap. Bank Manager. Married.

Routledge, Tom B. (S.H.), 1895–1898. Form IV. After leaving Wycliffe he went to the Armstrong School of Science at Newcastle and then to the School of Mines, Camborne. As a mining engineer he gained a first-class manager's certificate and at the time of his death (Dec. 1908), was engaged in sinking some new pits in Crumlin. He was an active member of the Cardiff Naturalists' and Archaeological Societies, and a Lieut. in the Territorials.

Routledge, William, *Bloomfield, Marton-in-Cleveland, Yorks.* (S.H.), 1896–1897. Form V. Engineer. Works Manager, Dorman, Long and Co., Middlesbrough. Member of the North Riding Territorial Assoc. Pres. of the Cleveland Inst. of Engineers. Member of Council of the Iron and Steel Inst. and of the Iron and Steel Employers' Assoc. Pres. of Social Service Clubs. Vice-Pres. of the Cleveland Technical Insts. Freeman and Liveryman of the Worshipful Company of Blacksmiths. Freeman of the City of London. Lieut.-Col. and D.A.D.O.S. 50th Northumberland Fusiliers. Married : (3 daus.).

Rowe, Charles Mortimer. (D.B.), 1890–1891. Form III. 1st XV Rugby became a partner in Messrs. Wood & Rowe, Coal Merchants, Stroud. Deceased.

Rowe, R. J. (H.), 1890–1891. Form V. Deceased.

Rowell, John Charles, *Ivydene, Chipping Norton, Oxon.* (S.H.), 1904–1911. Form VI. Probationer. 1st XI Cricket. 2nd XI Football. 2nd Lieut. R.N.V.R. Ironmonger.

Rowell, Robert Norman, *Ivydene, Chipping Norton, Oxon.* (S.H.), 1903–1907. Form IV. Lieut. R.A.F. Mentioned in despatches. Married.

Rowell, William Norman, *Ivydene, Chipping Norton, Oxon.* (S.H.), 1883–1884. Mayor of Chipping Norton 1904. Oxfordshire County Alderman. J.P. Chairman of County Public Health Committee. Thames Conservator for Oxfordshire. Engineer and Contractor. Married.

Roxburgh, Frank J. (S.H.), 1890–1895. Form IV. 1st XI Football. Returned to the West Indies.

Roxburgh, Kenneth L. (S.H.), 1890–1895. Form IV. In the West Indies.

Ruck, Capt. Charles F. Leyson. (H.), 1903–1904. Form V. Probationer. Sometime Demonstrator at Guy's Hospital. L.D.S., R.C.S. (Eng.), 1910. Capt. Indian Army. Dental Surgeon.

Rugman, Gilbert W. W. (Spr.), 1904–1907. Form IV. Deceased.

Russell, C. P. (H.), 1890–1891. Farmer. Died of consumption, May 14th, 1909.

Russell, Leonard, *Newland, Westbourne, Otley, Yorks.* (H.), 1890–1891. Form II. Draper. Married : (1 dau.).

Russell, W. F. (H.), 1890–1891. Form III. Died of consumption. February, 1907.

Rutherford, John Hunter, *R.A.F. Club,* 128 *Piccadilly,* W. 1. (Spr.), 1909–1910. Form III. Major R.A.F.

Rymer, Ernest Charles, *Philpotts Court, Tidenham, near Chepstow, Mon.* (S.H.), 1918–1921. Lower V. Music Prize. Farming.

Sadler, William Walter Linsell. (D.B.), 1895–1897. Form III.

Sage, Harry Edward. (S.H.), 1922–1925. Form V. Probationer. Electrical Engineer. Deceased 1930. ("Star," Dec., 1930).

Sainsbury, John Lessiter, 46 *Avenue Road, Trowbridge, Wilts.* (S.H.), 1923–1925. Form I.

Sainsbury, Richard Michael James, *Manor Farm, Chirton, near Devizes.* (S.H.), 1931–1934. Upper Remove. Farmer.

Salisbury, Benjamin Charles, *Maadi, Cairo, Egypt (Tel. Maadi* 93). (S.H.), 1892–1896. Form IV. R.A.S.C. Managing and Company Director. Now Assistant Master Intermediate School of Commerce, Daher, Cairo (Egyptian Government). Married.

Salisbury, Cecil Douglas, 120 *Queen Street, Cardiff.* (S.H.), 1908–1912. Form V. 1st XI Football. 2nd XI Cricket. Lieut. Manchester Regt.

Salisbury, Francis Henry, 26 *Charlton Road, Weston-super-Mare.* (S.H.), 1895. Form IV. Swimming Championship. R.A.S.C. Master Grocer (retired). Widower : (1 son, 1 dau.).

Salisbury, John Francis, 26 *Charlton Road, Weston-super-Mare.* (S.H.), 1928–1930. Lower V.

Salisbury, John James, 44 *Baldwin Street, Bristol.* (S.H.), 1890–1891. Form IV. Honours in Law Final. R.A.F. Solicitor.

Salisbury, Lester E., 120 *Queen Street, Cardiff.* (S.H.), 1908–1910. Form IV. 2nd XI Football. S. Wales M.B.

Salisbury, Dr Mark, 7 *Julian Road, Sneyd Park, Bristol* (h.). (S.H.), 1897–1900. Form VI. Senior. London Matric. House and Speaking Prizes. LL.D. London. Sometime Solicitor. Ordained from Wycliffe Hall, Oxford. Late Senior Chaplain at Quetta. Married.

Salisbury, Richard Michael James, *Manor Farm, Chirton, near Devizes, Wilts.* Farming.

Salisbury, Walter. (S.H.), 1900–1903. Form IV. Probationer. M.D., M.S. London. F.R.C.S. (Eng.). Subsequently qualified as M.C.O.G. F.A.S. and F.R.S.M. After periods of service at the Bristol Royal Hospital, the London and St. Thomas' Hospitals, he became senior resident M.O. of Queen Charlotte's Lying-in Hospital. Resident M.O. of the Women's Hospital and House Surgeon at the Royal National Orthopædic Hospital. In Northants he also filled several important posts in connection with the Borough and County Councils. During the War he was a Captain and Surgeon Specialist in the R.A.M.C. He died from influenza and pneumonia on January 7th 1934. ("Star," Dec. 1934, p. 22).

Salter, George Maynard. (S.H.), 1903–1905. Form III. Marine Engineer.

Sanders, John Emerton. (S.H.), 1909–1914. Form VI. Senior. Capt. 1st XI Cricket. 2nd XI Football. Prize for Speaking. Joined the 5th Gloucesters as a private. Only a few days after receiving a commission in the Lancashire Fusiliers he went into the action from which he never returned (1915). ("W. & W.", 89).

Sanders, Richard Leslie, *Willow Cottage, Gotherington, Cheltenham.* (S.H.), 1911–1917. Form V. 2nd XI Cricket and Football. Lieut. Dragoon Guards. Married.

Sandford, Clarence Charles. (S.H.), 1918–1920.

Sanguinetti, Valentine, Lee Shedden. (S.H.), 1894–1899. Form V. Died at his home in Jamaica a few years after leaving school.

Sarvis, George Frederick, c/o *Glanynys, Aberdare.* (S.H.), 1893–1894. Form V. Probationer.

Schupbach, Ernest, 94 *Philbeach Gardens, Earl's Court, S.W.* 5. (Spr.), 1920–1928. Upper VI. Prefect. Pres. of Lit. Soc. Vice Pres. of League. Higher Certif. 1st XI Football. 1st XV Rugby. 1st XI Cricket. Prizes for Speaking and Senior Lit. Comp. M.A. Cantab. (Hons. in Economic Tripos).

Schupbach, Frédéric Jacques Alexandre, c/o *Credit Lyonnais, Lombard Street, E.C.* 3. (Spr.), 1919–1924. Form VI. Senior. Vice-Pres. of League. Sec. of Lit. Soc. London Matric. Music Prize. In business. Director of Leather Co.

Scott, Alfred Thomas. (S.H.), 1895–1896. Form II.

Scott, Claude Halsbury, c/o *United Dairies, Salisbury, Wilts.* (H.), 1904–1905. Form V. Probationer.

Scott, John Richard Douglas. (D.B.), 1905–1907. Form VI. Senior. London Matric. He afterwards went to Canada, and became a clerk in the Traders Bank. Later he was one of the cashiers in the Canadian Bank of Commerce at Vancouver. Enlisting in the Canadian Army Medical Corps, he was sent to France, but afterwards invalided back to Canada, and lost his life by drowning at St. John's, New Brunswick. ('' W. & W.'', 90).

Scott, Keith Stuart, 17 *Dumfries Place, Cardiff.* (S.H.), 1914–1917. Form V. 2nd XI Football. Mechanical Engineer.

Scott, Stanley. (D.B.), 1900–1905. Form III.

Seaby, Herbert A., *Tuckahoe, Baker Street, Potter's Bar, Middlesex.* (Spr.), 1910–1914. Form VI. Probationer. Lieut. R.A.F. Numismatist (65, Gt. Portland Street). Married : (1 son, 1 dau.).

Seaby, Philip Charles, *Culverwood, Shinfield, Berks.* (h.). 10022 112*th Street, Edmonton, Alberta, Canada.* (Spr.), 1917–1923. Form VI. Probationer. 2nd XI Cricket and Football. Manager of Stationery Dept. for Alberta National Drug and Stationery Co.

Seaby, Wilfred Arthur, 57 *Blakesly Road, Yardley, Birmingham.* (Spr.), 1921–1926. Form V. Probationer. Assistant, City Museum and Art Gallery, Birmingham.

Selley, Arthur William, *St. Aubyn Street, Devonport.* (Spr.), 1903. Form V. Borough Treasurer's Office.

Selwyn, Stanley John, *Lindens, Brimscombe, Glos.* (h.). (D.B.), 1912–1919. Form V. Motor Engineer.

Sexton, Ernest George, *Barritts, Boxted, Colchester, Essex.* (H.), 1932–1934. Form V. 2nd XV Rugby. 1st XI Cricket. Junior Athlete. Middle-weight Boxing Champ. Sports Team. Market Gardening.

Shafto, G. R. Holt. (S.H.), 1884. Wesleyan Minister. Married.

Sharrock, George James, *Green Bank, Gathurst, Wigan, Lancs.* (S.H.), 1921–1923. Form II.

Sharrock, John Harvey, *Green Bank, Gathurst, Wigan, Lancs.* (S.H.), 1919–1922. Form II.

Sharrock, William Littlefair, *Green Bank, Gathurst, Wigan, Lancs.* (S.H.), 1917–1921. Form VI. Probationer. 1st XI Football.

Shaw, Bernard John, *The Firs, Stourton, Shipston-on-Stour* (h.). *Cadbury and Fry's Office, Accra, Gold Coast.* (S.H.), 1925–1930. Form VI. Prefect. School Certif. Jeune Cup. Foster Rifle. Connaught Shield Shooting Team. With Messrs. Cadbury & Fry, Bournville.

Shaw, Donald Hurst, *The Firs, Frithwood Avenue, Northwood, Middlesex.* (H.), 1924–1928. Upper V. House Monitor.

Shaw, George Douglas, *Cheerio, Hereford* (h.). *Friars, Chester.* (Spr.), 1916–1920. Form VI. Senior. Vice-Pres. of League. London Matric. 2nd XI Football. Music Prize. M.A. (B.A. Hons.), LL.B. St. John's College, Cambridge. Solicitor.

Shaw, Maxwell, *The Firs, Frithwood Avenue, Northwood, Middlesex.* (H.), 1925–1927.

Shaw, Reginald Mac Whitely, 12 *Yeading Avenue, Rayners Lane, Harrow, Middx.* (Spr.), 1919–1926. Form VI. Probationer. School Certif. 1st XI Cricket. 1st XI. Football. Senior Tennis Doubles. Surveyor. Married : (1 dau.).

Shaw, Robert William Trevor, 66 *Harefield Road, Stoke, Coventry.* (S.H.), 1924–1928.

Shearn, Henry Stock, *Alphan House, Midsomer Norton, Somerset.* (S.H.), 1924–1931. Lower Remove. 1st XI Cricket. Tennis and Shooting Teams. Capt. Midsomer Norton C.C. Motor Engineer.

Shepherd, Basil Radcliffe. (S.H.), 1897–1898. Form III. Went to S. America, where he joined a firm of Engineers and Contractors. Deceased.

Sheppy, John Percy, *Chestnut House, Congresbury, near Bristol.* (H.), 1893–1894. Form I. Corn Merchant. Widower : (2 daus., 1 gr. dau.).

Shipway, Frederick Martineau, 8 *Newport Street, Oldham, Lancs.* (Spr.), 1919–1924. Form II. Officer in Mercantile Marine.

Shipway, William George, 72 *Trelawney Road, Cotham, Bristol.* (Spr.), 1907–1911. Form VI. Senior. 1st XI Cricket. 2nd XI Football. Lieut. Glos. Regt. M.C. Wholesale Grocer and Sugar Merchant. Married.

Shirley, Samuel Arthur. (S.H.), 1882–1884. First arrival on the day the School opened. Senior. 1st XV Rugby. House Prize. J.P. Bristol City Council. Provision Merchant. Married : (3 daus.). Died 1936.

Shrimpton, Samuel Albert, 49 *Boulevard St. Michel, Paris.* (H.), 1897–1901. Form VI. Senior. Music Prize. R.Q.M.S., R.A.M.C. Paris Representative Allcock & Co., Redditch. Married.

Shrimpton, Stuart Norman, 18 *Bridge Street, Knighton, Radnor* (h.). 3 *The Avenue, The Cross, Worcester.* (S.H.), 1922–1928. Upper V. Prefect. School Certif. Architect.

Sibly, Thomas Franklin, *The Vice-Chancellor's Lodge, Reading.* (S.H.), 1893–1898. Form VI. Probationer. D.Sc. London. D.Sc. Bristol. F.G.S. Sometime Lecturer in King's College, London. Professor of Geology at University College, Cardiff, and at Armstrong College, Newcastle. First Principal of University College, Swansea. Vice-Chancellor of University of Wales (1925–1926), Principal Officer (1926–1929) and Principal of University of London (1929). Member of Royal Commission on University of Durham (1934–1935) and of Statutory Commission appointed by University of Durham Act. Now Vice-Chancellor of Reading University. Member of Council of Governors of Wycliffe College. Married : (1 son).

Sibly, Thomas Mervyn, *The Grove, Stonehouse, Glos.* (S.H.), 1893–1903. Form VI. Senior. Pres. of League and of Lit. Soc. London Matric. Speaking Prize. Capt. 1st XI Cricket and Football. Junior and Senior Athlete. Swimming Championship. Sometime holder of High, Long and Pole Jump Records. M.A. and Geog. Diploma, St. John's College, Cambridge. L.M.B.C., first boat. Capt. 9th Batt. Glos. Regt. Mentioned in despatches. Hon. Sec. Glos. Boy Scouts Assoc. Schoolmaster at Wycliffe College. Married : (1 son, 1 dau.).

Sibly, William Arthur, *Springfield, Stonehouse, Glos.* (S.H.), 1892–1902. Form VI. Senior. Pres. of League and Lit. Soc. London Matric. House and Speaking Prizes. Junior Athlete. 1st XI Cricket and Football. M.A. Lincoln College. Housemaster of Springfield since 1909. Headmaster of Wycliffe College since 1912. J.P. (Glos.). Member of Council of R.S.P.C.A.

Silvey, Bryan Ernest, *Compton Lodge, Cribbs Causeway, Westbury-on-Trym, Bristol.* (H.), 1925–1933. Form V. Chess Team. Coal Factor.

Silvey, Stuart John, *Compton Lodge, Cribbs Causeway, Westbury-on-Trym, Bristol.* (H.), 1925–1933. Science VI. Prefect. School Certif. 1st XI Cricket. 2nd XV Rugby. Hurdles Record. Connaught and School Shooting Team. Medical Student, Bristol University.

Silvey, Thomas Lindsay, *Compton Lodge, Cribbs Causeway, Westbury-on-Trym, Bristol.* (H.), 1924–1930. Form VI. Prefect. School Certif. With firm of Messrs. G. E. Silvey & Co., Coal Factors, Midland Road, Bristol.

Simmonds, Edwin Clifford, *Bryncliffe, Chepstow Road, Newport, Mon.* (S.H.), 1919–1922. Form V. Probationer. 1st XI Football.

Simpson, Alan Sopwith, *Woodbank, Mottram Road, Stalybridge, Cheshire.* (S.H.), 1912–1918. Form VI. Senior. Vice-Pres. of League. London Matric. M.R.C.S., L.R.C.P. University of Wales and London. M.B., B.S. (London). D.P.H. (Eng.). Assistant M.O. Grove Fever Hospital. Doctor. Medical Officer of Health, Stalybridge.

Simpson, Thomas Ivan, *Clarkshill, Low Road, near Carlisle.* (S.H.), 1912–1915. Form VI. Senior. Lieut. R.A.F. Farmer. Married.

Sims, George Blackwell, *Beausale House, near Warwick.* (D.B.), 1882–1886. Probationer. Farmer. Chairman, Stratford-on-Avon Branch National Farmers' Union. Married : (2 daus.).

Sims, Harold Vincent, *c/o Aldreth, Pearcroft Road, Stonehouse.* (S.H.), 1908–1913. Form VI. Senior. 2nd XI Football. Lieut., M.G.C. M.C. M.A., St. John's College, Oxford. Schoolmaster. Married.

Sims, Samuel S. (D.B.), 1883–1888. 1st XV Rugby. Merchant in Chili. Deceased.

Sims, W. R. (D.B.), 1889–1895. Form VI. Probationer. London Yeomanry.

Sims-Davies, Geoffrey, 9 *Toll Gate Road, Port Talbot.* (h.). (Spr.), 1924–1929. Upper IV. 2nd XV Rugby. Swimming Championship. Engineer. A.M.I.M.E. With Shell-Mex Co.

Sinclair, Thomas Marshall, *Victoria House, 42 Hogarth Road, Earls Court, S.W. 5.* (S.H.), 1911–1915. Form IV. Company Director and Accountant. Married.

Singleton, John Percy, *Holmbury, Thorncliffe Drive, Lansdown Road, Cheltenham.* (H.), 1915–1920. Form IV. Outfitter. Married : (2 daus.).

Sinnock, Paul. (S.H.), 1897–1901. Form VI. Was fruit farming in Nova Scotia. Deceased 1935.

Skinner, Walter Reginald Kingwell, *Bodorgan Manor, Bodorgan Road, Bournemouth.* (H.), 1907–1910. Form VI. Senior. 2nd Lieut. R.A.F. Dentist. Married.

Sleight, Albert Henry, 23 *Lawn Road, Hampstead, N.W. 3.* (H.), 1904–1905. Form VI. Senior. Prize for Speaking. Exhibitioner. Prizeman, M.A. (Hons. I, Modern Languages Tripos), St. John's College, Cambridge. Teaching Diploma, London University. Sometime Schoolmaster. Editor " Modern Language Review."

Sly, Arthur Cuthbert, *Arundel House, Channel View Road, Portishead, Somerset.* (S.H.), 1906–1910. Form V. Probationer. Lieut. R.A.F. Engineer with Imperial Tobacco Co. Married : (2 daus.).

Smale, John Arthur, 32 *Warley Hill, Brentwood, Essex. Lydney, Glos.* (h.). (S.H.), 1909–1911. Form VI. Senior. London Matric. 1st XI Cricket. B.Sc. Bristol. Lieut. R.A.F., A.F.C. Electrical Engineer with Marconi W.T. Co. Married : (1 son, 1 dau.).

Smart, Frederick James John, *Rhode House, High Street, Chalford, Glos.* (D.B.), 1916–1922. Form V. Probationer. 2nd XI Football. Grocer.

Smedley, G. A. (H.), 1900–1903. Form III.

Smedley, William Walter. (H.), 1901–1903. Form V. Senior. 2nd XI Cricket and Football. A.S.C.

Smith, A. A. N.

Smith, Alan Montague, *The Glade, Melksham, Wilts.* (S.H.), 1899–1904. Form VI. Senior. House Prize. 1st XI Cricket and Football. 2nd Lieut. D.C.L.I. Solicitor. Married : (2 sons).

Smith, Arthur Charles. (D.B.), 1895–1898.

Smith, Archibald Herbert Alexander, *Range Dairy, Illawarra Road, Moorbank, Liverpool, near Sydney, Australia.* (S.H.), 1899–1904. Form V. Dairyman. Married.

Smith, Alan Round, *Wayside, London Road, Cirencester. c/o L. Smith, Esq., Stonehouse, Glos.* (D.B.), 1904–1909. Form III. 1st XI Football. Sergt. 9th Lancers. 21st Machine Gun Squadron E.E.F. 1914–1919. Commercial Traveller. Married : (1 son).

Smith, Christopher Douglas. (S.H.), 1913–1918. Form IV. Probationer. 2nd XI Football. Manufacturer's Agent. Married.

Smith, Colin Puller, *The Hayes, Cleeve Lawns, Downend, near Bristol.* (R. and S.H.), 1929–1921–1936. Modern VI. Prefect. Higher Certif. 2nd XI Cricket. Senior Lit. Comp. Timber Trade.

Smith, C. T. Died in Gloucester about 1922.

Smith, David Cordwell, *Cambridge House, Ebley, near Stroud* (h.). 27 *Ashburnham Road, Luton, Beds.* (D.B.), 1932–1935. Form V. 1st XV Rugby. Motor Engineer at Vauxhall Works, Luton.

Smith, David Ivor, 11 *Victoria Avenue, Victoria Park, Cardiff.* (S.H.), 1894–1895. Form V. Surveyor.

Smith, Dennis, 2 *York Villas, Ebley, Glos.* (h.). 57 *Biggin Hall Crescent, Coventry.* (D.B.), 1925–1932. Science VI. House Monitor. London Matric. Electrical Engineer.

Smith, Douglas James, (S.H.), 1886–1887. Railway Manager in S. America.

Smith, Edward Angus, *Laneside, Westlecot Road, Swindon.* (Spr.), 1915–1921. Form VI. Senior. Pres. of Lit. Soc. London Matric. Prize for Speaking. Matting Manufacturer. Married : (1 son).

Smith, Edward Gethen, 79 *Promenade, Cheltenham.* (H.), 1893–1894. Form IV. 1st XI Cricker and Football. L.D.S., R.C.S. (Eng.). Dental Surgeon. Married : (2 sons).

Smith, Francis J. Geoffrey. (H.), 1898–1903. Form VI. Probationer. Spent some years learning his father's business of Flour Milling with Messrs. Workman, Cam. After a short period at Langley Mill became Manager of Albion Flour Mill, Walsall. During the War became a Captain in the A.S.C., but died in hospital July 29th, 1918 from nephritis, due to exposure. ("W. & W.", 91).

Smith, F. Moffatt. (S.H.), 1882–1886. Married.

HARESFIELD BEACON

(in the purchase of which for the National Trust the School had some share).

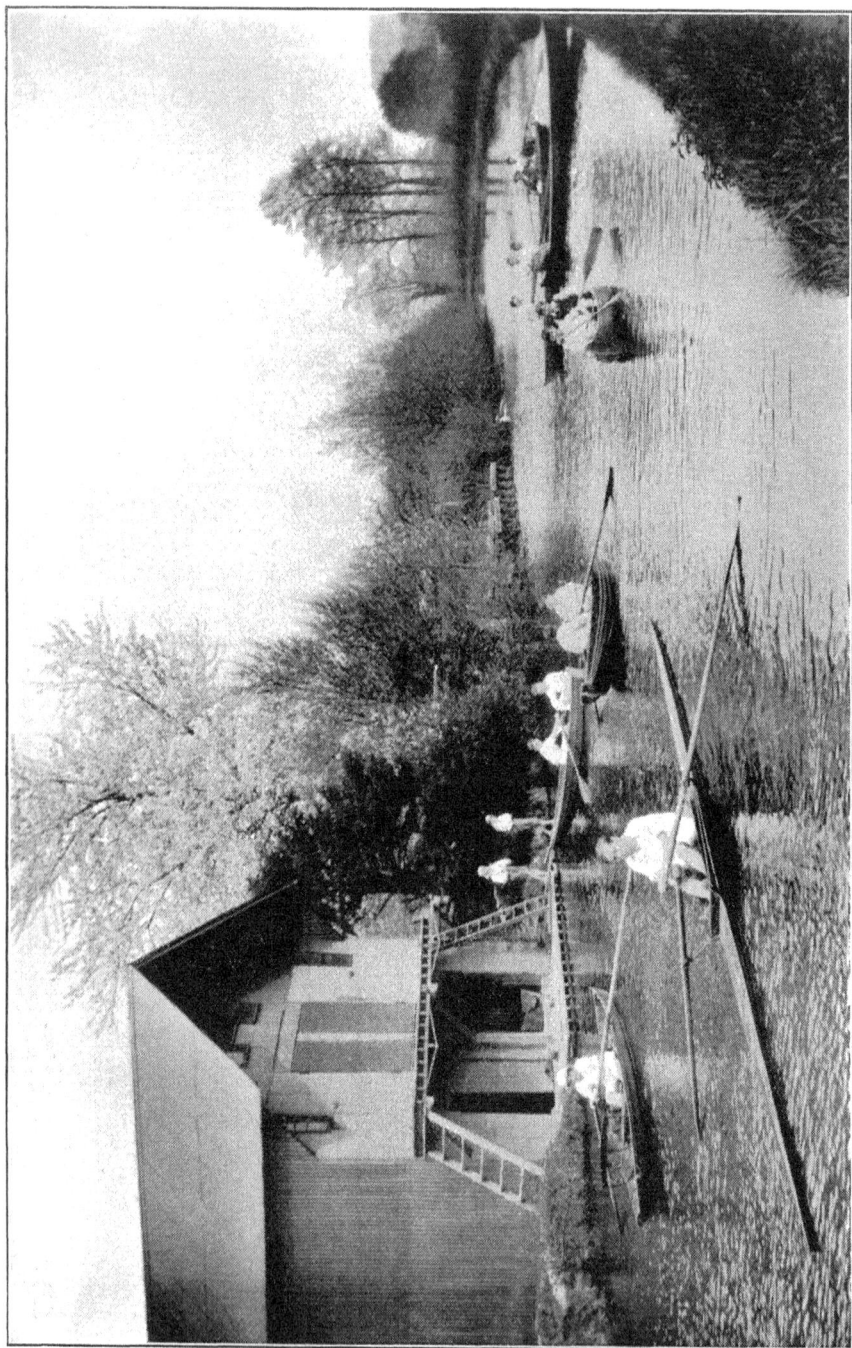

MIXED BOATING ON THE QUIET WATERS OF THE CANAL

THE NEW SCIENCE BUILDINGS CONTAINING SEPARATE LABORATORIES FOR CHEMISTRY, PHYSICS AND BIOLOGY, AND TWO LECTURE ROOMS

ROVER SCOUTS

(Not on the edge of 'the forest primeval,' but in a corner of the Wycliffe grounds).
E. Venning, F. Kenchington, D. Lewis, K. Williams, R. A. Binning, S. G. H. Loosley, C. H. Jowett

Smith, Geoffrey Martyn, *The Rowans, Carlton Gardens, Stroud, Glos.* (D.B. and H.), 1926–1933. Form VI. Prefect. Higher Certif. Prizes for Speaking and Music. With Cheltenham Repertory Company.

Smith, George Hardey, *Langley Mill, Notts.* (H.), 1894–1899.

Smith, George Sydney, 24 *Borough Road, Redcar, Yorks.* (S.H.), 1904–1906. Form V. R.G.A. Shipbroker and Iron Ore Merchant. F.I.C.S. Married : (1 son).

Smith, George William Hillier. (D.B.), 1886–1890. Director of Wholesale Dairy and Catering Firm. Married.

Smith, Harold William James, 54 *Charlton Road, Keynsham, Som.* (S.H.), 1902–1903. Form V. Manager for Imperial Tobacco Co. Married : (2 sons).

Smith, Henry Hardwick, 12 *Boulcott Street, Wellington, New Zealand.* (H.)., 1894–1896. Form VI. Senior. Pres. of Lit. Soc. London Matric. Capt. 1st XI Cricket and Football (unbeaten XI, 1895). M.A., M.B. (Cantab.), F.R.C.S. (Eng.). Senior Surgeon, Wellington Hospital, New Zealand. Married : (1 son).

Smith, Herbert John, *Hill View, Highworth, Wilts.* (S.H.), 1926–1932. Upper V.

Smith, Herbert Round, *Cirencester.* (D.B.), 1897–1901. Form III. R.G.A. Fruit Preserver. Married.

Smith, Hugh Colin, 212 *Drove Road, Swindon.* (Spr.), 1917–1923. Form VI. Senior. Pres. of Lit. Soc. Cambridge Senior. Music and Speaking Prizes. With the Oriental Fibre Mat and Matting Co. Married (1 son, 1 dau.).

Smith, Hugh Norman, *Broughton, Coronation Road, Rodborough, Stroud, Glos.* (D.B.), 1926–1934. Matric. Form. House Monitor. School Certif. 1st XI Cricket. Articled to Municipal and County Engineer.

Smith, James. (S.H.), 1882–1887. 1st XI Cricket and 1st XV " Rugger " Blue at Cambridge. M.A., B.Ch., M.B., Jesus College, Cambridge. F.R.C.S. Settled down in general practice at St. John's Road, Putney Hill. He died early in 1926. (" Star," August 1926, p. 22).

Smith, J. Davidson Eaton, *Lion Chambers, Huddersfield.* (H.), 1894–1898. Form VI. Senior. Pres. of Lit. Soc. Capt. 1st XI Cricket and Football. Junior and Senior Athlete. Sometime President of Huddersfield Rotarians.

Smith, John Hooper, 240 *Smithdown Road, Liverpool* 15. (D.B.), 1893–1895. Form II. Dairy Foreman. Married : (1 son, 1 dau.).

Smith, John Llewellin, *at Royal Gatehouse Hotel, Tenby, Pemb.* (S.H.), 1888–1890. Senior. Pres. of Lit. Soc. 1st XV Rugby. M.B.E. J.P. Glamorgan County Council 1924–1926. President South Wales Inst. of Architects 1913–1914. Architect. Married.

Smith, John Sidney. (H.), 1902–1903. Form IV. On leaving went into an engineering business. In 1915 became driver in Royal Flying Corps, but after being invalided home from Mesopotamia, died in Netley Hospital June 1916. (" W. & W.", 94).

Smith, John Wentworth, 11 *Palmeira Square, Hove, Sussex.* (S.H.), 1882–1886. Senior. 1st XV Rugby. Member London Stock Exchange.

Smith, John William, *Avon Lodge, Manor Park Road, Nuneaton, Warwicks.* (Spr.), 1918–1925. Form IV. 2nd XI Cricket. Draper.

Smith, Leonard James Graves, *c/o Aldreth, Stonehouse, Glos.* (D.B.), 1913–1919. Form III. With Borough Engineer, Colchester.

H

Smith, Leslie Arthur, *Carlton Gardens, Stroud.* (D.B. and H.), 1916–1923). Form VI. Senior. London Matric. 2nd XI Cricket. House Prize. Chartered Accountant.

Smith, Lewis Henry, *The Deyne, Amberley, Stroud.* (D.B.), 1887–1891. Coal Factor.

Smith, Lionel Charles, *Broughton, Coronation Road, Rodborough, Stroud.* (D.B.), 1926–1934. Matric. Form. House Monitor. School Certif. 1st XI Cricket. Articled to Surveyor, Stroud R.D.C.

Smith, Marcel. (Spr.), 1910–1911. On leaving joined his parents in Paris. During the War he became an interpreter in the Gloucesters, and was killed in France in September 1916. (" W. & W.", 92).

Smith, Norman. (S.H.), 1905–1906. Form V. Joined his brother in business at Edmonton (Canada) and also went on a surveying expedition in the North-West Territory. In 1914 joined the Canadian Artillery and was killed on the Somme in October 1916. (" W. & W.", 93).

Smith, Norman Henry Graves, *The Brambles, St. Martin's Approach, Ruislip, Middlesex.* (D.B.), 1905–1913. Form VI. Senior. 2nd XI Cricket and Football. Cambridge Senior. Lieut. Glos. Regt. Engineer. Married : (3 daus.).

Smith, Percy Edward. (D.B.), 1885–1891. Form V. 1st XV Rugby and 1st XI Cricket. Gloucestershire Rugby Team 1892–1899. Brewer. Married. Deceased.

Smith, Peter Douglas, *Dunedin, Charlton Road, Keynsham, Bristol.* (S.H.), 1929–1933. Form V. House Monitor. School Certif. 1st XV Rugby. With Imperial Tobacco Co.

Smith, Peter Norman. (D.B.), 1928–1930. Lower IV.

Smith, Reginald Cecil. (H.), 1885–1891. Brewer. Married.

Smith, Reginald John, 7 *King's Road, Penzance.* (S.H.), 1915–1919. Form IV. Probationer. House Furnisher and Removal Contractor. Married.

Smith, Robert Oswald, *Dunstead House, Langley Mills, Notts.* (H.), 1897–1899. Form V. 2nd XI Football. Miller.

Smith, Samuel John, *Boulsdon Croft, Newent, Glos.* (S.H.), 1908–1911. Form III.

Smith, Sidney Howard, *Beech Cottage, Rodborough, Stroud.* (D.B.), 1887–1888. 1st XI Cricket. 1st XV Rugby. Junior Athlete. All England Lawn Tennis Championship 1896. Retired Coal Factor. Married.

Smith, Stanley H., *The Mill House, Ambrosden, Bicester, Oxon.* (H.), 1930–1932. Form V Upper. Cambridge School Certif. 2nd and 1st XVs. Corn Merchant.

Smith, Sydney, 68 *Chester Square, London, S.W.* 1. (S.H.), 1886–1888. Discount Broker. Married.

Smith, Thomas Angell, *Southerndown, Highworth, Wilts.* (Spr.), 1922–1931. Matric. Form. House Monitor. 2nd XV Rugby. 1st XI Cricket. Bank Clerk.

Smith, Wilfrid Osborn Hardwick, *Mangamingi, Eltham, New Zealand.* (H.), 1897–1900. Form IV. Sheep Farmer. Married : (3 sons).

Smith, Wilfrid Stanley. (S.H.), 1895–1899. Form IV.

Snell, John Charles, *Townsend Farm, Brampton Abbotts, Ross-on-Wye.* (Spr.), 1903–1904. Form III. Farmer. Married : (4 sons, 2 daus.).

Snowsell, Norman E. (S.H.), 1906–1907. Form IV. Probationer. 1st XI Cricket and Football. Flour Miller.

Soane, Guy Victor St. John. (H.), 1914–1915. Form IIb.

Soane, Thomas N. (H.), 1914–1915. Form IIa.

Solomon, Richard Edward, *Westbrook, Westcross, Swansea.* (S.H.), 1918–1920. Form I. Produce Broker. Married : (1 son, 1 dau.).

Solomon, Sydney Arthur. (Spr.), 1910–1914. Form V. Probationer. Donor of the Solomon Cup for Shooting. Died of consumption in March 1921. (" Star," April 1921, p. 23).

Sotham, George Brian, *Groveley, Wookey Road, Wells.* (D.B.), 1916–1922. Form VI. Probationer. House Shooting Team. Accountant. Secretary of four Wells' Firms. Married : (1 son).

Southey, Robert Broughton. (H.), 1911–1915. Form IV. Entered the offices of the "Merthyr Express." Joined the Queen's Westminster Rifles, and transferred to the Machine Gun Corps. Was killed on Kemmel Hill, near Ypres, on April 11th 1916. (" W. & W.", 94).

Spackman, Arthur James, *Wycliffe House, Wanborough, near Swindon, and 44 Croft Road, Swindon.* (S.H.), 1920–1923. Form V. Probationer. 2nd XI Football. Building Contractor. Married : (1 dau.).

Spackman, Herbert Ralph, *Lothians, Marlborough Road, Swindon.* (S.H.) 1915–1918. Form IV. Probationer. 1st XI Football. 2nd XI Cricket. Swimming Championship. Building Contractor. Married.

Spackman, Howard Dixon, *Hodson Farm, Wroughton, near Swindon.* (S.H.), 1919–1922. Form V. Probationer. Building Contractor. Married.

Spinney, G. F.

Spoor, Arthur Twynham, *The Hydro, Bristol.* (H.), 1904–1908. Form IV. Probationer. M.A. Emmanuel College, Cambridge. M.R.C.S., L.R.C.P. (Lond.). M.O. i/c Physiotherapy Dept. Bristol General Hospital. Examiner to G.S.M.M.G. Married.

Sprigge, Christopher Edmund. (S.H.), 1928–1931. Matric. Form.

Spriggs, Bernard William. (H.), 1885–1887. Deceased 1904.

Spriggs, Sir Edmund Ivens, *Ruthin Castle, North Wales.* (H.), 1885–1888. Senior. London Matric. Scholar of Guy's Hospital. M.D., F.R.C.P. (Lond.). M.C.V.O. Formerly Physician to St. George's and other Hospitals. Lecturer and Examiner to Royal College of Physicians. Author of works on Medical subjects. J.P. Athenaeum Club. Now Senior Physician to Ruthin Castle Clinic. Married.

Spring, Herbert. (D.B.), 1922–1925. Form I. Articled to Auctioneer and Surveyor.

Squire, Edwin Ross, *Lloyds Bank House, Somerton, Somerset.* (S.H.), 1890–1893. Form VI. 1st XV Rugby. Capt. Lincs. Regt. M.C. Bank Manager. Married.

Squire, Ernest E., 24 *Gordon Road, Ealing, London, W.* 5. (H.), 1893. Form VI. Probationer. House Prize. Music Warehouse. Married : (1 son, 1 dau.).

Squire, Percy. (H.), 1888–1889. Died at Ealing 1889.

Stafford, Lawrence Tree, *Dunt Lane Farm, Hurst, Berks.* (S.H.), 1912–1913. Form VI. Probationer. Cambridge Senior. Royal Tank Corps. Farmer. Married : (1 son).

Stagg, Rowland Edward. (D.B.), 1915–1918. Form II. In Mercantile Marine.

Stamper, Gerald. (D.B.), 1899–1900. *In Canada.*

Stanfield, James Paget. (Spr.), 1915–1921. Probationer. Was articled to a Chartered Accountant in Liverpool. Died of pneumonia, January 1925. (" Star," April 1925).

Stanier, Charles Edward. (S.H.), 1892–1895. Form VI. Senior. Pres. of Lit. Soc. London Matric. 1st XI Football. Capt. 2nd XI Cricket. Junior Athlete. House Prize. Whitworth Scholarship. B.Sc. (Lond.). Assoc.M.Inst.C.E. Civil Engineer. Married : (2 sons, 1 dau.). Died 1936.

Stanier, James Gordon. (S.H.), 1897–1899. Form VI. Probationer. University College, London, Inter. B.A. LL.B. (Lond.), bracketed 1st in Honours Class I. Univ. Law Scholar. Solicitor at Winchester, and Lecturer in Dept. of Law, University College, Southampton. Canadian Army Medical Corps (Sergt.). Married : (2 sons, 2 daus.).

Stanier, William Arthur, *Newburn, Chorley Wood, Herts.* (S.H.), 1891. Form V. Probationer. Chief Mechanical Engineer, L.M.S. Railway. Pres. of Inst. of Locomotive Engineers 1936. M.Inst.Mech.E. Married : (1 son, 1 dau.).

Staniforth, John Norman, 24 *Connaught Avenue, Loughton, Essex.* (R. and Spr.), 1932–1936. Upper V.

Stark, John Loudon Strain, *Croft House, Selkirk, N.B.* (S.H.), 1916–1917. Form IV. Probationer. 1st XI Cricket. Edinburgh O.T.C. Colliery Agent and Contractor. Married.

Startup, Cuthbert Leethwaite. (H.), 1906–1910. Form III. Engineer.

Steedman, Mackenzie T. W., *Clovelly, Lampton Road, Hounslow.* (D.B.), 1897–1901. Form IV. Probationer. M.A. Clare College, Cambridge. M.R.C.S., L.R.C.P. Capt. R.A.M.C. Registrar Cumballa War Hospital, Bombay. Married.

Steel, Norman. (S.H.), 1905–1911. Form IV. Deceased.

Steele, William Henry Radmore, 273 *Fulham Road, S.W.* 10. (D.B.), 1890–1892. Form IV. Medallist, London School of Pharmacy. M.P.S. Chemist. Married.

Stephens, Charles Douglas. (D.B.), 1897–1898. Form VI. Senior. 1st XI Cricket. House Prize. Entered his father's business of cloth manufacturer at Lightpill, Stroud. In 1907 went out to Asia Minor as Assistant Treasurer of the Syrian Protestant College at Beyrout. Died of septic pneumonia in July 1913.

Stephens, Clifford Henry. (H.), 1924–1926. Form V. Probationer. Architect.

Stevens, Leslie William, *Haroldsfield Farm, Kingswood, Wotton-under-Edge, Glos.* (R. and S.H.), 1932–1933. Form III.

Stevens, Maurice, *Haroldsfield Farm, Kingswood, Wotton-under-Edge.* (R. and S.H.), 1932–1934. Middle IV.

Stevens, Reginald, *Haroldsfield Farm, Kingswood, Wotton-under-Edge.* (R. and S.H.), 1932–1934. Lower IV.

Stevinson, H. W. (D.B.), 1891–1894. Form II. In South Africa.

Stewart, Charles Edward. *In Natal.* (S.H.), 1910–1912. Form VI. Senior. Camb. Junior Hons. I. (1st in U.K. in Phys. Geog. and Nat. Hist.). 1st XI Cricket and Football. Senior and Junior Athlete. 1st R.N.B., Antwerp 1914. Foreign Representative. Married.

Stewart, Colin Murray, *Kirkfield, North Road, Parkstone, Dorset.* (S.H.), 1923–1926. Upper V. Senior. 2nd XI Football. 1st XV Rugby. Junior Athlete. Fl.-Lieut. in R.A.F.

Stewart, James, *Kirkfield, North Road, Parkstone, Dorset.* (S.H.), 1915–1918. Form VI. Senior. Vice-Pres. of League. Camb. Senior. 2nd XI Cricket and Football. Engineer on Tea Estate.

Stock, Richard Stanley. (S.H.), 1911–1912. Form I. Killed in a motorcycle accident 1925.

Stockwood, Thomas Alan Edward, *Wellington Road, Hakin, Milford Haven.* (H.), 1925–1930. Form VI. Prefect. School Certif. 1st XI Cricket. 1st XV. Shipbroker. Fellow Inst. Chartered Shipbrokers. Married.

Stoddart, William, *Glenroy, Park Lane, Gt. Harwood, Lancs.* (H.), 1924–1929. Form VI. School Certif. 2nd XV Rugby. L.R.C.P. (London). M.R.C.S. (England). Resident Physician Essex County Hospital, Colchester.

Stokes, Cyril Montague, *Beech House, Keynsham, Som.* (Spr.), 1909. Form III. In business.

Stokes, Eric Septimus, *Beech House, Keynsham, Som.* (Spr.), 1910–1913. Form III. In business.

Stokes, William Bomford, *Loughborough, Moreton-in-the-Marsh, Glos.* (Spr.), 1919–1921. Form V. Farming and Fruit Growing.

Stone, F. A. Deceased.

Stone, Jack, *Hill Croft, Rose Walk, Purley, Surrey.* (D.B.), 1902–1905. Form IV. 2nd XI Football. Lieut. Glos. Regt. Stockbroker. Married : (2 sons).

Stone, Lionel George, *May Street, Dulwich Hill, Sydney, New South Wales.* (S.H.), 1905–1908. Form II.

Strachan, Alan, *The Lodge, Worcester Road, Sutton, Surrey.* (S.H.), 1905–1910. Form VI. Senior. Treas. of Lit. Soc. M.D. Edinburgh. Physician. Surgeon R.N. 1917–1919. Married : (1 son).

Strange, Arthur Cecil. *In India.* (H.), 1913–1914. Form V. Probationer. Swimming Championship.

Strange, Edward Halford, *Belvedere, St. Lawrence, I. of W.* (D.B.), 1888–1891. Form VI. Senior. London Matric. House Prize. M.Sc. (Manchester). Technical Research Chemist. Married : (1 dau.).

Strange, John William, *Christowe, Minchinhampton, Glos.* (h.). (D.B.), 1918–1926. Form VI. Senior. Vice-Pres. of League. London Matric. School Certif. Prizes for Speaking and Literature (H. Park). B.Sc. London. In Research Dept. of H.M.V.

Strange, Thomas Arthur, *Christowe, Minchinhampton, Glos.* (D.B.), 1918–1926. Form VI. Senior. London Matric. Prize of Literature (H. Park). In business.

Strange, Wilfrid Arthur, *Christowe, Minchinhampton, Glos.* (D.B.), 1889–1893. Fruit Merchant. Married : (2 sons, 1 dau.). Died 1937.

Stratton, James Ernest. (S.H.), 1889–1892. Form VI. Senior. London Matric. M.D. London 1902. Late House Physician Wolverhampton and Staffs General Hospital. Married : (1 son, 2 daus.). Died 1936. ("Star," Dec. 1936).

Streader, Reginald Albert, *Brigstock, Streatley Lane, Four Oaks, near Birmingham.* (S.H. and Spr.), 1907–1910. Form V. 2nd Lieut. London Regt. Manufacturer's Agent. Married.

Streat, Philip Priestly, *Nelmside, 7 Ernest Road, Hornchurch, Essex.* (H. and Spr.), 1901–1904. Form IV. Probationer. London Rifle Brigade and Royal Engineers. A.C.I.I. Lecturer. Insurance Inst. of London. Married : (1 son, 2 daus.).

Stride, Horatio Barton, *Kenbar, Park Road, Shirehampton, Bristol.* (H.), 1910–1916. Form VI. Probationer. 2nd Lieut. Glos. Regt. Builder and Contractor. Married : (2 sons).

Stride, Robert Charles Barton, *Beech Avenue, Severn Beach, Bristol.* (H.)., 1905–1911. Form VI. Senior. Senior Cambridge. 1st XI Football. 2nd XI Cricket. Studied Engineering in Bristol University until 1914. O.T.C. (Bristol) and Transport Service in France. Married : (1 dau.).

Stride, William Henry Barton, 126a *Redland Road, Bristol* 6. (H. and Spr.), 1904–1910. Form VI. Senior. Vice-Pres. of League. Prize for Speaking. Dental Surgeon. Married : (2 sons, 1 dau.).

Stringer, Horace James, 5 *Westfield Road, Mate Mount, Mill Hill, London* *N.W.* 7. (H.), 1917–1921. Overseas Sales Manager Henlys Ltd. Married.

Strong, Frederick Carl, *P. O. Box* 217 *Windsor, Connecticut, U.S.A.* (Spr.), 1931–1933. Upper Remove. Student at Swarthmore College, Swarthmore, Pennsylvania, U.S.A.

Sutherland, David Arthur, 8 *Llythred, Swansea.* (S.H.), 1914–1918. Form V. Probationer. Married : (1 son).

Sutherland, William John Craig, 82 *Glanbrydan Avenue, Swansea.* (S.H.), 1909–1914. Form V. 2nd XI Cricket and Football. Sergt. Artists' Rifles, London Regt. Draper. Married.

Tabb, Ashby Bray, 55 *Bold Street, Liverpool.* (H.), 1883–1886. Married.

Tabb, Henry S., *The Garth, Batheaston, Bath.* (H.), 1890–1892. Form VI. Senior. London Matric. Managing Director of Paper Mills. Married.

Talbot, Edwin Charles, 1901–1902.

Tancock, James Paddon, *Highlands, Treloyan, St. Ives, Cornwall.* (S.H.), 1914–1921. Form VI. Senior. Pres. of League. Capt. 1st XI Football. House Prize. Outfitter. Married : (2 daus.).

Tanner, Samuel Foster, *Wexham Springs, Stoke Poges, Bucks.* (Spr.), 1924–1927. With Messrs. E. S. & A. Robinson, Bristol.

Taylor, Arthur Raymond, *Ewhurst, Dunottar Avenue, Eaglescliffe, Co. Durham.* (Spr.), 1922–1930. Matric. Form. Prefect. Vice-Pres. of League. Sec. of Lit. Soc. School Certif. 1st XI Cricket. 1st XV Rugby. Batchelar Cup. School Chess Team. Prizes for Music and Public Service. With Messrs. E. S. & A. Robinson, Bristol.

Taylor, Edward Roy. (S.H.), 1900–1903. Form IV. Apprenticed in London, before joining his father's business at Newport, Mon. Joined Welch Fusiliers in 1914. Commission in S. Wales Borderers 1915, later Captain. M.C. 1918 for attack on village of Maisseny. Killed during attack on Oise Canal, October 23rd, 1918. (" W. & W.", 95).

Taylor, Francis Arnold. (S.H.), 1902–1903. Form III.

Taylor, Geoffrey Barker, *Ewhurst, Dunottar Avenue, Eaglescliffe, Co. Durham.* (Spr.), 1921–1928. Upper V. House Monitor. Music Prizes. With Ashmore, Benson & Pearse (Engineers) of Stockton-on-Tees.

Taylor, Harold Francis. (H.), 1905–1908. Form III.

Taylor, John S. Crawford. (S.H.), 1895–1900. Form V or VI. Probationer. 2nd XI Cricket and Football. Chartered Accountant. Died 1933.

Taylor, Robin Gordon, *Kremsergasse* 4, *Vienna* VIII, *Austria* (h.). (H.), 1932–1935. Upper V. School Certif. Cadet in the British India Steam Navigation Co., 122 Leadenhall Street, London.

Teagle, Kenneth, 56 *New Road, Chippenham, Wilts.* (S.H.), 1929–1934. Form V. Auctioneer and Estate Agent's Pupil.

Teakle, David H., *Watledge Lodge, Nailsworth, near Stroud.* (D.B.), 1927–1934. Form VI. House Monitor. School Certif. Flock and Shoddy Manufacturing

Teakle, Percy Arkell, *Rooksmoor, Stroud.* (D.B.), 1901.

Terrett, Charles Robert, 26 *St. Alban's Road, Brynmill, Swansea.* (S.H.), 1884–1885. Manufacturer's Agent.

Theyer, Edward Isaac, *Parsonage Farm, Brockworth, Glos.* (D.B.), 1896–1897. Form III. Farmer.

Theyer, John Henry. (S.H.), 1895–1896.

Thomas, Allen Richard, *The Mount, Pentyla, Port Talbot.* (S.H.), 1924–1929. Upper IV. Draper.

Thomas, Brynmor David, *Wayside, Raglan Road, Port Talbot.* (S.H.), 1924–1928. Form V. 1st XI Cricket and Football. Caterer.

Thomas, Charles Leslie, *Cefn Park, Cadoxton Road, Neath, Glam.* (S.H., Spr. and H), 1907–1915. Form VI. Senior. Capt 1st XI Cricket. 1st XI Football. Lieut. M.G.C. President Neath Rotary Club. Solicitor and Notary Public. Partner in Lewis C. Thomas, Son & Morris, Solicitors. Married : (1 son, 2 daus.).

Thomas, Edgar Penrose, 4 *Mount Street, Swansea.* (H.), 1896–1901. Form V.

Thomas Edmund, *Upper Farm, Rhoose, near Cardiff.* (H.), 1904–1907. Form III. Capt. 1st XI Football. 2nd XI Cricket. Farmer.

Thomas, Eric Leslie Vivian, *Tolverne, Penzance, Cornwall.* (H.), 1909–1916. Form VI. Senior. Vice-Pres. of League. London Matric. Capt. 1st XI Football. 1st XI Cricket. Tennis Championship. House Prize. B.A., LL.B. St. John's College, Cambridge. 2nd Lieut. R.G.A. Penzance Borough Coroner. Solicitor. Married : (2 daus.).

Thomas, Ernest Gerald, *Myrtlebury, Caswell, Swansea.* (S.H.), 1907–1914. Form IV. Lieut. Welch Regt. Boxing Champ. 1914. Timber Importer. Married : (2 daus.).

Thomas, Ernest Whitney, 149 *Cromwell Road, Bristol* (h.). (S.H.), 1892–1895. Form V. Locomotive Works Manager in India.

Thomas, Frank Bernard Vivian. (H.), 1906–1914. Form VI. Senior. 1st XI Football. Prize for Excellence in Speaking. Received a commission in the 5th Duke of Cornwall's Light Infantry, and crossed to France in August 1916. On September 22nd he was killed by a sniper's bullet The pulpit in the Chapel at Wycliffe was given by his father in his memory. ("W. & W.", 96–100).

Thomas, Gwilym I. (S.H.), 1888–1890. Form VI. Senior. London Matric. Treas. of Lit. Soc. 1st XI Cricket. 1st XV Rugby. House Prize. After serving his articles with his brother, Mr Lewis Thomas, he practised as a solicitor in Merthyr Tydfil. In 1906 he was attacked by consumption, and died in January 1910.

Thomas, Henry Anthony, *The Mount, Pentyla, Port Talbot.* (S.H.), 1926–1933. Form VI. Prefect. Vice-Pres. of League. London Matric. 1st XI Cricket 1931–1933. 1st XV Rugby 1933. Prize for Public Service. Medical Student at Guy's Hospital.

Thomas, Howell B. (brother of Gwilym I.). (S.H.), 1888–1889. Capt. 2nd XI Cricket and 2nd XV Rugby. Capt. of Merthyr Tydfil Rugby Club for nine years. Was associated with his brother in the Thomas Merthyr Colliery. In the Autumn of 1911 he was attacked by peritonitis and died in January 1912.

Thomas, Herbert Walter. (H.), 1898–1900. Form III.

Thomas, Hugh Darlington, *Tanglyn, Mumbles, near Swansea.* (H.), 1923–1928. Upper IV. Jeune Cup (Record), Foster Rifle. Connaught Shooting Team.

Thomas, Hugh William Taunton, *Green Shutters, Old Mixon, Weston-super-Mare.* (S.H.), 1902–1904. Form V. Tailor. Married : (2 sons).

Thomas, John Ernest. (S.H.), 1894–1895. Form IV. Officer in the Royal Artillery during the War. Colliery Agent and Coal Exporter. Died 1928. ("Star," Dec. 1928, p. 8).

Thomas, Mervyn Lincoln, *Maescynrig, Merthyr Tydvil.* (H.), 1913–1914. Upper I.

Thomas, Norman Peter Landers, *Willowsmere, Park Drive, Swansea.* (H.), 1927–1933. Form VI. House Monitor. School Certif. 1st XV Rugby. Swimming Team. Swansea University Inter L.L.B. (London). Solicitor's Articled Clerk.

Thomas, Peter Nander Alan, *Thorncroft, Ray Park Avenue, Maidenhead, Berks.* (Spr.), 1930–1932. Upper IV. Law Student at Swansea Univ.

Thomas, Reginald, *Lochturffin, Mathry, Haverfordwest, Pem.* (S.H.), 1929–1933. Form VI. House Monitor. School Certif. 2nd XV Rugby. Fly-weight Boxing 1932. School Chess Team. Agricultural Course at Reading University. Farming.

Thomas, Reginald Charles, *Thorncroft, Ray Park Avenue, Maidenhead, Berks.* (Spr.), 1929–1932. Lower V.

Thomas, Ronald Llewellyn, *Penrhadwy, Vaynor, near Merthyr.* (S.H.), 1905–1912. Form VI. Senior. Pres. of League and Lit. Soc. London Matric. 1st XI Football. 1st XI Cricket. Senior Singles and Doubles Tennis. St. John's College, Cambridge. Capt. Welsh Regt. and Royal Flying Corps. Director Thomas Merthyr Colliery Co., Merthyr. Married : (1 son, 1 dau.).

Thomas, Trevor Norton, *The Fields, Southerndown, Bridgend, Glam.* (H.), 1928–1932. Form VI. School Certif. Junior Tennis. Midland Bank, Trevichy, Glam.

Thomas, Walter Price Clifford. (H.), 1901–1903. Form IV. Capt. Northumberland Fusiliers. M.C. Actor. Married. Died 1933.

Thomas, Wendell W., *Glenusa, Dinas Powys, Glam.* (S.H.), 1906–1913. Form VI. Senior. Pres. of Lit. Soc. Vice-Pres. of League. London Matric. 1st XI Cricket. Capt. 1st XI Football. High Jump Record. House and Speaking Prizes. B.A. St. John's College, Cambridge. Capt. S. Wales Borderers. Coal Owner. Married.

Thomas, William Henry. (S.H.), 1898–1904. Form VI. Senior. London Matric. After three years in an architect's office he joined the Slade School of Art. He had just fitted up a studio of his own when War broke out. He joined the H.A.C. He died of wounds received in action, at Gavrelle, near Arras, May 25th 1917. ("W. & W.", 100–102).

Thompson, Joseph Lowes, 80, *Stanpit, Christchurch, Hants.* (Spr.), 1930–1935. Matric Form. House Monitor. 2nd XV Rugby. Swimming Team. Life Saving Record. School Chess Team. Apprentice at G.W.R. Works, Swindon.

Thompson, William Frank Cranmer, *Lyn Cottage, Windsoredge, Nailsworth.* (D.B.), 1920–1922. Form IV. Boot-stiffener Manufacturer. Married.

Thompson, William Herbert Oliver, 36 *Prospect Road, Walmer, Port Elizabeth, S. Africa.* (S.H.), 1903–1905. Form IV. Probationer. Lieut. S.A. Brigade. In business. Married : (3 daus.).

Thompson, William J., *Croyland, Woking, Surrey.* (S.H. and H.), 1882–1884. Probationer. Sec. and Treas. of Lit. Soc. 1st XV Rugby. Farmer. Married.

Thorley, Donald Francis, *The Châlet, Valley Road, Streatham.* (Spr.), 1925–1926.

Thornton, Pensam, 49 *Wheelwright Road, Erdington, Birmingham.* (H.)., 1902–1903. Form II. M.D. Birmingham. M.C. Married : (2 daus.).

Thornton, Thomas Lockwood, 24 *Old Sneed Road, Stoke Bishop.* (D.B.), 1914–1915. Form VI. 1st XI Cricket and Football. War Service 1917–1919. Bank Manager. Married : (2 sons).

Tillett, Frederick Charles. (H.), 1893–1898. Form VI. Senior. Pres. of Lit. Soc. 1st XI Cricket and Football. Became a Consulting Engineer and later a Cardiff Shipowner. After the War he bought a part of the Osborne estate in the Isle of Wight (Barton Manor, once the home of King George V), and there farmed about 700 acres. He died very suddenly on November 14th 1926. (" Star," Dec. 1926).

Tilley, Albert Edward, 11 *Ferncroft Avenue, Hampstead, N.W.* (H.), 1884–1888. Senior. London Matric. 1st XI Cricket. 1st XV Rugby. F.C.A. Chartered Accountant.

Tilley, Charles. (H.), 1886–1888. Farmer. Married.

Tilley, Clifford James, *Summerside, Lucerne Road, Summertown, Oxford.* (S.H.), 1926–1928. Form VI. House Monitor. School Certif. St. *John's College, Oxford.* Honours in Philosophy, Politics and Economics. English Assistant in Schools at Berlin and Kiel 1933–1935. Grain importing since 1935. Married.

Tilley, Henry Arthur, *Shepton Mallet, Som.* (H.), 1888–1889. Farmer and Breeder of Old English sheep dogs. President of the Old English Sheep Dog Club. Hon. Life Member of O.E. Sheep Dog Club of America. Married : (1 son, 2 daus.).

Tilley, Leslie Howard, 54 *Bishop's Mansions, London, S.W.* 6. (H.), 1901–1903. Form IV. 1st XI Cricket. Played Hockey for Norfolk County. Cricket for M.C.C. Capt. Norfolk Regt. Company Director. Dramatic Critic and attached to Messrs. John Wisden & Co. Married.

Tilley, Percy John, 2 *Jaycroft Road, Burnham-on-Sea, Som.* (S.H.), 1927–1928. Form VI. School Certif. Junior Tennis Doubles. University College, London, studying for B.Sc. (Economics).

Timmins, Frank Leslie, 24 *Gordon House, Western Avenue, Ealing, W.* 5. (H.), 1916–1920. Form VI. Senior. Senior Cambridge. 1st XI Cricket. 2nd XI Football. Engineering Course at Birmingham Univ. In Sunbeam Motor Works, Wolverhampton 1923. General Manager London Valve Co, West Bromwich 1931. Facilities Manager Dagenham Motors, London 1932. General Manager, British Automatic & Associated Co., 14 Appold Street, London, E.C. 1936.

Tippett, P. G. (S.H.), 1894. Form III.

Titley, Charles Arthur, *Grenville College Avenue, Maidenhead, Berks.* (S.H.), 1898–1902. Form III. Canadian Scottish. Farmer. Married.

Titley, Francis Porritt, *Broad Blunsdon, near Swindon.* (S.H.), 1902–1905. Form III. Farmer.

Titley, William Addison, *Blunsdon, Swindon* (h.). *S. Rhodesia.* (S.H.), 1899–1905. Form IV. 2nd Rhodesia Regt. Farming.

Titley, William Anthony, *Blunsdon, Swindon.* (S.H.), 1898–1904. Form III. Dairy Farmer. Married.

Tomkins, Stephen Lawrence. (S.H.), 1902–1905. Form III.

Toogood, Arthur Sidney, *Knightwood, Stonehouse, Glos.* (R.H. and D.B.), 1931–1935. Matric. Form. House Monitor. London Matric. With General Accident Insurance Company.

Tovey, Geoffrey Harold, *The Priory, Midsomer Norton, near Bath.* (S.H.), 1927-1934. Form VI. Prefect. Vice-Pres. of League. School Certif. Capt. 2nd XI Cricket. 2nd XV Rugby. Prize for Public Service. Secretary, Waifs and Strays Society, Midsomer Norton. Medical Student, Bristol University.

Tovey, Hugh Stephen, 14 *Hillside Gardens, Wallington, Surrey.* (Spr.), 1927–1930. Matric Form. School Certif. Articled to Incorporated Accountant.

Tovey, Philip Godfrey, 14 *Hillside Gardens, Wallington, Surrey.* (Spr.), 1923–1928. Form VI. House Monitor. School Certif. B.Sc. King's College, London. Technical Assistant to Patents Agent.

Tovey, Ronald Norton, *The Priory, Midsomer Norton, near Bath.* (H.), 1924–1930. Lower IV. Captain Cotham Park 2nd XV Rugby. Auctioneer and Estate Agent.

Townsend, Harold Henry. (D.B.), 1910–1916. Form III.

Trapnell, Francis Cyril, 20 *Copers Cope Road, Beckenham, Kent.* (H.), 1889–1893. Form IV. Junior Athlete. M.D., King's College, Camb. Luther Holden Scholarship, St. Bartholomew's Hospital. Capt., R.A.M.C. Physician and Surgeon.

Tratt, Ronald James. (D.B.), 1904–1909. Form VI. Senior. Entered the Civil Service, and became a clerk in the Savings Bank. Joined Mobbs' Rugby Football Corps (7th Northants). Went to France in September 1915, and died in a German Field Hospital on September 30th, after being wounded during the great advance at Loos. (" W. & W.", p. 105).

Tregaskis, Ernest. (H.), 1895–1897. Form III. Farmer in Saskatchewan Married.

Tregaskis, H. G. Trevor. (H.), 1891–1895. Form VI. Electrical Engineer. Deceased.

Tregaskis, Leonard. (H.), 1895–1897. Form VI. Returned from farming in Canada to take a commission in the 16th Welch. He and his brother Arthur were killed in the great attack on the German lines in the West. (" W. & W.", 106).

Treloar, Peter Quintrell. (S.H.), 1919–1920. Form III.

Treloar, William Arthur Quintrell. *In Johannesburg.* (S.H.), 1919–1924. Form VI. Probationer. London Matric. Prize for Speaking. 2nd XI Football.

Tremaine, Dudley Laxon, *Barton Farm, Lower Guiting, near Cheltenham.* (S.H.), 1919–1922. Form II. Farmer.

Tremellen, Enner Thornley. (H.), 1900–1904. Form VI. Senior. 1st XI Cricket. After four years with the Borough Surveyor of Pontypridd joined the Inland Revenue Dept. as an Assistant Land Valuer. In 1914 he was gazetted 2nd Lieut. in the 5th Welch. He became a Captain and served at the Dardanelles and in N. Africa. He died in hospital in England in December 1917. (" W. & W.", 104).

Trewin, Howard James, *The Glebe, Holdfast, Upton-on-Severn.* (H.), 1910–1911. Form I. War Service : May to December 1918. Farmer. Married : (1 son, 1 dau.).

Trippe, Edgar Henry, *Lancarrow, 25 Maes-y-Coed Road, Heath, Cardiff.* (H.), 1911–1918. Form VI. Senior. Treas. of Lit. Soc. Prize for Speaking. Wholesale Woollen Merchant. Married.

Trippe, Reginald Bertram. (H.), 1911–1917. Form VI. Senior. Pres. of League. Sergt.-Major, Cadet Corps. Capt. 2nd XI Football. Literature Prize. Cadet R.A.F. Woollen Merchant. Died as result of an accident on July 17th, 1927. (" Star," August 1927, p. 13).

Trotman, Gilbert Beaman. (H.), 1900. Farming in Australia.

Trotter, John Frederick Felix. (Spr.), 1921–1927. Form VI. House Monitor. School Certif. Hearson Science Prize. Entered Imperial College of Science and Technology in October 1927. B.Sc. (Hons.), in Chemistry 1930. F.C.S. Was engaged in original investigation (Organic Chemistry) at the time of his death by misadventure on December 20th 1930. (" Star," Dec. 1930, p. 18).

Trump, Charles James, *Morfa, Westbourne Road, Penarth.* (H.),1891– 1894. Form VI. Senior. Camb. Senior. 2nd XI Football. Prize for " Best Shot." 2nd V.B. Norfolk Regt. 1904. Local Director at Cardiff for Monmouthshire and Glamorganshire Branches of Barclays Bank. Member of Council of Governors of Wycliffe College. Married : (1 son).

Trump, Herbert John. (H.), 1891–1896. Form VI. Senior. Was for many years mechanical and technical engineer with Dorman Long & Co. Ltd., Middlesbrough. Joined the Forces upon outbreak of War and served in France 1915 to November 1918. From Armistice to 1921, having then been offered and accepted permanent commission in R.A.O.C. (Regular Forces), he was with the Army of Occupation in Germany as a Major inspecting their munition factories under the Disarmament Commission. In this work his expert mechanical knowledge and ability to speak German was of great value and resulted in his being promoted in 1922 to the Experimental Warfare Establishment, Aldershot. He served 12 months in China with the Shanghai Defence Force, and ultimately, as Lieut-Col., became a member of the Mechanical Warfare Board at the Royal Arsenal, Woolwich. His health broke down and he died in May 1933, leaving a widow.

Trumper, Henry Ernest, 11 *Little James Street, Bedford Row, W.C.* 1. (S.H.), 1930–1933. Upper V. 2nd XV Colours. Scout Swimming Team.

Trumper, Leonard Cundell, *Woodlands, Devizes, Wilts.* (S.H.), 1922– 1925. Senior. School Certif. Hearson Science Prize. B.Sc. (Agriculture) University of Reading. N.D.A. 1st XIII Colours, Reading Univ. Lieut. 4th Wilts. Regt. (T.). National Farmers' Union, County Branch Secretary, Wiltshire. Corn Merchant. Married.

Trumper, Ronald Hayward, *Denewood, Devizes, Wilts.* (S.H.), 1915– 1918. Form V. Certif. in Agriculture, University of Reading. Corn Merchant. Married.

Truran, Arthur Percival. (H.), 1913–1916. Form IV. Deceased 1919.

Truran, Edgar, 49 *Pencisely Road, Cardiff.* (H.), 1903–1907. Form VI. Probationer. 1st XI Cricket and Football. Rowell Cup. R.G.A. Malta and Burma 1916–1920. Bank Cashier (Lloyds Bank, Cardiff Docks). Married : (2 daus.).

Truran, Herbert Colchester, *Lynthorpe, Western Avenue, Newport, Mon.* (H.), 1915–1918. Senior. 2nd XI Football. Band Sergt. Cadet Corps. Chartered Accountant. Married : (2 sons, 1 dau.).

Truran, Matthew Henry. (H.), 1911–1914. Form VI. Probationer. 2nd XI Football. Died in 1919.

Truran, Robert Illtyd, *c/o National Provincial Bank, Beaconsfield, and Oakroyd, Western Avenue, Newport, Mon.* (H.), 1915–1921. Probationer 2nd XI Football. Foster Rifle. Bank Clerk.

Trythall, Edward Richards, *Spring House, Hagley Road, Halesowen, Worcs.* (S.H.), 1915–1918. Senior. Violin Prize. L.D.S. Birmingham. Dental Surgeon. Married : (1 dau.).

Tucker, F. H. (D.B.), 1885. Deceased.

Tucker, Henry Riseley, *Ville Montrose, Heliopolis, Cairo, Egypt.* (S.H. and Spr.), 1912–1916. Form VI. Senior. London Matric. Lieut. E. Surrey Regt. B.A. (Hons.) Worcester College, Oxford. Master at Wycliffe 1924–1927. Now in a Government School in Egypt.

Turnbull, George Robert Austin, 165 *Redland Park Road, Redland, Bristol.* (O.B.), 1927–1928. Upper V. House Monitor. Senior Cambridge. 2nd XI Football. 2nd XV Rugby. Middle-weight Boxing. House Shooting Team. Junior and Senior House Relay and Cricket. Manufacturer's Agent.

Turner, John James, *Arrow Lodge, Kington, Hereford* (h.). (S.H.), 1931–1935. Lower V. House Monitor. School Certif. Rowed in 1st Four on Berkeley Canal (Glos. Regatta). Miller and Corn Merchant.

Turner, Joseph. (H.), 1900–1903. Form IV. Lieut. 1st Border Regt. Fruit Merchant.

Tweney, Ernest Alan St. Helier, *Calvert House, Mansel Terrace, Swansea.* (H.), 1927–1931. Matric Form. Dental Student at Guy's Hospital.

Tyler, Herbert Spencer, 52 *High Street, Weston-super-Mare.* (H.), 1913–1915. Form IV.

Valentine-Jones, William Fowles, *The Clays, Ashdon, Essex.* (H.), 1910–1917. Senior. Senior Cambridge (Hons.). London Matric. Music and Literature Prizes. B.A. Lincoln College, Oxford. I.C. O.T.C. and 3rd Gordon Highlanders. Barrister-at-Law (Inner Temple). First Publicity Representative on B.B.C. outside London 1926. Author of " Cotswold Corn," 1935. Married : (1 dau.).

Vance, Gilbert. (S.H.), 1889–1890.

Varma, Krishna Kumar, *Kanker State, C.P., India.* (Spr.), 1927–1930. Matric. Form. Prefect. School Certif. Senior Singles and Doubles. School Tennis Team. R.M.C. (Sandhurst). Lieut. in Indian Army.

Varrier-Jones, Sir Pendrill Charles, *Papworth Hall, Cambridge.* (H.), 1897–1902. Form VI. Senior. Pres. of Lit. Soc. Prizes for Speaking and Literature. M.A., St. John's College, Cambridge (1st Class Hons Nat. Science). Research Scholarship. M.R.C.S., L.R.C.P. (London). Wix Prizeman. Late House Physician at St. Bartholomew's Hospital. Founder and Medical Director, Papworth Village Settlement. Hon. Med. Director Enham Village Centre and Peamount Village Settlement. Late Hon. Med. Director, British Legion Village. President. After-Care Committee, Intern. Union against Tuberculosis. President of Wycliffe College.

Vaughan, C. (S.H.), 1888.

Vellacott, John Lewes Hole, *Trafalgar Lawn, Barnstaple.* (S.H.), 1892–1896. Form VI. Senior. London Matric. War Service : 1st Lieut. Duke of Wellington's Regt. 1915–1918. Solicitor. Deputy-Coroner for Barnstaple. Married : (1 dau.).

Venning, Edgar Sidney, *St. Lawrence, Seymour Park Villas, Plymouth* (h.). 73 *Aberdare Gardens, Hampstead, N.W.* 6. (S.H.), 1925–1928. Form VI. Prefect. Pres. of Lit. Soc. Vice-Pres. of League. London Matric. 1st XV Rugby. Senior Lit. Comp. Prize. L.D.S., R.C.S. (Eng,), Guy's Hospital (University of London). N.W. University, Chicago. Dental Surgeon.

Venning, Hedley Douglas, *St. Lawrence, Seymour Park Villas, Plymouth* (h.). *Wycliffe House, 58 Lewisham Park, London, S.E. 13.* (S.H.), 1929–1933. Science VI. Prefect. Treas. and Sec. of Lit. Soc. School Certif. Capt. 2nd XV Rugby. Junior Athlete. Piano Prize. Student at Guy's Hospital.

Venning, Norman Lawrence, *St. Lawrence, Seymour Park Villas, Plymouth.* (S.H.), 1928–1932. Form VI. Prefect. Vice-Pres. of League. London Matric. 1st XV Rugby. Capt. 1st XI Cricket. Junior Athlete. Violin Prize. Member Plymouth Orchestral Society. Student of Inst. of Civil Engineers.

Vibert, Arthur B. (S.H.), 1889–1892. Form VI. Probationer. 2nd XV Rugby. Provision Merchant.

Vibert, Benjamin. (S.H.), 1892–1893. Form VI. Senior. Pres. of Lit. Soc. London Matric. House Prize. 1st XI Cricket and Football. Married.

Vibert, Charles Drinkwater. (S.H.), 1885–1889. Senior. London Matric House Prize. Capt. 1st XV Rugby. B.A. London. Master at Wycliffe 1890–1894. Sometime Headmaster of Newport (I. of W.) Grammar School. Married.

Vick, John. (D.B.), 1896–1899. Partner in Messrs. Badham & Co., Iron-mongers and Hot Water Engineers, Gloucester. At the beginning of the War he became a sergeant in the Royal Gloucestershire Hussars, but died in Egypt on July 25th 1915. ("W. & W." 107).

Vick, Joseph Gordon, *Ellacombe, Bratton Clovelly, Okehampton, Devon.* (S.H.), 1918–1923. Form V. Probationer. 1st XI Football. Special Cup for Sports. Arm Test Record. Fellow of the Auctioneers and Estate Agents' Institute and Member of the Surveyors' Inst. Auction-eer, Surveyor and Estate Agent. Married.

Vigars, Frank Henry, *National Provincial Bank, Falmouth.* (S.H.), 1895–1898. Form I. Lieut. S. Wales Borderers. Capt. Brecknockshire Batt. (T.). Bank Manager. Married : (2 sons).

Vigars, John William, *Hartley, New South Wales.* (S.H.), 1895–1898. Form I. War Service with Australian Army. Hotel Proprietor.

Villar, Harry. (S.H.), 1895–1898. Form V. 2nd XI Cricket. 1916–1919 M.T., A.S.C. Cattle Dealer. Married : (2 sons, 1 dau.).

Vowles, Denis Loxton. (S.H.), 1921–1923. Form IV. Farmer. Deceased.

Vowles, Ernest Victor, *17 Herondale, Avenue, Wandsworth Common, S.W. 18.* (D.B.), 1920–1927. Form VI. House Monitor. Sales Representative for Hugh Stevenson & Sons, Manchester and London.

Vowles, Lionel Frederick G. (S.H.), 1894. Form III. Died of consumption.

Vowles, Robert Arthur, *168 Coldharbour Road, Westbury Park, Bristol.* (D.B.), 1918–1925. Form VI. Probationer. London Matric. With Messrs. E. S. & A. Robinson, Bristol.

Wailes, J. M. (H.), 1885–1887. Probationer.

Wainwright, John Hilditch, *15 Dunheved Road, North Thornton Heath, Croydon.* (S.H.), 1916–1922. Form VI. Senior. Vice-Pres. of League. Sec. Lit. Soc. and Field Club. Hearson Prize. 2nd M.B., St. John's College, Cambridge. Medical Scholarship to Westminster Hospital. M.R.C.S. (Eng.), L.R.C.P. (Lond.) 1927. Late House Physician Westminster Hospital.

Waite, Thomas Kenneth, *Engelberg, Cleeve Hill, Cheltenham.* (Spr.), 1915–1922. Form V. Probationer. 2nd XI Cricket. Jeweller.

Waite, Wilfred Eric, *Engelberg, Cleeve Hill, near Cheltenham* (h.)., *and 9 Imperial Square, Cheltenham.* (Spr.), 1922–1927. Form VI. Prefect. Sec. and Treas. of Lit. Soc. Sec. of Field Club. School Certif. Foster Rifle. Connaught Shield Team. L.D.S., R.C.S. (Eng.), Guy's Hospital Dental School. House Surgeon in Dental Dept. 1933. Dentist.

Wakefield, Henry Walter, 5 *Carfrae Park, Blackhall, Edinburgh.* (Spr.), 1918–1925. Matric. Form. Senior. 1st XI Cricket and Football. Junior Athlete. With Cardboard and Paper Manufacturers. Married.

Wakefield, Paul Manning, *Northwick Lodge, Worcester.* (Spr.), 1926–1931. Matric Form. 1st XV Rugby. 2nd XI Cricket. Motor Trade.

Walford (formerly Wilkins), Sidney Thomas, *Uphill, Leckhampton Road, Cheltenham.* (S.H.), 1902–1904. Form V. Probationer. Lieut. 12th Gloucesters' and Queen's Regt. Chartered Surveyor, Estate Agent and Valuer. Married : (1 son).

Walker, Douglas J. (H.), 1903–1904. Form IV. Deceased.

Walker, Francis Joseph, *The Gables, Woodchester, Glos.* (D.B.), 1904–1906. Form II. Royal Glos. Hussars and R.G.A. Umbrella Stick Manufacturer.

Walker, Herbert. (S.H.), 1894–1896. Form II.

Walker, Ronald Goodman. (H.), 1902–1904. Form III. Farming.

Walters, Tom Vivian, 3 *Belgrave Gardens, Walter Road, Swansea.* (S.H. and Grove), 1930–1934. Form VI. House Monitor. School Certif. Articled to Solicitor.

Walton, John, *The Square, Mere, Wilts.* (S.H.), 1912–1917. Form VI. Senior. 2nd XI Football. Draper. Director of John Walton & Co. Married.

Warner, Mark Capper, *The White Cottage, Hampton, Evesham* (h.). *Looksaw T. E., Carron P.O., Dovarz, India.* (S.H.), 1922–1924. Form IV. 1st XI Football. Tea Planter.

Warner, Walter William Francis, 63 *Foregate Street, Worcester.* (H.), 1926–1933. Matric. Form. House Monitor. School Certif. 1st XV Rugby 1932–1933.

Watkins, W. (S.H.), 1890.

Watson, Percy, 29 *Abbey Park Road, Grimsby.* (S.H.), 1890–1892. Form VI. Probationer. Electrical Engineer. A.M.I.E.E. Retired 1935. Married.

Watts, Arthur Josiah, *Highfield, Lydney, Glos.* (S.H.), 1902–1904. Form VI. Senior. Sec. of Lit. Soc. Camb. Senior. 1st XI Football. R.N.A.S., R.A.F. Inspector Cranwell Training Camp R.A.F. Engineering Section. Member Inst. Consulting Motor Engineers and of Inst. Motor Trade. Company Director. Married: (3 sons, 2 daus.).

Watts, John Hilton, *The Rocklands, Lydney, Glos.* (S.H.), 1903–1906. Form V. Probationer. 1st and 2nd XI Football. Managing Director in Road Transport Service. Chairman Lydney Area Advancement Assoc. Member of Wye Valley and Forest of Dean Publicity Board. President Lydney and District British Legion. Served in France and Belgium (12th Siege Battery, R.G.A.) 1915–1918. Married.

Watts, Stanley George. (S.H.), 1901–1902. Form I.

Watts, Wilfrid Douglas. (S.H.), 1914–1916. Form III.

Webb, Arthur Paxton, 54b *Addison Gardens, West Kensington, W.* 14. (S.H.), 1898–1904. Form II. Sergt. and Act. Asst. Surgeon R.A.M.C. In India and Persia. Chemist. Male Nurse. Hospital Attendant on R.M.M.V. " Highland Brigade." Married.

Webb, Bernard John, 19 *Grovelands Avenue, Swindon, Wilts.* (S.H.), 1924–1930. Lower Remove. Builders' Merchant.

Webb, Cecil Charles, *Auction Rooms, Tiverton, Devon.* (S.H.), 1908–1910. Form IV. R.A.M.C. Auctioneer and Valuer. Married : (1 son).

Webb, Charles John, *Station Road, Swindon.* (S.H.), 1892–1895. Form V. Builders' Merchant. Married : (1 son).

Webb, Harry. (S.H.), 1891–1892. Died from measles and inflammation of the lungs on February 24th 1892.

Webb, John Richard, 35 *Kelston Road, Whitchurch, Cardiff.* (H.), 1916–1918. Form IV. Probationer. 1st XI Cricket and Football. Architect. Married : (2 daus.).

Webb, J. W. (D.B.), 1890–1895. Form IV.

Webb, Nelson, Edgar, *Pear Tree Cottage, Stapley, Churchstanton, Chard, Som.* (S.H.), 1913–1915. Form VI. Senior. Vice-Pres. of League. Treas. Lit. Soc. London Matric. 1st XI Football. Capt. 2nd XI Football. Cpl. A.P.C. M.A. Lincoln College, Oxford. Sometime Master at Wycliffe. Married.

Webb, Stanley Whitman, 81 *Burton's Road, Hampton Hill, Middlesex.* (S.H.), 1899–1905. Form III. War Service 1915–1919. Art Salesman. Married : (1 son).

Weir, Douglas Aikman, *Constabulary Officers' Mess, Trinidad, B.W.I.* (S.H.), 1930–1934. Modern VI. Prefect. King's Scout. Cambridge School Certif. 1st XV Rugby. 2nd XI Cricket. Senior Singles and Doubles. School Tennis Team. Sub-Inspector of Constabulary. 2nd Lieut. Trinidad Light Infantry.

Weir, Ian George, *Plymouth, Montserrat, B.W.I.* (S.H.), 1925–1928. Upper V. 1st XI Football. 1st XV Rugby. 1st XI Cricket. Tennis Team. Jeune Cup. Foster Rifle. Sub-Inspector of Police.

Welch, John Edward. (H.), 1917–1922. Form V. Probationer. Corn Merchant.

Welch, Nicholas, 79 *Murray Avenue, Bromley, Kent.* (H.), 1921–1926. Form VI. Senior. School Certif. M.A., LL.B. Hons. Law Tripos., Christ's College, Cambridge. Solicitor.

Welch, Richard Vivian, 79 *Murray Avenue, Bromley, Kent.* (H.), 1923–1927. Upper V. Probationer. Manager, Commercial Union Insurance Co., Ipoh, Johore, Federated Malay States.

Wellman, Leslie Charles, *Treetops, Coulsdon Road, Coulsdon, Surrey.* (Spr.), 1920–1925. Form VI. Senior. Vice-Pres. of League. London Matric. House Prize. In Bank of England. Married.

Wells, Charles James de Lisle, *The Noake, Hucclecote, Glos.* (H.), 1925–1927. Form III.

Wells, Graham, *Haywardsfield, Charlton Lane, Brentry, Bristol.* (H.), 1921–1926. Upper V. Probationer. With Messrs. W. D. & H. O. Wills, Bristol. Married.

Wells, H. W. Sefton. (S.H.), 1893. Form IV. Stockbroker.

Wells, Sedley Archibald Stevens, *Windyridge, Rodborough, Stroud.* (D.B.), 1925–1928. Lower V. . Auctioneer.

West, R. A. R. (H.), 1888–1889.

Weston, Arthur Evans. (D.B.), 1890–1893. Form V. Went to America and became organist of an Episcopalian Church in Pittsburg. Deceased.

Weston, Leonard, *Applegarth, Much Marcle, via Gloucester.* (S.H.), 1908–1910. Form IV. Probationer. 1st XI. Cider Manufacturer. Married.

Whatley, F. Ernest Herbert. (S.H.), 1898–1902. Form V. 1st XI Cricket and Football. Became a Mining Inspector in Rhodesia. Deceased.

Wherrett, William Henry, *Cambridge, Glos.* (D.B.), 1896–1897. Form I. Farmer.

Whicher, Leslie. (S.H.), 1899–1902. Form IV. Became an engineer on a R.M.S.P. Liner, but died at Sydney, Nova Scotia in 1924.

White, A. E., 16 *Ansty Road, Ansty, Coventry.* (Spr.), 1905–1906. Form III. Builder. Married : (1 son).

White, Arthur Geoffrey, *Fromebridge Mill, Whitminster, Glos.* (D.B.), 1903–1907. Form III. Yorks. & Lancs. Regt. Miller and Farmer. Married : 1 son, 1 dau.).

White, Clifford, *Halmore, Cam, Glos.* (D.B.), 1903–1906. Farmer.

White, F. (D.B.), 1889–1891. Form V. Lampeter College. Ordained 1905. Rector of Canadian Parish.

White, Herbert Cyril, *Woodside, Fen End, Warwicks.* (H.), 1917–1922. Form VI. Senior. London Matric. Automobile Engineer and Company Director. A.M.I.A.E. Married : (1 dau.).

White, John A. M., 16 *Ansty Road, Ansty, Coventry.* (H.), 1932–1936. Form VI. School Certif.

White, R. Graham, 151 *Dock Street, Newport, Mon.* H.),1900–1901. Form V. Probationer. L.D.S., R.C.S. (Eng.). Dental Surgeon. Married.

White, Richard Stanley. (H.), 1894–1900. Form VI. P.A.S.E. and Fellow of Surveyors' Inst. Government Valuer.

Whittington, W. Rex. (Spr.), 1908–1910. Form V. Probationer. Architect.

Wiggins, Alan Kingsley, 1 *Dalby Square, Cliftonville, Margate.* (Spr.), 1911–1916. Form VI. Senior. Vice-Pres. of League. Pres. of Lit. Soc. London Matric. House Prize. Music and Speaking Prizes. Capt. 1st XI Cricket. 1st XI Football. M.R.C.S., L.R.C.P. (Eng,). Dental Surgeon.

Wiggins, Norman Ernest, *Oakley Lodge, Christchurch Road, Hampstead* (h.). 5 *King's Bench Walk, Temple, London, E.C.* 4. (Spr.), 1917–1920. Form VI. Senior. Pres. of League and Lit. Soc. London Matric. House Prize. Music and Speaking Prizes. Capt. 1st XI Cricket. 1st XI Football. Senior Cross Country. M.A., LL.B. St. John's College, Cambridge. Member of Inner Temple. Barrister-at-Law. Married : (2 sons).

Wight, Alfred Albert, *Woolstone Farm, Cheltenham.* (D.B.), 1895–1897. Form I. Farmer.

Wight, George Findan. *In New Zealand.* (S.H.), 1894–1895. Form V. 2nd XI Cricket and Football. D.C.M. in South African War. Assistant Headmaster. Married.

Wight, Henry Findon, *Petistree, Hills Road, Cambridge.* (S.H.), 1894–1896. Form IV. Surgeon.

Wight, John Eric, *c/o H. F. Wight.* (S.H.), 1897–1899. Form II. Automobile Engineer. A.M.I.M.E. Married.

Wight, Llewellyn, *Falconhyrst, Bradford Place, Penarth.* (H.), 1891–1895. Form IV. 2nd XI Cricket. Mining Engineer.

Wight, Melville William. (D.B.), 1907–1908. Form I. Farmer. Deceased.

Wight, Stuart Atholl, *Petistree, Hills Road, Cambridge.* (S.H.), 1897–1898. Form IV. Married.

A VIEW ACROSS THE VALLEY FROM THE SCHOOL FIELDS ON DOVEROW HILL

A SIXTH FORM GROUP, 1932

W. Foster, S. Silvey, R. Inglis, D. Young, A. M. Barnett, G. M. Smith, J. R. Ashton, P. R. Noakes, N. Venning,

D. Norman, G. Healey, J. A. Nott, D. B. Paine, The Headmaster, W. A. D. Young, A. R. Morris, N. Kenchington, V. Gifford,

THE STAFF AND BOYS OF RYEFORD HALL
(July, 1935)

THE BATCHELAR-BOWEN MEMORIAL BRIDGE
(This fine example of modern architecture connects the Junior School at Ryeford Hall with
its playing-fields and with Windrush and the Grove on the other side of the main road).

Wigmore, Ernest William Roland, *Goodrich, near Ross-on-Wye.* (Spr.), 1906–1907. Form III.

Wigmore, Montague Sydney. (D.B.), 1902–1907. Form IV.

Wilcox, Arnold W. Dove. (H.), 1891–1894. Form V. Leather Factor and Importer (with his father) in Bristol. Married after a few years, but developed lung trouble, of which he died.

Wilcox, Henry, *Thorington Rectory, Colchester, Essex.* (D.B.), 1887–1888. Probationer. 1st XI Cricket. M.A., St. John's College, Cambridge. Army Chaplain 1915–1919. Mentioned in Despatches. Married.

Wilcox, Joseph A. (D.B.) 1907–1908. Form III.

Wilkes, Leslie Martin, *Lyndhurst, Dursley, Glos.* (D.B. and H.), 1917–1923. Form VI. Senior. Draper.

Wilkes, Noel Ralph, *Market Place, Faringdon, Berks.* (D.B.), 1910–1912. Form III. Probationer. Service in France 1916–1918. Draper and Outfitter. Married.

Wilkes, Percival Edward, 25 *The Boulevard, Weston-super-Mare.* (D.B.), 1912–1915. Form III. Draper.

Wilkins, Arthur Hewlett, *Manchester House, High Street, Thornbury, near Bristol.* (S.H.), 1884–1888. Probationer. Draper. Chief Officer, Thornbury R.D.C. Fire Brigade 1898–1936. Volunteer 1916–1918. Married : (3 daus.).

Wilkins, Charles Roderic, 150 *Stoke Lane, Westbury-on-Trym, Bristol.* (H.), 1925–1928. Lower V.

Wilkins, Geoffrey Hope, 150 *Stoke Lane, Westbury-on-Trym, Bristol.* (H.), 1932–1934. Upper Remove. Builder.

Wilkins, Sidney Thomas. See **Walford.**

Wilkinson, Charles Stanley, *The Bryn, College Road, Sutton Coldfield, Birmingham.* S.H.), 1895–1897. Form IV. Probationer. Director of Halford Cycle Co. Married : (2 sons).

Wilkinson, John Kenneth, *The Bryn, College Road, Sutton Coldfield, Birmingham.* (Spr.), 1930–1934. Form V. With General Electric Co.

Willett, Alfred Lance, 2 *Priory Road, Tyndall's Park, Bristol.* (Spr.), 1904. Form II. Probationer. Lieut. " Bristol's Own " (12th Glos.) Corn Merchant. Married.

Willett, Arnold John. (Spr.), 1909–1912. Form VI. Senior. Pres. of Lit. Soc. 1st XI Football. 2nd XI Cricket. Senior Cambridge. House Prize. Went up to St John's College, Cambridge, but enlisted on the outbreak of War. Commission in Somerset Light Infantry. Was killed at Gallipoli in June 1915. (" W. & W.", 107).

Williams, Alan Hugh Meyrick, 25 *Fields Road, Newport, Mon.* (H.), 1934–1936. Form VI. Prefect. London Matric. Student of Commerce at London University. Solicitor.

Williams, Alwyn Mason, *Carinya, Beach Road, Newton, Porthcawl.* (H.). 1917–1920. Form V. 2nd XI Football. Tennis Championship, Traveller.

Williams, David Glyn, *The Nook, Southerndown, near Bridgend, Glam. and* 7 *Freeland Road, Ealing, W.* 5. (H.), 1919–1924. Lower V. Probationer. 1st XI Cricket. 1st XI Football. Music Prize. Bank Clerk.

Williams, Edward Geoffrey Montgomery, *Highway Cottage, Pennard, Gower, Glam.* (S.H.), 1923–1929. Matric. Form. Prefect. School Certif. 1st XV Rugby. Bank Clerk.

Williams, Edward Montgomery, *c/o J. M. Williams, 28 Lighthouse Road, Napier, North Island, New Zealand.* (H.), 1919–1921. Form V. Probationer.

I

Williams, Frank Robert, *Brynawel, Grove Road, Lydney, Glos.* (S.H.), 1922–1927. Lower V. House Monitor. 1st XV Rugby. 1st XI. Company Director.

Williams, Gordon Sydney, *Ragleth, Uplands, Swansea.* (H.), 1923–1925. Married.

Williams, Gwilym Tudor, *Cynon Cottage, Aberdare, Glam.* (H.), 1894–1896. Form IV. M.P.S., F.R.H.S. Analytical Chemist. Married.

Williams, Hedley Thomas, *The Garth. Park Street, Bridgend.* (S.H.), 1896–1898. Probationer. 1st XV Rugby. Retired from Bank, 1924. Married.

Williams, Hywel Penn Rhys, *Mor Hafren, Baylan Road, Port Talbot.* (S.H.), 1913–1917. Probationer. 1st XI Football. 2nd XI Cricket. Senior. Cross Country Champ. Bristol Univ. O.T.C. L.D.S., R.C.S. (Eng.), Dental Surgeon. Schools Dental Officer to Boroughs of Neath and Port Talbot. Married : (1 dau.).

Williams, John Colin Montgomery, *The Cliffs, Southgate, Gower, Glam.* (S.H.), 1919–1924. Form VI. Senior. Vice-Pres. of League. Pres. Lit. Soc. Sec. Field Club. London Matric. 1st XI Football. Jeune Cup. Foster Rifle. House, Herbert Park and Speaking Prizes. Played Rugby for Swansea 1st XV 1928–1929 and 1930–1931. Capt. Swansea 2nd XV Rugby 1930–1931. Chartered Accountant in Swansea. Married.

Williams, John Herschell. (S.H.), 1912–1914. Form V. Was apprenticed to Messrs. Barr & Stroud, Glasgow. When 18 years of age joined the Inns of Court O.T.C., and thence was gazetted to the R.F.A. Went to France in September 1916. Was killed on June 17th, 1917. (" W. & W.", 108).

Williams, John Montgomery, 28 *Lighthouse Road, Napier, North Island, New Zealand.* (S.H.), 1892–1893. Form V. Probationer. 1st XI Football. Vice-Pres. Swansea Chamber of Commerce. Chairman, Shipping Chamber of Commerce. Steamship Owner and Broker. F.I.C.S. Assistant and Deputy County Scout Commissioner. Married.

Williams, John Vernon, 15 *Clifford Street, Shrewsbury.* (H.), 1925–1927. Upper IV. 1st XI Football. 1st XV Rugby. Civil Servant.

Williams, Kenneth Robert, *Oakland House, Parkend, Glos.* (S.H.), 1922–1928. Lower V. Prefect. 1st XV Rugby. 2nd XI Cricket. Tennis Team. Draper.

Williams, Ralph Norman Haile, *Hazelwood, Nailsworth, Glos.* (S.H.), 1918–1922. Senior. Sec. of Lit. Soc. 1st XI Cricket and Football. 2nd M.B. St. John's College, Cambridge. St. Bartholomew's Hospital. M.R.C.S. (Eng.), L.R.C.P. (Lond.). Member of Gloucestershire Rugby XV. Trial Cap for England at Rugby. Medical Practitioner. Married : (1 son).

Williams, Roy M., *Victoria Street, Cinderford, Glos.* (H.), 1909–1910. Form IV. Royal Glos. Hussars 1915–1918. Served in Egypt, Gallipoli, Sinai, Palestine. House Furnisher. Married : (1 dau.).

Williams, Sigurd Montgomery, c/o *J. M. Williams, 28 Lighthouse Road, Napier, North Island, New Zealand.* (H.), 1923–1925. Upper III. Whole family has emigrated to New Zealand.

Williams, Thomas Gordon Haile, *Holmfield, Grove Road, Lydney.* (S.H.), 1918–1921. Grocer. Married.

Williams, Venable Montgomery, *Highway Cottage, Pennard, Gower, Glam.* (H.), 1885–1887. Probationer. 1st XV Rugby. Service on various Coal Boards 1914–1918. Director of Colliery and Steamship Cos. Married.

Williams, W. E. (S.H.), 1885.

Williams, William Glyn, *Gwynfa, Pentyla, Aberavon.* (S.H.), 1912–1914. Form IV.

Wilson, Cecil H. Erskine. (D.B.), 1895.

Wilson, Geoffrey Lewis, *Maynor, Thornhill Road, Streetly, Birmingham.* (H.), 1925–1929. Form V. Prefect. School Certif. 1st XI Football. 2nd XV Rugby. Engineering.

Wilson, James Bernard, *Maynor, Thornhill Road, Streetly, Birmingham.* (O.B.), 1925. Medical Student at Birmingham University.

Wilson, James Robin, *Raysholme, Oxenholme, near Kendal, Westmorland.* (S.H.), 1926–1934. Form VI. School Certif. Prefect. 1st XI Cricket. Shooting Team. Batchelar Cup. Pilot Officer, R.A.F.

Wilson, Tom George, *Raysholme, Oxenholme, near Kendal, Westmorland.* (S.H.), 1926–1934. Form VI. Higher School Certificate. Prefect. Vice-Pres. League. Pres. Lit. Soc. 1st XV Rugby. 1st XI Cricket. School Athletic, Chess and Shooting Teams. Prizes for Lit. Comp., Public Service. St. John's College, Cambridge. Lieut. R.A.S.C.

Winn, Charles Vivian, 16 *St. Mary's Road, Whitchurch, Glam.* (S.H.), 1931–1936. Matric. Form. House Monitor. School Certif. Capt. 1st IV. Engineering.

Wintle, Wadham Stanley, *Wick Farm, near Dursley.* (S.H.), 1907–1911. Form IV. Glos. Regt. Farmer.

Wise, Bertram, *Oakridge, Kingshill Road, Dursley, Glos.* (D.B.), 1917–1921 In Cloth Mills. Married.

Wise, Frederick, *Cicely Rubber Estate, Teluk Anson, Perak, F.M.S.* (D.B.), 1917–1920. Manager of said Estate.

Witchell, Herbert Edward, *Restholme, Warmley, near Bristol.* (S.H.), 1903–1905. Form IV. Probationer. Flour Miller. Married : (1 son.)

Witchell, K. M. (H.), 1885–1888. Probationer. 1st XV Rugby. Lieut. Light Horse in S. African War. In S. Africa. Solicitor.

Witchell, Mark Edwin Northam. (D.B.), 1918–1919. Upper III. Solicitor's Articled Clerk. Died March 19th 1928.

Witcomb, George Morris Bubb, *Ryall House, Upton-on-Severn, Worcs.* (H.), 1926–1932. Form V. 2nd XI Cricket. 2nd XV Rugby. Mile Record. Junior Cross Country Record. Farmer.

Withey, Harry George, *Parkside, Wykeham Road, Worthing, Sussex.* (S.H.). 1916–1922. Form VI. Senior. Pres. Lit. Soc. London Matric. Prize for Speaking. B.A. Lincoln College, Oxford. Later Master at Trinity College, Kandy. Now Curate at All Saints, Poplar.

Wolfe, Tom Keell, *Whiteway, Stroud, Glos.* (h.). 10 *Queen's Crescent, Blackhall, Edinburgh* 4. (D.B.), 1926–1934. Form VI. Prefect. Higher Certif. Prize for Lit. Comp. Student of Natural Health at Edinburgh School of Natural Therapeutics.

Wollaston, Richard Francis, *La Vieille Maison, St. Martin's. Guernsey, C.I.* (h.). (H.), 1928–1930. Matric. Form. House Monitor. School Certif. 1st XV. Rubber Planter at Kudat Jessellon, British N. Borneo.

Wood, Evan John. (S.H.), 1911–1919. Form VI. Probationer. 1st XI Cricket and Football. Cadet Sergt. A.S.M.

Wood, George Ernest. (H.), 1890–1895. Form VI. Senior. London Matric. 2nd XI Cricket and Football. L.R.C.P., M.R.C.S. Physician. Married. Deceased.

Woodcock, James Arthur, *Leominster Villa, Cainscross Road, Stroud.* (D.B.), 1921–1928. Upper V. House Monitor. 1st XV Rugby. Middle-weight Boxing. Constructional Gas Engineer.

Woodley, Herbert, *Preswylfa, Cardiff.* (S.H.), 1915–1918. Form V. Senior. Capt. 1st XI Football. 2nd XI Cricket. Open Tennis Doubles. House Prize. Meat Importer.

Woodley, William Thomas, *Park View, Griffithstown, Mon.* (S.H.), 1920–1926. Senior. Cambridge Senior. 1st XI Cricket and Football. Wholesale Purveyor. Married.

Woodman, Alec Charles, *Bristol House, Dyer Street, Cirencester.* (S.H.), 1917–1926. Form VI. Senior. Cambridge School Certif. 2nd XI Football. Leeds University (Textiles). Draper. Married.

Woodman, Alfred, 268 *Wells Road, Bristol.* (H.), 1888–1892. Probationer. 1st XV Rugby. 1st XI Football. Timber Merchant. Married : (3 sons).

Woodman, Bernard George Edward, *Manchester House, Winslow, Bucks.* (S.H.), 1921–1925. Form IV. Probationer. 1st XI Cricket and Football. Draper.

Woodman, Charles Frank, *Small Street, St. Philips Marsh, Bristol.* (H.), 1900–1904. Form IV. Timber Merchant.

Woodman, Cyril Graeme Churchill. (H.), 1914–1916. Form V. Probationer. 1st XI Football.

Woodward, Samuel Albert. (S.H.), 1897–1899. Form V. Probationer. 1st XI Cricket. Electrical Engineer. Married.

Woolcock, Bernard Vine, 12 *Kingsway, Luton, Beds.* (S.H.), 1920–1925. Form VI. Senior. London Matric. Motor Engineer. Methodist Local Preacher. Married.

Woolcock, Cleave Edward, *Blaythorne, Chadlington, Oxford.* (S.H.), 1921–1927. Form VI. Prefect. Vice-Pres. League. School Certif. House Prize. Assoc. Auctioneers' Inst. Auctioneer.

Woolcock, Stanley Richard, *Camford, Drove Road, Sholing, Southampton.* (S.H.), 1922–1927. Lower IV. Manager of Building Co. Married.

Woolley, William Downing, *Rhyd Hall, Tredegar, Mon.* (S.H.),1900–1902. Form VI. Senior. Sec. Lit. Soc. and Field Club. London Matric. House Prize. 2nd XI Football. Edward Medal. Humane Society's Silver Medal. Carnegie Hero Fund Certif. for Mine Rescue Work. Member Inst. Mining Engineers. Vice-Pres. S. Wales Inst. Engineers. Past Chairman of Mon. and S. Wales Coalowners' Assoc. J.P. Monmouthshire. Officer of Order of St. John. Married : (2 sons).

Woozley, Clifford J., *St. Brannock's, Lon Caebank, Sketty, Swansea.* (H.), 1914–1916. Form IV. In Lloyds Bank. Married.

Workman, Arthur John, *Huntingford, Charfield, Glos.* (S.H.), 1888–1892. Form VI. Probationer. Flour Miller.

Workman, Eric Lansdown, *Pendarren, Westrip, near Stroud, Glos.* (S.H.), 1905–1908. Form IV. Probationer. 2nd XI Cricket and Football. Timber Merchant.

Workman, Frank Ernest, *Woodchester Lodge, near Stroud, Glos.* (D.B.), 1888–1893. Form VI. Senior. Timber Merchant. Married : (1 son, 3 daus.).

Workman, Frederick Waite. (S.H.), 1888–1892. Took up gold prospecting in W. Australia. After farming in Somerset became partner in Messrs. A. J. Workman, Flour Millers, Huntingford, near Charfield. Died in 1907.

Workman, George Percival. (S.H.), 1886–1889. Sometime Capt. in Mercantile Marine. Director of Draycott Flour Mills. Married.

Workman, Gerald. (S.H.), 1915–1921. *In Australia.*

Workman, Herbert Edward, *Draycott House, Dursley, Glos.* (S.H.), 1888–1889. Form VI. Probationer. House Prize. Director of Draycott Flour Mills. Married.

Workman, J. C. Wait. (S.H.), 1885–1887. Joined his father in the flour-milling business, but was attacked by rapid consumption and died in 1888 in his eighteenth year.

Workman, John Clough, *Oakland House, Coaley Junction, Glos.* (S.H.), 1923–1929. Lower V. House Monitor. 1st XI Cricket. 1st XI Football. 1st XV Rugby.

Workman, Walter Purnell. (S.H.), 1891–1896. Form V. Probationer. Flour Miller. Married.

Worlock, Robert Thomas. (H.), 1893–1895. Form IV. Farmer. Deceased.

Worlock, William Robert George, *Wibley, Yate, Glos.* (H.), 1921–1924. Batchelar Cup. Farmer. Married.

Worth, Cedric Adolphus Werner, *Lickhill Manor, Stourport, Worcs.* (S.H.), 1922–1924. Form IV.

Worth, Edred Joseph E., *Lickhill Manor, Stourport, Worcs.* (S.H.), 1922–1925. Form I. In New Zealand.

Worth, Egbert, *Lickhill Manor, Stourport, Worcs.* (S.H.), 1922–1924. Form III. In Carpet Business.

Wright, Alfred Freeman, *Park Corner, Greenhill, Evesham.* (S.H.), 1918–1923. Form VI. Senior. Corn Merchant.

Wright, Cyril Temple Blundell, *The Square, Biggleswade. Beds.* (S.H.), 1919–1922. Form V. 2nd XI Football. Bank Clerk.

Wright, Percy Basil, *Park Corner, Greenhill, Evesham.* (S.H.), 1922–1928. Form VI. House Monitor. School Certif. 1st XI Cricket. Tennis Doubles and Singles. Corn Merchant.

Wright, Richard Louis, *Park Corner, Greenhill, Evesham.* (S.H.), 1924–1931. Form VI. Prefect. Vice-Pres. League. School Certif. Tennis Team. Harmston Music Prize. Piano Scholarship at Birmingham and Midland Inst. 1932–1933. Student, Freiburg and Hamburg Universities 1935–1936. With Messrs. Cadbury, Bournville.

Yates, R. A. Guy, *Glen Bank, Underdale Road, Shrewsbury.* (S.H.), 1925–1930. Lower V.

Young, David Robert, *Kingsheath, 13 Westbury Hill, Bristol.* (Spr.), 1931–1933. Form V and Commercial. House Monitor. School Certif. With Messrs. E. S. & A. Robinson, Bristol.

Young, George. (S.H.), 1902–1906. Form VI. Senior. 1st XI Football. Chartered Accountant.

Young, James Douglas Sale. (Spr.), 1928–1933. Form VI. Prefect. School Certif. 1st XV Rugby. Speaking Prize.

Young, William Alexander Douglas. (Spr.), 1928–1932. Form VI. Prefect. Pres. Lit. Soc. Higher Certif. 2nd XI Cricket. 1st XV Rugby. Heavy-weight Boxing Champ. Shooting VI. Foster Rifle. Jeune Cup (5 times and Record Average 95.5).

Zorian, Arshen Victor, *47 Lime Grove, St. Annes-on-Sea.* (Spr.), 1920–1925. Form V. 2nd XI Football. Journalist.

Zorian, Deran Ewart, *47 Lime Grove, St. Annes-on-Sea.* (Spr.), 1920–1924. Form VI. Senior. Northern Univ. Matric. Cambridge Senior. B.A. Manchester University. Chartered Accountant.

List of O.W.s Arranged Geographically

HOME

BEDFORDSHIRE
Jones, P. L.
March, H.
Woolcock, B. V.
Wright, C. T. B.

BERKSHIRE
Daniel, J. A.
Gardner, C. H.
Green, W. S.
James, D. G. W.
Keevil, W. L.
Maze, Eric
Seaby, P. C.
Seaby, W. A.
Thomas, N. P. A.
Thomas, R. C.
Titley, C. A.

**BUCKINGHAM-
SHIRE**
Bazzard, W. N.
Evered, D. A.
Evered, H. F.
George, R. D.
Kenchington, J. M.
Newth, J. D.
Robson, Eric
Sprigg, C. E.
Stafford, L. I.
Tanner, L. F.
Woodman, B.

CAMBRIDGESHIRE
Archbold, W. A.
Varrier-Jones
Wight, H. F.
Wight, J. E.
Wight, S. A.

CHESHIRE
Faulkner, R.
Galvayne, A. E. L.
Godfrey, J. H.
Jenner, A. E. A.
King, G. A.
Livsey, M.
Livsey, S.
Lloyd, J. F. P.
Morton, J. W.
Shaw, G. D.
Simpson, A. S.

CORNWALL
Brighton, W. C.
Giles, H. H.
Giles, T. T.
Grose, W. F.
Hillier, T. L.
Holman, F. L.
Hulbert, E. P.
Jarvis, R. C.
Martyn, H. K. G.
Michell, J.
Michell, T. B.
Pethybridge, H. W.
Pethybridge, J. H.
Pool, S.
Smith, R. J.
Tancock, J. P.
Thomas, E. L. V.
Vick, J. G.

CUMBERLAND
Duthie, R. A.
Simpson, T. I.

DERBYSHIRE
Adams, C. G. A.
Cash, O. H. G.
Horsley, G. M.
Lloyd, G. A. L.
Pethybridge, W. H.
Rawlings, H.

DEVONSHIRE
Binding, W.
Broadhurst, H. C.
Cardall, L. G.
Carder, A. T.
Caunt, F. W.
Davies, Evan
Dickenson, R. J.
Evans, P. J.
Foyster, E. R.
Foyster, P. A.
Gayner, R. C.
Hearson, J. H. S.
Jones, D. B.
Marsh, N. B.
Morris, C. A.
Parr, R. F.
Ractliffe, G. C.
Roberts, C. K.
Roberts, P. G.
Rogers, A. S.

Devonshire—*continued*
Rogers, J. F.
Selley, A. W.
Stanier, C. E.
Vellacott, J. L. H.
Venning, E. S.
Venning, H. D.
Venning, N. L.

DORSETSHIRE
Bond, J. D.
Carr, J. W.
Cotton, F. W.
Friedenson, T. L.
Gobey, S. C.
Moore, L. C. L.
Payne, J. V.

DURHAM
Harvey, F. E.
Taylor, A. R.
Taylor, G. B.

ESSEX
Allwood, E. S.
Bethleg, A. F.
Ciclitira, D. J.
Hathway, F. E.
Hawkins, J. S.
Hopkins, L. G.
Lloyd, G. D.
Lloyd, J. E.
Maslin, C. E.
Morris, A. R.
Morris, D. S.
Seaton, E. G.
Valentine-Jones,
  W. F.
Wilcox, H.

**GLOUCESTER-
SHIRE**
Adams, W. D.
Adkins, E. F. G.
Alcock, C. A.
Alcock, F.
Allen, P. G.
Anderson, J. H.
Anderson, J. S.
Anstey, T. F.
Anthony, A. P.
Anthony, G. H.

Gloucestershire—*continued*

Anthony, G. P.
Antill, S. M.
Appleby, A. W.
Appleby, Donald
Appleby, G. S.
Arkell, H.
Ashton, J. R.
Ayers, K, D.
Baker, H. D.
Banks, H. L.
Bannister
Barber, E. M.
Barnett, A. M.
Barnett, A. P.
Barnett, C. J.
Barnett, C. S.
Barnett, D.
Barnett, L.
Barnett, P. P.
Bartlett, B. G.
Bayley, L. W.
Beale, M. C.
Bennett, J. W.
Bennett, L. J.
Bennett, R. V. M.
Bennett, R. M.
Berry, O. L.
Bevan, J. G. M.
Bidlake, C. A.
Billington, J. W.
Bird, G. H.
Bird, H. G.
Bird, H. J.
Bird, R. C.
Bird, Stanley
Blackwell, E. L.
Blake, H. E.
Bland, G. H.
Blick, L. A. J.
Bown, J. H. E.
Bozworth, E. A. W.
Bradbeer, A. G.
Braine, H. A.
Branch, G. P.
Bretherton, W. G.
Brewer, E. D.
Brooks, C. H.
Bruce, F. W.
Bubb, G. C.
Buckle, P.
Budgett, F. G.
Burnett, D.
Butt, A. E.
Butt, G. F.
Cambray, R.
Camm, G. G.
Carter, C. R.
Chamberlayne, H.
Chamberlayne, J. A.

Chamberlayne,
  Maurice
Chandler, Edward
Chandler, G. C.
Chandler, J. R.
Chandler, S. J.
Chaplin, P. J.
Chatham, C. H.
Church, F. G.
Clark, J. H.
Clift, J. W.
Clissold, G.
Clissold, K. G.
Clissold, W. J.
Cloke, D. G.
Cloke, Ernest
Cloutman, N. F.
Coley, J. P.
Collins, L. W. G.
Cook, Alwyn
Cook, F. G.
Cook, J. A.
Cornock, C. J.
Cornock, J. N.
Cornock, W. B.
Cox, E. P.
Cox, F. J. B.
Cox, R. H.
Cridland, C. E.
Crocker, R. P.
Cullimore, G. E.
Cullimore, M. H.
Culverwell, John
Culverwell, J. R. S.
Culverwell, V. B.
Daniels, F. L.
Daniels, F. W.
Daniels, J. L.
Daniels, J. S.
Dash, D. B.
Dash, E. E.
Dashwood, V. de C.
Davis, B. C.
Davis, H. H.
Davis, R. A.
Davis, W. C.
Deakin, H. V. I.
Dennis, Preston
Desprez, C. S.
Dickenson, E. A.
Dickins, C. H.
Dickins, F. A.
Dix, G. C.
Dixon, A. P.
Downing, C. L.
Drew, G. H.
Drew, W. F.
Drew, W. T.
Dudbridge, L.

Dudbridge, M.
Dudbridge, N.
Dugdale, J. H.
Dugdale, R. O.
Duncalf, W. J.
Dunsford, G.
Edwards, F. G.
Edwards, F. H.
Edwards, J. H.
Edwards, J. R.
Evans, E. T.
Evans, W. H.
Exell, F. J.
Eyles, H. G.
Farr, F. J.
Fawkes, B.
Fearis, E. N.
Filer, R. G.
Fish, A. C.
Fish, H. M.
Foster, W.
Foweraker, R. M.
Franklin, A. G.
Gabb, C. R.
Gane, C. E.
Gardner, J. L.
Gardner, K.
Gardner, T. E.
Gardner, W.
Gayner, R. C.
Gibbons, C. P.
Gibbons, W. R.
Giles, C. A.
Gladman, D. A.
Goddard, W.
Greaves, G.
Greaves, S. J.
Green, H. L.
Gregor, J. B.
Greswell, R. F. C.
Griffin, R. P.
Grist, L.
Grist, S. H.
Grover, J. M.
Grover, R. S.
Guilding, L. J.
Guilding, W. J.
Gunter, H. A.
Hadley, B. C.
Hadley, G.
Hadley, J. E.
Hadley, R.
Hall, A. J.
Hall, F. G.
Hall, J. M.
Hammond, J. A.
Hanby, C. J.
Hanks, G. N.
Harden, A. J.

Gloucestershire—*continued*

Harding, L. N.
Harris, D. F.
Harris, J. E.
Harrison, J. A.
Harrison, R. T.
Hart, V. E. Ll.
Hatcher, V. B.
Hatherell, B. R.
Hawkins, H. H.
Hawkins, M. G.
Hawkins, T. G.
Hayes, J. C.
Hayward, W. M.
Hayward, C. N.
Heath, G. C.
Heath, J. L.
Heath, R. I.
Henly, H. J.
Henly, R.
Heyward, N. G.
Higgins, P. E₁
Hill, G. A.
Hill, M. R.
Hill, R. C.
Hill, R. M.
Hill, W. H.
Hince, J. E. F.
Hobson, A. P.
Hobson, E. G.
Hoddinott, H. M.
Holborow, R. J.
Holborow, R. W.
Hooper, H. E.
Hopkins, E. L.
Hudleston, C. R.
Hudleston, J. L.
Hudson, J. P. L.
Humpidge, K. R.
Ingram, W. J. M.
Ireland, H. J.
Isaac, A.
Jackson, R. G.
Jackson, W. G.
Jackson, W. H. C.
James, J. P.
Jamison, E. G.
Jarrett, M.
Jarrett, S.
Jeffes, C. E.
Jeffes, E. A. D.
Jeffes, G. R. L.
Jeffes, R. E. D.
Jeffes, Robert
Jeffes, R. H. F.
Jones, C. F.
Jones, J. L. F.
Jones, N. A.
Jones, N. H.
Keene, H. E.

Keene, R.
Kerby, N. G.
Keys, A. E.
Kimmins, E. R.
Kimmins, G. S.
King, H. J. H.
King, M.
Kingsley, C.
Kinnersley, L. G.
Kitchen, A. T.
Knott, A. J.
Lalonde, K. B.
Lance, K. J.
Lane, H. F. W.
Lane, Hubert
Lane, S. D.
Langford, K. E.
Langley Smith,
    E. L. H.
Langley Smith, W. H.
Langley Smith, W.
    Humphries
Lanham, W. H.
Lee, R. E.
Lister, G. A.
Lister, R. B.
Lock, G. M.
London, D. N.
Lovell, A. J.
Lovell, A. T.
Lovell, Tom
Luker, Cyril
Luker, W.
Lulham, A. R.
Luttrell, W. F.
Mann, F. O. H.
Manning, E. V.
Marshall, A. S.
Martin, R. T. B.
Mastin, L. A. C.
Matcham, R. C.
McCormack, D. P.
McCormack, J. D.
McFarland, J. W.
McLanahan, G. G.
Merrett, A.
Miller, C. P.
Miller, L. W. S.
Minors, L.
Morgan, G.
Morgan, W. W.
Morse, C. C. W.
Mullins, V. K.
Mullins, W. J.
Neale, J. H.
New, G. E.
Newcomen, A. B.
Newman, A. D.
Newman, C. P.

Newman, F. B.
Newman, H. M.
Newman, H. St. Elmo
Newman, J. B.
Newman, R. M.
Norris, C. G.
Norris, D. L.
Norris, J. S. L.
North, J. H.
Nott, J. A.
Ovens, E. A.
Paget, F. W.
Palmer, H. D.
Palmer, S. J.
Parkin, B. T.
Payne, A. F. R.
Payne, C. W.
Payne, S. R.
Peacey, A. F.
Pearse A. O.
Perry, S. D.
Phelps, E. S.
Phillimore, E. B.
Phillimore, W. G.
Phillimore, W. L.
Phillips, G. J.
Phillips, J. L.
Phillips, R. L.
Pike, N. W.
Plested, E. I.
Poulton, G. H.
Pratt, H. B.
Pratt, R. T. C.
Preston, R. A.
Price, A. R.
Price, S. D. H.
Pridham, C. W.
Pridham, J. C.
Prout, H. M.
Prout, R. M.
Prout, S. H.
Pullin, F. H.
Ractliff, A. H.
Reade, G. L.
Reece, P. J. M.
Reece, R. M.
Revell, C. J. M.
Revell, E. W. M.
Richards, A. M.
Rivers, H. P.
Rivers, M.
Rivers, W. J.
Robbins, C.
Robson, P. S.
Rymer, E. C.
Salisbury, J. J.
Sanders, R. L.
Selwyn, F. J.
Shipway, W. G.

Warwickshire—
continued

Harper, T. A.
Hatherley, N.
Holloway, H. H.
Joynes, F. W.
Kenchington, N. S.
Leath, S. B.
Leather, F. C.
Marmont, R. H.
Norman, D. C.
Parr, M.
Phennah, R. J.
Raymer, C. R. P.
Robinson, T. Ll.
Shaw, B. J.
Smith, C. D.
Smith, J. W.
Streader, R. A.
White, A. E.
White, H. C.
Wilkinson, C. S.
Wilkinson, J. K.
Wilson, G. L.
Wilson, J. B.

WILTSHIRE

Affleck, J.
Affleck, S.
Culverwell, G. L.
Curtis, H. A.
Dawson, G. J. C.
Evans, H. S.
Ford, F. W.
Francis, R. D.
Gauntlett, D.
Gauntlett, W. T.
Holborow, N. M.
Horder, A. S.
Jackson, K. V.
Long, G. R. W.
Lord, H. A.
Maggs, F.
Maggs, J. H.
Malings, W. G. F.
Marshman, T. W.
Pottenger, J. W.
Raynes, F. P. M.
Roberts, V. Lloyd
Smith, Alan M.
Smith, E. A.
Smith, H. J.
Smith, H. R.
Smith, T. A.
Spackman, A. J.
Spackman, H. R.
Spackman, H. D.
Teagle, K.
Tilley, C.
Titley, W. A.

Wiltshire—*continued*

Trumper, L. C.
Walton, J.
Webb, C. J.

WORCESTERSHIRE

Andrew, D. R.
Armstrong, R. J.
Bomford, D. R.
Bomford, E. R.
Bomford, R. B.
Cloke, E. P.
Collins, J. F.
Glasbrook, T. J.
Haines, A. J. F.
Hatherley, A. W.
Kenchington, F. W.
Liley, J. E.
Osborne, R. J.
Partridge, A. G.
Trythall, E. R.
Wakefield, P. M.
Warner, M. C.
Warner, W. W. F.
Worth, C. A. W.
Worth, E. J.
Worth, Egbert
Wright, P. B.
Wright, R. L.

YORKSHIRE

Adams, D. W.
Apperley, E. P.
Bennett, A. D.
Bennett, J. W.
Copp, H. E.
Gledhill, G. P.
Gooch, Y. E.
Graham, J. B.
Harroway, E. A.
Hartley, A. E.
Howell-Davies
Jenkins, W. A.
Kimmins, E. J.
King, C. E.
Mascall, R.
Mascall, V. C.
Pattison, C. L.
Pattison, P.
Phillips, C. E.
Routledge, W.
Smith, G. S.
Smith, J. D. E.
Smith, T. A.

WALES
BRECKNOCKSHIRE

Bishop, F. E.
Fawkes, K. S.

Brecknockshire—
continued

Goldsworthy, G. A. W.
Jayne, F. J.
Jones, David

CARDIGANSHIRE

Evans, I. L.
James, R. N.
Roberts, H. D.

CARMARTHEN-
SHIRE

Lewis, C. S.
Lewis, E. H.
Lewis, J. H.

FLINTSHIRE

Hampton, F. E.
Meldrum, J. H.
Spriggs, E. I.

GLAMORGAN-
SHIRE

Allen, H. R.
Beavan, W. G.
Bevan, R. V.
Bryant, L. W.
Case, B. L. S.
Collins, P. J.
Cook, A. A.
Cook, J. A.
Crockett, H.
Dakers, H. H.
Daniel, Archibald
Davies, E. M. G.
Davies, G. Hier
Davies, G. Howard
Davies, Hadyn P.
Davies, H. E.
Davies, J. H.
Davies, W. B.
Duck, F. A.
Durden, A. H.
Edwards, C. E.
Edwards, T. J.
Evans, T. M.
Eyon, H. H.
Gardner, R. S.
Gardner, W.
Giles, K. T.
Goldsworthy, W. H.
Grey, D. A.
Gunson, J. F.
Hannah, F. E.
Harris, A. E.
Hayes, G. F. R.
Hayes, J. W. G.
Hayes, R. S.

OVERSEAS

SUPPLEMENT GIVING DETAILS OF THOSE WHO LEFT AT EASTER OR IN JULY, 1937

Allinson, John Michael Anthony, *Journey's End, Minchinhampton, Stroud, Glos.* (Spr.), 1934–1937. Science VI. School Certificate. School Swimming Team. Music Prize. Dramatic Prize. Studying in Lausanne.

Braithwaite, John, *Park House, Park Road, Burgess Hill, Sussex.* (R. and Spr.), 1933–1937. Lower V-A. House Monitor. School Certificate. Electrical Engineer.

Clark, Alvin Raymond, *Thorold Lodge, Bitterne Park, Southampton.* (S.H.), 1930–1937. Modern VI. Prefect. Vice-Pres. of League. Sec., Treas., Lit. Soc. King's Scout. School Certificate. Captain 1st XV. 1st IV. Prizes for Public Service and Speaking. Articled to Solicitor.

Chamberlain, Richard John, *Crowmarsh Battle, Benson, Oxon.* (H.), 1934–1937. Upper V. School Certificate. School Tennis Team. Sen. Doubles. Articled to County Surveyor of Oxfordshire.

Collings, Frederick Arthur Burke, *Brook House, Water Lane, Brislington, Bristol* 4. (H.), 1932–1937. Science VI. Prefect. School Certificate. 1st XV. 1st IV. Foster Rifle. Capt. Scout Swimming Team. Prizes, Public Service and Opera. Science Student at Bristol University.

de Boehmler, Kenneth, *St. Joseph, San Fernando, Trinidad, B.W.I.* (S.H.), 1935–1937. Middle Remove. In Apex Company, Trinidad.

Dixon, Albert Noel, *247 Moorside Road, Flixton, Manchester.* (Spr.), 1934–1937. Lower V-B. 1st XI. 2nd XV.

Foster, Robert, *Hill View, Bourton-on-the-Water, Cheltenham.* (H.), 1933–1937. Modern VI. Prefect. Higher Certificate. 2nd XV. School Tennis Team. Prizes Daniels' Essay, History, English.

Fothergill, Arthur Brian, *Newlands, Kendal, Westmorland.* (H.), 1934–1937. Middle Remove.

Freeman, Peter, *Bell Hotel, Tewkesbury, Glos.* (H.), 1933–1937. Lower V-A. House Monitor. 2nd XI. 2nd XV.

Gladwin, Richard Thomas, *8 Oxford Street, Malmesbury.* (Spr.), 1934–1937. Science VI. Prefect. Vice-Pres. of League. 2nd XI. School Certificate. Articled to Wilson Lovatt, Civil Engineers.

Gledhill, John·Leslie, *Well House, Thongsbridge, nr. Huddersfield, Yorks.* (S.H.), 1934–1937. Lower V-A. Learning Woollen Manufacture.

Hopkins, Donald Cecil, *Uplands, Bexley, Kent.* (R. and S.H.), 1932–1937. Upper IV.

Hopkins, Richard Alfred David, *Uplands, Bexley, Kent.* (R. and S.H.), 1932–1937. Lower Remove. With General Motors, London.

Kelson, Wallace Howard, 1 *Eastfield Park, Weston-super-Mare.* (R. and S.H.), 1928–1937. Modern VI. Prefect. Cricket Captain. Sec. Lit. Soc. King's Scout. School Certificate. 1st XI. 1st XV. School Tennis Team. Prize for Speaking. English-Speaking Union Scholarship to U.S.A. Now at Pomfret School, Connecticut.

Liggatt, Alan Alexander, *Highfield House, Chase Ridings, Enfield, Middlesex.* (S.H.), 1934–1937. Lower V-A.

Malone, John Clement David, *West Square Street, Basseterre, St. Kitts, B.W.I.* (H.), 1932–1937. Modern VI. Prefect. School Certificate. Tennis Team. 2nd XI. 2nd XV. Athletic Team.

Marsden-Levy, Robert Henry, 30 *Rosary Gardens, London, S.W.* 7. (R. and S.H.), 1933–1937. Upper V.

Marshall, Hubert Edward, *St. Malo, Longleavens, Glos.* (H.), 1934–1937. Lower V-A. Bank Clerk.

Mather, Alan, 23 *Northumberland Road, Sheffield.* (Spr.), 1933–1937. Upper V. School Certificate. House Monitor. 1st XV. Athletic and Swimming Teams. Architectural Student Sheffield University.

McKinney, John Andrew, *Montrose, Nassau, Bahamas.* (S.H.), 1933–1937. Modern VI. Prefect. School Certificate. Swimming Team.

Parker, Ernest Patrick, *Rose Cottage, Newton, Porthcawl, Glam.* (Spr.), 1932–1937. Science VI. Senior Prefect. Pres. of League. Pres., Sec. and Treas. of Lit. Soc. Editor of " Star." Sec. Sports Committee. Boat Capt. Entrance Scholar. Higher Certificate. Capt. 2nd XV. Prizes Public Service, Literature, Excellence in Speaking. Undergraduate at St. John's College, Cambridge.

Poole, Harry Theodore Ruscombe, *Dawn, Whitecliffe Road, Parkstone, Dorset.* (H.), 1935–1937. Upper Remove. 2nd XI.

Pryce, Mostyn Rhys, *Hopelands, Stonehouse, Glos.* (R. and C.), 1932–1937. Upper IV.

Smart, Gerald Charles, *Ashcroft House, London Road, Stroud, Glos.* (C.), 1933–1937. Modern VI. House Monitor. School Certificate. Civil Service Clerk.

Spark, Ralph Alan, *Wellington House, 69 High Street, Norton-on-Tees.* (S.H.), 1934–1937. Lower V-A. 1st IV. Lightweight Boxing Championship.

Stride, Richard Thomas, 11 *Park Hill, Shirehampton, Bristol.* (H.), 1934–1937. Science VI. House Monitor. School Certificate. 2nd XV. Swimming Team.

Taylor, Colin George, *Wallnerstrasse* 8, *Vienna, Austria.* (R. and H.), 1929–1936. Upper V. £50 Scholarship to H.M.S. " Worcester."

Timpson, John David, *Maidenhill House, Stonehouse, Glos.* (H.), 1933–1937. Modern VI. Prefect. Vice-Pres. of League. Entrance Scholar. Higher Certificate. 1st XI. Prizes Drama, Excellence in Speaking, Public Service, Daniels' Essay. Now holding Scholarship at Principia College, St. Louis, U.S.A.

[It may be that some names, through inadvertence, have been omitted from this Register. In such a case the Editor would be most grateful if the O.W. concerned, or his friends, would communicate with him or with the Headmaster, giving as full details as possible.]

AN UNBEATEN FIFTEEN, DECEMBER, 1931
Matches played 17. Won 16. Drawn 1.
(Points for 496. Points against 38).

A. Morris   E. Clark   N. Clark   A. Barnett   P. Wakefield   E. Hodgkinson   J. Calverwell
H. K. Lewis   N. Venning   A. Young   D. Paine   J. Bown   F. G. Edwards   E. Jowett
J. Ashton   J. Cook

FOOTBALL IN THE BERRYFIELD
(Where four games can be played at the same time)

A CRICKET XI, 1933

T. G. Wilson   W. Luker   S. C. Gobey   P. J. Collins   J. B. Graham

L. C. Smith   J. H. Bown   A. M. Barnett   H. A. Thomas   S. J. Silvey

H. N. Smith

VIEWS OF THREE RECENT SCOUT CAMPS
Near Lulworth, Porlock and by the Wye in Wales

A CHRONOLOGICAL LIST OF MASTERS

1882 — 1937

(It is hoped that this list contains the names of all, other than occasional and visiting Masters, who have taught at Wycliffe for periods long or brief. It also includes the names of the ladies who lent a hand during the Staff shortage caused by the Great War).

———

G. W. Sibly, M.A. (Oxon.), 1882–1919, died in 1928.

John Bramley, M.A. (Lond.), 1882–1889, and 1903–1922, died in 1926.

F. H. Sherwell, B.A. (Lond.), 1882–1922.

James Bramley, B.A. (Lond.), 1884–1887, died in 1890. O.W.

J. T. Norman, 1884–1887.

Herr Dax, 1884–1885.

T. B. Dilks, B.A. (Lond.), 1885.

A. Wiseman, M.A. (Aberdeen), 1885–1886.

D. MacLeod, M.A. (Aberdeen), 1886.

J. H. Fowler, 1886.

Herr T. F. Lutz, 1886.

W. C. Arundel, M.A. (Oxon.), 1887–1888, died in 1911.

S. M. Reynolds, M.A. (Oxon.), 1887–1888.

H. B. Brown, B.A. (Lond.), 1887.

F. J. Edwards, 1887–1888.

J. Kemp, 1887–1890.

C. S. Harris, B.A. (Lond.), 1888–1890.

A. J. Robinson, B.A. (Lond.), 1888–1894, died in 1894.

H. S. Lovett, B.A. (Dublin), 1889–1892.

E. F. Hugill, B.A. (Lond.), 1889–1924, died in 1934.

F. Arthur Sibly, M.A., LL.D. (Camb.), 1889–1921, died in 1929.

J. Bawden Kitt, 1890.

C. D. Vibert, B.A. (Lond.), 1890–1894. O.W.

R. V. Ward, M.A. (Camb.), 1891–1937.

J. T. Jordan, 1891–1902.

K

Miss K. E. Jackson, 1892–1925.

W. G. Field, M.A. (Camb.), 1893.

T. Elmer, 1894–1895.

R. Bell, B.A. (Durham), 1894–1895.

A. L. Harris, 1895–1897.

A. F. Stray, M.A. (Lond.), 1895–1897, died in 1912.

W. J. Menendez, 1895. O.W.

J. S. Evans, B.A. (Lond.), 1897–1919, died in 1919.

S. W. Thornton, 1898–1900, died in 1919.

E. E. Dyson, 1899–1901. Has died.

Melville Müller (afterwards **Hastings**), 1901–1906, killed in action in 1918.

J. J. Purdey, 1903–1921.

A. G. Ham, 1904–1905, died in 1905.

G. Osborn, 1905.

Buchanan Smith, 1906–1910.

W. A. Sibly, M.A. (Oxon.), 1906–1937. O.W.

S. C. Glassey, B.A. (Birmingham), 1909–1910.

T. M. Sibly, M.A. (Camb.), 1910–1937. O.W.

A. L. Green, 1910–1911.

J. S. Barlow, 1911–1919.

D. E. Williams, M.A. (Sheffield), 1912–1915.

H. V. Bury, M.A. (Oxon.).

L. F. Rougeault, B.-ès-L., 1914–1916.

Miss May Shepherd, 1915–1919, died in 1927.

Mrs Large, 1916–1918.

N. E. Webb, M.A. (Oxon.), 1916–1917, 1921–1933. O.W.

Rev. Thomas Layng, M.A., 1917–1918, died in 1930.

J. A. Spence, B.A. (Dublin), 1917.

Rev. J. Mearing, B.D., 1917.

Miss E. K. Stone, B.A. (Lond.), 1917–1920.

P. Thuyn, 1918–1935.

Rev. R. E. Pryce, 1919–1937.

Mrs Burnard, 1919–1928, died in 1929.

G. F. Timpson, M.A. (Oxon.), 1919–1929.

Miss E. M. Turner, M.Sc. (Lond. & Sheffield), 1920–1921.

H. R. Tucker, B.A. (Oxon.), 1920–1921, 1924–1928. O.W.

A. W. Stewart, 1920–1937.

E. J. French, A.R.C.A., 1920–1937.

E. J. Bevan, M.A. (Camb.), 1921–1937.

G. L. Reade, M.C., M.A. (Camb.), 1921–1937. O.W.

H. V. Sims, M.C., M.A. (Oxon.), 1921–1923. O.W.

R. J. Young, B.A. (Lond.), 1922, died in 1931.

Miss Dorothy Sibly, 1922–1929.

T. S. Dixon, F.R.C.O., L.R.A.M., 1922–1937.

A. G. Caudle, B.Sc. (Birmingham), 1923–1937.

G. P. N. Goodwin, M.A. (Lond.), 1925–1937.

Mrs Goodwin, B.A. (Lond.), 1926–1929.

F. W. Stollery, B.A. (Camb.), 1928–1934.

B. T. Parkin, M.A., (Oxon.), 1928–1937. O.W.

C. V. Allen, M.A. Mus. Bac. (Camb.), F.R.C.O., 1929–1937.

J. C. Brooks, M.A. (Camb.), 1931–1936.

S. G. H. Loosley, B.A. (Camb.), 1934–1937.

C. J. Laviers, B.A. (Camb.), 1934–1937.

A. P. Polack, B.A. (Camb.), 1935–1937.

A. Elliott, B.Sc. (Lond.), 1935–1937.

I. L. Serraillier, B.A. (Oxon.), 1936–1937.

A. A. Robertson, B.A. (Oxon.), 1936–1937.

P. F. Seebohm, B.A. (Camb.), 1937.

J. Fleming, B.A. (Camb.), 1937.

(The Masters at the Junior School are not included in this list, but the names of the existing Staff there will be found on another page.)

BRIEF BIOGRAPHIES OF SOME WHO HELPED TO MAKE THE SCHOOL

Mr. G. W. Sibly

GEORGE WILLIAM SIBLY, founder and for the first thirty years (1882–1912) headmaster of Wycliffe, continued to act as housemaster of the School House during the staff shortage caused by the War, but on the return of his son Mervyn from the Front in 1919 he retired to Ivy Grove, and died there in 1928. During the last sixteen years of his life his physical powers were enfeebled by the *paralysis agitans* caused by a cycle accident in Ireland, but the development of the disease was slow, and an undimmed intellect enabled him to follow with keen interest all that concerned the welfare of the School and its Old Boys.

In a little memoir of about fifty pages, compiled by his children, the story of his life, work and personality may be read by any who are interested, so here it must suffice to speak very briefly of his achievements and character.

The second son of Mr Thomas Sibly of Taunton, Mr. G. W. Sibly, who was born in 1851, may be said to have inherited a schoolmaster's capacity in his very blood, although his first inclinations were towards the law. He went to Lincoln College, Oxford, in 1872, rowed in his college " eight," and gained the cup awarded at the University to the best shot of his year. He was, indeed, an all-round athlete, playing for Somerset in Rugby Football, and winning the " best average " bat at school in several successive years, as well as every event in the School Sports except throwing the cricket ball. A fine gymnast, he could vault anything he could reach, and he was also a pioneer among cyclists, riding a bone-shaker and a " high " long before the coming of the " safety." Boys who were at Wycliffe in the eighties and early nineties will remember his astonishing vigour at hand-fives, his great running dives into the Canal, and the long walks which he took with them across the hills on " whole holidays."

In the chapter entitled " The Story of Fifty-five Years " the record of this early period is given at some length, and it suffices to emphasise here the paramount part played by Mr. Sibly in the creation of the actual fabric and many of the general arrangements and traditions of the School, as most of us know it to-day. To this practical task he brought vast powers of work, and for the first twenty years at Wycliffe, lacking both clerk and secretary, he often toiled at accounts and correspondence far into the night, after a day spent in teaching and supervision, and an evening in which at least an hour was set aside for sitting with his wife and children. Many strong men would have broken under the strain, but Mr. Sibly was aided by a singularly temperate life (he had always been a teetotaller and non-smoker), his love of gardening and tree-planting, and by a certain quietude of strength which was seldom either ruffled or excited.

He possessed, too, a wonderfully clear head for finance, and the day's transactions, even in his petty-cash book, were always entered and balanced in the day. At the outset he adopted the plan of immediate payment for goods, and so speedily won the trust and respect of every tradesman in the neighbourhood.

His powers as a disciplinarian, an equable temper, and marked skill in managing men as well as boys, played no small part in his success. Though so quiet in manner, Mr. Sibly was always firm and strong in action, and very definite in his decisions.

He was ever distinguished by his absolute straightness and sense of justice, which was, indeed, so keen that he became almost pugnacious when he thought that his own or others' rights were being infringed. More than once, like some village Hampden, he led the parishioners of Stonehouse, armed with crowbars, to the removal of an encroaching fence or obstructing barricade, and he was a zealous champion of public rights of way.

He was singularly independent and courageous in his views, and the expression which he gave to them. Like his forbears, he was a staunch Wesleyan Methodist, and for forty years he took a leading part in local Methodism. He was a vegetarian for the last sixty years of his life, and retained to the end his beautiful rosy complexion. He was always a keen anti-vaccinist, and was more than once threatened with imprisonment, and saw his goods labelled for sale by public auction, because of his refusal to pay the fines imposed upon him for not submitting his children to what he never ceased to regard as an unnatural and useless practice.

Though never seeking office, he played a considerable part in local government. He was a member of the Parish Council for thirty years, and for some time its chairman. He was a District Councillor for a quarter of a century, and a Poor Law Guardian who never spared himself in the discharge of his duties.

So full a life left little time for social amenities, or for literary work and style. His correspondence was always brief and to the point, and sometimes brusque. But he was ever a devoted husband and father, cherishing his rather delicate wife with ceaseless solicitude until her death in 1915 left him to face the end alone. Yet not alone, for the devotion of his daughters still encompassed him, and in the progress of the School under the guidance of his sons he found a ceaseless source of interest.

At the School Jubilee celebrations in 1932 high tributes were paid to his work and worth, and a tablet was unveiled in the Chapel to his memory. Lord Rochester said :

" There was nothing idle or indifferent in him, and he was incapable of small thought or word about anyone. Quickly grasping the needs and possibilities of a situation, he brought to bear all the energy and enthusiasm of a vigorous personality and an alert intellect. Strict in integrity, discerning in judgment, devoted to service, he was esteemed alike in school and private life. Behind his modest disposition there were shrewd judgment, strong convictions and a sensitive conscience. His family life was characterized by great charm and refinement."

His son and successor, speaking in the Chapel of a few of his father's characteristics, said :

" Some of you never knew my father, and many of those now present only remember him as an old man, crippled as the result of an accident twenty years ago. But some remember him in the fulness of his prime, and a few in the wonderful strength and activity of his young manhood ; and all who knew him would wish to pay their meed of love, homage and respect."

He went on to speak of some of Mr. Sibly's chief characteristics :

" First I would place his courage. It required great courage to come to Stonehouse without capital, bringing a bride married a month before, and to found the School. Whether at Wycliffe or on holiday, whether dealing with boys or men, or even with a hostile public meeting, in the full tide of manhood or in enfeebled age, that courage never for a moment failed."

After telling of his father's powers of work, the Headmaster continued :

" And next I would note his modesty. Although he did much, he rarely talked about it, and he was always very humble. But combined with that modesty was a sturdy independence. . . . He ' never sold the truth to serve the hour,' and he walked unswervingly in the street called Straight. One could not conceive prevarication on his part, and as one looked into those keen and steady eyes one could hardly tell a lie. In money matters his integrity was absolute. He believed in paying cash for goods, and in ' paying on the nail.' He never anticipated his income or ran into debt. He abhorred all forms of gambling. Withal and above all, he was sustained from earliest boyhood to his last hours on earth by a profound unwavering faith in God, and in God's good purposes for man."

In closing this brief record, we quote a few sentences from the Memoir to which reference has already been made :

" Mr. Sibly never strove to shine in public life, or to sway his fellows by the arts of oratory, nor has he left any printed book behind. His name and fame, except in mid-Gloucestershire and among his old pupils and friends, remain almost unknown. . . . Yet few who knew him or read this record . . . will be found to deny him a title to noble manhood and eminent success. . . . In the last half of the nineteenth century many great businesses and reputations were built up, and human energy expressed itself in countless ways, but the measure of Mr. Sibly's achievement must appeal to all who knew it. By courage and character, by his practical sagacity, steady purpose and power of ruling boys and men, he founded and established a School after the fashion of his heart's desire. It was never a big school, as some schools go, but it has always been filled with some portion of his own spirit and outlook upon life, and as such we trust that it may be strong to endure."

The tablet placed in the School Chapel and reproduced on another page fittingly expresses the homage of many Old Boys to Mr Sibly's work, teaching and example.

MRS. SIBLY

MRS. SIBLY was the youngest daughter of the late Mr. Joseph Pillman, J.P., of Plymouth. She was educated at Hope House, and Flook House, Taunton, and it was there that, as a girl in her teens, she met Mr. G. W. Sibly. They were married in 1882, and returned from a honeymoon in the Lake District to open Wycliffe College in September of that year. Four children were born to them, and the care of her own family and of the many hundreds of boys who passed through the School House made large demands upon Mrs. Sibly's energy.

Although never very strong, she enjoyed moderately good health until the autumn of 1914, when symptoms of serious illness developed. An early operation was pronounced necessary, but the next few weeks were singularly peaceful, and for almost the first time in her life Mrs. Sibly received more than she gave. A London specialist, aided by three other doctors, performed the operation, but her heart failed, and she passed away at Wycliffe without recovering consciousness on February 4th, 1915, the eve of her 54th birthday. Hundreds of tributes from friends and Old Boys were received when the tidings of her death became known. We quote a very few.

" She has been doing kindnesses all her life, and her devotion to duty was absolute."

" Mrs. Sibly was so gentle, so compassionate, and so lived her gospel of good."

" That absolute purity of life and purpose is rare indeed. There are many who do good work, but few who so forget themselves in doing it."

" Though I do not belong to the Roman Church, she will always be only a ' saint ' to me."

Her classes for boys on week-nights and on Sunday afternoons, in which she combined Bible study with helpful conversation, her gift of flowers on Sunday mornings to boys who maintained her standard of pleasant and wholesome speech, her tenderness to those who were sick, her devotion to new and sometimes home-sick little boys, her belief in the whiteness of black sheep, her talks and gifts of helpful books to those who were leaving, and above all a gracious influence, felt as " the sweet presence of a good diffused," endeared her to generation after generation of Wycliffe boys.

She was extraordinarily conscientious and scrupulous. Toil for herself, her own convenience or inconvenience, and even probable misunderstanding, were studied not at all. Her only endeavour was to do the right thing. If one of her family cut a stick from a hedge, she was known to send a postal order anonymously to the owner. If goods on approval had been exposed to the chance of infinitesimal soiling, she felt it wrong to return them. If the August holidays had been blazingly hot, she yet insisted that every school mattress should be aired on each side for two hours before a fire. Although a poor night almost invariably gave her a bad headache next day, she would often make excursions to a distant part of the house to look at a boy who was sick.

Her sympathies were extremely broad and peculiarly personal, and she not only enjoyed the confidences of men and women of influence and position, but took an almost affectionate interest in all the tradesmen and employees whom she met, receiving in return their constant deep regard. She was accustomed to kiss her servants when bidding them good-night.

Her kindness to tramps and beggars and gipsies, and even to fallen men and women, was unstinted, and not all her charity was wise, but by implicitly trusting in others and giving to them her sympathy and fellowship, she helped many to trust in God and in themselves. Among the respectable and industrious poor, too, she had many friends. Often when out for a drive she would stop to give them a place in her carriage, while her gifts and kindness to lonely women extended to many places and to distant lands. Not only in such ways, however, was her charity shown, for in spite of weakness, and sometimes much weariness, she spent her life in seeking to serve all whom she believed it possible to help.

She possessed an acute mind and wider interest, was fond of music, and played the piano remarkably well. While she liked good literature, and especially to hear biographies and the novels of Dickens and Scott read aloud by her husband as she sewed by the fireside at night (such a practice is a true social and family cement) her favourite books were the New Testament, the Methodist Hymn Book, " The Indwelling Christ," " Being and Doing " and " Great Souls at Prayer." Twice a day, for half-an-hour she sought, in these and meditation, refreshment at " the secret source of every precious thing." Her religion was very deep, but not at all dogmatic and she claimed kinship with all who sought the fellowship of Jesus Christ and tried to follow Him.

Many epitaphs exaggerate, but that of Mrs. Sibly states the simple truth when it says " a perfect wife, a devoted mother, a sincere Christian ; for more than thirty years she gave to the friendless and the poor a heart at leisure from itself, and to the boys of Wycliffe College her constant love and care."

" DR. ARTHUR "

DR. ARTHUR SIBLY was the Housemaster of Haywardsfield from 1888 until the end of 1921. Born at Taunton in 1861 he passed from the school of which his father was headmaster to St. John's College, Cambridge. Though a good Rugby player, Dr. Arthur's tastes were always chiefly intellectual, and he threw him- self with zest into the literary and cultural life of the University. After taking his degree in Law in 1883, he remained for some time at Cambridge as a Law coach, was called to the Bar, and became a member of the Inner Temple. Had he practised as a barrister, his great ability as a forensic pleader and his splendid powers of speech would have taken him far.

Just at this time, however, Mr. G. W. Sibly was seeking a successor to Mr. Bramley at Haywardsfield, and Dr. Arthur accepted the vacant post. It was a happy chance which brought the two brothers together in this way, for their qualities were comple- mentary rather than similar, and together they made the School as we know it.

Mrs. Arthur, to whom he was married in 1889, combined, in her office as house-mistress, much social charm with very great efficiency. She was equal to any emergency, whether of illness or entertainment, and at one time she took a considerable part in the public life of the locality.

After leaving Stonehouse at the close of 1921 he lived in the old family home at Taunton, but continued to take a considerable part, in public life. He died unexpectedly at the end of 1928, on the night following Christmas Day, and by his own direction his ashes were cast into the Atlantic from the cliffs of King Arthur's Castle at Tintagel, a spot which held for him many hallowed memories.

Dr. Arthur was from the first a most competent Housemaster, and for thirty-three years he ruled Haywardsfield with power and dignity and a sympathy born of much insight into the character and hearts of boys.

By means of the prizes which he gave for the study of good literature, by reading aloud—he possessed a fine, sonorous voice—in the Senior's class which he held on Sunday afternoons, and latterly by the "musical half-hour" which followed Sunday tea, he helped to instil into the mind of many a boy a love of good books and beautiful music. He was also a fine actor and often a first-rate reciter.

His scientific knowledge, though not very profound, was extraordinarily wide, and he had a great power of imparting that knowledge in an interesting way, whether by lantern lectures or otherwise. For more than thirty years he was President of the Field Club.

But it was in the sphere of morals that Dr. Arthur's greatest influence was exerted. Possessed of intense spiritual earnestness himself, it was the supreme endeavour of his life to impart an equal enthusiasm for virtue to all whom he might influence, and especially to the older boys whom he met in his class each Sunday. His genius was apostolic rather than social. The rôle of an apostle is not without its pitfalls, and he sometimes aroused opposition, especially amongst older and critical minds. He himself seldom saw life in half-tones. White to him was always splendidly white, and black was very black indeed. Dr. Arthur possessed, however, in a high degree the quality of moral courage, and it was he who, often in the teeth of clenched antagonisms, guided the frail barque of the League's first beginnings into the smooth waters of security and success.

Outside the School, too, he achieved much. He was amongst the first to advocate enlightened teaching on the subject of sex, was the joint author of "Youth and Sex" in the People's Library and his pamphlet "Private Knowledge for Boys," first written for use at Wycliffe, was adopted for official use by the Council of the Alliance of Honour, and has been welcomed by many eminent leaders of public opinion, including Lord Baden-Powell and the present Archbishop of Canterbury.

He left his mark, too, on the educational life of England. From 1904 to 1919 he was almost continuously either Chairman or President of the Private Schools' Association, and he secured the incorporation of an important amendment, drafted by himself, in Mr. Fisher's Education Act of 1917.

Like his brother, he was a whole-hearted anti-vaccinist, and he issued a challenge, with the offer of all expenses paid, to a debate on this subject with any doctor in the West of England. He was also an ardent humanitarian, and was vehemently opposed to vivisection, like two of his own greatest teachers, Tennyson and Browning.

Some found his intense earnestness a little overpowering and his judgment, tho' not his intention, was at times at fault, but the sort of influence he exercised is well expressed by quotations from four out of many letters received after his death. All the writers are O.W's who were under his care at Haywardsfield.

> "It is not an easy matter to write of one who has had so great a part in one's own life, and to whom one owes such a debt for patience, trouble and kindliness shown, but I want to add my tribute to him who for so many years gave so much of himself for others. There are a host of men out in the world—and many others who have gone over—in whose lives Dr. Arthur's teaching, and influence have played a greater part than even they know, and it is amongst these especially that he will be most remembered for his good deeds, the friendship, consideration, kindness and help which he showed them even at times when authority, sternness and discipline had to appear."

> "Dr. Arthur was not only one of the oldest of my friends, but his friendship was in so many ways unique. Many a man looks back to his Housemaster with something like filial gratitude, but I wonder if any gripped us as Dr. Arthur gripped us in those days. He left us with a new direction and meaning to life, and then one never lost touch afterwards."

> "He was a very great schoolmaster, attracting, disciplining, moulding men with a sureness of touch that puts him, in his own sphere, among the giants, with Arnold, Thring and Lacordaire."

> "He was a very great deal more to me than a schoolmaster, and has helped me in many ways since I left school. He was the greatest man I have ever known, or ever expect to know "

In the light of such testimony, which could be multiplied, there stands revealed some portion of Dr. Arthur's influence for good upon the School which he helped to shape.

MR. JOHN BRAMLEY

MR. JOHN BRAMLEY may well be counted among the makers of Wycliffe, for he came with Mr. Sibly to Stonehouse as his senior assistant master in 1882 ; he was the first Housemaster of Haywardsfield, and at a later date of Springfield too, and except for eleven years of headmasterships elsewhere, his work and interest were associated with Wycliffe until his retirement to Taunton in 1922.

The death of Mrs. Bramley in 1915 was a great grief to him. She had been with him in every post of responsibility, and was unwearied in her devotion to the health and comfort of the boys who, at Haywardsfield and Springfield, came within the circle of her care.

As a class teacher, especially of Latin, he was exceedingly interesting and lively. As a housemaster at Wycliffe and as a headmaster elsewhere, he was widely loved and esteemed, and always very painstaking, but somewhat too trustful to be entirely successful, for the guilelessness of his own nature made him slow at times to recognise and combat wrong which needed correction. Apart from this, both in school and out he was extraordinarily prompt and punctilious in the performance of duty.

As a Wesleyan Methodist he was for nearly fifty years a " local preacher," and he filled in turn almost every office open to a layman, infusing all of them with his own spirit of genial brotherliness. He, more than anyone else, was responsible for the building of the Chapel in which the School now worships. He was a Liberal of the old school, and a J.P. for Gloucestershire. He was a teetotaller and non-smoker all his life, and a supporter of every humanitarian movement. He was very fond both of music and literature, and never happier than when reading aloud his beloved Charles Dickens. He was a skilful raconteur, and laughed so heartily when telling jokes and stories—really funny ones—that his audience was speedily reduced to a similar state of merriment. At the same time he was a man of moods, and in private he was sometimes subject to depression. In all his public and social life he was distinguished by friendliness and brotherliness, with an utter freedom from snobbery. He had a cheery word or friendly enquiry for almost every man, woman, or child he met, and wherever he went he left behind him a trail of smiling faces and cheerful thoughts.

Miss Valentine

MISS VALENTINE, or " Madam," as she was often called, came to the School House as matron in 1883,

> " A perfect woman, nobly planned,
> To warn, to comfort and command,"

and for a quarter of a century, until her wonderful powers began physically to fail, she remained a helpful, inspiring and hallowing force at school. She possessed great ability, unfailing tact, unruffled dignity, much physical beauty, a cool and resourceful brain in cases of accident or serious illness, tireless energy, and a large capacity for methodical work.

For older boys she made her little sitting-room a pleasant rendezvous, and to others she regularly read aloud after tea on Sunday evenings, either in that room or beneath the mulberry tree. She almost invariably attended the Debating Society and the Sunday evening prayer-meeting, and occasionally took an active part in both. When she laid down her work at Wycliffe in 1909, an annuity was given to her by past and present boys and masters, as a small token of esteem and love. Her kindness never failed, nor was her judgment found wanting, and when she died at New Barnet eight years later, on May 1st, 1917, many hundreds of O.W's at the Front and elsewhere felt that they had lost a " pal."

Mr. J. S. Evans

MR. EVANS was a master at Wycliffe from 1897 until his death at the end of 1919. The son of a farmer in the Eastern Counties, John Samuel Evans graduated at London University at an early age, and after brief experience elsewhere, he came to Wycliffe as master of the Fourth Form and Upper School Scripture master. Latterly he became the senior master teaching Mathematics. A hard worker himself in school hours, he expected others to work hard too, and many boys first learnt the meaning and value of hard work when they came beneath his rule in " the Fourth." As a disciplinarian he was most capable and just. He never lost his temper, and seldom had cause to punish, but every boy knew that his word was law, and he was also a master of the sometimes dangerous power of sarcasm.

When he first came to Wycliffe he was in the prime of manhood, a fine all-round cricketer, and a good football player. After his marriage in 1910 golf and his garden, in which he took great delight, became his principal recreations. In his early years amongst us he was young, with much of a young man's attitude towards life, but he mellowed with the years, and his sympathy, patience and regard for the things of the spirit grew apace. He was typically English, very manly, " rich in saving common-sense," and most discerning in his judgments of others. He abhorred anything which partook of meanness or slackness or sham, so he was quick to speak his mind and at times to criticise.

Though he appeared extraordinarily robust, a partial breakdown in 1915 was followed by a more serious one in 1917, which for a time led to his absence from school and from the command of the Corps, his special war-time interest. He stuck to his work with grim determination as long as he was able, and was devotedly nursed by Mrs. Evans, but he died unexpectedly on December 1st, 1919.

Many tributes were paid to his memory. " A true sportsman in every sphere of life," wrote one Old Boy, and another said, " He always played the game."

Miss K. E. Jackson

MISS JACKSON'S teaching work at Wycliffe extended over a period of thirty-three years, from 1892 until 1924. Since that date she has been in charge of The Nook, now used as a hostel for masters, and of late years she has been the guardian of the School Book Room.

At first, and for many years afterwards, Miss Jackson taught the Lower First or Preparatory Form, drilling generations of youngsters for " the march of mind," teaching them how to work and how to obey. There were not a few who found her rule at first severe, but many a boy and man has cause for gratitude as he looks back on the lessons of industry, order and obedience learnt in her presence. Her teaching was so good that in time it extended to the Upper III Form, and during the staff-shortage occasioned by the War she also took a considerable part of the Upper School English. Her discipline, as far as class-teaching was concerned, was as good as that of any master in the School.

In many other ways she shared in the general life of Wycliffe. A keen gardener, she tested Scouts for their Gardener's Badge. She was for long a member of the School Choral Society, and still attends the meetings of the Debating Society, whose award of prizes for speaking she has helped to decide during four decades.

With many interests, not least in books and gardening, and with a personality of outstanding strength, there are those who have at times found her a little hard or *difficile*, but she has been a great servant of the School during forty-five years, and those who know her best are aware of many kindnesses, often wrought by stealth.

MR. F. H. SHERWELL

FOR forty years Mr. Sherwell was music-master at Wycliffe. He came with Mr. Sibly when the School was first opened in 1882, and retired from the greater part of his work in July 1922, though he is still living in Pearcroft Road, and lends a hand in various ways.

In the early years of the School, Mr. Sherwell, who was a good all-round cricketer and football player, was regularly seen in the XI and XV. For a long period he was secretary of both these games, and afterwards of the Association Football Club, and Treasurer of the general Sports' Fund. He had charge of choral singing, and the concerts and musical evenings arranged by him totalled several hundred in number. He gave an interest in music to many, and was a competent player himself, although his technique was more developed than the artistic temperament. In addition to all this, he was the master of the Fifth Form, and regularly took a class for boys on Sunday afternoons, as well as nearly thirty piano pupils and several ordinary school duties. Certainly the amount of work which masters, if not boys, accomplished in these early years was little short of prodigious.

On the occasion of his marriage in 1903 a beautiful service of silver plate was presented to him by past and present Wycliffe boys. For although lively moments in his class-room were not unknown, he was genuinely interested in boys and fond of them, and many have reciprocated both his interest and his affection. He has corresponded much with Old Boys, and in their minds his memorable personality and figure stand out as an almost indispensable part of the Wycliffe of an earlier day. He is still with us, happy in having Mrs. Sherwell at his side, and he is the only man now living who can say of Wycliffe, " I saw the start."

MR. E. F. HUGILL

MR. HUGILL, like Mr. Bramley, was first a boy at Kingswood School and afterwards a master at Taunton and Harrogate. After a fleeting earlier visit he settled at Wycliffe in 1889, as assistant housemaster at Haywardsfield, and he remained with us until he reached the age of seventy, after more than thirty-five years had elapsed.

For the remaining ten years he lived in his sisters' home at Marlborough, active and interested to the last. He came to Wycliffe for the Old Boys' Re-union in July 1934, but three weeks later, when cycling (in his eightieth year) on the main Bath Road, he was killed by a motor-car. Death was instantaneous, and surely thus came kindly to one whose life had been crowned with years and peace.

During school hours at Wycliffe most of his work lay with the Second Form and many boys will also remember him as the master " on duty " on Saturday afternoons, and as Dr. Arthur's assistant at Haywardsfield. " Drive " and method were never his most marked characteristics, and his skill in imparting knowledge was not equal to his capacity for amassing it, but in private life he was a most interesting and informative companion. For fifty years, mostly passed at Wycliffe, Ernest Hugill was an assistant school-master, with an income as modest as himself, but none the less he was rich indeed. He may not have been a great class teacher, but he taught, in a fever'd artificial age, how true wealth consists not in the abundance of a man's possessions, but in his breadth of interests and delight in simple things. All his life he was thus happy in possessions truly great.

First among these was his love of reading and literature. He was a devoted reader of the *Manchester Guardian* and of the *Bookman*. In his room at Ivy Grove books gradually carried all before them, until at last only one small drawer remained for clothes and other personal belongings.

A little after love of books came his love of Nature. He knew the note as well as the appearance of almost every English bird, and the name of nearly every flower. He delighted in crag-climbing, at which, indeed, his ardour at times exceeded his skill, for he thrice knew what it feels like to dangle from a rope on the precipices of Great Gable. Love of the great mountains never made him despise the little hills. Every day, rain or shine, saw him on Doverow's top, often not once, but twice or thrice. At a modest computation he climbed that hill not less than twenty thousand times during his thirty-five years at Wycliffe.

Churches and monuments, the histories and mysteries of some famous house or abbey, personal and literary associations, always intrigued him greatly. He had a passion for dipping into old churches, and possessed a fine collection of brasses of his own rubbing.

Spare of frame and light of limb, vigorous exercise on foot or cycle never came amiss to him, and often in the vacations he entirely eschewed trains. He had even mastered the dangerous art of reading while cycling.

When he resigned his post at Wycliffe, O.W.s combined to give him a valuable present, which they asked him to accept for " his gentle courtesy in word and deed." With the family home as haven, the *Manchester Guardian* in his hand, the song of birds and the Wiltshire Downs about him, there was small need to wish him happiness.

MR. R. V. WARD

IN the foregoing pages an attempt has been made to describe, vividly and truthfully, the work and personality of all the masters who, for a space of twenty or thirty years and more, built and served the School, but who now rest from their labours. One faithful servant of Wycliffe, Mr. R. V. Ward, who first came to Stonehouse in 1891, is still working in our midst, though no longer taking classes. Mr. Ward's teaching, painstaking rather than exciting, was chiefly with the Lower Third Form, and later in part with the Upper Fourth, but he will mainly be remembered as an untiring public servant, doing with conscientious zeal every task which came to his hand. These were many, and have included the care of the School Shop, the rather unpopular business of collating fines in olden days and " rounds " in these, the Treasurership of the Library, with all the routine work associated with this and the various Reading Rooms, and much besides which did not catch the public eye, but which called for faithful performance. It has been a great gain to the smooth running of Wycliffe that Mr. Ward could always be depended on to hear that call, and to give methodically and ungrudgingly of his best.

Mr. Ward was for long a useful bowler in the 1st XI, keeping a most accurate length, a keen and skilful photographer—he was the President of the first Photographic Club—an enthusiast in various hobbies, and a frequent traveller in Switzerland and other lands, from which he brought back many delightful pictures.

In the 1927 edition of this Register we expressed a hope that Mr. Ward would continue to serve the School for many years, but we dared not then anticipate all the services which he has since given. Not only has he continued to fulfil much routine work, but he has become one of the greatest benefactors the School has known. Most noteworthy of all has been his gift, at a cost of about £3,500, of a Swimming-Pool to Wycliffe. In the little speech which he made at the opening ceremony on Whit-Monday (June 1st 1936), Mr. Ward said that when he first saw Wycliffe on an Autumn

BY LAKE AND MOUNTAIN, 1931.

1. Sunbathing 10,000 ft. above the sea, with the Gorner Glacier below. 2. 'Excelsior,' with the Matterhorn beyond. 3. Roped to cross the Theodule Glacier. 4. The top of the Pass and the frontier of Italy. 5. After rain, on the Gemmi Pass. 6. Between Leukerbad and Leuk. 7 and 8. By Lake Lugano.

THE ORGAN

(Dedicated in July, 1932, to commemorate the fiftieth anniversary of the first foundation of Wycliffe).

SOME WYCLIFFE MASTERS
(1882—1922)

Dr. Arthur Sibly   Mr. E. F. Hugill

Mr. J. S. Evans   Mr. John Bramley

A BEAUTIFUL MEMORIAL GIFT
The Chancel and Reredos

afternoon in 1890 he little dreamed that he was soon to begin an association which had lasted to the present day. Forty-five years were a big slice out of any man's life, but the lines had fallen to him in pleasant places, and out of gratitude to the late Mr. G. W. Sibly, his successor and the School he felt that the time had come to make some tangible return for all that the School had meant to him.

Nor have Mr. Ward's services ended there, for although these personal and historical notes are written by another hand, it is by him that all the spade-work involved in the production of this new Register has been done.

May he long remain in our midst, to bless us with some new surprises, and keeping still the zest which enables him to fill the passing hour with interests and ardour unabated.

MR. MELVILLE HASTINGS

(Better known to Wycliffe boys as Mr. Müller or " Max.")

MR. MÜLLER was a master at Wycliffe from 1901 to 1906. Shortly after that date he changed his name by deed-poll to Hastings, the town of his birth, and a year or two later he went to Canada. Thence he returned with " Princess Pat's " famous fighting regiment early in 1915, and on September 28th 1918, being then a lieutenant in the 52nd Canadian Infantry (commanded by Col. W. W. Foster, D.S.O. and O.W.) he was mortally wounded during the final offensive on the Western Front.

His war record, and the remarkable series of letters which he wrote from the Front, are found in " Wycliffe and the War," and it is not our purpose to deal with these things now. Neither can he be exactly counted among the makers of the School, and yet we think that some brief tribute should be paid to a remarkable personality.

In one or two crucial questions his standards were different from those of the School, but none could fail to recognise his remarkable and sterling qualities. He was an effective teacher, with methods of discipline and exposition all his own. He despised poetry, but was devoted to Macaulay and the dictionary. In football he played a very vigorous, bull-like game at centre-half. For cricket he did not care so much, disdaining pads (as also " gas " at the dentist's) as " unmanly," but some of us can still see him rolling the tennis courts year in and year out, and rushing about to help, now here, now there. Double duty was a joy to him, and if anyone was sick or overworked he was always the first to volunteer, and indeed, to *insist* on giving aid.

Whatever he may have thought when first he came to Stonehouse, his ultimate love and admiration for the School were great

L

indeed. His sister wrote from Canada to say that she had found, treasured amongst his effects, a bundle of papers containing everything connected with Wycliffe received during seven years in the New World. When he came back across the Atlantic to fight, he looked upon the School as his only home in England, and more than once, in 1916 and 1917, he walked in straight from the trenches, to find a few days' peace and refreshment. All his writings breathe this affection :

"I'm going to Wycliffe. I know where I am going. Within her precincts there is a-hovering an atmosphere as of green fields, and mountain breezes, and it's good for me to be there."

"If you know of a better 'ole, well, 'op right to it. I don't, and that's why I am going there to-day."

A month after his death we received from Canada a card, printed in fateful anticipation with the words : " Melville Hastings deceased," and then, in his own hand-writing : " Best wishes to the best place I ever struck. Good-bye."

May we close this with an extract from his own brief memoir, " Trench Philosophy " :—

"Let us pray rather to be made men, strong brothers of the Strong Son of God, English gentlemen. I have proved the power of such a prayer, and the truth which says ' I fear no foe with Thee at hand to bless.' You can search deep dugouts alone, bayonet along trenches alone, be unafraid of shattering shells, lead, not follow ; be in fact at once sufficiently an English gentleman to be afraid to be afraid."

THE CONSTITUTION OF THE SCHOOL

WHEN Wycliffe was placed on a permanent foundation in 1931, the School received a new constitution and became a legal 'corporation.' Its President is Sir Pendrill Varrier-Jones (O.W.), and the financial and general direction of its affairs (apart from the specific control vested in the hands of the Headmaster and those to whom he delegates authority) belongs to a Council of Governors, almost all of whom are O.W.'s. Members of the Council retire in rotation, but are eligible for re-election at the Annual Meeting. The present Council consists of :—

J. HERBERT EDWARDS, *Chairman*	Edwin B. Gauntlett
Ralph J. Armstrong	Dr. Somerville Hastings
Hubert W. Batchelar	J. Cecil Hayes
W. Norman Bubb	Raymond S. Hayes
Claude A. Carr	Harold Mather
David W. Coates	J. D. Newth
Frederic L. Daniels	H. Leonard Porcher
Ifor L. Evans	Mildred A. Sibly
Crofton E. Gane	Dr. T. Franklin Sibly
Fernley Gardner	Charles J. Trump

Secretary : Sydney T. Toogood, Knightwood, Stonehouse.

Auditors : Messrs. S. J. Dudbridge & Sons, Stroud.

The following Committees have been appointed to deal with special interests. Some are only called on the same day as the Council, whose meetings are usually held at Stonehouse in February and July and in London in November. Others meet more frequently as required.

Finance and General Purposes Committee	Finance Sub-Committee
	Planning Committee
Education Committee	Health Committee
Social and Welfare Committee	Chapel Committee
Scholarship Committee	

SCHOOL STAFF, September, 1937

MAIN SCHOOL

Headmaster :

W. A. SIBLY, M.A., Lincoln College, Oxford. J.P. (Glos.)

T. M. Sibly, M.A. and Diploma in Geography, St. John's College, Cambridge.

G. L. Reade, M.C., M.A., St. John's College, Cambridge.

T. S. Dixon, F.R.C.O., L.R.A.M.

E. J. Bevan, M.A., St. John's College, Cambridge.

*R. V. Ward, M.A., St. John's College, Cambridge.

A. G. Caudle, B.Sc., Birmingham.

Rev. R. E. Pryce, F.R.G.S., Trinity College, Carmarthen and Bishops College, Cheshunt.

E. J. French, A.R.C.A., London.

G. P. N. Goodwin, M.A., University College, London.   M.L.A.

B. T. Parkin, M.A., Lincoln College, Oxford.

C. V. Allen, M.A., Mus.Bac., Clare College, Cambridge.   F.R.C.O.

S. G. H. Loosley, B.A., St. John's College, Cambridge.

C. J. Laviers, B.A., Trinity College, Cambridge.

A. P. Polack, B.A., St. John's College, Cambridge.

I. L. Serraillier, B.A., St. Edmund Hall, Oxford.

P. F. Seebohm, B.A., Caius College, Cambridge.

J. Fleming, B.A., Trinity Hall, Cambridge.

* Has retired from class teaching.

Chaplain : Rev. Alan Kay, M.A., Cambridge

JUNIOR SCHOOL

Master-in-Charge :

K. C. BIRD, M.A., Lincoln College, Oxford.

R. B. Evans, M.A., Magdalen College, Cambridge.

Miss Wright, B.A., London.

G. H. Burdess, Westminster Training College, London.

W. A. C. Bullock, B.Sc., King's College, London.

C. G. V. Taylor, B.A., New College, Oxford.

Mr. J. V. Murdin is the cricket professional and groundsman, and Messrs. A. W. Stewart and H. Jenner instruct in Woodwork and Metal-work.

MORE WYCLIFFE PERSONALITIES

Mr. R. V. Ward
Miss Jackson

Miss Valentine
Mr. F. H. Sherwell

THE SWIMMING POOL—A GIFT TO THE SCHOOL BY MR. R. V. WARD

THE MIKADO, 1937

(Gilbert and Sullivan Operas have been given at Wycliffe in recent years).

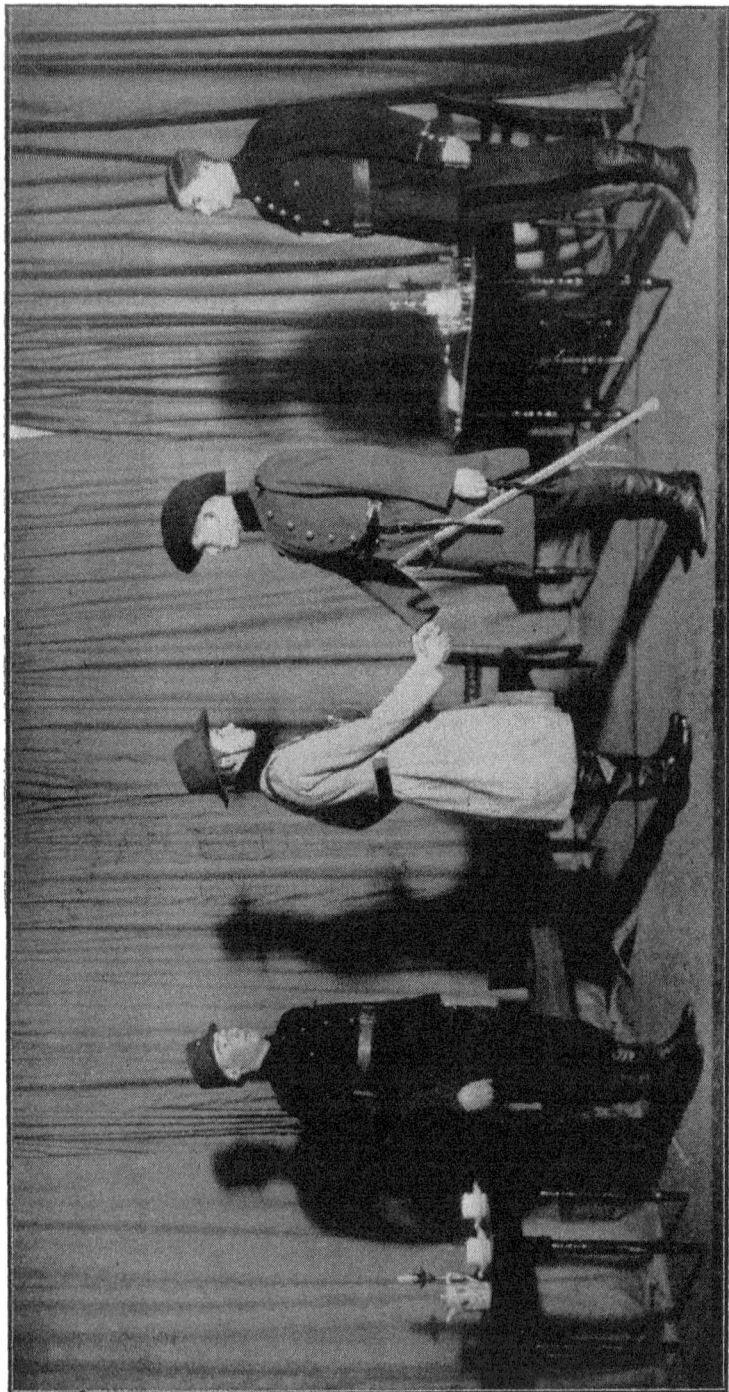

GENERAL GRANT ACCEPTS THE SURRENDER OF GENERAL LEE.

(in the play " Abraham Lincoln ")

MISCELLANEOUS NOTES

The O.W. Society

THE Old Wycliffian Society, with a membership of about 500, has grown continuously in recent years, and it is hoped that ultimately it may possess 1,000 members. The Hon. Secretary is Mr. W. Norman Bubb, whose business address is 5 Philpot Lane, London, E.C. 3. He has held this post since the Society was reconstituted after the War, and all concerned have cause to be grateful to him. The subscription is 10/6 a year, or £1 10s. od. for three years. This sum also entitles members to receive the *Wycliffe Star* three times a year. By means of this comprehensive magazine of between 90 and 130 pages, with some 20 to 30 pages devoted to " O.W. Notes," Old Boys are kept in touch both with the School and with one another.

The Annual Dinner is held in London, usually at the Connaught Rooms, on a Friday towards the end of November, and at the time when this Register is published the Dinner Secretary is Mr. H. W. Pethybridge, 58 Lewisham Park, London, S.E. 13.

In addition to the parent Society in London there are affiliated branches with headquarters at Bristol, Cardiff and Manchester. It is hoped that a fourth branch, for Old Boys in Mid-Gloucestershire, may soon be formed, and there is talk of other branches in the Midlands and in Yorkshire. The names and addresses of the Secretaries of the Local Branches are :—

Bristol & West of England : T. L. Silvey, Compton Lodge, Cribbs Causeway, Westbury-on-Trym, Bristol.

South Wales : D. Alan Gray, Bryn Eithin, 2 Arran Place, Cardiff.

North of England : S. M. Healey, Selsley, Manchester Road, Heywood, Lancs.

(Subscriptions are best paid to Mr. W. N. Bubb, but can be received by the Local Secretaries or by the School).

Local Dinners are held in alternate years in February at Bristol and Cardiff, and there is also a dinner at Manchester in March, sometimes every year and sometimes every other year. There are occasional dinners at Oxford and Cambridge.

Summer Gathering at Wycliffe

At the time when this Register is printed an alteration of the date of the Annual Old Boys' Day is under consideration by the

School Council, the O.W. Society and the authorities at Wycliffe. For many years this was on a Tuesday, and of late it has been held on the second Friday in July, but many are of opinion that neither of these dates is very convenient for the majority of O.W.s. It is suggested that in future the date should be the second Saturday in July, the present date of the Stroud match, but the final decision will not be known until the end of the year, too late for inclusion in this Register.

In any case **the Summer Gathering of O.W.s in 1938** will be held at Stonehouse on **Saturday, July 8th,** and not on the Friday.

Individual notices of this Reunion are not usually sent to O.W.s, but these have a standing invitation to be present. In 1938 hospitality will be provided by the School throughout Saturday, July 8th, all O.W.s being invited to meals on that day, including the Supper in the evening. For those who cannot by reason of time and distance get home again after the Gathering, and who have no friends with whom they can stay in Gloucestershire or neighbouring counties, the School will endeavour to provide sleeping accommodation on the Saturday night and breakfast on Sunday morning, but all who desire this are asked to give previous notice in writing to the Headmaster or the Housemaster. Such accommodation cannot be guaranteed, and in any case hospitality cannot be extended beyond the Sunday morning, seeing that the domestic staff at the various Houses is fully occupied providing for the ordinary wants of the School. All O.W.s are welcome at the service in the Chapel at 10.30 a.m. on the Sunday, as indeed at any Chapel Service during term time throughout the year.

While it seems probable that in future (and not only in 1938) the second Saturday in July will be chosen for the Old Boys' Reunion, O.W.s are asked to make certain of this fact by consulting the *Wycliffe Star* or by writing to the School.

On July 8th, 1938 there will be two cricket matches, one between a combined Past and Present XI and Stroud and the other between a Wycliffe XI and an XI of Old Boys. Weather permitting, the Stroud match will be from 2.0 till 7.0 and the Old Boys' match from 11.30 to 6.30. Half a dozen tennis courts will also be available for O.W.s, and it is hoped to arrange a programme of events in the new Swimming Pool.

All O.W.s are invited to Prayers in the Chapel at 7.30 on the Saturday and to the Supper at 8.0. It helps greatly in making the necessary arrangements if O.W.s will sign their names in the book provided as soon as possible after their arrival at the School.

Present boys are not allowed to ride in cars driven by O.W.s or to leave the School grounds on Old Boys' Day.

O.W. Football Match

A match between an O.W. XV and the School 1st XV takes place in December, usually on the second Saturday in the month. O.W.s desiring a game should give as long notice as possible to Mr. T. S. Dixon. In making up the O.W. XV records of recent play will be taken into consideration.

Wycliffe House

This is a residential hostel for young men working in business, hospitals, etc., in London. Although not directly connected with Wycliffe, it was largely founded by a former School Chaplain, and there have always been a number of O.W.s in residence. The address is 58 Lewisham Park, S.E. 13, and fuller details may be obtained by writing to the Superintendent.

Some youthful O.W.s have also found a welcome at Regnal House, 6 Eccleston Street, S.W. 1.

O.W. Colours

These colours can be obtained from Messrs. Thomas Plant and Co., 22 The Promenade, Cheltenham, or from the School Shop by writing to the Secretary, Ivy Grove, Stonehouse, Glos. Prices at the time when this Register was printed were as follows, but are liable to vary from year to year :—

Blazer	45 /-
Crest	4 /6
Cap	5 /6
Silk Sash	13 /6
Barathea Tie (extra long)	3 /6
Art Silk Neck Wrap	9 /6
Art Silk Neck Wrap (Colours through) ..	15 /-
Wool Neck Wrap	10 /6
Cashmere Neck Wrap	15 /6
Sweater (plain stitch)	18 /6
Sweater (twist stitch)	21 /-
Grey Slip-over	10 /6
Cuff Links	3 /6

The blazer is of specially woven cloth, and all O.W.s are now entitled to wear the School Crest on its pocket.

Messrs. Plant and the School Secretary are prepared, on the recommendation of the Headmaster, to send goods on approval to any Old Boy in any part of the world.

School Telephones

While the last thing which busy schoolmasters desire is a frequent summons from classroom and other engagements to answer telephone calls, the following numbers may be noted for use in an emergency :—

School Office and Sanatorium	.. Stonehouse	223.
Mr. T. M. Sibly, The Grove	.. ,,	211.
Mr. T. S. Dixon, School House ..	,,	220.
Mr. E. J. Bevan, Haywardsfield ..	,,	238.
Mr. K. C. Bird, Ryeford Hall	.. ,,	102.

It should be remembered, though, that the School Office is closed during part of the holidays, and almost invariably in the evenings, as also that the boarding houses are often shut up altogether in August and sometimes for a week or so in January, April, September and December.

THE SCHOOL'S FAITH AND PURPOSE

(Preaching in the School Chapel on February 9th, 1936, the Headmaster attempted to formulate the Wycliffe ideal, and his words may appeal to many O.W's no less than to present boys. After a reference to the interest and complexity of life which resulted from the variety of personality to be found in every school, he said :)

" Yet here we are, called by Chance and Fate—or, if you prefer it, Time and the will of Heaven—from many different homes and lands and places, so that we may tackle, for a few years at least, the supremely difficult art of all living together in health and happiness, in growing wisdom and in true honour.

Can we make, not only for the majority but for practically all our number, a real success of it ? Can we find some guiding principles by which the whole machine can be kept running sweetly and smoothly ? I believe we can.

But if so the first thing we must possess is honour for one another. Let there be no snobbery or ' despisery ' in any, or for any, of our number. Inevitably, when so many are gathered together, we shall find a few, especially among those who are younger, whose manners lack the repose ' that stamps the caste of Vere de Vere,' and some whose accent and voice would not wholly commend them to the B.B.C. when that body was in search of a new announcer. There will generally be some who seem to those who teach them extraordinarily dull. . . . There are others who present peculiar difficulties to any who long to help them towards a wise and noble life. . . . I have heard people say sometimes, ' So-and-so is a bit common, isn't he ? ' or ' He doesn't come out of the top drawer.' But the Twelve Apostles were most of them very common indeed, and certainly few of them belonged originally to any sort of top drawer, but in the companionship and friendship of Jesus base metal was transmuted into gold, and there are very few boys at Wycliffe or elsewhere whom love and sympathy and encouragement and wise leading may not guide to something good and true.

A really bad boy is a rarity. ' Tough Nuts' are more common. Sometimes I have had a few in my own House, boys who seem to find it difficult to understand that school life can be something so much finer and nobler than a cat-and-mouse business, or that honour for the rule they know may bring happiness and satisfaction to all concerned.

But to come back to our programme.

RELIGION IN SCHOOL LIFE

The School of my ideals will be built upon a foundation of real religion, but I use that word in a wider and less exclusive sense than some of my friends might do. Even as things are, the masters and boys who constitute the greater part of Wycliffe have an extremely varied religious inheritance, and, in a few cases, of personal religious experience as well. The background of your homes, the faith of your fathers or mothers, leads you towards Methodism or the Church of England or Congregationalism or to the Baptists, Quakers, Roman Catholics, Christian Scientists, and for some of you in other directions too. For a few of your number your religion is expressed along the lines of the Oxford Group, and happily, helpfully and sincerely so. Others cannot easily go that way, and may even be repelled by it, but yet they too want to know God, if haply they may find Him. There are yet others who see in the Sacraments and in the ministrations of a dignified ritual the best outward expression of their faith.

In the Wycliffe of my ideal I have no wish for uniformity or expectation of conformity, but I look for a very real appreciation of the other fellow's point of view. Let us all remember that

' The love of God is broader
Than the measures of man's mind '

and that there is room for you all in the Faith of the Future and in the religious fellowship of this School, provided only that here, too, is found no pharisaism or ' despising ' in any quarter, that you truly seek to live in love and charity with your fellows, and—here is the important thing, here is the real condition of a practical faith and fellowship—that you are sincerely and constantly prepared to listen for, and hearing to obey, that voice of Conscience which God has given to us all ; that you possess the spirit of an essential reverence for ' that Power in darkness whom we guess ' ; that you are ready to live, even to the point of self-sacrifice, for some cause greater than yourself, and to express your faith in daily and devoted service.

If only these things are true, I am sure we can claim a fellowship one with another, no matter how varied our ecclesiastical labels may be.

Personally I believe that in this great Book can still be found the fullest and the noblest revelation of God and of His will for us, and that we all do well to study and to ponder it, but, speaking for myself, I do not believe that Truth ends with the Bible. I believe that creation and revelation are processes which are continuous and never-ending. I believe in the prophets and apostles of the nineteenth and twentieth centuries as well as in those of Judea long ago. I believe that Carlyle and Ruskin, Tennyson and Browning and Whittier, Dickens, Galsworthy, Rabindranath Tagore and many

more, even perchance, in their nobler moods, H. G. Wells, and
Bernard Shaw, are teachers of truth which is inspired, and so must
be divine. I believe that God fulfils Himself in many ways, and
that He has spoken to His children by divers prophets and teachers
ever since the world began. Above all do I believe that right
action is more important than full knowledge, and that, if only
sincerely and humbly we try constantly to do God's will, as we
understand it, from day to day, fuller light and life and knowledge
will be given to us as we journey on.

I have taken so much time in speaking of religion as the foundation of school life because, in some form or other, religion is indeed
fundamental. More briefly let us look at other matters on which
we do well to be united and resolved.

HARD WORK ESSENTIAL

A good school surely should be a place where hard work is
honoured. There are a hundred reasons why that should be so.
The sacrifices of our parents, the interests of our fellows, our own
pleasure in our studies, our future success or failure, are but a few
of them. The slacker, if he would only stop to think about it for
a minute, is a traitor to the whole community. He is spoiling other
fellows' chances as well as his own. Like a bad apple in a box, his
own rotten work threatens to turn the work of others rotten too.
He does much to prevent that great happiness which we can all
find in work well done. Such a boy or man is Public Enemy No. 1.
If he does not get well soon he should be isolated or sent away,
quite as much as if he were suffering from fever or measles.

Happy indeed is that school where masters and boys together
have learnt that work is a noble thing, and that there are few joys
in life greater than that of a good job finely done, and where the
public opinion of the school as a whole, or of a house or a class in
particular, will no more tolerate a ' spoil-work ' than it would a
' spoil-sport.'

TRUTH IN WORD AND DEED

No less must this School, if it is to realise its possibilities to
the full, be built upon the practice of truth in word and deed, or of
honesty out and out. If men and boys can be trusted, all things
are possible, but when truth goes, if it is not speedily recaptured, all
things go. If a boy is ready to tell a lie whenever he thinks it
convenient to do so, or to practise deceit, which is only another
name for lies in action, the whole body of our life together receives
an ugly wound. . . . Such things ought not to be. You may,
some of you, think that these instances of untruth are not of much
consequence, but in reality they strike at the whole basis of our
happy life together. They spring either from slackness or from

cowardice, or from greed and a lack of common honesty. When the other fellow cannot be trusted to tell the truth, or to respect the property of those about him, a school must rapidly degenerate into an affair of magistrates and masters, prefects and policemen on the one side, and would-be law breakers and culprits on the other, and as a result checks of one sort and another and restrictions of liberty, with general or particular penalties, are bound to follow.

Cannot you all see the possibility of something much better and bigger and nobler ?   A school where all are to be trusted in speech and act, where, as Rovers and Scouts and boys of Wycliffe, your word is always to be relied upon ; a place where falsehood of every sort is seen and known as the mean and contemptible and cowardly thing it really is ; a school where public opinion regards all liars as ' outsiders ' ; a place where we can all have absolute confidence in one another ?   Probably that is true of many of you already. Is it beyond the bounds of possibility that we may make it so of all, so that Wycliffe may ever be a veritable temple of Truth ?

The Call to Service

Seventeen years ago, when the Great War had ended, I tried to define a ' programme of peace ' for this School. We have already touched on some points in that programme, and there is no time to develop them all.

But I expressed then, and would repeat now, that one purpose of a good school must be to give to all who teach and study there some aim of social service, combined with the will and power to serve. ' Humanity has struck its tents,' said General Smuts not long ago, ' and is everywhere on the march.' Here in England, and throughout the world, people are hungry for leadership, and opportunities of serving your fellows and the State abound. I would like to think that no boy would ever leave Wycliffe without a strong resolve and some actual power to give unselfish service to the greater world beyond the walls of School. Some of you already make a beginning in this direction, by means of your work as Scouts and Rovers and your interest in Toc H and in practical Church and Christian service, but everywhere the fields are white unto harvest, and labourers of the right sort are all too few. I hope that every one of you will do something to help, and will be found in the number of those who ' look up and not down, and lend a hand.'

Safeguarding Liberty

I believe it to be no small part of the mission of this School to cherish its individuality, its liberty to experiment, and even its eccentricities. Most people and most schools are afraid to be original. I rejoiced to hear one of my colleagues, who was educated at another older and more famous school, say in School Prayers two nights ago that he had found something different, surprising, and

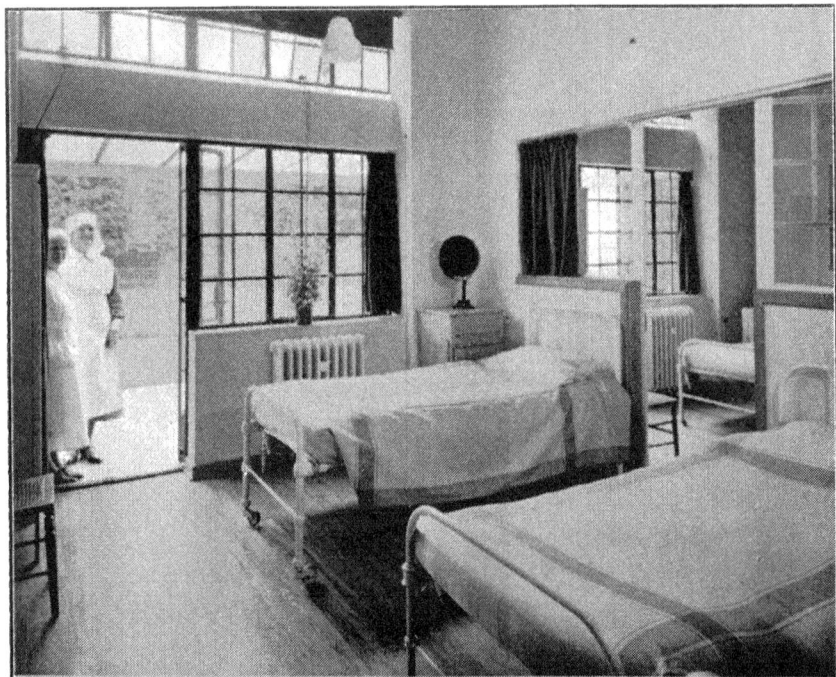

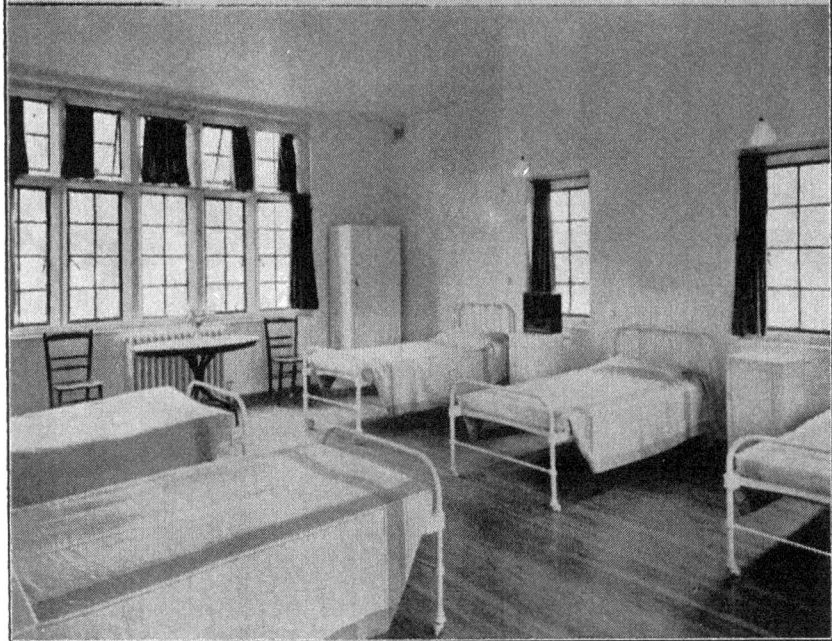

IN THE SCHOOL SANATORIUM

1. A Ward with two beds (and two 'ministering spirits'). 2. One of the larger Wards, so attractive as to make its occupation almost a pleasure.

THE MAIN AND MIDDLE FIELDS FROM THE AIR   [*Photo: Aerofilms*]

(In the centre stands Haywardsfield, with the Sanatorium, Ivy Grove and Chapel to the right. Across the road is Springfield, with the row of cottages since demolished to give room for the extension of the House and gardens. At the extreme right is the new Science Building, and just above is the Assembly Hall and the School House partly hidden by trees. A keen eye can discern a cricket match, two other cricket games and nets, and eight tennis courts. The Swimming Pool and the Berryfield, with its four football grounds, are just off the picture.)

WYCLIFFE BOYS BY THE ARCH OF CONSTANTINE IN ROME.

(April, 1935)

(During the past seven years parties of Wycliffe Rovers and Scouts, varying in number from 25 to 86, have visited and camped in Greece, Algeria, Italy, Sicily, Germany, Egypt and Palestine, as well as other lands nearer home).

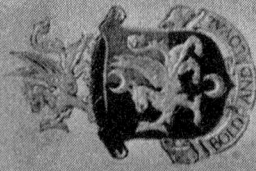

THIS·TABLET·HAS·BEEN·PLACED
HERE·BY·SOME·OF·HIS·OLD·BOYS
IN·EVER·GRATEFUL·MEMORY·OF
GEORGE·WILLIAM·SIBLY
FOUNDER·&·FOR·THIRTY·YEARS
HEADMASTER·OF·WYCLIFFE·COLLEGE
WHO·BY·HIS·TEACHING·AND·EXAMPLE
INSPIRED·THOUSANDS·OF·THE·YOUTH·OF
ENGLAND·TO·DO·JUSTLY·LOVE·MERCY
AND·WALK·HUMBLY·WITH·GOD

ONE OF THE MEMORIALS IN THE CHAPEL

rather unique in Wycliffe, something which he was sure was well worth preserving. Let us be pioneers and experimenters, not only in school journeys to Greece, to Africa and Sicily, but in reasonable reforms of dress and diet and health, and in all rational adverturings of the human spirit.

An Appeal for Kindness

I hope that Wycliffe will ever be a place where a sunny kindliness reigns supreme, where true friendship—but not of any sentimental, mawkish type—abounds, where new and little boys will be secure from bullying, where animals are treated with an understanding compassion, and where even for fun or so-called ' sport ' not one of you would ever seek his pleasure through their death or pain. Broadly speaking, I believe that that is true even now, but occasionally one comes across a horrid and sadistic exception, and in any case true kindness must not only be passive but active too, finding its expression in an ardent championship of every cause of mercy.

No Mean Ideal

To sum up and to conclude, I want us all to cherish here, and continually to put into practice, the belief that school life can be something better, happier and more beautiful than many schools in fact have found it, the belief that boys and masters, working together, are capable of responding gladly and freely to a higher code than that prescribed by convention. It is our faith that sunshine and morality, energy and serenity, friendship and reverence, tradition and experiment, truth and liberty, can best go hand in hand, and that only when they do so are each and all truly safe.

When rules are respected because their essential reasonableness is understood, and where the desire for right conduct and fine work is so general as to be almost universal, we may yet realise a school where all will endeavour in the daily round to do what is right because it is right, little influenced by the fear of punishment or the hope of gain.

Just as there is a patriotism which is splendid and sublime, a patriotism which is ever jealous of a country's fame for justice and right dealing, so every member of this School should possess a rightful pride in the School's good name.

It is yours to guard the good things committed to your care. Some of us feel rather sick when we see (what happily is rarely seen) a School XV playing badly and so half-disgraced, or a Cricket XI coming out like a flock of frightened sheep. We feel that they are letting Wycliffe down. Far more important for the welfare and fame and future of Wycliffe is your regard for the School's good name for righteousness, truth and courtesy.

We may never be a big school or, in the ordinary sense of the word, a famous school, but the opportunity is ours, both yours and mine, to make Wycliffe a good and so in truth a great school. Shakespeare makes Henry V speak somewhere of his followers and himself as

' We few, we happy few, we band of brothers,'

and how much may be achieved in these later days by those who work together with a single aim !

If only all of us, masters and boys, can be bound together by a common purpose and a high resolve, what may we not both be and do to make this School for all the land, for all the world, a source of light. A little light, maybe, but yet to friends working together, by God's grace all things are possible.

Living for some such aims, cherishing such a faith, we need not fear the menace of the years, but rather

' in simpleness and gentleness and honour and clean mirth '

we shall go confidently forward, ready to greet, and eager to take our part in shaping, a ' brave new world.' "

A Collect for the Old Boys of the School

(as used in the Service on Sunday mornings)

BEFORE Thy throne of grace, O Father, we would remember all who have met and worshipped here. Be with them in their goings-out and comings-in, and wherever they minister to the needs of men. Companion them always, even unto other lands, and to the far-off outposts of the empire. In friendship and pleasure, in their homes and social life, in public and Christian service, give them grace and guidance. Help them to bear their witness bravely, to do their duty faithfully, to act kindly and live purely, and to walk humbly with Thee, being persuaded that neither death, nor life, nor things present, nor things to come, can separate them from Thy love revealed in Christ Jesus our Lord. *Amen.*

www.ingramcontent.com/pod-product-compliance
Lightning Source LLC
Chambersburg PA
CBHW030933150426
42812CB00064B/2837/J